Capitalist Restructuring, Globalisation and the Third Way

T0271890

This book addresses the contemporary debate about the Third Way in European social democracy. By analysing the paradigmatic case of social democracy – 'the Swedish model' – this book challenges the recent 'third way' perspective. The author argues against the widely held belief that the nature of contemporary capitalist restructuring and globalisation has rendered 'traditional' social democracy obsolete.

Engaging with the comparative welfare state literature and drawing on the conceptual framework of regulation theory and Gramscian international political economy, this book argues that:

- There is nothing inherently neo-liberal about the technological forces behind contemporary 'post-Fordist' capitalist restructuring and globalisation, and these forces could be mobilised to address contemporary social problems in a manner that is compatible with the norms of social democracy and democratic socialism.
- The power of neo-liberal ideology *as such*, and its effect on the subjective outlook of social democratic elites, is crucial. It has played a decisive role in the neo-liberal structural bias of transnationalisation of production and globalisation of finance.

By applying concepts from critical international political economy, this book makes a significant contribution to this highly topical debate about globalisation.

J. Magnus Ryner is lecturer in the Department of Government at Brunel University. He has previously been affiliated with York University in Toronto, the University of Amsterdam and, as Jean Monnet fellow, at the European University Institute in Florence. He co-edited the *International Journal of Political Economy: Special issues on global neoliberalism and the political economy of restructuring in Europe*, in 1998.

Routledge/RIPE Series in Global Political Economy

Series Editors: Otto Holman, Marianne Marchand (*Research Centre for International Political Economy, University of Amsterdam*), Henk Overbeek (*Free University, Amsterdam*) and Marianne Franklin (*University of Amsterdam*)

This series, published in association with the *Review of International Political Economy*, provides a forum for current debates in international political economy. The series aims to cover all the central topics in IPE and to present innovative analyses of emerging topics. The titles in the series seek to transcend a state-centred discourse and focus on three broad themes:

- the nature of the forces driving globalisation forward
- resistance to globalisation
- the transformation of the world order.

The series comprises two strands:

The *RIPE Series in Global Political Economy* aims to address the needs of students and teachers, and the titles will be published in hardback and paperback. Titles include:

Transnational Classes and International Relations
Kees van der Pijl

Gender and Global Restructuring
Sightings, sites and resistances
Edited by Marianne H. Marchand and Anne Sisson Runyan

Global Political Economy
Contemporary theories
Edited by Ronen Palan

Ideologies of Globalization
Contending visions of a new world order
Mark Rupert

The Clash within Civilisations
Coming to terms with cultural conflicts
Dieter Senghaas

Routledge/RIPE Studies in Global Political Economy is a forum for innovative new research intended for a high-level specialist readership, and the titles will be available in hardback only. Titles include:

* *Also available in paperback*

Capitalist Restructuring, Globalisation and the Third Way

Lessons from the Swedish model

J. Magnus Ryner

London and New York

First published 2002
by Routledge
2 Park Square, Milton Park, Abingdon, Oxfordshire OX14 4RN

Simultaneously published in the USA and Canada
by Routledge
711 Third Avenue, New York, NY 10017

First issued in paperback 2014

Routledge is an imprint of the Taylor and Francis Group, an informa business

Transferred to Digital Printing 2006

© 2002 J. Magnus Ryner

Typeset in Baskerville by BC Typesetting, Bristol

British Library Cataloguing in Publication Data
A catalogue record for this book is available from the British Library

Library of Congress Cataloging in Publication Data
Ryner, J. Magnus.
  Capitalist restructuring, globalisation, and the third way/J. Magnus Ryner.
    p.   cm. – (Routledge/RIPE studies in global political economy)
  Includes bibliographical references and index.
    1. Socialism. 2. Socialism–Sweden. 3. Welfare state. I. Title. II. Series.

HX44.5.R96 2002
330.9485–dc21   2001048587

ISBN 978-0-415-25294-2 (hbk)
ISBN 978-1-138-81104-1 (pbk)

till morfar och i minne av mormor

Contents

Illustrations

Figures

Tables

Series editors' preface

In the mid-1990s, Social Democratic parties in Western Europe miraculously arose from the dead. One after the other, they entered government after having spent many years in the electoral shadows of such towering conservative opponents as Margaret Thatcher and Helmut Kohl. The foremost examples, of course, were the resurrection of the British Labour Party under Tony Blair and the return to power of the German SPD under Gerhard Schröder. A precedent had already been set by the Dutch Labour Party under Wim Kok (one of the longest serving Prime Ministers in the European Union) which was quickly followed by the surprise return of the French Socialist Party to power under Lionel Jospin (albeit in co-habitation with the Gaullist President, Jacques Chirac). This return of the Social Democrats as an attractive electoral force in Europe coincided in 1993 with the election in the United States, after twelve years of Republican administrations, of the Democrat Bill Clinton.

Hence in these four years all major Western countries experienced a political shift to what a decade earlier would have been called (and still is by conservative die-hards) the 'Left'. Something very fundamental had happened: the Left had changed clothes. As Wim Kok said (in the only speech he ever made on party ideology), Social Democracy had 'shed its ideological feathers' and was now concentrating on the practical job of running the capitalist economy. Social Democracy had found a 'Third Way'.

In this book, Magnus Ryner presents a critical analysis of this ideological transformation and its theoretical underpinnings. If any name is linked to the intellectual parentage of the Third Way, it is that of Anthony Giddens. In the first chapter, Ryner shows how Giddens' critique of the 'old Left' and its Keynesian beliefs is premised on a very specific reading of the supposed failures of Sweden's Social-Democratic government in the 1980s. Giddens and Gosta Esping-Andersen (Giddens' key source on this issue) argue that the Swedish case provides indisputable proof that Social Democratic Keynesianism was fatally flawed and destined to collapse under the impacts of globalisation.

The better part of Ryner's book is then devoted to a detailed analysis of the Swedish case as exemplary of the demise of Keynesian Social-Democracy throughout Western Europe. Ryner reaches very different conclusions from Giddens and Esping-Andersen. He shows that the supposed 'failure' of Keynesianism either did not actually occur or could have been avoided at a relatively modest cost. The defeat of Keynesianism and the resulting victory of neo-Liberalism in Sweden, as was indeed the case – mutatis mutandis – in several other European countries, was not the result of the innate flaws of Keynesian macro-economic management, nor of the inescapable need to 'adapt' to the competitive pressures of the globalising economy. It was, rather, the outcome of a long drawn out 'war of position'; a concerted economic, political and ideological assault orchestrated by vested Swedish capitalist interests and their 'organic intellectuals'. This assault was directed against the traditional organisational strongholds and ideological foundations of Social-Democracy.

In his subsequent attempts to explain the ideological reincarnation of many Social-Democratic leaders as ardent neo-liberals, Magnus Ryner presents a refined and nuanced theoretical argument. He shows how structural forces, individual idiosyncrasies and rational calculatoins by party officials along with historical continuities, produced this remarkable transformation. Ryner's concluding argument is an eloquent plea for the resurrection of Social-Democratic Keynesianism as an alternative to the unfettered rule of market forces in Europe. Traditional organisations of the Left, Trade Unions and Social Democratic party organisations especially, should not be written off. Ryner argues that they can, and should, play a key role in the construction of a Left European Social Democracy.

We are convinced that Ryner's argument can play an important role in the debate about the future of the Left in Europe. It provides a balanced analysis that allows us to transcend one of the most debilitating elements in that debate, namely the question of the national versus the European solution. Ryner convincingly shows how these can – and must – be treated simultaneously. This book should be read not only by students and scholars of European politics, but also by Trade Union and party activists on the Left.

Henk Overbeek, Otto Holman, Marianne Marchand,
Marianne Franklin

Acknowledgements

This book is the product of research that has been done over quite a few years and in many places. The bulk of the empirical research on the Swedish case was completed as part of my Ph.D. dissertation, which I wrote at the Graduate Programme of Political Science at York University in Toronto and (the then) the Swedish Centre for Working Life (*Arbetslivscentrum*) in Stockholm. The work on the comparative context and relating the Swedish case to current debates on the Third Way in European social democracy was done during my post-doctoral research. This research took place at the Research Centre of International Political Economy (RECIPE) at the University of Amsterdam and at the Department of Social and Political Science, European University Institute (EUI). The final drafts were written at the Department of Government, Brunel University. These are all intellectually stimulating places where I learnt much from many fellow intellectual travellers and friends. It is impossible to mention everybody who created the stimulating milieu in these places, so I thank you all, mentioning no-one in particular but forgetting no one. But I must give special thanks to my house-mates, Sharon Wong and Jamie Lawson who put up with many of my idiosyncrasies over the years. I would also like to thank warmly Sheila Strong and Marlea Clarke, who at different times were particularly close to me, for their emotional support.

A number of individuals and institutions were involved directly in the support of my research. I would like to take this opportunity to express my sincere gratitude to them. It would have been financially and logistically impossible for me to complete my work without the generous support of the Jean Monnet Fellowship Programme of the EUI, the Faculty of Social Cultural Sciences (PSCW) of the University of Amsterdam, the Ministry of Education of Ontario, and two grants from the Social Sciences Research Council of Canada (SSHRCC). With respect to my field research, I would like to thank Anders L. Johansson, then Director of the Swedish Centre of Working Life' for inviting me to utilise the good offices of the Centre during my research trips to Sweden. I would also like to thank all those who, despite their busy schedules, agreed to be interviewed for their generosity and openness.

xiv   *Acknowledgements*

With regard to concrete guidance and comments on my work, I must above all thank my Ph.D. dissertation supervisor, Stephen Gill. I benefited especially from his uncanny ability to strike a balance between providing the guidance that the novice researcher needs and for allowing and respecting my autonomy and the inner need that ultimately had to determine the direction and content of my research. I am also grateful to Stephen, as well as Kees van der Pijl, for suggesting that I recast my work in terms of the Third Way debate. I would also like to thank the other members of my dissertation committee, Leo Panitch and Robert W. Cox. I am never sure whether Leo will ever consider me a 'comrade', but I hope that the text shows that when he taught me not to forget the importance of neo-Marxist state theory it made a lasting impression on me. Were it not for the fact that his modesty discourages it, I would be more than happy to consider myself Robert Cox's disciple. Finally, thank you to Rianne Mahon for her support over the years. There is hardly any researcher with whom I feel more of a 'kinship' in terms of normative orientation, as well as approach, as Rianne. Many international observers have come to study the 'Swedish model' over the years. Few have actually understood it with as profound an insight as Rianne. Other teachers who were not immediately involved in the project but whose teaching made the project possible include Robert Albritton, Daniel Drache, Robert Campbell, John Wynne-Hughes, Edgar Samuel, Blair Dimock, David Kettler and Sue Golding.

In much more recent years I must thank the editorial board of the RIPE/ Routledge Series on Global Political Economy for putting me through a process (to which I sometimes was reluctant) that I believe made this a much better book. I am especially grateful to Henk Overbeek for his excellent editorial comments at the final stages of writing and to Otto Holman for giving me advice in the beginning of the process on how to structure the book to achieve our objectives.

Apart from the aforementioned, I have benefited from comments given to me at academic conferences, and by advice and comments on specific aspects of my research. For this, thank you to Gregory Albo, Carolyn Basset, Leo Bieling, Robert Boyer, Marlea Clarke, Edward Comor, Colin Crouch, Roland Czada, Panayotis Damaskopoulos, Stephen Gelb, Jeffrey Harrod, Björn Hettne, Gerd Junne, Chris Klein-Beeckman, David Law, Jamie Lawson, Martin List, Robert A. Marshall, Craig Murphy, Mark Neocleous, Ronen Palan, Heikki Patomäki, Katherine Scott, Jochen Steinhilber, Byron Sheldrick, Tim Sinclair, Graham Todd, Geoffrey Underhill, Georg Simonis, Bastiaan van Apeldoorn, William Walters, Sören Wibe and Sharon Wong.

Finally I would like to thank relatives and family whom I have always been able to count on when I needed their support. I would in particular like to thank my wife Sushuma Chandrasekhar for her loving understanding.

My grandparents have played a particularly important role in my life. I am forever grateful to my late paternal grandfather, Vilhelm Ryner, for encouraging my academic faculties. I firmly believe with Gramsci that political science ultimately is normative and is dialectically related to common sense wisdom derived from experiences of justice, injustice, visions and hope in everyday practice (that is, 'feelings and passions becoming knowledge and hence understanding'). This is why I above all would like to express my devotion to my grandfather, Anders Engström, and my late grandmother Anna-Greta Åman-Engström. It is from them, and their life experience that began in the working-class 'communities in struggle' of the *bruk*, that I received the 'passion' to write this book. It is to them that the book is dedicated.

Parts of chapter 1 have been translated and reproduced from an article entitled 'Der neue Diskurs ueber den Dritten Weg: Zur Dynamik des social-demokratischen Neoliberalismus' in H. J. Bieling and J. Steinhilber (eds) *Die Konfiguration Europas* (Westphaelishes Dampfboot, 2000). It has been reprinted here with the kind permission of the publishers.

Parts of chapter 5 and 7 have been taken from an article published elsewhere: 'Neoliberal Globalization and the Crisis of Swedish Social Democracy', *Economic and Industrial Democracy* 20 (1) (1999), and has been reprinted here with the kind permission of Sage publications.

J. Magnus Ryner

Abbreviations and acronyms

AMS   *Arbetsmarknadsstyrelsen* (Swedish Labour Market Board)

CDU   *Christdemokratische Union* (Christian Democratic Union, Germany)

IUI   *Industriens utredningsinstitut* (The Industrial Institute for Economic and Social Research, Sweden)

LO   *Landsorganisationen i Sverige* (The Confederation of Swedish Trade Unions)

SACO   *Sveriges akademikers centralorganisation* (The Swedish Confederation of Professional Associations)

SAF   *Sveriges arbetsgivareförbund* (Swedish Employers' Confederation)

SAP   *Svergies socialdemokratiska arbetarparti* (The Social Democratic Workers' Party of Sweden)

SEB   *Skandinaviska Enskilda Banken*

SHB   *Handelsbanken*

SI   *Sveriges industriförbund* (Confederation of Swedish Industries)

SNS   *Studiesförbundet näringsliv samhälle* (Centre for Business and Policy Studies)

SPD   *Sozialdemokratische Partei Deutschlands* (Social Democratic Party of Germany)

TCO   *Tjänstemännens centralorganisation* (The Swedish Confederation of Professional Employees)

VF   *Verstadindustriförbundet* (The Association of Swedish Engineering Industries)

Introduction

This book addresses the contemporary debate about the Third Way in European social democracy, through an analysis of the crisis of the Swedish model in the 1990s. The premise of this approach is that the Swedish case continues to be a paradigmatic case containing broader and more general lessons about the nature of social democracy, its constraints and its prospects.

Third Way advocates argue for a neo-liberalisation of social democracy. This argument hinges on the premise that 'traditional social democracy' is inherently untenable, given contemporary forces of technological change and globalisation. I will show that this position rests implicitly on a particular reading of the crisis of the Swedish model in the 1990s – a model that until that time had been highly influential on social democratic thinking world-wide. I will challenge that reading, and show that rather than being the outcome of intransitive forces, the crisis was fundamentally political in nature. Furthermore, in this political crisis, the neo-liberalisation of Swedish social democracy itself played a decisive role. In other words, the Swedish case suggests that the 'modernisation' that Third Way advocates have interpreted as a rational and inevitable submission to functional neo-liberal pressures is in fact due to contingent political practices of social democratic elites, pursuing a particular kind of neo-liberal strategy ('compensatory neo-liberalism'). This is of significance because it suggests that the constraints identified by Third Way advocates are in fact socially constructed and transitive constraints, created through human practice that can be changed through alternative practices. This opens up the space to consider alternative modernisation projects for the European left that are more consistent with its (so be it) 'traditional' commitments to social citizenship and de-commodification.

The book begins its pursuit of this argument through a review of recent Third Way discourse in chapter 1, focusing on the arguments of the cosmopolitan intellectual of the Third Way *par excellence*, Anthony Giddens. Such a review makes it possible to situate the study on the Swedish model in a broader discussion about the nature of democracy and freedom as well as economic rationality in contemporary modern mass society. This theme is continued in chapter 2, which focuses on economic rationality and the comparative political economy 'post-industrial', or as I prefer, 'post-Fordist' restructuring of welfare capitalism. Drawing on a wide-ranging analytical and comparative discussion, the overall argument of these two chapters is that there indeed is a case for democratisation and pluralisation of the social democratic welfare state (what Giddens calls 'no rights without democracy'). However, rather than abandoning the principles of social citizenship, de-commodification and welfare state universalism, my contention is that these norms provide the necessary basis for such a transformation. Such an argument depends, of course, on the economic viability of these norms that has been questioned by the conventional neo-classical 'Eurosclerosis' thesis, which Third Way advocates adopt uncritically. Chapter 2 is devoted precisely to refuting this thesis through a comparative political economy analysis which establishes the Swedish model to (still) be a paradigmatic case.

The remainder of the book is devoted towards substantiating the thesis advanced in the first two chapters, through a detailed analysis of this paradigmatic case. Chapters 3 and 4 describe the formation, the institutional *modus operandi*, and the historical-structural conditions of existence of the Swedish model, which had its 'golden age' in the 1950s and 1960s. Operating from the premise that an analysis of a crisis presupposes an understanding of what is in crisis, this is in part a scene-setting exercise for the subsequent chapters that are concerned with the patterns of determination of the crisis in question. A second and related objective is simply to give a more detailed account of what social democracy *qua* the Swedish model actually entailed, in order to counter the superficial and stylised understandings that currently characterise discussions about the Third Way. In particular, I seek to high-light the sophisticated conception of socio-economic rationalisation that underpinned the Swedish model, and how this related to patterns of capital accumulation as well as social discipline, representation and legitimation. The lack of understanding of the Swedish model is quite surprising, given the abundant literature on the subject. Chapters 3 and 4 essentially amount to a synthesis of this literature. However, given the importance of 'globalisation' in contemporary discussions, my account differs from previous accounts in that it specifies the international relationships that the Swedish model presupposed.

Chapters 3 and 4 show how the Swedish model worked. The remainder of the book is concerned with the contradictions and limitations that brought it into crisis, as well as with the socio-economic and socio-political forces that were provoked as a response. In terms of time-scales, the crisis of the early 1990s is situated within a broader narrative of crisis and search for a new institutional equilibrium that goes back to the origins of the so-called 'Fordist' crisis in the late 1960s.

Chapter 5 is concerned with the nature, meaning and extent of 'globalisation' as it intervenes in the political economy of capitalist restructuring. The objective in this context is to clarify what the term actually refers to and to discern more exactly how it relates to the crisis of social democracy and the

Swedish model. The chapter affirms that the breakdown of the 'embedded' welfare–liberal world order of the immediate post World War II period is central to the crisis of the Swedish model, and indeed, transnationalisation of production and globalisation of finance have radically altered the conditions that it presupposed. At the same time, the political and contingent nature of many of the central tenets of globalisation is also identified. The chapter argues that the particular type of globalisation that is occurring is connected to a transnational hegeomonic political project that responded to what was conceived in ruling class circles as a crisis of governability in the 1970s. Hence, 'new constitutionalism', centred around monetarist macroeconomic governance, has become a central regulatory norm around which social restructuring is taking place throughout the world, including Sweden. The chapter ends by identifying some of the limits and contradictions of new constitutionalist governance and considering the strategic terrain for counter-hegemony.

By chapter 6 the book is finally in a position to substantiate empirically the claims made about the Swedish model, especially in chapters 1, 2 and 5, through an account of the evolving politics of crisis and response in Sweden from the late 1960s to the present. The chapter begins by returning to the question of legitimation deficits in the welfare state, discussed in the review of Giddens under the heading of 'no authority without democracy'. It is argued that this was indeed the theme of the left-wing social movement that first brought the Swedish model into crisis, and this points to the discrepancies between the ideal and the real in Swedish social democracy. It is also argued, however, that elites in Swedish political society, where the blue-collar Confederation of Swedish Trade Unions, LO, played a leading role, initially responded to this crisis of legitimacy and representation by a politics of reform and accommodation that included increased social consumption, industrial democracy and collective capital formation. In my estimation, if fully institutionalised, these reforms may very well have not only addressed the problems of legitimacy, but may also have made this compatible with the new terms of economic rationality. The point is, however, that these reforms never amounted to a coherent institutional response because of the manner in which they challenged the prerogatives of capital as they were entrenched in the historic class compromise that underpinned the Swedish model. In short, this reform agenda was *politically* defeated through a counter-mobilisation led by organised Swedish business which at the same time experienced a profound transnationalisation. In many respects, this response by Swedish business to the challenges to fundamental 'rights of business' in capitalism is hardly surprising. Perhaps more interesting is the manner in which Swedish social democracy not only retreated from its radical position in the 1970s, but also came to play a leadership role in the compensatory neo-liberal restructuring in Sweden in the 1980s and 1990s. Central in this respect was their neo-constitutionalist economic strategy that was formulated and executed by a narrow group of officials in the

Ministry of Finance and the Central Bank. I would argue that this change demobilised the left-wing response politically, and at the same time the contradictions between this narrow elite project and the terms of ideological legitimacy within social democracy and the corporatist state in Sweden triggered the deep economic crisis in the early 1990s.

Chapter 7 is concerned with the question, how and why are social democratic elites incorporated into a neo-liberal hegemonic project? It is argued that the literature has paid insufficient attention to the question of why social democratic state managers had become so receptive to neo-liberal governance in the first place. I would argue that receptiveness only becomes intelligible when we, following Foucault (1970), shift our attention from the content of policy discourse to its form. That is, when we shift our attention from *what* is argued to the *manner* in which matters have to be argued in order to *be taken seriously* in political circles. Here we note a fundamental change in the form of economic discourse in Swedish social democratic circles in the golden age of the Swedish model itself. This shift seems to be, as Poulantzas (1978) suggested, intimately connected with the practice of capitalist state management as such. Paradoxically, Giddens, the critical-realist sociologist, in his attempt to broaden the appeal of social democratic neo-liberalism, broadens the narrow and austere positivist limits of the discourse, and opens it up for contestation and challenge, to which this book is a modest contribution.

A note on theory and method

The purpose of this book is to shed light on a concrete subject matter, and not to engage in self-conscious reflections on epistemological and ontological premises. Nevertheless, conception and observation cannot be separated, and the analysis obviously rests on a particular conceptual framework. Since the framework I adopt – Gramscian critical theory – is not generally accepted, it creates a dilemma for this study. On the one hand, for the sake of clarity of argument, one does not want to engage in theoretical detours that stray away from the immediate subject matter. On the other hand, given that the approach cannot be taken as self-evident, there is a need to state, explain and defend the epistemological premises of the study and the research procedure.

The way that I have chosen to deal with the dilemma has been to minimise explicit theoretical discussions and to embed this discussion in the substantive exposition. At the same time, I provide an appendix that contains a more self-conscious reflection on epistemological premises and research procedure. This is intended to be a point of reference for those who are interested in exploring these foundations of the argument, and it is an attempt to make the case for my approach for those who are not immediately convinced. References to the appendix are made in the main body of the text when appropriate.

By way of introduction, it can be said that the study sets forth to identify, within a particular sphere of action, humanly constructed social production and power relations that on the surface of things seem to manifest themselves as objective constraints, or 'coercive illusions', on human political aspirations. Indeed, to identify these relations as socially constructed and thereby remove their sense of objectivity and inevitability is, in a basic sense, the essential objective of critical theory (Connerton 1976).

To advance such an analysis, the study adopts as its key concepts, the Gramscian concepts of 'historic bloc' and 'organic crisis'. These should be understood as historical-structural concepts fundamental to the analysis of social formations in particular periods. According to Gramsci, they are the key concepts of an analysis of 'relations of force' in society (Gramsci 1971: 175–85, 210–18, 365–66). By 'historic bloc', Gramsci means a stabilised, institutionalised relationship between socio-economic 'structure' and political-ideological 'superstructure'. This crystallisation is embedded within a certain 'historic compromise' between, and osmosis of, tendentially conflictual social forces; and/or an exclusion or marginalisation of forces that are too weak to assert themselves.[1] This compromise/osmosis/marginalisation is not politically neutral. On the contrary, it is politically and ideologically charged. It reflects a balance of material and ideological power – the 'hegemony' of a dominant synthesised complex of social forces (the 'power bloc'). 'Organic crisis' is the negation of historic bloc and thus expresses its opposite. It refers to a situation of fundamental social conflict and contest, and the absence of cathartic resolution of the conflict between contending social forces. As Cox (1981) has pointed out, the historical-structural institutionalisation of historic blocs needs to be thought of in terms of a synchronic equilibrium of the co-determined levels of social relations of production, forms of state (understood in an extended sense to entail state–civil societal relations) and world order.

Historic bloc is the fundamental organising concept of the entire book. However, as the exposition progresses refinements are introduced. Hence, in chapter 1, the concepts of 'organic' and 'cosmopolitan' intellectuals are introduced to specify political practices in mass societies that are pursued to articulate the subjective and objective moments of social reality to enforce hegemony and the stability of a historic bloc. In chapter 2, the concept is refined to facilitate the analysis of socio-economic reproduction; hence, the regulation theoretical terms, 'regime of accumulation', 'modes of regulation', and 'hegemonic project'. Finally, in chapter 4 the conceptualisation of the institutional form of the capitalist state is refined through the notion of 'patterns of social representation' and attendant concepts.

1 Recent discourse on the Third Way

Introduction

It is an irony of contemporary European politics that the essentials of a neoliberal project – the subordination of society to market discipline – is being consolidated by social democratic governments (eg. Crouch 1997). This articulation of social democracy with economic liberalism, pursued in a political project referred to as the Third Way, sets high demands on ideology in the Gramscian sense, as a multi-levelled phenomenon that contains and fuses a wide range of more or less coherent discursive forms from 'common sense' to 'philosophy' (Gramsci 1971: 326–43, 348–51, 367; Hall *et al*. 1977: 46–52; Mouffe 1979: 185–88, 190–92, 195–98; Simon 1982: 58–66).[1]

Ideology in this sense is a material practice, with the function of 'cementing' (or better, interpellating) multifarious, stratified and antagonistic segments of society into a broad political direction. Politicians and mass parties play a strategic role in this practice as 'organic intellectuals', as it is they who take on the task of ensuring this coherence. In this practice they deploy a number of discursive techniques at different levels of communication and action in civil and political society. These discursive techniques, ranging from 'spin-doctoring' in the tabloid media, to internal party work, to policy formulation, assume different forms depending on the specific context of civil and political society at which they are directed. In terms of content, provided that it is possible to achieve operational coherence at the policy level, heterogeneity in 'the message' and even factionalism is not necessarily a weakness, but rather a strength, since this increases the range of interests and identities that can be integrated into the political project. In other words, the successful mass-party elaborates and mediates different and heterogeneous interpretations of 'common sense', with a coherent and operational political strategy within the state (and other public authority agencies) that also is consistent with socio-economic developments. As Häusler and Hirsch (1989: 306) put it in their study of 'catch-all' parties in Germany:

The party system represents the component of the regulative network of institutions within which antagonistic and pluralistic attitudes are pro- duced, articulated, adjusted, formed and connected in such a way that relatively coherent state action, safeguarding the reproduction of the system as a whole, is rendered possible and legitimate . . . The parties' regulative capacities are due to large degree to their internal structure: they hardly ever constitute hierarchically and rigidly organised, closed, homogeneous and single-purpose oriented apparatuses, but rather decentralised, heterogeneous, organisational networks, relatively open to their environment. Parties represent complexes of a multitude of 'vertically' (internal factions and groups) and 'horizontally' (regional and local subdivisions) divergent separate organisations. Their hetero- geneous internal structures enable parties to entertain 'pluralistic' rela- tions within an intricate and contradictory institutional 'environment' ['civil society'] . . . Parties remain open to the state apparatus whose personnel they actually or potentially recruit, as well as towards a diverse societal environment. [This heterogeneity] represents a decisive precondition for its regulative function of articulating and processing antagonistic interests and norms.

But, as they continue:

Simultaneously, however, this structure produces a permanent contra- diction that has to be dealt with internally between the incorporated plurality of interests on the one side and programmatic and political unity and administrative capacity to act on the other.

It is with reference to this last point that social scientists and philosophers, under certain conditions, may also play a crucial role, alongside spin- doctoring and piecemeal, technocratic, 'nuts and bolts' policy formulation. Philosophers and social scientists may provide ideological discourse with a special logical coherence, direction and authority, by drawing on 'scientific' and philosophically grounded arguments. Hence, the capacity of politicians to address the 'permanent contradiction between the incorporated plurality of interests on the one side and the programmatic and political unity and administrative capacity to act on the other' might be enhanced. The economic corps has played a crucial role for neo-liberalism in this context. However, after the end of the 'euphoric' (Thatcherite) phase of neo- liberalism, it seems that this economistic discourse has not proved to be adequate for social legitimation (see Bieling 2001).

It is interesting to note therefore that the cosmopolitan intellectual[2] of the Third Way *par excellence* is a sociologist, whose past lies in the milieu of the 'New Left', and who seeks to fuse neo-liberal economics with more 'social' and communitarian sentiments. I am referring to Tony Blair's allegedly 'favourite intellectual', the Director of the London School of Economics,

Anthony Giddens. His *The Third Way: The Renewal of Social Democracy* (1998) has the stated aim of being an ideological treatise for a 'modernised' social democracy. There can be little doubt of his success. There is ample evidence that the aforementioned endorsement of the British Prime Minister is more than self-promotion on the back of the jacket of a book, and that he plays a leading role as such for New Labour in Britain (Hall 1998; Rose 1999, cf. Straw 1998). Furthermore, the fact that social democratic neo-liberalisation does vary on specifics within a certain range in different European political societies (just as the formulation of the Third Way message varies according to different referent groups within a country) does not prevent Giddens' treatise from serving a 'cosmopolitan' philosophic-ideological function for other social democratic parties outside Britain. Indeed, Wolfgang Merkel (2000) gives a detailed account of the variations of social democratic neo-liberalisation in different European countries, including the more corporatist Dutch 'Polder model' and the politics of retrenchment in Sweden in the 1990s. But he also shows that Giddens' Third Way is a common source of intellectual reference and justification. Merkel's benevolent review of the Third Way is itself an indication of the fascination for Giddens' Third Way in Germany after the SPD's electoral victory in 1998 (on this, see Sandner 2000). A more significant indication of this is the joint Blair–Schröder (1999) paper on general policy principles addressed to 'Europe's social democrats' during the elections to the European Parliament in 1999. Even those who oppose the Third Way are compelled to specifically address Giddens (eg. Petrella 1999; Lafontaine 1999).

In this chapter and the one that follows, I will review and critique the discourse of the Third Way exactly on the level where Anthony Giddens seeks to pitch it: as a social-scientific/philosophical justification of a neo-liberalisation of social democracy. This strategy of review and critique has two merits. First, the self-reflexivity and logical coherence of the social-scientific and philosophical discourse allows me to specify exactly in what sense the Third Way is neo-liberal, and how it attempts to articulate neo-liberalism with social-democratic principles. Second, a critique pitched at this level becomes a direct antithesis to the academic-intellectual version of the Third Way discourse. This, it is hoped, will contribute to an understanding of how an alternative left strategy of social democratic articulation, more in line with the European democratic socialist tradition, might render compatible successful social mobilisation and programmatic policy unity and capacity.

In the next section of this chapter, I review Giddens' theory of the Third Way. In this review, I will in particular discuss Giddens' rejection of de-commodification and social citizenship in the universal welfare state as the basis of a viable social democratic political strategy. This is because the maintenance of these principles are, contrary to Giddens' contention, the very precondition for the democratisation and pluralisation of politics that

Giddens also insists are necessary to address legitimation and governability deficits in his call for 'no authority without democracy'.

The remainder of the chapter is organised so as to support this argument. I do so, firstly, through a direct critique of Giddens' position where I point to the inherent contradictions between his principle of 'no authority without democracy' and Giddens' other principle of 'no rights without responsibilities' (which is based on an uncritical reading of neo-classical economic critiques of the welfare state). I conclude that Giddens' attempt to combine participatory and developmental democracy with neo-liberal economics is implausible.

Finally, in the concluding part of the chapter, I introduce the reader to the Swedish model, which is generally accepted as the closest approximation of an ideal social democratic welfare state, based on the principles of universal social citizenship and de-commodification. I do so by invoking the works of Ulf Himmelsrand and his collaborators as well as that of Bo Rothstein and others. On the basis of the results of their research on the Swedish case, I advance a positive and concrete case in favour of the universal social citizenship state and de-commodification. *Contra* Giddens, I argue that this type of welfare state provides an appropriate institutional form to address the legitimation and governability deficits of the welfare state. As a result of this exercise, only Giddens' critique of the economic-rational aspects of the universal social citizenship state remains unaddressed. Given the importance of the Swedish welfare state for the social democratic ideal type, it is not surprising that the Swedish case is particularly pertinent in this context as well. Indeed, Giddens' economic critique of 'traditional social democracy' fundamentally rests on a reference to the 'moral hazard thesis' of the economist Assar Lindbeck as developed in his diagnosis of the crisis of the Swedish economy in the 1990s. I will return to this argument in chapter 2, where I argue that it is based on a faulty reading of Swedish politico-economic developments in the 1980s and 1990s. However, the last section of this chapter will refute the contention that traditional social democracy had no conception of 'supply-side' economic rationality by pointing to the notion of 'misrationalisation' in social democratic ideological discourse.

The Third Way of Anthony Giddens

Left, right and the hegemony of neo-liberalism

It should be made clear from the beginning that when it is suggested here that Anthony Giddens contributes to the hegemony of neo-liberalism, it does not imply that his views are identical to Thatcherism/Reaganism. This is worth pointing out, because many recent commentators on the Third Way have sought to refute the idea that the Third Way is neo-liberal. As indeed Merkel (2000: 100–101) points out, *contra* market fundamentalists Giddens accepts that there is a need for a social safety-net, as trickle-down economics is unlikely to ensure a tolerable level of welfare for the poorest strata of society. Giddens himself is adamant that he is not interested in dismantling the welfare but in reconstructing it (Giddens 1998: 113). He also subscribes to a form of participatory and 'developmental' democracy that would be quite alien to the more 'protective–democratic' ethos of Thatcherism, and is more consistent with the ethos of the libertarian factions of the New Left of the 1960s and 1970s.[3] In this context, Giddens is also concerned about the reproduction of morality and ethics in society. Echoing the thinking of Daniel Bell (1976) on the right and Jürgen Habermas (1976) on the left, he doubts that markets are capable of producing the necessary ethical framework for trust and work-discipline that the market economy requires. Giddens is also taken by Putnam's (cf. 1993) idea that such ethical norms can serve as a 'public good' that in fact enhances the functioning of the economy (social capital) – a point that is lost on neo-classical utilitarians, with their economistic outlook. According to Nicolas Rose (1999: 474–78), it is in this preoccupation with the manufacturing and reproduction of ethics as the legitimate political endeavour of an 'enabling state', flanking the 'community', that we find the novel 'inventiveness' of Third Way politics.

Of course, it is debatable how distinct Third Way politics is on this score. As Rose himself points out: the moral content of the Third Way bears a striking semblance to the neo-conservative morality of the nineteenth century: 'the domesticated family, the disciplines of work, the educational inculcation of moral and technical capacities and competencies, the stabilising cathexis of the home' (ibid: 480–81) (and one could challenge Merkel to find any neo-liberal intellectual who is merely utilitarian and does not concern him/herself with traditional values). Indeed, according to Hall (1998: 12), one of the most striking features of Third Way discourse is its return to the nineteenth century conception of the unemployment problem. With Third Way discourse, this is once again understood as a moral problem of the individual who is unemployed, as opposed to the Keynesian understanding of unemployment as an indicator of a (manageable) problem of the economic system. It should be pointed out, in this context, that Bentham's nineteenth century workhouses were residual welfare-state measures of sorts, deployed exactly with the intention of inculcating a work ethic, and they are manifestations of an awareness that *laissez faire* must be planned (Polanyi 1957).

Nevertheless even if it is accepted that Giddens and Third Way discourse differ from Thatcherism and Reaganism, this does not mean that it is not commensurate with neo-liberal hegemony. Hegemonic politics is not primarily about articulating a common vision, but rather about '[articulating] different visions of the world in such a way that their potential antagonism is neutralised' (Laclau 1977: 161). It is exactly this that Giddens does. If successful, the effect of his particular variant of a politics of commodification, and a politics of no alternatives would be to broaden and consolidate the appeal of neo-liberalism. It would consequently include, for example, the established workers in transnational corporations, teachers, social workers, those in the voluntary sector and perhaps intellectuals of the '1968' genera-tion, who have now reached middle age. There would be contestation and difference in such a hegemonic socio-political bloc (what Gramsci calls a 'power bloc'), but there would be an intersubjective agreement about the necessity of subordinating social life to commodity-economic discipline.

In order to get a more concrete sense of how this neo-liberal interpolation works, we can refer to Giddens himself, who is quite conscious and deliberate with respect to this in his characterisation of the Third Way as a politics 'beyond' the old 'left and right'. This becomes especially clear in his dis-cussion of the meaning of 'left' and 'right' as adopted from Norberto Bobbio:

> When parties and political ideologies are more or less evenly balanced . . .
> few question the relevance of the distinction between left and right. But
> in times when one or the other becomes so strong that it seems 'the only
> game in town', both sides have interests in questioning that relevance.
> The side that is more powerful has an interest, as Margaret Thatcher
> proclaimed, in declaring 'there is no alternative'. Since its ethos has
> become unpopular, the weaker side usually tries to take over some of
> the views of its opponents and propagate those as its own opinions. The
> classic strategy of the losing side is to produce a 'synthesis of opposing
> positions with the intention in practice of saving whatever can be saved
> of one's own position by drawing in the opposing position and thus
> neutralizing it'(cf. Bobbio 1996: 16). Each side represents itself as going
> beyond the old left/right distinction or combining elements of it to
> create a new and vital orientation, [and thereby a new left-right
> polarity].
>
> (Giddens 1998: 41, cf. Bobbio 1996)

Hence, in *The Third Way* Giddens proceeds to lay out a 'new left polar-position'. But this is to be understood as a polarity within the 'politics of no alternative' as defined by Thatcher: 'a synthesis of opposing position, which draws in the opposing position and neutralises it, to save whatever can be saved'. It is exactly in this neutralisation, however, that the hegemony of the opposing position is affirmed. It has become 'common sense'.

The economics of the Third Way

What, then, more specifically is Giddens' understanding of the 'politics of no alternative'? And especially, in what sense can one say that he accepts the politics of a neo-liberal common sense? Giddens argument can be subdivided into the categories of 'economic-rational constraints' and 'legitimation constraints'.

With regard to economic-rational constraints, even according to Merkel, who otherwise goes to some length towards distancing the Third Way from neo-liberalism:

Giddens and New Labour share with neo-liberalism the rejection of statist macroeconomic intervention in the market economy. They also accept the fiscal-conservative policy of budget consolidation, eschew increases in social expenditure and advocate the independence of the European Central Bank.

(Merkel 2000: 100, my translation)

Giddens himself is actually more subtle concerning some aspects of a free market system than this characterisation suggests. Giddens is rightly concerned about the myopic and speculative character of deregulated global financial markets, which he reasonably argues requires a framework of public multilateral regulation (Giddens 1998: 147–53). Merkel, however, captures the way that Giddens' thinking is interpreted in political circles, including the pronouncements of social-democratic 'modernisers', such as Blair, Schröder and Bodo Hombach, who have few propensities to question the role of global financial markets as objective and reliable arbitrators of economic rationality (eg. Held 1998: 25; cf. Blair 1998; Blair and Schröder 1999; Hombach 2000: 9–13). Nevertheless, and more fundamentally, Giddens accepts the microeconomic aspects of the neo-liberal economic argument. He considers traditional social-democratic social and economic policy to be anachronistic as he maintains that it undermines competitiveness in the modern global economy. This is because the institutions of social protection against market effects that traditional social democracy has promoted allegedly generate disincentives, sub-optimal economic behaviour, and inefficiencies. Consequently, such protection, reflected in the expansion of public sector expenditure, should be avoided. Hence, Giddens offers a sophisticated rationale for Blair and Schröder's contention that 'public expenditure as a proportion of national income has . . . reached the limits of acceptability' (Blair and Schröder 1999: 164). Given that British and German public expenditure is much lower than that of Denmark, Norway and Sweden, it should be noted that this implies that these social democratic leaders consider the public expenditure of the Scandinavian social democratic welfare state regimes to be unacceptably high.

The neo-liberal aspects of Giddens' argument, then, pertain specifically to issues of economic rationality. He states quite plainly that the 'old style' social democratic claim that capitalism can be humanised by public intervention has been rendered *passé* by the 'death of Marxism', sealed by the collapse of the Eastern bloc. Moreover, social democratic theory – also in its Keynesian variant was, he claims, always inadequate because of its lack of concern for, and conceptualisation of, the supply-side aspects of markets, pertaining to innovation and productivity. According to Giddens, both Marx and Keynes took productivity for granted. Traditional social democracy was also inadequate, he continues, due to its underestimation of the importance of markets as informational devices. These inadequacies were revealed in the 1980s, 'with intensifying processes of globalisation and tech-nological change'(Giddens 1998: 4–5).

Giddens' economic critique of 'old style' social democracy focuses on the theme of risk and its role in society. The welfare state, as advocated by social democrats, has up until now been based on the minimisation of risk for the individual, based on the idea of social pooling. Individuals have been able to 'unconditionally' claim social entitlements from public programmes in case of, for example, illness, unemployment and old age. While Giddens does not advocate an outright abolition of risk pooling, he does argue that such protection against risk cannot and should not be absolute or 'uncondi-tional'. Welfare policy should not only minimise risk, but also:

> harness . . . the positive or energetic side of risk and provide . . . resources for risk taking. Active risk taking is recognised as inherent in entrepre-neurial activity, but the same applies to the labour force. Deciding to go to work and give up benefits, or taking a job in a particular industry, are risk infused activities – but such risk taking is often beneficial both to the individual and to the wider society.

> (ibid: 116)

For Giddens, risk taking is essential, given the imperatives of technological innovation in the competitive globalised economy. With respect to this point, he is particularly critical against 'unconditional' social citizenship entitlement, traditionally advocated by social democrats, and institu-tionalised in the Scandinavian welfare states. In this context Giddens relies on a reference to the work of the Swedish economist Assar Lindbeck on the crisis of the Swedish economy to substantiate his argument. It should be noted that this reference is the only reference he offers as evidence. Lindbeck is an influential advocate of neo-liberal reform in Sweden, and played a prominent role in the policy formation of the Conservative-led coalition government headed by Carl Bildt in the early 1990s.[4] Lindbeck interpreted the crisis of the Swedish economy in the 1990s essentially to be one of 'moral hazard' caused by the Swedish welfare state. According to the moral hazard thesis, public insurance protection against unemployment and illness makes people alter their behaviour in ways that makes them sub-optimal market actors. This results in higher levels of absenteeism and lower levels of job-search (ibid: 114–15, cf. Lindbeck 1995). This is held to undermine economic competitiveness, and by extension, the economic preconditions of the welfare state.

Pluralism, democracy and the welfare state

When it comes to legitimation constraints, however, Giddens argument is not neo-liberal. It is rather reminiscent of the arguments of some neo-Marxists in the 1970s, especially Habermas (1976) and Offe (1985).[5] According to this argument, the neo-conservative ambition to totally dismantle the welfare state fails to recognise that the golden epoch of *laissez faire* in the nineteenth century rested upon a particular substructure of tradition that is now gone. The patriarchal extended family and quasi-feudal community were important in this context. These secured important reproductive functions, such as child rearing, health care, age care, and care for the poor. They provided informal networks that ensured that exposure to life risks did not threaten social order. This particular construction of a communal life also ensured the reproduction of 'self-evident' norms (especially through religion) that provided the necessary motivational inputs for the economy (work ethic) and for the cementing of consent to public authority (law and order). This substructure was undermined by the process of market-driven restructuring itself, and the welfare state has taken over many of these essential functions. There is no going back to this pre-modern society and the welfare state serves necessary reproductive functions that the market itself cannot provide. In this sense the welfare state is 'irreversible' (Giddens 1998: 70–77). This is the central premise behind Giddens' claim for the need to develop a 'left polar position' within the 'politics of no alternative' as defined by neo-liberalism.

But, according to Giddens, this is not an argument for post-war nostalgia. Following the arguments of the aforementioned neo-Marxists again, Giddens turns the argument of the 'undermining of tradition' against 'traditional' social democracy and the Keynesian welfare state. For example, its conception of full employment presupposed a 'traditional' form of family, with a male 'breadwinner' and housewife, which is no longer tenable. Furthermore, its bureaucratic, uniform and centralised solutions to social service provision were of an undemocratic, authoritarian and increasingly anachronistic character. Apart from these aspects of social policy, pertaining mainly to the 'inner' socialisation of human nature, both neo-conservatives and social democrats have been inadequate in their treatment of 'outer-socialisation': the manner in which human activity transforms the ecological 'environment'.

This part of Giddens' argument is derived from Ulrich Beck's notion of 'risk society'. The basic idea behind this notion is that the ecological sphere has been manipulated and transformed ('socialised') by human activity to such an extent that there is no 'original nature' to which to return any more. Hence, humans in modern society have to cope with the question of how they 'construct' ecology and how they manage ecological risk. However, the ecological interventions and their human implications are so complex that it is no longer possible to rely on experts and the bureaucratic state to devise a regulatory framework based on unambiguously objective scientific conclusions. Given the nature of 'outer socialisation', there will always be scientific controversies and probabilities of risk that in the last instance require a subjective evaluation on behalf of society as a whole. Such an evaluation can only can be generated fairly and legitimately through active civic involvement in ecological risk assessment (ibid: 59; cf. Beck 1994).

Discussing these developments under the heading 'individualism', Giddens argues that the effect of these socialisation processes and transformations have been a 'proliferation of lifestyles' requiring more cultural pluralism (Giddens 1998: 34). In addition, the patriarchal family structure, with a stay-at-home housewife, has been undermined. A kind of anti-politics has also emerged, where people abandon their involvement and loyalty to mass-political organisations, like parties and trade unions. This does not mean that people have become egotistical and apathetic. Present generations show a greater sensitivity towards moral concerns than previous generations, 'but they do not accept traditional modes of authority and legislation of life-styles' (ibid: 36) associated with the parties and interest group organisations that emerged in the early part of the twentieth century. Rather, they tend to be drawn to single-issue politics (ibid: 49–53).

These developments, Giddens continues, pose a threat to social solidarity as organised through present institutions and policies – especially as the conditions of the homogeneous working-class community have been undermined. But at the same time the developments in question suggest that new forms of solidarity are possible, and a politics of the Third Way should seek to devise the appropriate institutions and policies to foster this (ibid: p. 37). For Giddens, as well as the neo-Marxists of the 1970s, the general formula in this context is to democratise political authority structures, including the welfare state, in order to create spaces for human self-fulfilment.

> Social cohesion cannot be guaranteed by the top-down action of the state or by appeal to tradition. We have to make our lives in a more active way than was true of previous generations, and we need more actively to accept responsibilities for the consequences of what we do and the life-style habits we adopt.
>
> (ibid: 37)

Policy-norms: 'no authority without democracy'; 'no rights without responsibilities'

The themes of self-fulfilment call for a politics where 'no authority' is granted 'without democracy'. Hence, Giddens advocates devolution, decentralisation, freedom of choice, diversity and pluralism, as well as a limit on scientific and bureaucratic management in the denaturalised world. On the other hand, considering also his aforementioned analysis of the economic constraints, he also calls for a politics of 'no rights without responsibility' as opposed to 'unconditional' social citizenship entitlements: positive welfare intervention by a 'social investment state'.

Active labour market policy ([re]training of the labour force and 'life-long education') are included as measures of 'positive welfare' and 'social investment'. But so also is proactive encouragement of entrepreneurial initiatives. The premise here is that 'Europe still places too much reliance upon established economic institutions, including the public sector, to produce employment' (Giddens 1998: 124). Under the social investment heading comes also the idea of abolishing statutory pension ages. Due to the general improvement of health, the elderly should not be forced into retirement, but should be allowed to continue to work. Furthermore, Giddens envisages a more individualist and flexible type of pensions saving. Pensions should be individualised both on the savings and withdrawal side in order to allow people to organise their work in the life cycle according to their individual needs and tastes. This means that welfare states should allow, and rely on, an increased proportion of private pension savings. This type of arrangement, Giddens maintains, would mobilise the old as a resource, and would serve to prevent the fiscal crisis associated with the increase of pensioners today (ibid: 118–20).

Concerning flexibility of entry and exit in the labour market, Giddens advocates measures that would allow people to pursue individual strategies to combine work with reproductive functions and life-long learning (through 'family friendly workplace policies' such as child-care, telecommuting and work sabbaticals) (ibid: 118–26). Furthermore, since Giddens belongs to those who doubt that it is possible to return to full employment in the post-war sense, he also envisages 'active redistribution of work'. But this, for him, should be left to the practices in the private sector, as effective public legislation is unlikely 'without counterproductive consequences' (ibid: 126–27).[6] It should also be pointed out that Giddens is not averse to labour market regulations ('labour market rigidities like strict employment legislation do not strongly influence unemployment'). But they can only be accepted if they do not encourage moral hazard. More generally, Giddens argues that benefit systems connected to the labour market 'need to be reformed where they induce moral hazard, and more risk-taking attitude [needs to be] encouraged', because above all, according to Giddens '[h]igh unemployment is linked to generous benefits that run indefinitely' (ibid: 122).

At the same time, Giddens insists that 'adequate' state pensions will remain a necessity for the sake of 'social cohesion'. It is unclear, however, what 'adequate' might mean when risk-minimisation is replaced with risk-management as the guiding principle for policy. This is connected to a continued commitment to the view that it is necessary to have programmes that are 'universal'. 'Universal' is in this context understood in a very specific and limited sense: basic entitlement should ensure that those on the bottom of the social income hierarchy do not become so destitute that they are 'excluded from the mainstream of society'. At the same time, programmes should also provide those in the upper income brackets with a sufficient utility, to ensure they do not 'exit' public schemes altogether, and lose their (tax) 'loyalty' to them. Examples of programmes that should be configured for this end are those in the areas of education and health (ibid: 107–08). Anti-poverty programmes will also continue to be necessary, but they should be designed so as to facilitate 'community care' (ibid: 110).

It should be emphasised, however, that the most significant measures available for the pre-emption of social exclusion in a 'society where work remains central to self-esteem' are labour market policies. And, given the technological revolution on the labour market with its attendant secular trend towards reduced demand for unskilled labour, the solution to this problem must be the aforementioned investments in life-long learning, retraining, and the elimination of moral hazard caused by overly generous social benefits (ibid: 122). Hence the individual is supposed to be compelled to take individual responsibilities in order to assert her or his rights.

Critique

I will not argue against the Beckian conception of risk society, nor Giddens' general argument concerning 'no authority without democracy'. The critical-theoretical research by Habermas, Offe and others on the combined legitimation- and rationality-crisis of the Keynesian welfare state convincingly support the essence of such arguments. The problem is rather that this aspect of Giddens' argument is irreconcilable with the neo-liberal aspects of his argument – those pertaining to 'no rights without responsibilities'.

Of course, Giddens would deny this. And, indeed, he does have an argument that links his neo-liberal economics with his radical participatory politics. He makes the link through a particular, and problematic, reading of Beck's 'risk society'. This reading allows him to treat the imperative for democratic civic involvement in ecological risk management as equivalent and synonymous with the need for individuals to manage their pension, unemployment and health insurance. In this context, ecological risk, social risk and economic risk are treated as if they had the same ontological quality: taking responsibility for the environment and one's mutual fund become one and the same.

> Providing citizens with security has long been a concern of social democrats. The welfare state has been seen as the vehicle of social security. One of the main lessons to be drawn from ecological questions is that just as much attention needs to be given to risk. The new prominence of risk connects individual autonomy on the one hand with the sweeping influence over scientific and technological change on the other. Risk draws attention to the dangers we face – the most important of which we have created for ourselves – but also to the opportunities that go along with them. Risk is not just a negative phenomenon – something to be avoided or minimised. It is at the same time the energising principle of a society that has broken away from tradition and nature.
>
> (ibid: pp. 62–63)

This connection of financial, social and ecological risk is necessary to hold the neo-liberal economics and the radical democratic aspects of Giddens'

argument together. However, this extension of Beck's conception of ecological risk to social and economic risks is a conflation.

From the point of view of political and ideological practice this conflation
is ingenious, because it reconciles within the neo-liberal social democratic
project, conflicting demands, pertaining on the one hand to economic
imperatives, and on the other to imperatives of legitimacy, social representation and civic participation. As a result, it justifies on a philosophical
and theoretical level a broad alliance of interests that otherwise would not
be reconcilable. This parallels the practical politics of 'New Labour' in
Britain, and its aim to be all-inclusive. Chantal Mouffe (1998) and Stuart
Hall refer to this as an attempt to construct a 'politics without enemies',
which actually ignores real and concrete political cleavages and antagonisms
in an unequal society. According to Hall, New Labour:

> speaks as if there are no longer any conflicting interests which cannot be
> reconciled. It therefore envisages a 'politics without adversaries'. This
> suggests that by some miracle of transcendence the interests represented
> by, say, the ban on tobacco advertising and 'Formula One', . . . ethical
> foreign policy and the sale of arms to Indonesia, media diversity and the
> concentrated drive-to-global-power of Rupert Murdoch's media
> empire have been effortlessly 'harmonised' on a Higher Plane, above
> politics.
>
> (Hall 1998: 10)

As such, Third Way discourse, both in its New Labour variant and in
Giddens' discussion of risk, functions as an elaborate rationale for mediating
and pre-empting social conflicts that may arise from real and concrete
cleavages and contradictions. Yet, as Stuart Hall continues, a project that
intends to radically modernise society that does not disturb any existing
interests 'is not a serious [radical] political enterprise' (ibid).

Of course, one cannot deny that 'positive sum games' and social compromises are possible. Indeed, it is difficult to envisage any social democratic
politics, past, present or future, without them. But such positive sum games
are based on particular conditions. Giddens' conflation of risk obscures
rather than clarifies an analysis of these conditions, and pretends that there
is scope for positive sum solutions where there are none. (On the conception
of the socio-economic aspects of these conditions, see the section on a theory
of capitalist regulation in chapter 2.) It is far-fetched indeed to suggest that
Beck's conception of ecological risk is of the same ontological quality as the
kind of risk that is associated with the management of financial assets, which
so severely constrain welfare states through globalised financial markets.
The same goes for the kind of risk that wage-labour faces on the labour
market. Furthermore, the 'human energies' required in the pursuit of a job
and in the choice of a mutual fund, on the one hand, and on the other hand
in civic involvement and in the reasonable consideration of our actions in

light of ecological risk are hardly one and the same. In fact one can reasonably follow the classical works by Marx and Polanyi on the nature of alienation in the capitalist wage relation to argue that these 'human energies' stand in a relation of mutual conflict and contradiction to one another. This is especially true for the socially unprotected worker without 'human capital', who enters the labour market under subordinate conditions. Moreover, if it is at all possible to reconcile them, it requires a continued commitment to the 'traditional' social democratic project of humanisation of capitalism – that is, de-commodification. Giddens does not give us a single reasonable argument as to why and how the contradictions analysed by Marx and Polanyi have been resolved and no longer obtain. To invoke the collapse of the Soviet Union as a means of dismissing these arguments ('the death of Marxism'), as Giddens does, is not valid, as the collapse in question has no bearing on the analysis in question.[7]

As Martha Nussbaum (eg. 1990) has argued, the fundamental point was already present in the work of Aristotle. According to him, leisure is required for civic involvement and ethical deliberation in the polity. This means that 'free and equal' citizens must be certain that the satisfaction of their basic human needs is guaranteed and hence is not dependent upon success in the marketplace. These needs include the goods required for the reproduction of the human body and a reasonable protection against pain. But furthermore, the potential cognitive capabilities, their capacities for practical reason, affiliation with fellow human beings, and relatedness to nature must also be fully encouraged and nurtured; and, the autonomy of humans as individuals must be respected. Only when these needs are satisfied can humans leave the 'realm of necessity' and enter the 'realm of freedom' as citizens capable of civic involvement in a democratic polity. What is more, in a democratic society, these needs have to be secured for *all* citizens. In particular the development of the capacities of practical reason and affiliation – the 'architectonic functions' – are required for humans to organise themselves democratically and ethically in society. In the *Economic and Philosophical Manuscripts* (1844), it was Marx's point exactly that the leisure required, and these architectonic functions, could not be adequately produced for the rugged possessive individualist of capitalist society. Adequate amounts of leisure and security are certainly not granted to the wage labourer in precarious consumer-service employment (a type of employment that, as argued in chapter 2, is becoming increasingly typical in contemporary capitalist society). Furthermore though, those who are affluent in capitalist society are also constantly compelled to face the risks and competition of the market. As a result, all their energies also have to be concentrated on the reproduction of the conditions that are necessary for their existence, and the development of the architectonic functions are thus neglected. If it is at all possible to ensure that the architectonic functions required for ethical deliberation and involvement in capitalist society are developed, it would have to be through the counteracting force of welfare state. And, indeed, social welfare reform constituted exactly a response to this Marxist challenge of bourgeois society. These measures would have to be deliberately geared towards a de-commodification that is forceful enough to ensure that the architectonic functions are present for all citizens in a democracy (Nussbaum 1990).

The problem with Giddens' conflated extension of Beck's management of ecological risk to the management of risk in the labour and financial markets, is that the latter type of risk correspond exactly to the kind of commodification of human life that undermines the architectonic functions. The result of this is that Giddens sets utterly unreasonable demands on the citizen. One wonders where one might find Giddens' heroic competitive, flexible and mobile individual who at the same time is a nurturing parent, rooted in a community, in which he/she has time and energy to invest civic involvement. That is, an individual who could arbitrate, for example, in complex scientific debates about the wisdom of allowing genetically manipulated produce. It would be a repressed super-ego indeed that in this context would refrain from engaging in power-charged strategic language games driven on by economic interests imposed by necessities as defined by the terms of market participation. When the individual then fails to live up to these demands, it is presumably the role of 'etho-politics' to discipline (and punish?) the *individual*. It is as if the entire weight of the social contradictions of modern capitalism is to be borne by the individual, who has no social rights at all to claim 'without responsibilities'. The highly unequally distributed incidence of this weight, that stems from the unequal terms on which individuals participate on the labour and capital markets, is too obvious to require further elaboration.

In contrast to the conclusions that Giddens draws from Beck's analysis of 'risk society', I would put forward those of Claus Offe (1996: pp. 31–57). Like Giddens, Offe argues that Beck's risk society requires explicit ethical civic involvement, and in this context he invokes the Habermasian notion of 'discourse-ethics'. To be sure, Habermas has developed a powerful critique of bureaucratic intervention in everyday life, because such interventions tend to undermine the informal communal networks in which intersubjective moral norms – Aristotle's architectonic functions – are reproduced. But Habermas' critique is not only one of state bureaucracy. This is only one aspect of a broader critique of the tendency in modern society to overextend technocratic 'systems-steering' of society. In contrast to Giddens, Habermas and Offe continue in this context to be concerned also with the dangers of the commodity logic of the capitalist economic system and its 'colonisation' of these communal networks. In recent work, Offe is particularly concerned with the threat of social marginalisation that is inherent in private insurance. Such insurance gives powerful incentives to those with purchasing and market power to exclude others, in order to reduce risks and costs on premiums. More generally, neo-liberal deregulation promotes residual measures, where only 'those in need' will be protected. This, however, tends to constitute different welfare constituencies as fragmented and marginal groups, who can easily be targeted as minority 'special interests' when further cutbacks are called for, or as neo-liberal political constituencies call for tax cuts. This perpetuates rather than mitigates the fragmentary tendencies of post-traditional society (Offe 1996: 105–20; 147–200). Whilst Giddens claims that the Third Way is committed to prevent such social exclusion, he does not provide any reasonable evidence that it is up to this task. This also applies to the question of organisation of work and the labour market. To be sure, new technology allows for reduction of work time and more skilled and 'humanising' work practices but, as I will discuss in further detail in the next chapter, neo-liberalism is likely to pre-empt rather than promote such a 'post-Fordist' development.

Offe situates this analysis within a broader critique of the specific mode of social regulation that neo-liberal capitalism promotes. Such modernisation subordinates all other aspects of social life to the exigencies of the market system. Certainly, one effect of this development has been a revolutionary expansion of production possibilities and an increase in the range of choice of individuals. However, this development has generated a complex array of external effects, while the capacity to counter these external effects is undermined by the same development. In part, the capacities to counteract the external effects are reduced because capitalism fragments social agency and undermines the terms of discourse ethics. But there is also a regulative dimension to the problem: since all other forms of social action are subordinated to the market, the complex set of external effects can only be countered *ex post* through residual measures when the effects already have occurred. This leads to a daunting regulatory agenda with many policy conflicts that cannot be resolved. In contrast to this, Offe calls for forms of regulation that prevent these external effects *ex ante* (Offe 1996: pp. 1–30).

To sum up, there is a lot of merit in much of what Giddens has to say about social democratic renewal – about environmental risk, diversification of life-styles and the undermining of traditional authority – which makes democratic deepening not only desirable but also arguably necessary. But he ignores the empirical evidence and the theoretical arguments that point towards the destructive effects that self-regulating markets have on the conditions required for such developments; and he to underestimates the need for countervailing regulation – the old fashioned project of a humanisation of capitalism.

Traditional social democracy reconsidered

The case for the continued relevance of traditional social democracy understood in terms of welfare state universalism, social citizenship and de-commodification can be made with reference to the most sophisticated of the works on the Swedish model, the so-called Scandinavian power-mobilisation school; that is, the work by Ulf Himmelstrand (1981) and his collaborators. Himmelstrand *et al.* took very seriously the 'extended contradictions' of the welfare capitalism that Habermas and Offe had identified. Himmelstrand *et al.*'s response was not to deny that the welfare state had played its part in generating these. Furthermore, they were aware of the fact that the Swedish welfare state of the 1970s also had its limitations and problems and that it was not exempt from the aforementioned contradictions. Nevertheless, they argued that the institutional framework of universalism and de-commodification that social democracy as a hegemonic force had generated in Sweden created favourable conditions and potentials for redressing these problems. They understood the welfare state in reformist Marxist terms as an ambiguously progressive legacy, which had led to an improvement in the life chances of the mass population, but that also had its limits and contradictions. However, the universal welfare state, they argued, created the power resources required to address these contradictions and hence further the reformist socialist project.

First, Himmelstrand *et al.* pointed to the importance of the institutions of the universal welfare state for the political reproduction of organised labour as a collective actor (ibid: 105–209). This was not only a question of devising full employment policies, unemployment insurance schemes, solidaristic wage policy, and universal benefits so as to reproduce the industrial working class as a collective actor (though, it was that too). With careful empirical analysis they showed that these institutions counteracted the tendencies of fragmentation of working-class agency in the post-modern and post-industrial phase of development. In particular, these institutions encouraged the growing stratum of white-collar professionals in the expanding public service sector to identify themselves as 'wage-earners'. This 'extended working class', they argued, could potentially exercise 'ethico-political leadership' over society as a whole, and make the universal welfare state part of the 'common sense' through which post-modern demands for ecological renewal, pluralism, and decentralisation could be made. This could potentially create the space for social democracy to propose decentralisation through measures such as 'industrial democracy' and decentralisation of social service delivery within a reconstituted welfare state that remained committed to universal entitlements.

True, traditional social democratic organisations, such as the blue-collar trade union federation (LO), is unlikely to be the agency to redress the problems of the post-war welfare state in an immediate sense, beyond questions of work environment and industrial democracy. But subsequent work has shown that struggles of so-called 'new social movements' for gender equality[8] and immigrant rights,[9] for example, can actually or potentially be comparatively propitiously pursued within the universal welfare state. Hence, these struggles might be productively articulated to the hegemonic project of such an extended working class. As a result, these groups tend to develop loyalty to the universal welfare state and the principle of social citizenship. What is more, although people acquire a plurality of subject-positions, their position in the extended working class as reproduced by the universal welfare state implies that these are related to class unity at the level of work. For example, Jenson and Mahon (1993) have pointed to the tendency towards 'wage-earner' feminism in the Swedish trade union movement, which shows particular concerns for issues of nurturing, caring and reproduction in society. More recently, Rothstein (1998) has argued that it is only a universal welfare state that can formulate its norms of entitlement on a sufficiently *abstract* level in order to be independent of a particular conception of the content of the 'good life'. This would seem to be necessary in order to allow for a sufficiently wide range of concrete expressions of the good life as implied by the subjective pluralism that characterises contemporary society. On the basis of these works, one can argue that there is no reason to presume that 'traditional' social democratic institutions cannot potentially cope with what Giddens calls 'individualism'. Rather, the decommodifying *universal* welfare of the Swedish type seems particularly well suited for this.[10] There is, however, no guarantee that these potentials are realised. In chapter 6 we will point at the disintegrative effect the neo-liberal macroeconomic policy has had for such politics in Sweden.[11]

Secondly, Himmelstrand *et al.* argued that this hegemonic extended working class provided a good potential socio-political basis for addressing the governability crisis of the welfare state. When embedded in the aforementioned welfare state institutions, such a working class can potentially develop an integral perspective of social life and its environment. The *habitus* of a highly organised working class is such that it potentially integrates a wide range of contradictory incentives and concerns. Whilst it might not be in a position to find an 'optimising' strategy to deal with the contradictions of modern life, it is in a better position to develop a wide-ranging 'satisficing' strategy. As wage-earners the members of such a class obviously have an incentive to ensure high wages and a good work environment. Furthermore, they also have an incentive in long-term innovation in enterprises, since their work depends on this. But in order to integrate these contradictory incentives, the organised working class needs guarantees that profits will be reinvested so as to ensure such employment, and this led Swedish trade unions to demand a radical variant of workers' ownership in the shape of the so-called 'wage-earner funds'. In addition, Himmelstrand *et al.* argued that workers in their capacity as inhabitants of communities were affected by environmental degradation and, in materially secure conditions, where the welfare capitalism ensured them a certain standard of living, they could potentially be mobilised for an environmentally sustainable development (Himmelstrand *et al.* 1981: 130–38). Again, the organisations that most immediately represent the workers as workers, the trade unions, were not to be seen as the immediate agents of such a complex articulation. Rather, this role would fall to the social democratic party. This party, synthesising and representing a 'general will' of a broader movement whose branches include the trade unions as well as other popular movements (*folkrörelser*),[12] and linking this movement to the state, would be charged with the role of constructing an integral strategy of economic, social welfare and ecological reform, and a reform of the subjective definition of solidarity.

In other words, the security of the universal welfare state and the minimisation of social risk would allow such a working class with sufficient leisure and freedom to consider in an integral manner these 'external effects' and contradictions of advanced capitalism. Moreover, industrial democracy – counteracting the de-skilling of Taylorist production – and the progressive reduction of working time would encourage the development of architectonic functions for a more active citizenship.

It should be emphasised that the universal–abstract conception of social citizenship is needed to integrate different fractions of this wage-earner collective as well as other non-class subject positions that they might occupy (as women, parents, immigrants, etc.) to prevent social divisions and distributive conflicts between different groups. It is only through this broader conception of social citizenship that one can envisage a 'discourse ethics' emerging, that would allow citizens to cope, for example, with the environmental risks that Giddens raised by invoking Beck (see Offe 1996). But to be meaningful at all in this context, universal entitlements need to be set at generous levels, and services need to be of a high quality. This means that they are costly and that they require high tax-rates (Rothstein 1998a). It also means that redistributive questions are best resolved *ex ante* at the level of the wage relation. (Universal benefit systems are not effective for redistribution as such, but they provide social protection potentially without state intrusion into the lives of citizens.) Such *ex ante* redistribution, however, requires a tight discipline on capital. In other words, social wage relations need to be modified *ex ante* before the capitalist labour market generates its external effects on the life-world.

Underpinning this is a particular ideological–intellectual knowledge perspective. In Swedish social democracy, these ideas centred on a notion of 'misrationalisation' in advanced capitalism. The notion was introduced to Swedish socialists from a particular reading of Austro-Marxist Otto Bauer in trade union debates on strategy in the 1930s (De Geer 1978). According to Bauer, misrationalisation occurs when there is a discrepancy between private-economic rationalisation (implemented by individual enterprises in order to increase its profits) and societal rationalisation. The reduction of costs of production for the individual capitalist is not the same as the reduction of costs for society. Bauer argues that in advanced, functionally differentiated and organically complex capitalism, the tendency is towards increased instances of misrationalisation. This tendency has its origin in the fact that wage labour is a commodity in capitalist society that the capitalist purchases only as long as s/he needs it. However, the costs for (re)production of labour power falls on society as a whole (and in the case of *laissez faire*, the cost is distributed to each individual wage-labouring household). The discrepancy between private and social rationalisation can only be bridged where economic production and social reproduction are unified within the same organisational principle or meta-principle (for Bauer, the socialist state).

In this ideological conception, rationalisation as a principle is affirmed. However, the naive equation of rationalisation with the unleashing of market forces is profoundly problematised. What Swedish social democrats took from Bauer as a guiding principle in their pragmatic search for appropriate welfare state mechanisms, was the idea that economic and social rationalisation had to be viewed from an integral and holistic perspective. Furthermore, they accepted the argument that a common organisational meta-principle was needed (often referred to as 'planning'), and that the reproduction of labour was at the core of the problematic. What was required was an *integral welfare state* (*pace* Mishra 1984), that had at its regulatory core institutions that could promote economic rationalisation at the same time as this rationalisation was checked for social concerns. Swedish social democrats postulated certain political goals of social security, that were held to be consistent with socialist principles as they were achievable within the present development of productive forces. From this vantage point, they enquired empirically and experimentally what form of social organisation was the most suitable to meet the ends in a given instance. Market actors that could not deliver were to be eliminated, and where appropriate, replaced by public or cooperative forms.

This principle is not easily applied in practice, and in subsequent chapters we shall see how socio-economic power relations resulted in particular interpretations of the meaning of 'misrationalisation' where certain concerns were excluded. One central problem here, of course, is that the consistent application of the principle is politically explosive in what in essence remains a capitalist socio-economic order. It implied a serious challenge to the absolute discretion of private ownership of the means of production. As a result, Swedish capitalists have continuously fought off the most radical and logically consistent political implications of this thinking, such as the wage-earner funds and Gunnar Myrdal's notions of democratic planning in the immediate post-war period. Nevertheless, Swedish social democracy in the post-war period was sufficiently strong to maintain this principle through the mode of regulation that was based on the co-called 'Rehn–Meidner model', which related supply- and demand-side aspects of economics to the redistributive principle of de-commodification. (This will be discussed in detail in chapter 4.) In other countries, the capacity to control the 'supply side' has been weaker – perhaps particularly in Britain, where Labour in the end only came to subscribe to a vulgar variant of demand-side Keynesianism, without any elements of integral planning. But this 'retreat to the demand side' expressed a compromise from a position of weakness. Seen from this perspective, Giddens' characterisation of a demand-side orientation as the essence of social democratic ideas is not only wrong, but also ironic – it is not the essence of traditional social democracy, it represents the dilution of traditional social democracy, which resulted from its compromise with social liberalism.

In contrast to this 'integral' welfare state perspective, Giddens in fact conceives of what Titmuss (1971) called a 'residual' welfare state. In the residual model, the market mechanism is not modified *ex ante* but construed as the basic mechanism of social organisation. Welfare state measures are merely used as 'correctives' *ex post* when people cannot for 'valid reasons' manage to make ends meet through market participation. This type of welfare state thinking is not new. It is the type that has tended to characterise western capitalist societies, especially in the Anglo-Saxon world. Furthermore, the extent of its prevalence is inversely related to the mobilisational power of the organised working class and social democracy (Esping-Andersen 1985a). If anything, Giddens – and neo-liberals more generally – merely advocate a purer type of residualism. Such a welfare state, however, is full of Offe's *ex post* contradictions. Though justified in a society that on the level of ideals privilege 'individual freedom', this type of welfare state by necessity must be selective and intrusive, as it is forced to economise on scarce welfare state resources. Hence the freedom of its clients is restricted and violated. This is as a result of the constraints that the unregulated capitalist market economy sets on it, in terms of limited rates of taxation, and inequalities implied in unregulated labour markets. As neo-Marxist political economy established back in the 1970s, this type of welfare state is not propitious to the freedom required for democratic participation and inclusion in social life. It is Giddens' disregard of these contradictions between the terms of capital accumulation and his goals for social inclusion and democracy that constitute the essential problem with his Third Way.

2 The social democratic welfare state and the political economy of capitalist restructuring

Chapter 1 made the case for the continued relevance of the universal welfare state based on norms of de-commodification, or the 'social citizenship state', of which the Swedish welfare state is the closest approximation to the ideal type (Esping-Andersen 1985a). The argument was not that the social democratic welfare state is without problems with regard to pluralism and democracy. But, invoking particularly Himmelstrand *et al.* (1981) and Rothstein (1998a,b), the argument was that the institutional form of the social democratic welfare state provided a propitious framework and context for a socio-political transformation that could address the legitimation problems of contemporary advanced capitalist society. Universalism with high levels of entitlement are required to ensure that policy implementation remains simple (and hence avoids bureaucratic 'governability crisis'); to ensure that state intervention does not become intrusive and infringe on diverse lifestyles (here the distinction between entitlement levels and monistic implementation is important); and to sustain a social solidarity based on the popular hegemony of an 'extended working class'. In short, *contra* Giddens, chapter 1 constitutes an advocacy of the project of a humanisation of capitalism without apologies.

But chapter 1 did not address the question of the economic viability of this welfare state in the era of 'global competition'. In other words, Giddens' neo-liberal argument against the economic rationality of 'traditional social democracy' has yet to be addressed. That is the objective of this chapter. It will be argued that the 'traditional' social democratic project of a humanisation of capitalism is still a viable project in the 'late-modern', 'post-industrial', or more to the point, 'post-Fordist' world. What is more, an analysis of Swedish political economy in the 1980s and the first part of the 1990s that goes beyond the superficialities of the mainstream demonstrates this.

Post-industrialism, models of welfare capitalism and global competition

Whilst globalisation is an important theme for Giddens in *The Third Way*, his argument against the economic rationality of traditional social democracy is in essence a microeconomic one. His critique focuses on the level of the individual and his/her performance on the labour market. Welfare benefits, based on the principles of social citizenship and risk-minimisation generate, according to Giddens, economically dysfunctional behaviour, as these schemes encourage individuals to consume social services excessively whilst they perform sub-optimally and dysfunctionally as factors of production. For example, individuals tend to reduce job-search efforts; they prolong claims to unemployment insurance; they call in sick too often or remain on sick-leave for too long and hence they prolong claims to health insurance; and they have incentives to claim pensions prematurely. Such micro-economic irrationalities then undermine the competitiveness of corporations in the global marketplace. As a result, the material basis of the welfare state is undermined. Globalisation, understood in terms of reduction of trade barriers and barriers to capital movements, has reduced the possibility of tolerating such economically dysfunctional behaviour (Giddens 1998: cf. Lindbeck 1995; see also Lindbeck *et al.* 1994).

I will return to Giddens' argument later in this chapter and seek to refute it. It cannot be addressed immediately because it does not reflect the best possible case against the norms of de-commodification. Giddens' account does not analyse in sufficient detail the pressures that the welfare state faces. Furthermore, his account of the welfare state is too stylised and does not analyse in detail important variations between different types of welfare states. There are, however, more nuanced and detailed analyses of the welfare state that are in basic agreement with Giddens. These must be addressed before I can provide a more convincing defence of the socio-economic rationality of the social democratic welfare state. Gøsta Esping-Andersen's (1996) recent work is in basic agreement with Giddens, and this work should perhaps be taken especially seriously since Esping-Andersen is an erstwhile avid defender of the de-commodifying universal social democratic welfare state. Indeed, the usage of the very concept in contemporary discussions can be attributed to him.

According to Esping-Andersen, welfare states face a dramatically increased trade-off between social protection, equality and economic rationality, because of changing demographics, fundamental shifts in the capitalist socio-economic structure and increased global competition. Esping-Andersen argues that advanced welfare states face a basic dilemma: how should they cope with ageing populations, lower fertility rates, and differentiated 'life-cycles' on the one hand, and with a slower rate of growth that he (invoking Baumol 1967) suggests is inherent in the shift from a manufacturing-centred industrial economy, to a service-centred post-industrial economy on the other, whilst at the same time they face the increased constraints of global competition. For Esping-Andersen, the essence of the problem is constituted by demographic trends. With a projected 50 per cent increase in the age-dependency ratio between 1996 and 2020, given present-day entitlements and rates of economic growth, welfare state capacities will be over-stretched.

To meet current commitments, an increase of social expenditure equivalent to an extra 5–7 per cent share of GDP would be required. This indicates the severe fiscal strain that secular demographic trend exerts on welfare states (Esping-Andersen 1996a: 7, cf. European Community 1993: 24 and OECD 1988a). Given the imperatives of global competition, increased taxation hardly constitutes a feasible route towards raising the required additional resources, according to Esping-Andersen. Increased rates of productivity growth could, however, provide the basis for the required additional expenditure. Productivity growth would need to underwrite an *additional* increase of 0.5–1.2 per cent of real taxable earnings on top of what current rates of productivity growth allows. This would be sufficient to finance additional expenditure (Esping-Andersen 1996a: 7).

But Esping-Andersen suggests that such additional productivity and real social wage growth are difficult to achieve in the post-industrial economy. In post-industrialism there is an increased trade-off between employment, equality and high rates of productivity growth. This is because high value-added jobs in manufacturing are becoming increasingly scarce as a result of increased capital intensity, generated by the introduction of automation technology. The new jobs are increasingly to be found in the low productivity service sector, where wages consequently have to be lower. The alternative to the creation of a low-wage economy is mass unemployment, which further exacerbates the tendencies towards fiscal crisis, because of increased claims on unemployment insurance funds. Given his conclusion that the afore-mentioned trade-offs have become more severe, he advocates welfare and labour market reforms that are similar to those suggested by Giddens.

The post-industrial dilemma and Esping-Andersen's three 'policy regimes' of welfare capitalism

Esping-Andersen supports his argument with reference to different types of advanced welfare capitalism. Here he uses the famous typology of three 'policy regimes' that he developed elsewhere (Esping-Andersen 1985a; 1990: esp. pp. 26–32, 38–54). In that work, Esping-Andersen showed that the distinct institutional characteristics of different types of welfare state regimes were determined by, and tended to reproduce, distinct socio-political political power structures. One of Esping-Andersen's ideal types is the 'conservative', or 'Christian democratic' welfare policy regime, which finds its approximate concrete expression in the continental European states (such as Germany, Austria and the Netherlands). In this model, conservative social forces, connected with the state and the church, and with their roots in pre-capitalist society, took the lead in welfare state development in the late nineteenth century. Following the lead of the Bismarck reforms of the 1880s, these forces mediated between the forces of capitalist development and the emerging socialist working class, in order to ensure that the dis-integrative effects of the former did not lead to a socialist revolution. The essential social purpose in this context was to counteract what they considered to be the morally degrading and anomic effects of capitalist commodification, and to ensure that the proletariat was organically integrated into national society as a loyal subject of the state. This type of welfare policy regime, then, keeps commodification in check in order to maintain 'traditional values' such as the family, church, and the respect towards preordained status and hierarchy between social groups. Here workers are granted corporative status and protection in the national community, in exchange for 'responsible behaviour'. The main components of social policy in this regime are corporatist interest intermediation in collective wage-bargaining and occupation-based (status-determined) social insurance.

The liberal welfare policy regime is another of Esping-Andersen's ideal types, and it approximates developments in, for example, the USA, Britain and Canada. Here the *raison d'être* of welfare policy is to maintain and reproduce the ethos of possessive individualism. To be sure, the liberal welfare state was also designed in terms of 'public goods' to protect people against contingencies such as illness, accidents and unemployment. But the protection – simulating individual insurance contracts – was designed to maintain rather than mitigate the cash nexus (between individual contribution and benefits) and the individual wage labourer as a privileged reference for socio-economic identity. This type of welfare state tolerates trade unions under the guise of 'freedom of association', but is reluctant to give them official status or acknowledge the wage relation as an 'unfree' relation that requires a collective mobilisation of workers to counteract the power of capitalists. Welfare policy is organised along voluntary, individualist–actuarialist lines and public intervention is kept to a minimum. The state only contravenes the market logic through a residual means-tested 'safety net' – social assistance, intended for those 'problem cases' that are not capable of providing for their own protection through market performance. The liberal welfare policy regime is synonymous with what chapter 1, invoking Titmuss (1974), labelled the 'residual welfare state'.

Esping-Andersen reserves the label 'social democratic' welfare policy regime to the ideal type that approximates welfare state design in the Scandinavian countries. It was only in these countries that the labour movement of the second international became hegemonic and succeeded in making welfare policy reflect the concrete strategy of the politically conscious reformist working class. The essential *raison d'être* of the social democratic policy regime is to provide a social income or wage that is independent of wage labour, and that is granted as a universal entitlement of 'social citizenship'. Such 'de-commodification' was intended to generate working class unity and loyalty to the social democratic project and to extend the appeal of this project beyond the working class to 'the people' in general. Like the conservative regime, this regime provides de-commonification, but rather than allocating particularist entitlements and assigning particularist 'places' for social groups in society, this de-commodification strategy attempts to project

universalism. The policies of this de-commodification include transfer payment and services that provide universal entitlements or income maintenance, a collective bargaining regime supporting solidaristic wage policy,
flanked by a macroeconomic policy commitment that blunts the disciplinary
stick of the threat of unemployment by providing an unconditional commitment to full employment.

These welfare state regimes were created in the course of the development
of industrial capitalism and the institutionalisation of distinct Fordist
models of economic growth. However, Esping-Andersen argues that these
institutional arrangements have also set the framework for distinct, path-
dependent trajectories of post-industrial capitalist development, some of
which Esping-Andersen considers to be more viable than others. He argues
that the Christian democratic welfare policy regime of continental Europe
faces some fundamental contradictions. These result from the fact that this
institutional form has not responded to the decrease of labour demand in
the industrial manufacturing sector, generated by increased capital intensity
and automation, by an offsetting increase of labour-demand in an expanding
post-industrial service sector. Rather there has been a reduction of the
labour supply and the volume of employment.[1]

Two institutional determinants, both intimately related to the shape of
welfare state arrangements, are held to be central in this context: the 'rigid'
nature of wage determination in the corporatist labour market; and social
policy encouraging the reproduction of the traditional family and the male
breadwinner model (Esping-Andersen 1996b). Apart from failing to address
poverty generated by the increased incidence of breakdown of the traditional
family,[2] these determinants have generated an unsustainable trajectory of
'jobless growth', characterised by mass unemployment and fiscal crisis.
Comparatively high and 'rigid' negotiated wages, asserted by the corporatist
collective bargaining regime on the economy as a whole, have led to capital
intensive corporate restructuring in the export-oriented manufacturing
sector. At the same time, these high wage-levels have retarded the development of the service sector, given the limits to productivity growth in services.
Furthermore, this type of welfare state deliberately encourages the maintenance of the traditional family, and has not pursued the heavy public
investment in, for example, public childcare that might have boosted the
service sector. Whilst this development results in high productivity growth
and high wages for those who remain employed (the 'insiders' of the labour
market), labour is to a significant extent shedded. Christian democratic
welfare states have responded to this excess labour supply, through early
retirement schemes, a reduction of working hours, and high levels of unemployment insurance payments. The problem is, however, that these benefits
are funded through increases of payroll taxes (employers' and employees'
contributions), which increase wage costs further, and compel companies to
pursue labour shedding further. According to Esping-Andersen, the continental model is engaged in a hopeless battle to remain fiscally solvent, as

growth rates can no longer be maintained to generate sufficient revenue for its transfer payment programmes. This is especially so because increased capital intensity means that the payroll-tax revenue/growth rate ratio tends to decrease whilst demographic changes increase demands for expenditure and reduce revenue.[3] Additionally, the unemployment problem becomes increasingly acute, which generates further fiscal pressure. The scope to switch to alternative forms of taxation, such as the taxation of capital, is held to be very limited in an era of global competition and transnational capital mobility (Esping-Andersen 1996b; see also Streeck 1995).

According to Esping-Andersen, the neo-liberal route of deregulation of the Anglo-Saxon residual welfare state as practised in the United States and Britain in the 1980s and 1990s is a more viable response to post-industrialism. Here, curtailment of union rights, labour market deregulation, and a reduction of social benefits have resulted in an increase of employment growth and a reduction of unemployment. This has created the conditions for the development of a labour-intensive service sector, which depends on low-wage flexible labour but that also offers high skill and high (albeit often flexible and insecure) wages at the apex of its occupational stratum.[4] Esping-Andersen argues that fiscal pressures and unemployment problems can be resolved in this model. The emerging service sector has proved to be capable of absorbing surplus labour, which, in turn, offloads fiscal burdens from the state. Furthermore, pensions become increasingly a private matter, generated through private savings and managed by mutual funds. Indeed, pension-fund management plays an important role in the emerging service economy. In this context, the difference between the normative and institutional relationship to the traditional family in the liberal and the conservative regimes is of critical importance. In the liberal regime, there has been a dramatic increase in the labour force participation rate and the employment rate of women – in large part in low-end service jobs, but also in some high-wage professional jobs (Esping-Andersen 1990: 201–02).[5] This increases the tax base, which significantly contributes to the relief of the aforementioned demographic pressures on social expenditure (Esping-Andersen 1996a).

On the basis of this comparison, Esping-Andersen argues that re-commodification, retrenchment, and a certain convergence towards the liberal welfare policy regime will be necessary if welfare capitalism is to be stabilised. Compared to Giddens, however, he is refreshingly blunt about what the distributive implications of this type restructuring will be. In a pessimistic tone, he predicts that the result of such neo-liberalisation will be increased polarisation and segmentation between core and periphery in the labour market (leaving little room for Giddens' 'social cohesion' of the Third Way). Drawing on the American and British experience, he points out that the trend towards 'flexible' and reduced wages has produced 'unprecedented levels of poverty' (Esping-Andersen 1996: 8). He (rightly) does not even entertain the prospect that this type of welfare state might generate more participatory forms of democracy.

Esping-Andersen's recent work is also strikingly pessimistic about the post-industrial prospects of the social democratic welfare-policy regime. Here there has been a dramatic shift in his argument between the publication of *The Three Worlds of Welfare Capitalism* in 1990 and *Welfare States in Transition* in 1996. Indeed, in the former work he argued that the social democratic policy regime did provide the basis of a viable post-industrialism, which maintained and perhaps even enforced and extended the norms or de-commodification and social citizenship. He argued that mass unemployment could be avoided in the social democratic model through tax-funded public investments in labour-intensive social welfare services. He pointed especially towards the expansion in 'reproductive' services and female employment in Sweden in the 1970s and 1980s, ensured by public child-care programmes, education, and in the expansion of public care and services for the elderly. Employment expansion proceeds without significant wage-segmentation in this policy regime, because public service workers are unionised, and wages are determined through inter-sectoral, co-ordinated and solidaristic wage bargaining. Resources are thereby transferred to the low productivity, service sector, oriented towards the national economy, from the export-oriented high-productivity manufacturing sector. This transfer is ensured in two ways: first, high taxes (income taxes, corporate taxes, sales taxes and payroll taxes) are used to finance public service sector production. Second, coordinated and solidaristic wage-policy implies that workers in the export-oriented manufacturing sector forfeit some of the wage increases that productivity increases in their sectors would grant, in favour of wage increases above productivity rates in the public service sector.

Esping-Andersen supported his argument with some striking empirical evidence that set Swedish developments since 1960 apart from the developments in the USA and Germany. In contrast to Germany, in Sweden, high and negotiated wage growth in the manufacturing sector did not correlate with reduced participation rates and employment. Rather, post-industrial employment grew at the same rate in Sweden as in the USA, with a dramatic increase in female employment in health, education and welfare making up for low rates, comparable to the German rates, in the low-end consumer service sector. The total employment rate also increased in Sweden, although at a lower rate than in the USA. Moreover, a significant part of employment growth was growth in part-time employment. On the other hand, participation rates in Sweden were much higher even than in the USA, and the part-time ratio was significantly lower than in Germany.[6]

In *The Three Worlds*, Esping-Andersen argued that this social democratic form of post-industrial welfare capitalism was also fiscally viable. Tolerance of higher tax-rates obviously helped and full employment obviously contained unemployment insurance expenditure. But furthermore the welfare policy regime ensured a more sustainable transition from the traditional family structure. High female participation rates and exceptionally high fertility rates would ensure an adequate expansion of the labour supply, a

Table 2.1 Basic economic indicators, Sweden

	1986–90	1991–95	1996	1997
Real GDP growth	3.8	0.5	1.3	1.8
Govt financial balance	3.1	−7.9	−3.6	−1.8
Unemployment	2	7.2	9.6	9.9
RULC change	8	1.6	4.7	0.9
Productivity growth	1.8	2.7		

Source: OECD (1999) *Economic Outlook 66*, Annex Tables 1, 13, 22, and 30 and OECD (1997) *Historical Statistics*, Table 3.7.

Real GDP: average annual percentage change.
Financial balance: average annual balance as percentage of GDP.
Unemployment: standardised rate of unemployment.
Relative Unit Labour Cost: average annual change.
Productivity growth: average annual change of GDP/person employed.

higher tax base and a lower dependency ratio, which in turn would address the problem of demographic pressures. These developments were facilitated by public child-care and extensive provisions for parental leave that would allow women to 'harmonise careers with fertility' (Esping-Andersen 1996: 13, see also 76).

It is evident, however, that Esping-Andersen was impressed by the rapid developments towards severe fiscal imbalances, high levels of unemployment and years of low GDP-growth that emerged in Sweden almost immediately after the publication of *Three Worlds* (Table 2.1). In his subsequent dismissal of the socio-economic viability of this policy regime, the same microeconomic interpretation, as in Giddens' *The Third Way*, relying on the same school of neo-classical economists for the diagnosis, is articulated. Invoking the moral hazard argument, he states that 'high wages and taxes are widely believed [sic] to spur negative work incentives and hidden employment' (ibid: 13, n. 15), and he concludes:

> [the] Achilles heel of the system . . . is the growing tax burden that a huge public labour market incurs. With high rates of productivity growth the system can be sustained: when productivity of private investments are sluggish, severe cost problems emerge. This is exactly the situation that especially Sweden faces today: declining fiscal capacity combined with rising pressures on public job creation/or income maintenance. Swedish policy makers and unionists can no longer avoid wage flexibility and major social benefit cuts.

(ibid: 13)

I will return to and critique this 'belief', for which, Esping-Andersen admits in a footnote, it is hard to 'come by hard evidence' (ibid: 13, n. 15) in the second half of the chapter. But before this can be done, it is necessary to discuss in further detail Esping-Andersen's prescriptions for the continental 'Christian democratic' welfare states. Such a discussion is important, because European social democratic 'modernisers', in charge of welfare state restructuring in Europe at the time of publication of this book, depart from conclusions like those generated by Esping-Andersen's analysis. They have eschewed ambitions to transform Christian democratic welfare states in a Scandinavian social democratic direction. Instead, they seek a partial convergence with the Anglo-Saxon liberal welfare policy regime. In this context, the practical experiences of Dutch restructuring (the 'Polder Model') have generated particular interest among social democratic modernisers, not the least in Europe's economically dominant state, Germany.

Neo-liberalism with a human face?

Esping-Andersen concludes that the realities of post-industrialism require a convergence towards the Anglo-American policy regime despite its costs in terms of poverty and inequality. However, he does hold up the hope that if this policy is modified with one component of the social democratic model, an active labour market policy of retraining of the workforce, then the worst of the inequalities can be checked. Indeed, insofar as people are likely to change jobs more often over the life-cycle, life-long learning might result in equality over the life-cycle as people move from low-skill to high-skill employment (Esping-Andersen 1996a: 261–65). This would amount to a kind of 'neo-liberalism with a human face'. Here Esping-Andersen's prescriptions dovetail with those of the social democratic modernisers, who provide the current intellectual input for welfare state reform in continental Europe. A prominent representative of these intellectuals is Wolfgang Streeck, a Max Planck Institut professor and adviser to the German Social Democratic government, in the tripartite negotiations 'Alliance for Jobs' (*Bündnis für Arbeit*). Streeck would merely add that 'responsible' corporatist bargaining has also a role to play, if unions accept wage segmentation and 'competitive corporatism' in exchange for a reduction of unemployment and an effort to avoid the starkest inequalities (eg. Riester and Streeck 1997). For these analysts, the Dutch Polder Model of restructuring in the 1990s has been held up as a possible case of best practice to emulate. More broadly, the Dutch model has become a favourite case in social democratic modernisation discourse in Germany and elsewhere. For example, its merits have been revisited over the last few years in fora such as *Die Zeit*, the left-liberal/social democratic quality weekly newspaper, published in Hamburg. Here, the Polder Model is seen as an affirmation of the possibility of implementing market-oriented, supply-side reforms whilst maintaining a somewhat retrenched but nevertheless well developed welfare state (eg. Perner 1999).

While explicitly avoiding the term 'Polder Model' and the hubris surrounding the aforementioned discussion in the German press, Visser and

Table 2.2 Basic economic indicators, the Netherlands

	1986–90	*1991–95*	*1996*	*1997*
Real GDP growth	3.1	2.1	3	3.8
Govt financial balance	−5.7	−4.3	−1.8	−1.2
Unemployment	7.4	6.4	6.3	5.2
RULC change	0.7	1.9	0.8	1.1
Productivity growth	1.1	0.4		

Source: OECD (1999) *Economic Outlook 66*, Annex Tables 1, 13, 22, and 30 and OECD (1997) *Historical Statistics*, Table 3.7.

Real GDP: average annual percentage change.
Financial balance: average annual balance as percentage of GDP.
Unemployment: standardised rate of unemployment.
Relative Unit Labour Cost: average annual change.
Productivity growth: average annual change of GDP/person employed.

Hemerijck's (1997) detailed study – in part inspired by German fascination – provides a benevolent account of the Dutch welfare state restructuring in the 1980s and the 1990s. Theirs is a story about how a Christian democratic continental welfare state has managed to generate employment growth and resolve fiscal crisis (Table 2.2). A crucial reason for this 'relative success' has been wage moderation, negotiated between the corporatist 'social partners' (a process started by the Wassenaar Accord in 1982). Wage moderation resulted, in part, from an exchange between unions and business. But it was also in part the result of an exchange between unions and the government, where the latter reduced taxes and the level of non-wage charges for social insurance as a reward for wage moderation. This proved to be possible due to an increase in the tax base generated by an increase of part-time work in the service sector. This reduction of non-wage costs in turn increased demand for social services which contributed to further service employment. Fundamentally, this development included negotiated wage segmentation, where wages for new jobs were set at low increments on the negotiated wage-scale. Here the government used the threat of not accepting the negotiated settlements as the wage norm for the non-unionised sector to enforce the usage of the lower increments. According to Visser and Hemerijck, the increase in part-time work has been what generated female employment, and made it possible to combine child rearing with paid employment.

Another important aspect of Dutch reform has been a tightening of the eligibility criteria for long-term health insurance and early retirement, in order to shift social policy from income maintenance of the long-term unemployed towards employability. Finally, the Dutch state has started to pursue an active labour market policy of retraining, through public and private labour bureaux. These also contribute towards wage segmentation since they are used as temp agencies by employers, whose lower wages and benefits are regulated through the contracts of the bureaux, and not directly by the businesses for whom the workers in question perform their work (ibid.).

No doubt, the Netherlands remains a more egalitarian and welfarist society than, for example, the United States, and therefore Dutch fiscal and macroeconomic re-stabilisation should not be altogether dismissed. Also, the combination of part-time work and child rearing is not without interest when one considers questions of work-sharing, demands for civic participation and reproduction in a post-traditional society. Therefore, Visser and Hemerijck's modest pronouncement of 'relative success' is more convincing than the hubris generally associated with the Polder Model.

The achievements of the Dutch model ought to be relativised, however. Employment rates may have increased, but this is from one of the very lowest levels in Europe. Hence, it is highly misleading to suggest that the Netherlands offers a superior solution to the problem of generating sufficient employment so as to solve the post-industrial welfare dilemmas. It is especially dubious to contrast its 'success' with Swedish 'failure'. Even at the height of the Swedish unemployment crisis in the mid-to-late 1990s, a higher proporion of the adult population was in employment than in the Netherlands (Figure 2.1). Secondly, the higher employment levels in the Netherlands come at the price of increased income polarisation. Visser and Hemerijck may be correct to argue that Dutch wage-inequality still lies somewhere 'between' Sweden and Germany on the one hand, and the USA and the UK on the other. But the percentage *increase* of wage dispersion in the Netherlands (as measured by '90–10 ratios') was just slightly below that of the UK and much higher than that of the USA, and these countries stand out as the 'income-polarisers' of the OECD countries.[7] Considering the P90/P10 ratios are calculated in terms of full-time employment and the extent of Dutch reliance on part-time employment, this probably understates wage polarisation in the Netherlands. Thirdly, with an average annual productivity-growth rate below 1 per cent from 1990 to 1995, the Dutch record of productivity growth can hardly be considered impressive (Table 2.2). If one of the criteria of social democratic modernisation is higher productivity growth, then the Polder model is a failure. Finally, claims that the Dutch model is gender-progressive should be treated with great scepticism. The policies are not designed to relieve women from reproductive work. Rather, they seek to make waged work compatible with women's (assumed) child-rearing duties, and hence make it possible for them to take on a 'double burden'. This is also a double burden they are increasingly compelled to take if their partners are employed in precarious work. The main point here is that even if progressive males agree to share this burden, the work time a household requires for generating sufficient wages and reproductive labour has increased for the family as a whole.

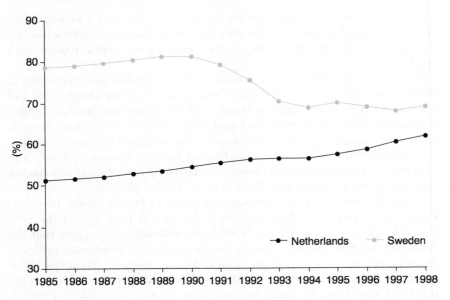

Figure 2.1 Employment rate in the adult population: the Netherlands and Sweden, 1985–98.

Source: own calculations based on OECD (1999) *Economic Outlook*, Tables 19 and 22.

Capital and the state, on the other hand, incur no extra labour force reproduction costs, and average wage costs decrease. In other words, the rate of exploitation of women and men has increased.

As well as recognising the relative nature of Dutch welfare state achievements, it is important to ascertain whether the Dutch model could be emulated elsewhere. To their credit, Visser and Hemerijck eschew making any claims to that effect (1997: 184). In the Dutch case, a facilitating condition seems to have been its export structure. The Netherlands has managed to reduce its energy import costs as a result of gas reserves in the North Sea. This has allowed the Netherlands to tie its currency to the mark, and to maintain low import costs. Consequently, wage moderation has been easier to achieve. The Netherlands also specialises in particular niches of international service trade with a high value added. In particular, the Netherlands functions as a service centre and a transportation hub for the German economy. Finally, insofar as wage competition with Germany has been important to the Dutch model, this is of course not an option for Germany. More generally, undercutting the costs of others is necessarily a particularist strategy for someone in relation to another entity and it can therefore not be a general answer to the problem of post-industrialism.

Beyond post-industrialism: regulation theory and post-Fordist restructuring

The final point in the last section indicates an important blind-spot of the one-sidedly comparativist focus of the literature reviewed so far in this chapter. This literature contains a fallacy of composition and fails to account for the problem of competitive austerity in contemporary capitalist restructuring. That is when

> each country reduces domestic demand and adopts an export oriented strategy of dumping its surplus production [by keeping wage increases below productivity growth and pushing down domestic costs], for which there are fewer consumers in its national economy given the decrease in workers' living standards and productivity gains all going to the capitalists, in the world market. This has created a global demand crisis and the growth of surplus capacity across the business cycle.
>
> (Albo 1994: 147)

Competitive austerity is central to the diagnosis of the problems of welfare capitalism of the so-called 'regulation school'. According to the regulation school, economic policy that accepts global competition uncritically as the adjudicator of economic rationality and that is based on one-sided supply-side strategies pre-empt more welfarist approaches to technological change. As a result its call for welfare state retrenchment becomes a self-fulfilling prophesy (Lipietz 1989).

It is also possible to invoke the regulation school to critique the notion of post-industrialism as a concept intended to make sense of capitalist restructuring. The problem with this notion is not so much that 'manufacturing matters'; clearly, both manufacturing and services are important in contemporary capitalism. The problem is rather that the notion of a 'service' is too heterogeneous to capture the dynamics of capitalism. It refers to too many different instances of economic activity to be useful as an abstract concept. No doubt, service employment has become more important for advanced capitalism in the last twenty years. But there is no single self-referential logic that has driven this development. Rather, the growth of service employment is linked to several logics that are contingently related. At the most, these logics are related to one another only through a set of highly mediated processes that are not identified by the post-industrialist literature (Sayer 1992). Some increases in service employment are due to the disembedding of the international monetary order, which has led to a sharp rise in the need for risk management in financial services (Sassen 1991). Another increase in demand for labour in services is indeed, as Esping-Andersen suggests, due to the breakdown of traditional family patterns, which generates demand for child-care, care of the elderly, cleaning services, etc. Some increase in the demand for services is due to income polarisation generated by neo-liberalism itself. For example, the rise of an intensively consuming middle class has led to the expansion of the entertainment industry and the provision of 'spectacles' (eg. Davis 1984). Neo-liberalism has also generated an increased demand for services due to the increasingly punitive methods which are associated with its methods of regulation of the marginalised population. This includes the increase in demand for prisons (Wacquant 1997). More generally, a problem with the notion of post-industrialism is that it falsely assumes a determinist logic of socio-economic development.

A theory of capitalist regulation

The regulation school provides a more fruitful approach to the analysis of capitalist restructuring. Regulation theory relates technological and industrial change to the particular social form of capitalism with its attendant contradictory and crisis-prone circuit of expanded reproduction. It explains how such change may or may not help sustain the coherence of this circuit and hence maintain order in capitalist society.

Michel Aglietta (1998) has succinctly explained the premises and key concepts of this approach in the postscript of the new English edition of his seminal *A Theory of Capitalist Regulation* (1979). The theory starts from the premise that money is 'the primordial social link' in capitalism. Following the analysis of Marx, this is because the link between actors takes place through the exchange of commodities, whose value is expressed through the 'universal equivalent' of money (Marx 1867). This makes capitalism growth-dependent as well as inherently contradictory.

Capitalism is growth-dependent because it depends fundamentally on specialised financial institutions to provide credit for investments in economic activity, and the motivation of these institutions is to make more money out of money. This in turn is a *raison d'être* that is passed on to productive enterprises as an imperative, because they need to make profits, if for no other reason than to settle their debts to their creditors. This is expressed through Marx's famous formula M–C–M'.

This growth dependence tends to generate contradictions, and a rather basic contradiction is inherent in the system. The making of more money out of money is only materially possible on an aggregate (or 'social') level through the exploitation of wage labour, understood in the specific sense that labour as a subordinate class produces more than it receives in return in wages. This is possible in capitalism, because the private property regime has separated the workers from the ownership and control of the means of production that is necessary for their survival. As a result they sell themselves on the labour market for a price below the value that they actually produce in the labour process (because their 'supply' of labour-power is not determined by this value, but by their opportunity cost for not working, determined by the imperative to provide for the necessities of life). This is the root of the basic social contradiction in capitalism. This contradiction has a distinctly economic dimension, which constitutes the analytical focus of regulation theory: the imperative of making more money out of money requires a continuous expansion of aggregate consumption. However, such expansion tends to be frustrated by the fact that individual capitalists necessarily minimise wage costs to sustain profits (the rate of labour exploitation). Hence, the prospects of the expansion of consumption required to realise (or 'validate') expanded reproduction tends to be undermined by the exploitation of labour, which also constitute the mass of consumers.

On the basis of this Marxist ontological position, regulation theory has developed its key concepts – regime of accumulation, mode of regulation and hegemonic project – in order to explain how such a mode of production, which is so prone to instability, can sustain itself. The economic dimension of the aforementioned basic contradiction of capitalism necessarily compels capitalists to constant innovation (a revolutionising of the means of production [*pace* Marx] or creative destruction [*pace* Schumpeter]) to maintain profit rates. Indeed, without such innovation, expanded reproduction cannot take place and the system enters a state of crisis. Following Schumpeter, regulation theorists argue that such innovation tends to be defined by particular technological paradigms that prevail in particular epochs, with their attendant core-products and core production-processes (eg. the textile industry and the putting-out system in the mid-nineteenth century, the automobile and the conveyor belt system since the 1930s). It is the nature of these *norms of production* that determine whether the basic contradiction of capitalism can or cannot be successfully counteracted, together with the *norms of consumption*, and together they constitute a particular regime of accumulation.[8] Because of the contradictory role that people play in the system as consumers and wage labourers, there is no guarantee that the paradigm that defines the norms of production automatically produces a compatible paradigm for the norms of consumption. It may be that competition compels firms to cut costs or increase productivity so as to generate surplus capacity. Indeed, regulation theory interprets the depression of the 1930s in these terms: a highly productive norm of (mass) production, based on industrial mechanisation, had then been implemented, but consumer demand was not sufficient to equal this production.

This tension between norms of production and consumption implies that the capitalist market economy needs to be encased in a broader stabilising institutional framework, which also needs to ensure basic requisites for a market economy such as the honouring of contracts and the respect for property. It is this institutional framework that regulation theorists call the mode of regulation. In part, it is of course possible that capitalists themselves solve aspects of these regulatory problems through collective action. But for the most part, the mode of regulation is constituted, and depends upon, collectively binding decisions within the territory of operation which can only be ensured through the sovereignty associated with the state. The exact object of regulation is contingent on politics and the prevailing ideology

(Jessop 1990b: 316–19). However, at the very least the capitalist mode of production demands that the mode of regulation deals with the regulation of the wage relation, the regulation of finance, the reproduction of the management of the currency, property and contracts (Lipietz 1987: 27).

Regimes of accumulation can either be 'extensive' or 'intensive'. Intensive accumulation means that the making of more money out of money, that is expanded reproduction, is ensured through increased productivity (that is, through the increased value of output per unit of labour power). Extensive accumulation is based on an increase in the labour time required to ensure the reproduction of labour power, which manifests itself through a downward pressure on wages. The distinction is important from the point of view of class relations, because intensive accumulation regimes provide the potential for positive sum games between capital and labour, where wage- and profit-rates can increase simultaneously. Extensive accumulation implies a zero-sum game, where profitability only can be maintained through the suppression of aggregate wage-rate increases (ibid: 26). With reference to my critique of Giddens in the previous chapter, it is only through such an analysis than one can ascertain whether the regulation of economic reproduction is compatible with distributive 'positive sum games' between classes.

The meaning of the term 'regime of accumulation' is often misunderstood in empiricist social science. It is important to point out that it is not a description of immediate empirical phenomena. Rather, it guides empirical investigations by reflecting on the more abstract generative structures and structural functional requisites inherent in capitalism and the relation of these to the technology of the forces of production. This is to provide more empirical concepts with sufficient analytical depth to reflect on conditions of existence that are not immediately observable (see Appendix pp. 197–98 for further elaboration).

The analysis of empirical-historical manifestations of capitalism can only take place through the concepts of 'accumulation strategy', 'hegemonic project' and 'growth model' (Jessop 1990a,b). Modes of regulation do not emerge automatically as functional effects of the imperatives of regimes of accumulation. They are rather the outcome of prevailing socio-political strategies advanced by concrete political subjects in competition, conflict and co-operation with other concrete political subjects over the nature of the collectively binding decisions of society. These subjects are understood in a Gramscian sense as conscious subjects, whose outlook, to be sure, depends on their particular social position and interests, but who reflect on the problems as they emanate from these positions in an intellectual and immanently creative way. Hence the subjective dimension is to be understood as having an independent effective reality, which interacts, and is not wholly determined by objectivity (see Appendix). 'Accumulation strategy' refers to the particular regulation strategy of the many possible strategies that is chosen to deal with problems of capital accumulation, and this strategy depends on the successful articulation and advancement of a particular economic ideology. Since regulation depends on collectively binding decisions, accumulation strategies also need to be embedded in the state institutions, whose legitimacy in society depends on the particular articulation of the 'general will' and the 'general interest' of society, that is, the particular articulation of a 'hegemonic paradigm' (Jessop 1990b: 193–218; 311–16). The particular mode of regulation that is thus configured by the accumulation strategy and the hegemonic project regulates the 'growth model' of a society. The growth model is a more concrete expression of a particular economy of a particular society than the regime of accumulation, because it reflects on contingencies such as particular product specialisms, natural endowments and other individual peculiarities that are not captured by considerations of the capitalist mode of production in general, even considered in a particular phase of historical development.

Together the aforementioned concepts provide an analytical refinement of the Gramscian concept of 'historic bloc' as discussed in the introduction (see also Appendix), which allows for a consideration of the terms for material reproduction in society.

Fordism and post-Fordism

On the basis of this theoretical interlude, we can discuss the alternative conception of regulation theory to the question of the welfare state and post-industrialism. Rather than understanding contemporary restructuring in terms of post-industrialism, it understands it in terms of a transition from Fordist to post-Fordist regimes of accumulation. Here one should highlight a crucial difference between the two perspectives concerning the material prospects of sustaining welfare capitalism. In contrast to the pessimistic post-industrial perspective on productivity, regulation theory does not envisage an inherent decrease in productivity growth. Rather new technology offers increased scope for productivity growth; the issue is rather to find an institutional framework that can facilitate such growth and simultaneously addresses the question of distribution of the product.

According to regulation theory, the Fordist regime of accumulation constituted the socio-economic basis of the policy-regimes of welfare capitalism identified by Esping-Andersen as well as their crisis. This regulationist account is well known: in the Fordist phase of capitalism, the norm of production was organised according to Taylorist principles,[9] applying product-specific machinery on a large scale. The productivity increases that resulted, together with *ex ante* integrated Fordist wage norms, Keynesian economic policy, and sometimes Beveridge-style social policy, ensured that this type of intensive regime of accumulation provided non-inflationary growth and increased standards of living.[10] Hence, it provided the basis of a positive-sum game and 'historic compromises' between organised labour and capital. Mass consumption could thereby validate mass production, which in turn underwrote mass consumption through productivity increases (repressing inflationary tendencies in Keynesian regulation and more fundamentally the real costs of investment goods – in Marxian terms the 'organic composition of capital') (Aglietta 1979; Lipietz 1985: 35–41; Boyer 1997).[11]

Stagflation signalled the breakdown of Fordist circuits of valorisation in the 1970s. Many factors intervened in the economic crisis (including, for example, the oil crises, the breakdown of the Bretton Woods system, inflationary Keynesianism and mounting government debt). Nevertheless, as Lipietz argues, in the last instance the crisis was determined by the fact of Taylorism reaching its organisational frontier of production process innovation. Significant economies could no longer be yielded through the Taylorist method of fragmenting work-moments and the separation of conception from execution. Especially important in this context was the legitimation and motivation-constraints manifested through labour force resistance. (Workers resisted change through absenteeism, sabotage, or wildcat strikes.) As a result, returns to capital decreased and continued demand expansion could not be underwritten through productivity increases. This expressed itself through stagflation and fiscal crisis (ibid: 41–46).

Regulation theory understands the new phase of capitalism, not in terms of a single unfolding post-industrialism but in a more open-ended way, in terms of a set of potential post-Fordist trajectories of capitalist accumulation. The prospects of these competing post-Fordist trajectories depend on supporting modes of regulation, accumulation strategies and hegemonic projects. The conclusion of regulation theory research has been that, whilst technological developments are by no means socio-politically neutral, there is nothing inherently neo-liberal implied in the logic of this contemporary dynamic of socio-economic restructuring. Regulation theory research has reached these conclusions in its search for emerging norms of production, through theoretically informed empirical research of different experimental corporate responses in the OECD region to the 'stagflation crisis' of the 1970s and the attendant profits squeeze. These responses entailed different mixes of cost-cutting strategies and production–technological innovation, and they have set the conditions for a new phase of capitalist development based on new core products and processes.

At the most abstract level, post-Fordist production is based on cybernetic automation of industrial processes, and a breakdown of information bottlenecks. This allows an increased capital intensity and a breakdown of information bottlenecks which in turn make possible corporate organisation over a larger geographical space, a reconnection of conception and execution without productivity losses (especially through computer-assisted integration of design, management and manufacturing ['CAD/CAM']), as well as more flexible adjustment to demand (Kaplinsky 1984). One of the most important contributions of regulation theory has been its ideal–typical sketch of different possible regimes of post-Fordist capital accumulation. Here, macroeconomic implications are inferred from the observation of microeconomic experimentation in the 1980s (Leborgne and Lipietz 1988).

Certainly, *flexible neo-liberalism* provides the basis of one possible post-Fordist trajectory. Here the economies of CAD/CAM and 'general purpose machines' are facilitated through the elimination of collective bargaining and the usage of individual contracts, incentives and threats, and numerically flexible wages, all used to create an 'enterprise-corporate' culture. Flexible liberalism implies labour market polarisation, with a shrinking core workforce with enterprise-corporate contracts and a growing periphery of precariously employed workers. However, on the basis of corporate experiments in parts of Sweden, Germany and northern Italy, Leborgne and Lipietz argue that another trajectory is more compatible with trade unionism. In sharp contrast to what Esping-Andersen, drawing on neo-classical economics, assumes, the premise of the 'negotiated involvement' model is that numerical flexibility of wages is not essential for post-Fordism, but that they can continue to be set through bi- or tripartite collective bargaining. Rather, co-determination provides an organisational form for 'functional flexibility' – or 'networking and skill to adjust volume to demand without productivity-losses' (Amin 1994: p. 20–21) – compatible with the application of CAD/CAM technology and general purpose machines. In this model, active labour market policy facilitates workforce training and mobility, and collective bargaining provides for a solidaristic distribution of work, wages and leisure, in exchange for public goods, such as the stable supply of a skilled workforce and public provisions cutting social overheads (such as health and child-care). The final ideal-type is the 'neo-Taylorist' model where new technology is merely used in a Fordist way to increase capital intensity and to extend further the separation between conception and execution.

Considered from the point of view of the functionalist requisites for expanded reproduction, the different models have different macroeconomic strengths and vulnerabilities. One central strength of the negotiated involvement model is that collectively bargained wages and social entitlements (operating as 'automatic stabilisers') could still integrate expanding production with demand and consumption *ex ante*. This would mean that flexible adjustment and economies of scope could be combined with other economies, like capacity utilisation and returns to scale, adequate investment levels, and a stable environment and time-horizons for 'learning by doing'.[12] At the same time, however, this model seems to presuppose stable and expanding aggregate demand. Apart from the role that demand expansion in and of itself plays for productivity increases, this is because of the limited scope for cost cutting during contracting demand in the negotiated involvement scenario. Hence it requires a Keynesian dimension. This is further reinforced by the fact that it is associated with tight labour markets that increase the capacity of labour to sustain solidaristic wage policy and assert demands for meaningful co-determination in the production process. Furthermore, wage rigidity tendentially shifts the burden of adjustment to capital as it requires capital accumulation at lower profit/value added ratios, and/or as it sets higher demands for innovation – a 'Schumpeterian dimension'. This, in turn sets a higher demand for stable and predictable access to sources of finance, and other public goods such as vocational training.

At the same time, non-market relations associated with the regions that have developed production based on negotiated involvement may resolve 'collective action' problems and provide positive externalities that facilitate precisely such economies. Corporatist arrangements, whether under the auspices of the Swedish Labour Market Board (AMS), or Germany's apprenticeship system, do facilitate the supply of skilled labour (Standing 1988; Streeck 1992). Positive externalities of a long-term commitment to finance of production, and coordination and diffusion of innovation (as well as the propensity to organised interest intermediation), are also generally associated with intimate, sustained, organisational 'voice' linkages between financial institutions and firms (such as 'house-banks') (Zysman 1983; Pontusson 1992: pp. 152–53; Streeck 1995). Such finance linkages are also generally associated with lower requisite levels of interest payments to finance investments (Zysman 1983), which counteracts the pressure on profits exerted by negotiated wages. Finally, welfare state services, more highly developed in Scandinavia than on the continent, provide the foundation for labour-intensive growth despite automation, operate as a stabiliser of aggregate demand, and can provide user–producer linkages in social systems of innovation (Edqvist and Lundvall 1993).

A weakness of the flexible liberal model is that (especially downward) wage flexibility set *ex post* may mean that it encounters difficulties in generating sufficient demand for a sustained new growth phase, and it may be associated with wide business-cycle fluctuations.[13] It may also have difficulties in generating adequate public goods such as vocational training (Albo 1994: pp. 150–53). But the former problem might possibly be compensated for by intensified consumption by the upper middle class, and a reduced turnover time in consumption, particularly in the service sector. Moreover, the financial sector has also become very flexible in terms of managing slumps and booms, through risk-management and credit extension (Harvey 1990, Chapter 10 and 11).[14] It should be noted, however, that these are services for which it exerts rents, although the financial sector itself is responsible for much of the risk (Strange 1989).[15] One should also not forget territorial expansion as a possible mechanism to sustain accumulation.[16] Moreover, of course, numerical wage flexibility allows for wage reductions as an instrument to sustain profit rates. Together these measures may prove to be sufficient to displace contradictions in capital accumulation.

The nature of the financial sector is a critical factor upon which the direction of post-Fordist capitalist development hinges. The present predominant trend towards more market-based and globalised finance operates tendentially both as an obstacle to negotiated involvement and as an impetus for flexible liberalism. The balance of payments constraints and the shortening of time horizons in investment associated with globalisation and marketisation of finance constitute severe obstacles to the welfarist, Keynesian as well as Schumpeterian, requisites of negotiated involvement. With regard to the latter requisite, increased markets for risk management, and increased competition in corporate finance spurred on by informatics, provide incentives for a breakdown of voice-based links between banks and firms,[17] as well as a relative focus on financial transaction as such (including mergers and acquisition), as opposed to production process innovation.[18] With regard to the former requisites, rents exert inhibiting costs on the prospects for public sector expansion as well as fiscal and monetary stimuli, especially in the present context of high debt ratios. Whether this takes the form of higher deficits, increases in inflation (in relation to other currencies), or taxes, currency markets will punish such moves with higher interest rates and 'risk-premiums' on currencies. Moreover, in a context when all states try to run surpluses to reduce their debt burden, the result is a reduction of demand-growth in the world economy and 'competitive austerity'. At the same time, the increased importance of risk management as an economic activity, and the rent it exerts, provides the basis for an expanding financial services industry, organised along flexible liberal lines (Sassen 1991). This may provide neo-liberal accumulation with a 'core product'. The consequence of all these trends is that global finance operates as a formidable bias for flexible liberalism and against negotiated involvement. Hence, the question of regulation of financial markets is central to the question as to whether flexible liberalism or negotiated involvement prevails as the hegemonic regime of accumulation. In this context it is significant to note, as even Giddens grants, that the globalisation of finance was not unleashed by a pre-determined endogenous economic logic, but rather by contingent political decisions and non-decisions (Strange 1989; Helleiner 1994). Hence, unlike social democratic modernisers we have good reason to treat 'globalisation' not as an objective economic logic, but as a socially constructed phenomenon that can be questioned, and whose re-regulation ought to be a high priority on the political agenda.

Regarding the neo-Taylorist model, a regime of accumulation based 'purely' on its principles is unlikely. Due to expensive overheads it requires stable market outlets, but undermines these through increased capital intensity, unemployment and a breakdown of the Fordist *ex ante* wage-relation. However, the model remains relevant because a 'fallacy of composition' is possible (what is irrational on the macro level, might be rational for the individual components), engendering an 'organic crisis of production'. But perhaps more importantly, there is evidence to suggest that no concrete case of economic restructuring follows the ideal types 'purely', but articulates elements from all models.[19] Taylorist practices might survive as a subordinate mode in the dual economy or 'sunset' sectors (notably in the consumer service sector). Moreover, corporate strategy may employ elements of the different models in attempts to combine economies of scope and scale. For example, corporations may combine flexible processes with scale and mergers designed to retain price-setting privileges in their markets (Amin and Malmberg 1994). The mixing of Fordist/Taylorist elements makes scale more relevant, and decreases the capacity of market adaptation of flexible liberalism to fluctuating and sluggish demand. However, insofar as strategies of scale have become transnational, it also generates further balance of payments constraints for the reflationary aspects of a negotiated involvement strategy, as well as constraints on industrial policy.

Reconsidering the economic prospects of the social citizenship state and de-commodification strategies: the Swedish case

We are now in a position where we can return to consider Giddens' and Esping-Andersen's understanding of the contemporary economic limits of the universal social citizenship state and social democratic de-commodfication strategies. In this context, Sweden is a critical case to consider. This is implied in Esping-Andersen's work of the 1990s, where the Swedish welfare state was seen as the case approximating the ideal type of a viable social democratic response to the challenges of post-industrialism. By 1996, however, in the wake of a rapid deterioration of Swedish economic performance he, like Giddens, accepted the neo-classical economic argument against this welfare state, based on moral hazard thesis with its attendant postulates about the allegedly dysfunctional microeconomic performance of the Swedish labour market. However, regulation theory postulates on negotiated involvement as a viable form of post-Fordism challenge this interpretation.

To put matters more concretely, according to Giddens' (in fact, Lindbeck's) 'moral hazard' argument, social citizenship type entitlements in health and unemployment insurance systems generate economically dysfunctional behaviour on the labour market. They generate problems such as absenteeism and an inflexible adjustment to labour demand, which is incompatible with global competitiveness in an era of technological change (as discussed on p. 13). Esping-Andersen, in essence, advances the same argument, but connects it to a more concrete analysis of what he understands to be the productivity and demographic constraints of the new post-industrial economy (see the quote on p. 34). In this section, I seek to falsify this thesis, and advance an alternative thesis: as Leborgne and Lipietz suggest, the institutions of the Swedish welfare state contain the potential to develop a negotiated involvement variant of post-Fordism. Such post-Fordism is compatible with the maintenance of a highly developed public service sector with unionised wages that are cross-subsidised by the manufacturing sector. Moreover, such a post-Fordism contains the productivity potential to underwrite the expenditure that is necessary to meet Esping-Andersen's demographic challenges. The implication for this would be that not only does this type of welfare state contain the potential to address the legitimation problems of modern society as I argued in the last chapter, but it also contains an economic rationality that is compatible with technological change.

But how should one explain the crisis of the Swedish economy in the late 1980s and early 1990s? It is the thesis of this book that this crisis was not due to an inherent incompatibility with the forces of technological change. It was rather generated by a more contingent dynamic: the failure to institutionalise a mode of regulation to stabilise a growth model based on negotiated involvement, which in turn was an effect of a political shift towards a neo-liberal accumulation strategy and hegemonic project. This section is devoted towards refuting the Giddens/Esping-Andersen/Lindbeck thesis and to establish that the potential for negotiated involvement was present in Sweden in the 1980s and early 1990s.

Any reasonable review of the evidence must face up to the fact that Sweden underwent a severe economic crisis in the 1990s (Table 2.1). According to the *Economic Surveys* of the OECD, in the wake of serious labour unrest and wage-push inflation, Sweden entered the world recession of 1991 with a 'cost crisis' and high inflation. The subsequent restructuring became very dramatic as the social democratic unconditional commitment to full employment was abandoned and economic policy was reconfigured so as to prioritise price stability. As a result of these developments Sweden experienced negative growth between 1991 and 1994. The open unemployment rapidly increased from 1.5 to 9 per cent in only a few years and the employment rate decreased. An important factor in this story was fiscal crisis. When the expenditure for unemployment insurance rose, it became evident that social expenditure cuts had to be implemented to balance the budget. Apart from reducing social entitlements and services, this added further momentum to the depression and the reduction of employment (OECD *Economic Surveys: Sweden* 1994: 11–38). In this context it is important to point out that the expansion of employment in the 1970s and 1980s had distracted attention from the fact that average productivity and GDP growth had been very sluggish throughout the period. It is not uncontroversial to conclude that, in the end, the post-industrial policy of wage solidarity had not worked. Productivity growth in the export-oriented manufacturing sector had not been rapid enough to underwrite wage increases in the domestic service sector. A cycle of inflationary wage rounds and devaluations had displaced this institutional weakness until the late 1980s. But from the 1980s this was no longer possible in the era of global finance. Indeed, in previous research I have arrived at this conclusion myself (Ryner 1994: 245–58).

But what caused this? The argument that Giddens and Esping-Andersen uncritically adopt from neo-classical economists – that this negative economic development can be reduced to the static inefficiencies caused by regulatory distortions of the labour market, including all 'moral hazard' (Lindbeck *et al.* 1994) – is highly spurious. Given its prevalence, it is remarkable how little empirical support there actually is for this thesis. This has

been argued not least by Esping-Andersen's erstwhile co-author, Walter
Korpi (eg. 1996).

Moral hazard and sclerosis in Swedish labour markets and in production practices?

Given the moral hazard thesis, we would expect Sweden to have a comparatively unfavourable 'Beveridge curve', which illustrates the 'clearing'
capacity of the labour market by measuring the relationship between
vacancies in relation to unemployment (an indicator of the labour supply).
It follows from the moral hazard thesis that one would expect a relative
inertia in the filling of vacancies on the Swedish labour market, since overly
protected workers would be less prone to take the available jobs as they
become available, or adjust their skill portfolio to meet demand. But the
Beveridge curve does not confirm this in the Swedish case. Compared to
other OECD countries, Sweden had the most 'favourable' development of
the Beveridge curve from 1960 to 1990. In other words *only in Sweden did the
vacancy rate at a given rate of unemployment* not *increase significantly during this time*
(Homlund 1993: 419–20; cf. OECD 1992: 62–66; see also Korpi and Palme
1993). Moreover, the rapid increase in unemployment in the early 1990s,
from one of the lowest levels of the OECD to the very high EU average,
cannot be explained by a deteriorating Beveridge curve. There was no
sudden increase in the vacancy rate over unemployment. Rather the movement towards increased unemployment takes place 'along' the Beveridge
curve, which is an indicator of a reduction of demand for labour (which was
hardly surprising given the years of negative growth and the free fall in
aggregate demand) (Holmlund 1993: 421).

More broadly, a wide range of studies applying a variety of indicators and
methods showed that the Swedish labour market of the 1980s, the period
immediately prior to the crisis, functioned comparatively well (Bosworth
and Rivlin 1987; Åberg 1988: 76–84; Standing 1988; OECD *Economic Surveys:
Sweden* 1989: 55–80). The latter, of course, is quite consistent with the idea
that an active labour market policy more than compensates as a mechanism
of labour mobility in the absence of numerical flexibility (when wages are
partly de-commodified through wage solidaristic bargaining). Concerning
the question of productivity, while it is true that productivity growth
declined in Sweden in the 1970s, 1980s and early 1990s, there is no evidence
for a causal relation between this decline and market distorting regulations
(SOU 1991: 7–144; Wibe 1993).

This, together with the finding that labour mobility increased in Sweden in
the 1980s, was the conclusion of one research report that Bertil Holmlund
(1993) submitted to the Lindbeck Commission. But his conclusions were not
reflected in the final report. The final report rather followed the conclusions
of Lars Calmfors, whose argument was in line with the 'sclerosis thesis' of
Lindbeck. Calmfors conceded that the empirical results were uncertain. In a

critique of the argument about a favourable Swedish Beveridge curve, he argued that it overestimates Swedish flexibility because individuals who are in public vocational retraining programmes are counted as employed. His revised Beveridge curve indicates that Sweden's performance is *the same* as in the rest of the OECD world (Calmfors 1993: 156–59). That is, it is not better. On the other hand, with a comparatively de-commodified welfare policy regime, it is not worse either. This can hardly be considered strong evidence for the moral hazard thesis.

However, Calmfors also addressed two other forms of labour market functionality and flexibility that are of interest because they will lead us to a discussion of the broader issues of instituting a viable growth model *à la* the regulation school. First, on the question of the relationship between the inflation rate and the rate of employment, he invoked his previous research with Driffil, which has commanded considerable international attention. Hence he reiterated that both highly decentralised and highly centralised wage determination correlate with comparatively low inflation rates at a rate of high employment (ibid: 118–22; see also Calmfors and Driffil 1988). In other words, on this score also Calmfors argues that the traditional Swedish model of wage determination performed comparatively well (and hence ought to be compatible with Esping-Andersen's social democratic route to post-industrialism, rejected in 1996). But Calmfors also noted (and correctly so) that the Swedish wage determination system had shown signs of fragmentation since the 1970s. This explains the trend towards wage-push inflation, since Sweden has moved towards the more unfavourable and inflationary 'middle-position' between high levels of decentralisation and centralisation. On the basis of his research with Driffil, one would assume that the inflation problem could either be tackled through decentralisation – that is a move towards a neo-liberal labour market – or centralisation – that is, a consolidation of solidaristic wage policy. The implication of this would be that societies can *choose* between neo-liberalism and social democracy. However, contrary to the Calmfors/Driffil thesis, Calmfors unequivocally prescribed that Sweden should move towards the decentralised, more market-oriented type of wage setting.

His reasoning behind the latter conclusion is highly pertinent to our discussion because it leads directly to the question of post-Fordism. Calmfors was concerned with yet another type of labour market functionality, concerning the motivation and skills of individual workers and the attendant effects of this on productivity. While he conceded that the traditional centralised Swedish Rehn–Meidner model might have facilitated 'mechanical' productivity increases in the past, he argued that this is incompatible with contemporary terms of productivity, which rely on 'human capital'. He argued that such economies could only be realised through individual incentives generated by differentiated and individual wages. In his pursuit of this line of argument, he explicitly invoked, via a reference to the work of Piore and Sabel (1984), the term 'post-Fordism' (Calmfors 1993: 122–25). The problem with this conjecture is that Piore and Sabel make a point of avoiding such determinism. Despite other disagreements with the regulation school, they agree that there is a range of possible post-Fordist trajectories (Piore and Sabel 1984: 251–80). In other words, they agree with regulation theory, and Calmfors and Driffil for that matter, that structural economic developments allow for socio-political choice.

Despite Sweden's problem of generalising productivity growth so as to make it reflect aggregate indicators, the argument that Sweden's labour market and wage determination system is incompatible with post-Fordist efficiency and productivity growth can be falsified. Case study research on workplace organisation in Sweden in the 1980s support Leborgne and Lipietz' (1988) argument that such a bargaining system, together with a well developed retraining policy and co-determination between labour and capital, can facilitate post-Fordist efficiency and productivity, as discussed under the heading of 'negotiated involvement'.

The most prominent and well researched case to cite in this context is that on Volvo's plants in Kalmar and Uddevalla (indeed Leborgne and Lipietz have gone so far as to call negotiated involvement 'Kalmarism') (Berggren 1992; Pontusson 1992b; Sandberg 1995, 1998). This research has demonstrated that bipartite co-determination of the division of labour, work tasks, work time, staffing levels and promotion ladders can be combined with macro-corporatist wages in a production paradigm that harnesses the potential economies of new technology. This also means that unions have some scope to ensure that technology is designed so as to minimise labour shedding in favour of negotiated work-time reduction. Hence the enterprise can rely on highly skilled and motivated work teams to autonomously organise production according to orders, specified in terms of customisation of the product and delivery time. In return, workers have a secure, stimulating and self-fulfilling work environment in which they can learn and grow (and develop their architectonic functions, one might add) and over which they have a degree of influence. The Uddevalla-plant in particular moved away from the mass-production conveyor-belt paradigm in favour of general purpose machines that in principle reintroduced a high tech variant of crafts production (each production worker in a work team could in principle produce a car on her/his own). Productivity increases were impressive. After only two years of operation, the Uddevalla plant superseded the neo-Taylorist Gothenburg plant in productivity. With its 32.8 hours/car in 1992, the plant was still less productive than the 25 hours/car of Toyota in Japan. But this was still during the early life-time of the plant, and with a 50% rate of productivity increase in 1990–92, there was substance behind the confidence of plant managers that the gap between their plant and the paradigmatic plant of 'Toyotism' would be closed. The potential of the plant is indicated by the fact that one worker in Uddevalla built one car in 10 hours on his own.[20]

Whilst these are studies of only two plants owned by one corporation,[21] it should be noted, as work sociologist Michel Freyssenet points out, that there is no reason to assume that the logic of the techniques applied at Uddevalla are specific to automobile manufacturing. Rather

> in seeking to attribute ordinary human cognitive and co-operative dimensions to work activity [and thereby making multiple motion compatible with high productivity, Uddevalla's organisation] can be described as a different way of marrying manual activity with mechanisation and automation, leaving the complex part of the productive process in the hands of the direct worker. In a dynamic manner it can be interpreted as another automation process, susceptible of generating a new social form of automation applicable to all production process phases and to all activity branches.[22]
>
> (Freysennet 1998: 112)

On the basis of this interpretation, I would contend that we can generate a more tenable argument as to why the Swedish model entered a period of crisis in the early 1990s, and hence we can specify more precisely what the constraints on social democratic renewal are. As argued in the previous section, regulation theory holds that a growth model needs to be encased in an institutional framework, a mode of regulation that is compatible with its central norms. My argument is that it was the failure to implement such a mode of regulation in the 1980s and 1990s that pre-empted a negotiated involvement solution in Sweden.

The hypothesis can be specified with reference to the functional strengths and weaknesses that we can derive from the structural properties from the negotiated involvement type of post-Fordism specified in the previous section. As in Fordism, *ex ante* wage regulation could still serve the function of integrating mass production and mass consumption in the negotiated involvement model. The assumption would be, of course, there would be adequate process innovation to ensure productivity increases. But at the same time stable aggregate demand expansion may serve to facilitate the dynamic determinants of productivity increases (Boyer 1991): 'learning by doing', adequate investment, capacity utilisation and economies of scale. These are the so-called 'Kaldor–Verdoorn effects' that have been notable by their absence in the monetarist era of the 1980s, despite the technological revolution (Boyer and Petit 1991). On the other hand, the negotiated model is much more vulnerable to breakdown resulting from contracting and unstable demand, because of its limited capacity for cost-cutting. In this sense it seems to require a 'Keynesian dimension', in the sense of stable and expanding demand, as well as a predictable institutional framework in which corporate and financial planning, public policy and negotiation can proceed. Moreover, it requires a certain balance of power between labour and capital.

The actual fate of the Kalmar and Uddevalla plants in the recession of the 1990s lends plausibility to this argument. These were still relatively small and experimental plants in a large corporation, which in the recession faced surplus capacity. This made defensive and short-term corporate consolidation decisions around the core of the corporation (in Gothenburg) more important (Hancké and Rubinstein 1995). In short, the security and stability of the market needed to continue this bold experiment were not there. In this context it is also important to note that unemployment increased. This reduced the need to attract workers with a good work environment and it also forced the unions into a defensive position (Sandberg 1995: 16–17). To this one should add the fact that Volvo were in the process of merging with Renault at this time, which was directly hostile to these production concepts (ibid: 14–16). In any case, the decision could not have been based on firm performance, since Kalmar was Volvo's most productive plant, with Uddevalla quickly catching up (ibid; Berggren 1995).

The remainder of the book will illustrate how this general line of argument can be used to analyse the crisis of Swedish social democracy. This crisis can be understood in terms of the pre-emption of negotiated involvement as a trajectory of capitalist restructuring which in the last instance is determined by socio-political power relations that are advancing a neo-liberal accumulation strategy and hegemonic project. It will be argued that the term 'globalisation' could be used as a shorthand explanation for the crisis of Swedish social democracy. However, contrary to the economistic and determinist conception of globalisation that Giddens' and Esping-Andersen's discussions imply, I will emphasise the political dimensions and power relations of globalisation that stand in a contingent relation to the logic of post-Fordist forces of production. I will do so by relating globalisation to neo-liberal hegemony. These are power relations that have generated what the Austro-Marxist Otto Bauer would have called 'social mis-rationalisation' – a socially sub-optimal appropriation of productive forces.

3 The formation and consolidation of social democratic hegemony in Sweden

The intellectuals of the Third Way project argue that social democracy and the left should abandon de-commodification and social citizenship universalism as guiding political norms in the present phase of modernisation and globalisation. The previous two chapters sought to refute this argument. In chapter 1, it was argued that these norms continue to be of central relevance, and should provide the guidance for a pluralisation and democratisation of the welfare state. Chapter 2 made the case for the continued socio-economic viability of such de-commodification and social citizenship in an era characterised by globalisation and 'post-industrial', or more to the point, 'post-Fordist' restructuring.

Thus far the argument has been advanced with reference to the dynamics of capitalist restructuring in general. In this context, although the Swedish case, as the exemplar of the social citizenship welfare state, has been particularly important as a reference point, it has been discussed as part of a more global and comparative perspective. This has had the benefit of highlighting how the Swedish case is relevant to the broader questions of the crisis of welfare capitalism. But it has also had the inevitable side-effect of making the discussion of this critical case rather sketchy and stylised. The remainder of the book seeks to redress this problem. It will be devoted towards a more in-depth analysis of the Swedish case, which will consolidate and provide substantial evidence for the general argument advanced in chapters 1 and 2.

This chapter deals with the question of the nature and meaning of 'traditional social democracy' as it developed from its origins in the crisis of the classical liberal world order of the late nineteenth century, and as it played a part in the consolidation of the 'Fordist' 'golden age' after World War II. Again, the focus on the institutionalisation of the Swedish model is particularly pertinent since (apart from Norway) it is the only country in which the social movement associated with the Second Socialist International actually assumed a hegemonic national popular leadership in civil society and hence played a directing role in welfare state formation.

This chapter has two fundamental purposes. One of these purposes is to correct Giddens' caricature account of traditional social democracy. It is alleged in his account that traditional social democracy had no conception of socio-economic rationalisation that took into account the 'supply side' of the economy. Furthermore, he implies that its legacy has nothing to contribute towards the more active and participatory form of citizenship that 'no authority without democracy' implies. In chapter 1, I critiqued this caricature with reference to the work of Ulf Himmelstrand *et al*. In this chapter I seek to substantiate that argument through a concrete historical analysis of the formation of social democratic hegemony in Sweden and the institutionalisation of the Swedish model. The other objective of the chapter is, together with chapter 4, to complete a scene-setting exercise that is necessary for the analysis of the subsequent chapters. If we are to understand the crisis of Swedish social democracy, it is necessary to understand exactly what it is that is in crisis. For that purpose, the chapter seeks to carefully reconstruct the nature of the institutional arrangements of the Swedish welfare state that were developed under social democratic national popular leadership. Furthermore, the chapter seeks to highlight the historical-structural conditions of existence of these institutional arrangements, with reference to the balance of social forces (which necessarily includes a consideration of both material and normative structures) operating at the levels of social relations of production, forms of state and world order (Cox 1981: 217–34) (see Appendix pp. 195–98).

The formation and consolidation of welfare states took place in a distinct period of history throughout the 'advanced capitalist world', beginning with the Bismarck reforms of the 1880s and ending in with the post World War II settlements (eg. Pierson 1998: 99–120). This suggests that although welfare states have developed within nation states, their development is part of a more transnational dynamic. Karl Polanyi (1957a: esp. 130–34) has suggested convincingly that they are the outcome of a 'double movement', where the commodity economic logic of capitalist development necessarily provokes a countervailing logic of 'socialisation' due to its disintegrative effects (see van der Pijl 1998: 7–30).[1] On a more concrete level, the welfare state emerged in the wake of the crisis of the nineteenth century liberal international system developed under British hegemonic leadership.

Industrial capitalism developed at the end of the nineteenth century within the socio-political framework set by Pax Britannica. Great Britain developed a 'virtuous circle' of capital accumulation based on the application of increasingly 'industrialised' and rationalised processes to certain key sectors, beginning with textiles. These were conditioned and perpetuated by a favourable terms of trade in an increasingly liberalised international trade regime (secured through the generalisation of the 'Most Favoured Nations' principle codified in the Cobden–Chevalier Treaty), that transferred surplus, savings and hence finance to Britain. Central to the system was the Gold Standard, for which the pound sterling was the anchor currency and for which the City of London was the central financial hub. Since the pound sterling was considered 'as good as gold', Britain's favourable terms of trade, its lead in productivity, and imperial access to gold reserves ensured that international liquidity could be expanded to underwrite the expansion of trade and economic growth beyond the metals base of gold, without degenerating into inflation. The main source of liquidity came in the form of bills of exchange and bonds denominated in pounds sterling that were secured through Britain's gold reserves (Schwartz 1994: 165–70).

But in the late nineteenth century this system began to disintegrate due to its contradictions, and it was in this context that the welfare state was formed. Market 'widening' and 'deepening' did, to be sure, counteract overproduction and underconsumption tendencies in the (extensive) regime of accumulation, as did the paradigmatic shift in core products and processes towards steel and chemical industries in the 'second industrial revolution'. However, these transformations made the institutional framework highly vulnerable. First, Great Britain was losing its lead in the international division of labour, as especially the USA and Germany surpassed Britain in the new core-commodity sectors. Hence the productivity gap was narrowed, and the ensuing negative effects on Britain's terms of trade began to erode the capacity to use the pound sterling as the currency to underwrite the growth of international trade. The outbreak of World War I served as a catalyst in this context, as it transformed Great Britain into a debtor nation. After this juncture, it was not possible to maintain a gold standard based on the pound sterling, and its brittle re-constitution in the inter-war years came to an end in 1931 when Britain went off the gold standard, an act that led to a collapse of international trade. On a deeper level, new production technology and practices were less amenable to a 'free market'. Steel and chemical industry implied very complex and expensive production requiring high investment levels in 'asset-specific' productive capital (Williamson 1975, cited in Cerny 1995). It also implied an increased importance of economies of scale, with its attendant propensity towards oligopoly and vulnerability to fluctuations in demand. This fuelled protectionism and state interventionism, which was inconsistent with *laissez faire*. Ultimately, it engendered the mercantilist, nationalist and statist propensities of contender states like Germany in the period of economic stagnation 1873–96, but also in Britian itself (Gourevitch 1986). The literature of international relations and international political economy has long argued that it is with reference to these factors that one can understand the collapse of the transition from the '100-year liberal peace' to the atavistic period of 'rival imperialism', which culminated in World War II (eg. Cox 1987: 151–210).

But the origins of the welfare state are also part of this story, and are intimately related to another aspect of the aforementioned dynamic of contradictory restructuring. As Herman Schwartz (1994: 168) has pointed out, in sociological terms, the penetration of international capitalism under Pax Britannica remained shallow in the capitalist core and the semi-periphery. The circuit of capital accumulation was initially centred around trade circuits between settler colonies in the periphery, and a small number of cities in the core. The vast mass of the population of core states (with the exception of Britain, whose violent commodification of 'everyday life' was analysed by Polanyi), had their subsistence reproduced through rather autarkic peasant–lord relations on the countryside.[2] Here participation in the commodity economy remained a lucrative complementary activity to the production and consumption of the basics for human survival up to the latter part of the nineteenth century. This meant that the economic adjustment and restructuring that international trade and the gold standard necessarily demanded, especially from deficit countries, did not threaten the fundamentals of social cohesion. This changed, however, as commodification deepened in the second industrial revolution, when the European peasantry underwent proletarianisation. It is in this context, then, that the 'workers' question' is raised, and social democracy as a social movement is formed. This is also the time when welfare state reform reaches the political agenda as part of the overall transition of world orders from Pax Britannica to rival imperialism (Cox 1987: 164–89). In this context, the Bismarck reforms of the 1880s are paradigmatic.

This was a period of heavy industrialisation and profound social dislocation where 'everyday life' was transformed from its traditional context, and where mass populations were integrated into nation-state projects in a process that E. H. Carr (1945: 1–34) called 'the socialisation of nationalism and the nationalisation of socialism'. The welfare state was central to this process of social integation (Flora and Heidenheimer 1981; Wilensky 1975). It is indeed important to note that the welfare state did not emerge as an inherently democratic institution, as the notion of *Soldaten der Arbeit* illustrates. The articulation of liberal democracy, the welfare state and industrial capitalism was not stabilised until the consolidation of 'Fordist compromises' after World War II. However, if there was one social movement at the time that subscribed to the notion of democracy and articulated welfare state practices and modernity in these terms, it was the social democratic labour movement. Furthermore, its conception of 'integral democracy' was much more radical, participatory and unambiguously located in what in chapter 1 was labelled the 'developmental democratic' tradition, than the one that eventually became the outcome of the Fordist 'post-war settlement'. That is, when social democracy *compromised* with other social forces in the context of a capitalist mode of production. In Sweden, for instance, the labour movement emerged in the 1880s in the context of the rapid transformation of agrarian society, together with the free church and temperance movement, as one of the 'popular movements' or *folkrörelserna*. In this context, it became the leading force in a social alliance that mobilised around the issue of democratisation of society.

This chapter sets out how the Swedish labour movement succeeded in achieving hegemonic status in Swedish civil society in the first part of the twentieth century. In other words, I explain why and how it became the leading political force in the process through which the organic crisis (cf. Introduction and Appendix) of the 'nineteenth century system' was resolved.

I also indicate how, as this movement accommodated itself to the socio-economic imperatives of Fordist industrial regulation and forged a class compromise with Swedish capital, its developmental-democratic ideals in part were attenuated and displaced in an ideological re-articulation. The outcome of this class compromise was, however, the universal welfare state which, despite these compromises, did provide tremendous material gain for the mass of the population. This welfare state also, as Himmelstrand *et al.* have argued, provides a propitious institutional form for further democratic development, exactly because it is based on the principle of 'de-commodification' or, as the early Swedish social democratic intellectuals preferred to call it, 'de-proletarianisation' (Tilton 1991: 370, cf. Steffen 1920; Karleby 1928).

Power mobilisation and the social democratic welfare state: a reconceptualisation

The 'power-mobilisation thesis', associated with Ulf Himmelstrand *et al.* (1981), the early work of Esping-Andersen (1985a,b; 1990) as well as with Walter Korpi (1978; 1983) and John Stephens (1979) provides a parsimonious model that accounts for the causes and implications of this distinctiveness of the welfare state in Scandinavia. This theory is highly materialist. It understands classes as rational actors, whose interests can be derived from their essential locations in the social relations of production. It defines power resources in terms of material capabilities, which in the case of labour includes mass mobilisation in trade unions and political parties. Hence the possibility exists that labour can counter the 'economic power' of capitalists with 'political power' in the liberal democratic states. When understood in this way, balance of class power is the independent variable for power mobilisation theory and the welfare policy regimes (discussed with reference to Esping-Andersen in chapter 2) express 'distributive outcomes' which is the dependent variable. The hypothesis that the balance of class forces thus understood determines the distributive outcomes is tested through the quantitative, variable-oriented comparative method with many cases, complemented with qualitative case studies. According to the power-mobilisation thesis, the Swedish working class has been distinctly successful in its political mobilisation of labour as a collective actor. The social democratic party has become the 'natural party of government' and the trade union movement has achieved an unprecedented degree of organisation of the labour force. This has allowed the two 'arms of the labour movement' to centralise and coordinate their power resources in the design of the industrial relations system, social policy and economic policy, thus counteracting the 'economic power' of capital with the 'political power' of organised labour. The outcome of this has been the universal welfare state, based on the norms of de-commodification. This institutional design of the welfare state not only provides the working class with a higher degree of social protection, it also tends to reproduce the power resources of the working class, since it configures the incentives of the working class to mobilise itself as a unified force, and it also brings the middle class into its orbit (the 'extended working class'). Hence, there is an institutional feedback effect from the dependent to the independent variable.

In broad terms, power-mobilisation theory provides a compelling account of the distributive principles of the Swedish welfare state as well as certain important aspects of the reproduction of working class power resources, at least in the Fordist period. But power-mobilisation theory, emphasising the 'output' and 'feedbacks' of the welfare policy regime, only sheds light on part of the story. Power-mobilisation theory wrongly assumes that a state with a social democratic 'natural party of government' straightforwardly reflects some 'working class interest' whose identity is *a priori* determined. Such straightforward interest representation cannot be assumed. First, this is because it ignores the imperative of a capitalist state to sustain capital accumulation through a coherent mode of socio-economic regulation. The tension between accumulation and legitimation imperatives renders the relationship between social democratic state policy and labour representation much more complex and contradictory than power-mobilisation theory suggests (Pontusson 1984: 69–107).

It is also wrong to assume an inherent and social democratic working class identity, interest and ideology. This is to succumb to what Gramsci called the 'vulgar economism' of the orthodox Marxism of the Second and Third Internationals. The discrediting of orthodox Marxism and the validation of Gramsci's argument has been decisively established by the relationship between consciousness and material practice that is implied in Lacan's discovery of the intimate relationship between psycho-analysis and social linguistics (Hall 1988).

Power-mobilisation theory no doubt characterised central aspects of working class identity and interests in Sweden during the golden age of the Swedish model. But these were discursively constructed identities, interests and ideologies, specific in time and space (Jenson and Mahon 1993: 77). Moreover, the story of the welfare state is not only that of the state, capital and labour as social subjects. Other social relations and subjects are also relevant, such as gender relations. An adequate account of labour politics in the golden age of the Swedish model cannot focus solely on policy outputs and their feedback effects. One must also pay close attention to how labour was represented in relation to other interests, and in relation to the imperative of capitalist accumulation. This requires a specification of the way in which working class identity was constructed in a hegemonic social paradigm.

Politics of productivity

The Swedish model can be viewed as a variation of a broader trend of formation of accumulation strategies and hegemonic projects institutionalising

Fordist growth models. The socio-economic rationale of Fordism was specified in chapter 2. Its growth models emerged in the West in the 1930s and the 1940s through what Charles Maier (1991: 169–202) has called a 'politics of productivity'. The politics of productivity was typically forged by power blocs composed of forces associated with industrially oriented capital, organised labour, organised farmers, and technocratic reformist intellectuals. They ensured low unemployment levels and high social wages for organised labour and price controls for farmers in exchange for the acceptance of the right for management to manage, and peaceful industrial relations. An important precondition of the politics of productivity was the subordination of 'circulation forms' of capital (which tended to favour market clearing and price stability or 'sound money'), to 'productive capital' (which in Fordist/Taylorist conditions tended to favour returns to scale), facilitated by the collapse of the gold standard, the 1929 Wall Street Crash, the New Deal and wartime economic planning (van der Pijl 1984: 76–177).

The power blocs of the politics of productivity were either forged internally in social formations as a response to the depression in the 1930s, or they were imposed after the World War II through American international hegemony. Whilst not by any means without external theoretical and ideological influences, Sweden's power bloc was forged 'organically' and internally in the 1930s (Marklund 1988).

'Formative events' (*pace* Rothstein 1992: chapter 6) in the formation of this power bloc include the election of a social democratic minority government in 1932 and the affirmation that this government received when it was returned to power with a majority in 1936, as well as the 'Cow Deal' (*kohandeln*) that SAP (*Sveriges socialdemokratiska arbetariparti*, the Social Democratic Workers' Party) struck with the Agrarian Party to ensure Parliamentary support for its policies.[3] The 'Cow Deal' ensured broad Parliamentary support for family policy and unemployment insurance reform[4] as well as for the 'new economic policy' (retrospectively labelled 'Keynesian'), based on boosting employment through a deficit-funded public works programme where the going union rates would be paid. To the 'new economic policy' one should also add the devaluation of 1931 which, following the lead of the pound sterling, took the Swedish Crown off the Gold Standard. This was not a deliberate part of the Cow Deal, since an acute balance of payments deficit had actually forced the preceding liberal minority government to take this measure which went against its beliefs.[5] However, its social democratic successors saw this necessity as a virtue (Kock 1961: 104–05, 107–08), and it is generally recognised that the devaluation contributed more to the reduction of unemployment than the public works programme did. The Agrarians agreed to support these policies, in exchange for price controls and protection for the agricultural sector. The success of these policies paved the way for SAP's return to office with a majority in 1936 and the consolidation of social democratic hegemony.

Another critical event was the so-called Saltsjöbaden Accord of 1938 between the Employers' Federation of Sweden (SAF) and the Confederation of Swedish Trade Unions (LO), which set the institutional framework for 'joint-central regulation' (Fulcher 1991: 132–53) in wage determination.[6] After World War II, the social democratic government and the trade unions consolidated the institutional framework of the Swedish model against the backdrop of these accords of the 1930s. The Postwar Programme of 1944 set the framework for further reform in social policy and instituted a welfare state based on the principles of de-commodification and universalism (Olsson 1987). Finally, the Rehn–Meidner model formulated an overall concept of socio-economic regulation and governance that codified the inter-relationship between 'solidaristic wage policy', social policy and macro-economic management of the economy. The latter model was developed in the late 1940s under the leadership of the two trade union economists after which it is named. It became the basis for trade union wage policy in 1951 and was accepted by the government as the 'joint policy of the two branches of the labour movement' in 1958, when it became the paradigm for state macroeconomic management (Martin 1984: 203–13).

In the Swedish case, unlike the American case, forces demanding social protection from the market became particularly salient. This was because the social democratic labour movement managed to maintain an alliance with agrarian forces, and pre-empt what emerged in the United States: an alliance between financiers, industrialists, and agrarian interests, that watered down the interventionist density in the mode of regulation in favour of market norms (Weir and Skocpol 1985: 141–48). This point is of crucial significance for understanding the social basis of the Swedish mode of regulation. It made possible in Sweden a 'Kaleckian' Keynesianism, with a principled commitment to full employment. In the typical liberal, American and 'vulgar' Keynesianism that emerged after the war, employment merely became one variable in the policy matrix of stability, constrained by certain prerogatives of 'free enterprise'. According to Kalecki, full employment could only be sustained through ambitious public investment programmes and certain selective planning measures, required to deal with the inflationary tendencies of bottlenecks. Industrialists, he argued, would resist such a policy. They would oppose an extensive public investment programme in principle. They would also oppose a policy of sustained full employment, as it would eliminate the disciplinary mechanism of 'the sack'. On the other hand, they would favour the promotion of private investment through countercyclical monetary and fiscal policy in recessions, but align with rentier interests around the 'peril of inflation' in booms. The result of this 'political business cycle', Kalecki prophetically envisaged, would be a Keynesianism that fell short of a full employment commitment (Kalecki 1943: 322–31). By contrast, Sweden's 'new economic policy', based on an unconditional commitment to full employment, public work at going union rates, and the 'Ghent model' of unemployment insurance (in addition to a social policy designed to reduce the dependence of workers on the cash nexus one might add), was deliberately designed to promote de-commodification (Unga 1976). To the extent that the aspects of the market forces were incompatible with full employment in this context, they were to be replaced with 'planning' mechanisms.

Why did a 'Kaleckian' mode of regulation emerge in Sweden? To answer this question one needs to explain why the Social Democratic labour movement, not the bourgeoisie, came to exercise ethico-political, national popular and hence hegemonic leadership in the power bloc. Why did Swedish Social Democrats – to borrow a term from Jonas Pontusson – develop a 'successful hegemonic disposition' (*pace* Pontusson 1988: 26–46) whereas none of the bourgeois factions of Swedish society did so? This question, in turn, requires a consideration of the balance of social forces in relation to ruptures and longer-term legacies associated with the Polanyian 'double movement'. One also needs to consider the strategies advanced by organic intellectuals during formative events in the 1930s and 1940s. Through such an exploration one can explain why Swedish capital accepted such a labour-inclusive power bloc and mode of regulation.

The factors behind social democratic hegemony in Sweden

The double movement in Sweden: the crisis of 'Bernadottism' and the origins of labour movement hegemony

The lack of an effective hegemonic disposition in the Swedish bourgeoisie can in part be understood with reference to Sweden's pre-modern legacy. As was the case with most of the European 'contender states' to the Anglo-Saxon hegemonic power as well as the semi-periphery (van der Pijl 1998), Sweden's economic transformation to capitalism occurred first gradually from a corporative *Ständestaat* (*pace* Poggi 1978: ch. 3) type of mercantilism through what Gramsci called a 'passive revolution'.[7] This passive revolution seems to have originated with Gustav III of Holstein Gottorp's *coup d'état* in 1772. But it is perhaps best labeled 'Bernadottism' (as a variation of the Marxian notion of Bonapartism) after the Napoleonic general; General Bernadotte was elected Crown Prince of Sweden in 1809 and became king in 1818 as Carl XIV Johan. He and his successors Oskar I and Carl XV, and the 'enlightenment' section of the aristocracy that occupied the bureaucracy, closely guarded their prerogatives, privileges and pre-capitalist forms of corporative representation. But they gradually liberalised socio-economic relations through, for example, the Freedom of Enterprise Laws of 1846 and 1864, and through a bilateral trade agreement with France in 1865 that incorporated Sweden into the Cobden–Chevalier free trade area. Hence, Sweden's capitalists were either excluded from political representation, or they were incorporated into one of the estates. They were appeased through the introduction of 'economic liberties' that allowed them to pursue their economic endeavour (Samuelsson 1968: 155–83; Therborn 1989: 79–87). The bourgeoisie developed little in terms of an independent political force, and it certainly did not develop a 'Jacobin' capacity for popular mobilisation. Hence, it did not develop the capacity to forge an ethico-political leadership of subordinate groups in society, and to interpellate them into a bourgeois conception of the general interest. The discourse of Bernadottism was conservative, in the sense of having a hierarchical conception of organic unity, where workers were viewed as 'uncultured', almost sub-human, 'thugs' or as 'children' (Frykman and Löfgren 1987).

When the corporative *Ständestaat* parliament was abolished in 1866 as part of the process of passive revolution, Sweden's structures of representation finally resembled the bourgeois constitutional monarchy 'typical' of the nineteenth century. But ironically, this reform, coming at the twilight of the liberal century of world history ushered in an era of political reaction. Electoral eligibility was based on strict property criteria, and it became a bastion for conservative landholders, farmers, and magnates in the iron and lumber industries. These groups were to jealously guard their political privileges, and resisted pressures to integrate the propertyless into political society (Samuelsson 1968: 155–83). At the turn of the century, the Swedish *Riksdag*, along with the Prussian *Landtag*, had the most conservative rules of representation in Europe (Schiller 1975: 199). Internationally this era coincided with the decline of liberal internationalism, and the emergence of rival imperialism (Sweden reverted to protectionist regulation in the 1880s). Under the reign of Oskar II (1872–1907), Sweden tended towards the German cultural and geopolitical sphere of interest.

But social transformations associated with modernisation and industrialisation ushered political pressures that would prove too difficult to contain within the Bernadottite framework. After Wilhelmine Germany's collapse in 1917, the Bernadottite power bloc had definitely run its course, and the hegemonic capacity of the bourgeoisie would henceforth remain weak. This vacuum would provide a space where a social democratic hegemonic project could assert itself. At the turn of the century, the state could quite plausibly be construed in the manner suggested in social democratic agitation: as the 'executive committee of the bourgeoisie'.

It was within the context of the crisis of this Bernadottism that Swedish social democracy began to develop its successful hegemonic disposition. Social democracy spread to Sweden from Germany via Denmark in the 1880s and 1990s. From there it inherited a Marxist doctrine. But the Swedish labour movement emerged on a terrain laid by other popular movements such as the free church and temperance movement. These movements had begun to preach a 'gospel of solidarity', and a morality of self-development and discipline through popular mobilisation and education.[8] They found particularly fertile terrain for their work in the countryside, where capitalist development caused great social dislocation among the rural poor, but where there also was a long tradition of self-organisation inherited from the old free-holding peasant communities. The labour movement developed in inter-action with these movements – indeed many of its leaders emerged from them – and by the turn of the century it had become the most prominent organisation of this counter-hegemonic popular movement culture. By World War I, the labour movement exercised leadership in an alliance consisting of the popular movements, liberals and socialists, organised around the demand for universal suffrage. In 1917, in the turmoil surrounding the Russian revolution and the collapse of Wilhelmine Germany, the conserva-tive forces gave in and accepted universal suffrage, under a perceived revo-lutionary threat (Andrae 1975: 232–53).

In the area of industrial relations, the 'economic wing' of the labour movement, the trade union movement, made significant headway in the first decade of the century. A Social Democratic federation of trade unions, LO, was formed in 1898. While the union movement suffered a strategic defeat in the general strike/lockout of 1909, unions had by that time made significant headway in being acknowledged as representatives of their members (Casparsson 1951). This signalled a transition in production rela-tions from free enterprise labour markets in the cities, and the quasi-feudal, quasi-capitalist patriarchal production relations in the iron and lumber communities (the *bruks*). By 1909 unions had won a series of conflicts over the definition of freedom of association as implying the right to represent their members in negotiation. In this context, they had also gained signifi-cant support from liberal and social conservative circles that invoked the corporative 'ancient rights' (in nationalist romantic discourse) of Swedes to organise themselves. (The pre-capitalist peasants had not been serfs and had enjoyed a measure of representation as the 'Fourth Estate'.) These circles saw unions as a potential vehicle of corporative social integration (harmony of interests) of the proletarian masses. In this context, the educative and disciplinary effect the unions had on 'worker thugs' was also often invoked. When SAF (*Sveriges arbetsgivareförbund*, the Employees' Confederation of Sweden) formed in response to a series of concerted strikes in support of uni-versal suffrage in 1902, and managed to make significant wage concessions and defend management prerogatives in work organisation, as codified in the famous Paragraph 23,[9] they nevertheless also acknowledged develop-ment of a bipartite mode of wage determination. While this bipartite rela-tionship was by no means equal, it nevertheless made it more difficult for capitalists to define their case in terms of some 'general interest' above their corporative interest – especially when lockouts became their preferred method of enforcement.

Once introduced, liberal democratic institutions rooted themselves rather quickly in the 1920s. The period after 1923 was also an era of continued rapid growth and industrialisation in Sweden. Nevertheless, from the perspective of socio-economic regulation, it was also a period of impasse. The interests of the organised union movement clashed with a business class determined to defend its prerogatives on the labour market. The parliamentary situation was also fluid and unstable, because once universal suffrage had been established, the Liberal–Social Democratic coalition broke down on questions of social policy, and above all labour law and industrial relations. On these issues, the Liberals were at odds with what they considered to be the extreme pro-union positions of the Social Democrats that defied basic economic laws. Weak minority governments succeeded one another. Neither Conservatives, Liberals, Agrarians, nor Social Democrats could attain working majorities.

The labour movement also faced a doctrinal crisis. After 1917 it had definitely struck a reformist route, and argued for the advancement of social change through the liberal democratic state. But what did this mean in practice? Apart from not being able to muster enough votes to achieve a parliamentary majority, the movement was hard pressed to define the meaning of 'reform in a socialist direction'. Like other social democratic movements of the time, it was rendered quite paralysed by a determinist Marxist diagnosis and neo-classical policy tools. Lofty ambitions of 'socialisation' and 'industrial democracy' ground to a halt with a public commission that failed to produce operative policies.

During the depression of the 1930s, however, when unemployment dramatically increased, the labour movement successfully secured its hegemonic position. The breakthrough came in the period between 1932 and 1936, when SAP had abandoned full-scale socialisation of the means of production as a method to address capitalist crisis, and successfully implemented their new employment policy and their social reforms through the Cow Deal. In political and ideological terms, the Social Democrats administered well the political capital they gained from this success. The reforms of the 1930s were articulated in terms of an unfolding and unfinished project which had started with political democratisation in 1917 and now had reached the stage of social democratisation, which in turn would set the stage for economic democratisation some time beyond the foreseeable future. On the level of mass politics, a term coined by Prime Minister Per-Albin Hansson, 'People's Home' (*folkhemmet*), where no one was to be treated either as a 'favourite' or as a 'stepchild', proved to be particularly enduring and politically compelling. Articulating more traditional conceptions of family justice and the 'harmony of interests', it showed the Social Democratic project to be beyond class interests and equivalent to more universal conceptions of fairness. It is no exaggeration to label the notion of the 'People's Home' a Sorelian myth, which gave direction and cohesion to the labour movement and enabled it to project its political concepts beyond itself to the 'ethico-political moment' of civil society at large.[10]

Swedish capitalism: a non-hegemonic accumulation strategy

Although the Oscarian era was politically reactionary, Sweden nevertheless experienced quite a remarkable phase of economic growth and development during this time. Certainly, this development is an important backdrop to the social transformation that would lead to the undermining of the Bernadottite power bloc. But this pattern of economic growth is also an important factor in determining the particular shape that Sweden's politics of productivity would take.

Swedish industrialisation first took off in the 1880s, within the political framework of the Bernadottite 'strong state', with roots in the absolutist period of the seventeenth century. Perhaps one can view Swedish industrialisation in the twilight of Pax Britannica as an analogy of the miracle of the East Asian 'tigers' in the twilight of Pax Americana. Sweden became a raw material supplier within the international division of labour of Pax Britannica (lumber and iron). As the second industrial revolution commenced, Swedish terms of trade improved dramatically as the demand for Swedish lumber and iron increased. Moreover, the state had invested in an extended railway network, and in public education. Earlier in the century agriculture had been rationalised through enclosure reform. These developments generated the financial requisites for industrialisation through vertically integrated linkages between iron forging, steel making and engineering, and lumber, pulp and engineering, flanked by a rationalising agriculture dominated by yeoman farmers emerging out of the 'Fourth estate' peasantry (Samuelsson 1968: 172–96, 207–21; Jörberg 1975: 92–135).

This pattern of industrialisation provides an important backdrop to Sweden's distinct mode of Fordist growth. Articulation of mass production and mass consumption in the context of national Keynesian welfare states implies that accumulation is autocentric. Hence, accumulation is ensured through the development of relatively self-referential and differential domestic productive systems. In this context, international trade may play an important but nevertheless auxiliary role in capital accumulation. Despite the progressive increase of international trade in the post-war period, capital accumulation conformed to the Fordist ideal type in the large industrialised countries. They developed differentiated industrial structures first behind the trade barriers of the immediate post-war period, and then maintained industrial diversity because increased trade was of an intra-industry as opposed to inter-industry nature (Mjøset 1987: 70–71; Ruggie 1983: 216–17, cf. Cooper 1980: 74–78). In addition, significant international connections were restricted to trade relationships. Productive and financial capital tended to be of a national character, up until the development of the 'off-shore' Euro-dollar markets in the late 1960s. Swedish post-war development, however, probably along with all the other 'small European states' analysed by Katzenstein (1985), diverges from this pattern as far as the relationship between capital accumulation and trade is concerned.

The productive system of post-war Sweden (and of the other Nordic countries) can perhaps be labelled a 'disarticulated' or 'peninsular' Fordism (Mjøset *et al.* 1986: 72–73, 76–89; Mjøset 1987: 410; Andersson 1990: 26–29; Ryner 1997: 25–27). Here, mass production was relatively undiversified, whereas mass consumption was diversified and the circuit of capital accumulation was very trade dependent. Thus in disarticulated Fordism, mass production was dependent upon demand in the world economy, and mass consumption was dependent upon imports, financed by foreign exchange earned from high value added commodities in the export sector. Moreover, the export sector was composed of a relatively narrow range of dominant commodities and corporations.

The term 'disarticulation' is borrowed from Samir Amin's version of dependency theory. Amin explains how a high degree of trade exposure in the core (autocentric as opposed to autarkic accumulation) is possible without leading to dependency and underdevelopment (extroverted accumulation). Perhaps anticipating Aglietta's work, Amin defines autocentric development as the capacity of a social formation to counteract the over-production/underconsumption tendency of capitalism, by expanding domestic demand in a manner which simultaneously counteracts the tendency of the organic composition of capital to increase. A necessary condition for this is that there is a synchronic expansion of productivity, particularly in the investment goods sector, and of real purchasing power. In this context, exports may be seen as providing a supplement to the domestic market, even at quite high levels of trade exposure, as long as a social formation can regulate the productivity–consumption relationship. According to Amin, the peripheral formations have never had this capacity because their technological potential for productivity increases is limited, and domestic demand is fundamentally disarticulated from supply (Amin 1976: 76–78, 191–97).

The Nordic growth models are curious because they seemed to achieve autocentric development despite disarticulation. The product and process composition of their production developed a high technological potential for productivity increases in relation to scale. However, domestic demand could only influence this through the mediation of export performance. On the other hand, other factors and forms of policy routines ensured that auto-centric accumulation became central in the Nordic modes of growth. These included more selective forms of economic intervention (eg. industrial policy in Norway and Finland, labour market policy in Sweden), coordination of economic policy and wage determination through corporatist arrangements, heavy regulation of monetary policy, complex user–producer networks of industrial innovation, and close to no foreign ownership and control over the means of production (Andersson 1990: 26–27; see also Katzenstein 1985). The next chapter will further elaborate on the ensemble of policy routines that constituted the mode of regulation of the Swedish model.

Since the export sector is so strategic for accumulation, and since it is narrow, it is important to study the specific composition of the export sector. Most of Sweden's post-war export-oriented corporations and products originated with the country's late and rapid industrialisation process. They developed from natural advantages in the production of what often were 'staples' commodities, produced from lumber and iron. Swedish Fordism depended on the expanding scale, process innovation, and the improvement of products in these industries (Edquist and Lundvall 1993: 271–74).

The engineering input industry, which initially emerged as a supplier of Swedish firms producing semi-processed goods such as lumber and steel, became Sweden's most important export industry, employing just under half of the industrial work force. Sweden became a key exporter of electrical-engineering products (Asea, Ericsson, AGA), mechanical-engineering products (SKF, Sandvik, Atlas-Copco, Boliden), shipping (Kockums, Göta-verken) and agricultural processing (Alfa-Laval, Tetra-Pak). In addition, Sweden subsequently developed important exports in some consumer durable industries such as automobiles and housing durables (Volvo, SAAB, Electrolux, IKEA). In the post-war period manufacturing would make up about 40 per cent of Swedish exports. Semi-processed goods (steel, pulp and paper), and raw materials (iron ore and lumber), while diminishing in relative importance, nevertheless remained important export sectors.

This is not to say that internal mass consumption would not become important for domestic mass production. The success of Swedish corporations such as Tetra-Pak, IKEA, Electrolux, Ericsson, Asea, SAAB and Volvo in developing their products depended on the user–producer networks and demand induced by public domestic consumption (through, for example, agricultural subsidies, defence, telecommunications, nuclear power programmes and housing provision) and real wage increases. In latter years health provision has led to spin-offs in the pharmaceutical industry (Astra and Pharmacia). However, the key to the viability of these firms has never-theless been export performance, not domestic demand. Swedish mass production and consumption was mediated by the world market. The export sector has never been a mere auxiliary for domestic Fordism.[11]

Swedish capitalists did not exercise hegemonic leadership in the politics of productivity, but they did develop a coherent and successful accumulation strategy. Hence the hegemonic position of the social democratic labour movement is not inconsistent with the existence of capitalist relations of production, or a capitalist 'ruling class' in the structuralist Marxist sense. The Swedish capitalist class developed and maintained internal coherence, exercised power *vis à vis* labour, and influenced policy through organisations such as the Federation of Swedish Industries (SI), the Association of Bankers (*Bankföreningen*), and particularly through their employers' organisation, SAF. SAF can be understood as a cartel that enables the capitalist class to pool the power resources inherent in individual capitalist firms, based on con-trol over the means of production, market control, and the structural power of capital emanating from the valorisation process (Therborn 1989: 146–49). Rather than mobilising an ideology of 'national popular leadership', SAF's strategy in the context of the Swedish model *vis à vis* the state was to influence policy by providing 'technical advice' through participation in public commissions, tripartite boards, and through the creation and financing of research institutes such as SNS (*studieförbundet näringsliv samhälle*) and IUI (*industriens utredningsinstitut*) (Söderpalm 1976: 43–59, 144–53; Lewin 1967: 375–83).[12] The key purpose of this accumulation strategy was to defend their prerogatives over the production process and ownership, and to maintain an adequate rate of profit. In addition, as we shall see, in situations when it was perceived that these prerogatives were threatened, Swedish capitalists managed to intervene successfully in the public debate.

The 'historic compromise' between capital and labour, upon which the Swedish politics of productivity was based, thus ensured private ownership of the means of production, and the absolute discretion of owners to decide what, where, how and for whom to produce and invest. Since the inter-war period, Swedish capital can be characterised as heavily concentrated, and densely organised, as bank-centred finance capital (i.e. an intimate articulation of productive and financial capital). Characteristic of Swedish capital, especially export capital, since the 1930s, has been the manner in which corporations are tied into a handful of relatively discrete 'spheres' through investment banks/holding companies, through cross-ownership, and cross-membership of management and executive boards. These tended to be institutions controlled by a handful of family financial dynasties ('the 15 families') (Hermansson 1989: 79–84).

This development can also be traced to Sweden's industrial development at the turn of the century. Industrialisation was financed by loan capital. Banks, emerging out of trading houses that had mediated Swedish commodity trade in the mid-nineteenth century, borrowed money abroad, mediated credit to domestic firms, and earned their profits through interest rate differentials. Industrial capital was initially not particularly concentrated, and it was not centralised until the 1920s and the early 1930s when the banking spheres acquired shares and consolidated and reorganised productive capital. At first, this happened rather serendipitously. The stock market did not absorb new industrial shares after the post World War I recession of 1921–22. As a result, the banks absorbed the shares that they had issued on behalf of firms. A second concentration thrust happened in the depression and in the wake of the so-called 'Krüger crash' (see note 5) of the 1930s, when banks took over shares as companies defaulted on their loans. Again, this was an unintended consequence for Svenska Handelsbanken (SHB), whereas the Stockholms Enskilda Bank (SEB) of the Wallenbergs pursued this type of strategy deliberately (Lash and Urry 1987: 29–35). Government legislation complicated matters. In the wake of the Krüger crash the government was concerned about the risks to the monetary system of share-owning banks and prohibited this. However, the financial capitalists had acquired a taste for share ownership, which appeared especially lucrative given the low rates of interest, and they found a way to maintain the links. They did so by creating holding companies (Investor in the case of the SEB-Bank, Industrivärden in the case of the SHB-bank and Custos in the case of Skandinaviska), controlled by the bank-owning families, which would hold the shares in question (U. Olsson 1995: 9).

One can be more precise about the relative strength of the different spheres and families. One family, the Wallenbergs, has by far been the most dominant economically. It has governed the Stockholms Enskilda Bank/Investor (SEB) sphere, in coalition with a handful of smaller families (such as the Ax:son Johnson, Söderberg and Wehtje). The two other spheres were the Skandinaviska/Custos sphere, which was also a family-controlled sphere, and the Handelsbanken/Industrivärden (SHB) sphere. The latter was more of an institutional investor, without tight family control. In terms of the value of the corporations controlled, the Wallenberg/SEB sphere was as large as the other two combined. This relative domination of the SEB sphere was enforced when the Stockholms Enskilda and Skandinaviska banks were merged in 1972 into a Wallenberg-controlled Skandinaviska Enskilda Bank. Thus, by the 1970s only two spheres remained, and the SEB sphere was about twice as large as the SHB sphere (Hermansson 1989: 91–98; Olsen 1994: 199–203) The third largest holding group, about half the size of the SHB sphere, was the consumer cooperative (KF), with holdings exclusively in the domestic sector.

The formation of a bank-centred economic structure is an important factor behind the joint central, negotiated mode of economic regulation. A bank-mediated articulation of financial and productive capital (where industry is connected to a 'house-bank') tends to facilitate a 'voice'-mediated credit structure, where the economic consciousness of financiers converges with that of industrialists (Zysman 1983). This provided for a more long-term view in finance and investment decisions, with particular emphasis on the prospects of the development of the productive (Fordist) system.[13] The high degree of centralisation also ensured a measure of corporate planning for capital as a whole. This is an important backdrop to the embracing of central wage negotiations led by SAF (Ingham 1974: 35–65), and probably also to the fact that SAF could generate collective agreements acceptable to capital, despite LO pursuing a solidaristic wage policy, which squeezed out individual sectors and firms.

It is, however, not possible to understand the emergence of joint central regulation and the emergence of the employers' federation, SAF, as the primary organisation of business representation without recognising that this took place in the context of a non-hegemonic accumulation strategy. In other words, SAF had to respond to the hegemonic position of the labour movement that developed in the 1930s, and social democratic executive power that seemed permanent for the foreseeable future. It was assumed that the bargaining power of LO would be enhanced primarily through unemployment insurance legislation and full employment policies. In this context, more centralised negotiations were seen as a way to pre-empt price competition for scarce labour power (Swenson 1991).

This strategy was only accepted begrudgingly by the Wallenbergs as a necessity. They were also lukewarm towards IUI and SNS. Corporations in the Wallenberg sphere had played a central role in a more confrontational strategy towards the new social democratic government in the early part of the 1930s. This strategy was organised through the so-called 'Director's Club', which was formed amid fears that the new economic and social policies would result in labour shortages and increased labour costs. The strategy was to fund the Liberal and Conservative Parties in the 1936 election and to support their campaign which was based on the argument (drawing on works of established economists like Heckscher and Cassel) that the 'new economic policy' contradicted elementary economic rationality. After the re-election of SAP, however, the more accommodating strategy towards the labour movement emerged as dominant in Swedish business circles, preparing the ground for the Saltsjöbaden Accord (Söderpalm 1976: 31–38).[14] But it was the more pragmatic officials within the organisation of SAF itself, such as its Director Gustaf Söderlund, rather than the owners and CEOs themselves, who prepared and advanced this political re-orientation (Söderpalm 1976: 38, 43–46, 48–50).

Despite their dominant material position, representatives from Wallenberg sphere would not play a proportional direct role in SAF.[15] Rather, the more enthusiastic supporters of SAF's strategy came from pragmatists in the SHB sphere, such as Tore Browaldh, a disciple of Gunnar Myrdal who emphasized the 'social responsibility' of corporations (Browaldh 1976: 17–96, 153–247).

The discourse of 'rationalisation'

One should not view the aforementioned developments and compromises of the 1930s too mechanically. Significant ideological re-articulations occurred during the inter-war period, which facilitated the Cow Deal and the Saltsjöbaden Accord. Particularly important was the interpellation of capital and labour into the discourse of 'rationalisation' that emerged in the wake of the increased salience of 'scientific management'. This points to the importance of the emergence of a new stratum of experts at this stage of capitalist socio-economic development, that van der Pijl (1998: 138–43) calls 'cadres'. Cadres are actors whose social function it is to ensure social and systems integration in society so as to counteract the disintegrative effects of commodification in capitalist society. In other words, they are a social group whose existence is rooted in the need for socialisation (in the sense of *Vergesellschaftung*, see note 1). The 'demand' for such social integration increased in the wake of the crisis of Pax Britannica, because the increased scale of corporations demanded that capitalists themselves engaged in deliberate planning. But in addition, there was also an increased need for the state to take on socially integrative functions, to prevent disease and to ensure the basic level of health and education that was required from labour as a valuable input in the industrial processes. In essence, these were the functional pressures behind the eventual formation of the welfare state (Wilensky 1975). Furthermore, the motivation and loyalty of the mass population to the social order also had to be reproduced, as the traditional framework of moral reproduction of the village was undermined through industrialisation. Interestingly, as the labour movement became increasingly powerful, its organisation also took on some of these functions. For example, trade unions, in representing labour in wage negotiation, also became an organisation that socially integrated labour in capitalist society. As the social democrats also began to think seriously about state power and reformist strategy, they also began to recruit and develop within themselves an increasingly powerful stratum of cadres.

As a result of this development, a new pattern of social representation emerged in the early part of the nineteenth century, where specialised cadres began to represent social groups. The 'consensus' of the Swedish model can be seen as a product negotiated and agreed by different cadres, representing the different social groups, and the discourse of rationalisation provided them with a common intersubjective framework through which they could define common norms, including norms of how to deal with differences and conflict. Now, there were fundamental differences between different cadres representing different interests, and hence the 'consensus' should not be seen as one of total agreement. The different social classes and groups had not only different interests but also different understandings of the meaning of the Swedish model. It could be seen as a modernisation of capitalism rendering class struggle and ideology irrelevant, a pragmatic 'middle way' between capitalism and socialism, or as a stage on the way to socialism. In other words, although the Swedish model undoubtedly had a distinct language, the different social forces spoke it with different dialects (Jenson and Mahon 1993: 79, cf. Pekkarinen 1989). Hence, to invoke Laclau again, hegemony was not so much about a common outlook as it was about neutralising the antagonisms between different outlooks. Different groups were interpellated and 'rationalisation' was the central articulating principle.

The history of the social development of this articulating principle has in particular been charted by the dissertations of Hans De Geer (1978) and Anders Johansson (1989). Initially it was the emerging engineering profession, influenced by Taylorist production norms developing in the USA (but also in France by Fayol), that was the main proponent of rationalisation. Industrialists became increasingly receptive to their ideas after 1907. This was in the context of labour supply shortages that were caused by emigration and by what Taylor called 'soldiering': work slowdowns orchestrated by organized workers on the local level. Mechanisation and scientific management became means for industrialists to redress these problems. It decreased demand for labour and provided a method for control over the labour process, which in turn could increase labour and production-process intensity. It is probably no coincidence that these developments coincided with the aforementioned December Compromise of 1906 (note 9). Given the strike rates of the 1920s and 1930s, the continued shortage of labour supply, and the hegemonic position acquired by SAP, SAF sought to protect management prerogatives, and provide access to a stable and affordable supply of labour power through the Saltsjöbaden Accord. In terms of concessions, SAF decided not to fight against the goal of the labour movement to promote employment above all. SAF also agreed to tripartite regulation of health and safety standards, that could be justified with reference to the scientific rationality of psychology and medicine.

The Federation of Industrialists, SI, was formed in 1910 to promote rationalisation. Initially, it was promoted in conservative terms as a means of 'national rebirth' (consistent with the Oscarian ethos). The discourse often had corporatist overtones, and it was argued that social institutions should be adjusted to industrial demands (De Geer 1978: 62–70).[16] At the same time, the rise of the discourse of rationalisation led to a decline of the patriarchal and despotic ethos of management of the nineteenth century, and thereby set the groundwork for an acceptance of bipartism as well as liberal democratic parliamentarism. Industrialists from the emerging engineering sector were pushing the Conservatives to accept universal suffrage in 1917. The legacy of patriarchy in the labour process did not disappear altogether, though. Whereas American and Taylorist ideas predominated in the mechanical aspects of labour process organisation, social conservative ideas (*pace* Fayol) remained influential because of what they had to say about corporate 'psychology', and the guiding and moral leadership role of the manager (ibid: 103).

After the recession of 1920–23, state managers also became increasingly interested in rationalisation. This increased interest was in part the result of the economic consequences of the introduction of the eight-hour working day. This legislation was brought in by the liberal–socialist coalition immediately after World War I. The Academy of Engineering (IVA) was formed as a business–government joint venture. It was to develop competence in psychotechnology. Intellectuals from this academy with their 'scientific objectivity' would play an important mediating role between labour and capital in central public commissions in the 1930s, for example the Committee for Labour Studies Questions in 1933. Moreover, the Conservative government of 1928, influenced by the Mond–Turner talks in England, initiated a Labour Peace conference between LO and SAF. This conference was an important precursor to the Saltsjöbaden Accord.

The labour movement was interpellated intellectually into the discourse of rationalisation through the notion of 'organised capitalism', for which the most prominent intellectual proponent was the Austro-Marxist Otto Bauer (ibid: 262–65, 268–71; Unga 1976: 63–67; Esping-Andersen 1985b: 17–24). This form of thought developed in the 1920s as a result of the abortive Austrian revolution and the power Austrian social democrats acquired in ('Red') Vienna. These developments raised questions about the character and meaning of socialist reform, and about reformist strategy.

Since Swedish social democratic intellectuals faced similar problems, they paid close attention to the intellectual developments in Austria. This reformist brand of Marxism has been mentioned in preliminary terms in chapter 1. It combined an economic analysis of uneven development with piecemeal social engineering. It argued that capitalist rationalisation implied a gradual development to a more affluent, rational and organised society, that would demand social planning as the productive forces developed. It was agnostic on the question of the form of adequate state intervention and planning, and held that social experimentation and empirical data would determine an adequate private–public mix at any one stage of socio-economic development. (Austro-Marxist theory abandoned a dialectical conception of knowledge in favour of a positivist one.) The conception of the state as the 'executive committee of the bourgeoisie' was also abandoned. Once the labour movement had ascended to the commanding heights of the state, the latter was conceived of as an instrument that could be used to achieve the aims of the working class. The issue was not perceived as the state as such. Rather it was seen as an issue of who actually occupied executive power in the state (Sunesson 1974).

Central to this ideology was the concept of 'misrationalisation'. The development of monopoly capitalism would unleash new productive forces, that would require a more social form of organisation. But these could not be rationally organised by market forces, since they did not correspond to the increasingly 'social' character of economic life generated by the productive forces. As monopolisation increased, prices would become distorted. Increased capital intensity would also lead to overaccumulation and disproportion between supply and demand. When such misrationalisation occurred, the labour movement should intervene and promote and organise state intervention towards 'social need'.[17]

Austro-Marxism was only one source of inspiration for social democratic intellectuals as they sought policy guidance, although it provided the big picture and legitimation since it suggested how piecemeal reform related to their vision of social transformation and reform. Domestic influences included the functionalist Uppsala philosophy of Axel Hägerström, the economics of Knut Wicksell and the 'Stockholm School' (which included Gunnar Myrdal and Bertil Ohlin). The ideas of British liberals, such as Beveridge and Keynes, also caught the attention of Swedish social democrats (Olsson 1994: 45–50; Erlander 1972: 117–35). Social democrats were interested in these ideas because they suggested methods through which state intervention could actually redress the misrationalisation Bauer discussed in general terms. Wicksell provided a theory of counter-cyclical monetary policy, but above all he provided an economic rationale for income redistribution. The Stockholm School and Keynes provided an economic rationale and methods to combat unemployment.[18]

Rationalisation and the rearticulation of developmental democracy

The version of politics of productivity that underpinned labour's participation and acceptance of the terms of the Saltsjöbaden, had gained increased prominence among trade union intellectuals, such as Sigfrid Hansson, through the 1920s and 1930s. The need to render the eight-hour working-day reform compatible with wage increases, and the downward pressure on wages resulting from the economic crisis of the early 1920s and increased capital intensity in production, were the underlying pressures that such a political orientation was intended to address (Alf Johansson 1989: 51–52, 54–58, 61–92). Associated with this was a shift in the conception of work. During this period work was construed as a virtue, whereas previously 'the realm of freedom' in social democratic discourse had been associated with leisure. Moreover, the conception of work was de-problematised as the notion of alienation was displaced to the periphery of social democratic discourse. The demand for industrial democracy which had been central in the 1920s was gradually marginalised, or more to the point, it was discursively conflated with health and safety norms (eg. Helldén 1990: 58–151).

Centralisation was long resisted by unions on a local rank-and-file level. Branch-level agreements rendered ineffective their struggle against intensification of the pace of work, increased redundancies of skilled labour, and a hollowing out of meaningful work tasks as Taylorist norms were implemented. Centralisation also contradicted the popular movement norms of self-organisation and direct democracy. However, during the depression of the 1930s this resistance disappeared. A number of factors explain this. First, skilled work-tasks were eliminated and eventually the crafts workers that had been at the forefront of local resistance were replaced by a new generation of semi-skilled 'Taylorist' workers, with less of a craft identity and a sense of a craft to protect. Secondly, and relatedly, Taylorisation was at that time considered inevitable. Thirdly, the high level of unemployment made the rank and file open to a new strategy. Fourthly, and most importantly, the uneven development of wages in the export and home sector led to the demand for solidaristic wage policy and distributive justice, which required centralised coordination. Norms of local democracy and influence over pay scales were sacrificed for the sake of this broader goal. At the same time, workers envisaged a more integral strategy: a programme of social welfare reform would be ensured through parliamentary representation and municipal politics, and wage struggle through central mobilisation (Alf Johansson 1989).

It is important to note, then, that the politics of productivity implied a rearticulation of the discourse of integrative democracy. The old discourse associated with the 'birth' of the labour movement had emphasised participatory procedures to ensure personal development, local empowerment and mobilisation. At the same time this discourse was rather vague on the specifics of the large-scale reforms that would be implemented once the labour movement 'acquired power'. This discourse now gave way to another articulation which ended up virtually excluding any participatory democratic procedures. Instead, it focused quite exclusively on the role of providing the material means considered necessary to lift up the populace to a level of affluence which would eventually give them the capacity to be fully fledged citizens. The procedural forms considered adequate for meeting these goals were not participatory democratic, but centralist, technocratic and 'scientific'. Democratic control was understood in rather narrow terms as indirect representation in Parliament and the municipalities, and through elected functionaries of unions and other organisations.

Much faith was put in the capacity of 'experts' – scientists, engineers, architects – to define reform policies. Particularly in social policies relating to population and family issues, 'social engineers' were influential. These social engineers were influenced by Rousseauian and utopian-socialist values in their conception of family and community development and gender relations, as well as a functionalist conception of means–ends rationality. Much faith was put on scientific rationality, and if people resisted change that was judged to be scientifically correct, there was a sense that they should be 'forced to be free'. The state had a role to play to make sure that, for example, housing standards were adequate, and that certain norms were met in children's upbringing.[19] The most insidious legacy of this was the forced sterilisation programme of categories of people (often diagnosed as mentally ill, but even vaguer definitions of problem cases were used, including those including '*folk*') who were not considered appropriate as parents.[20]

The Myrdalian discourse was not the only discourse informing social democratic social policy. It existed, sometimes in an uneasy relationship with another discourse, advanced by the Minister of Social Affairs, Gustav Möller. Möller, who in contrast to the Myrdals was not an academic but had risen from the party ranks, was much more sceptical about the possibility and desirability of bureaucratic steering. Möller and his advocates did not believe that the state should formulate detailed substantive norms to regulate everyday life. They believed in simple universalist norms and programmes that would reduce complexity in implementation and eliminate side effects such as steering problems and bureaucratic discretion. This suspicion of bureaucracy was, for example, the rationale behind the Ghent model, where union cadres managed unemployment insurance. For Möller *et al.*, universalist programmes were also seen as less authoritarian and stigmatising, and were thus favoured because the purpose was not to target the 'deserving poor', but to increase the realm of freedom and security of the populace at large through civil social rights.

Möller was inspired by the Danish Social Democrats Bramsnæs and Steincke, and construed welfare state reform in Marxian terms as partial human emancipation at a stage when productive forces were still inadequately developed. Such reforms were seen as a strategy to develop the productive and human resources of society for further (socialist) emancipation in the future. This strategy required that reforms were general, rather than specific, that administrative tasks were primarily given to popularly established organisations and their cadres, that the power of the juridical state apparatus was reduced and that old state apparatuses were closed down and replaced by new ones.[21]

It is probably no coincidence that social policies pertaining to labour issues were primarily in the Möllerian mode, whereas many of the policies pertaining to family and population were influenced by the Myrdals. The relative role of indirect representation versus scientific authority in the definition of policy ends varied depending on the relative location of the issue and the social force concerned in the power bloc. 'Women's issues' tended to be defined by the social engineers, bureaucrats, and politicians not directly associated with those to be regulated (Hirdman 1989: 159–75, 216–39). Labour issues were defined by unionists. Although labour politics was becoming more centralised than before, unionists nevertheless had to consider more directly the sentiments of its membership. We will return to this issue in the discussion of unequal representation in the next chapter.

Summary and conclusion

This chapter has explained why social democracy managed to become a hegemonic force in Sweden, and it has begun to account for its content. It has also accounted for how Swedish capitalists nevertheless managed to forge a coherent Fordist accumulation strategy despite these socio-political conditions. Finally, the chapter has explained why the notion of rationalisation was the articulating principle of the 'consensus' behind the Swedish model. The notion of misrationalisation indicates that Swedish social democracy had a well-developed conception of economic systems rationality and its relation to social democratic goals. At the same time, we have also seen how the definition of democracy was narrowed in the process. Nevertheless, Swedish social democracy successfully assumed national popular leadership in the process associated with Polanyi's 'double movement' and institutionalised a particularly progressive mode of Fordist regulation and politics of productivity. The next chapter will account for the functional logic of this mode of regulation.

4 Social democratic regulation
The Swedish model

The decisive transition towards Fordist politics of productivity began in the 1930s, but its institutionalisation was not assured until after World War II. As in the rest of the western world, the Swedish politics of productivity progressively evolved and gained internal coherence in the 1940s and early 1950s. In this process, a set of policy routines, capable of mediating imperatives of sustained capital accumulation and Fordist capitalist growth with imperatives of social legitimacy, redistribution and social representation, were progressively institutionalised. The policy routines that crystallised included, above all, centralised and coordinated wage bargaining between LO and SAF, and a strategy of solidaristic wage policy pursued by LO. They also included counter-cyclical demand management, and a selective labour market policy pursued by the government with the purpose of achieving the overarching economic policy aim of full employment. The culmination of coherence of this ensemble of policy routines was achieved in the late 1950s, when the Rehn–Meidner model was adopted as the common economic policy doctrine of SAP and LO. This chapter describes the institutional *modus operandi* of this institutional framework and specifies how it presupposed certain conditions of existence in the social relations of production, forms of state and world order that indeed did obtain in this period and up to the late 1960s.

The immediate post-war period: from the Post-war Programme to the Rehn–Meidner model

The tendency towards institutional equilibrium notwithstanding, the immediate post-war period of 1946–49 was one of ideologically charged conflict over SAP's and LO's common Post-war Programme, formulated in 1944. This development paralleled international developments immediately after the world war, before the Bretton Woods framework and the Cold War crystallised conditions. We shall return to this at the end of the chapter, which will shed light on the international context of the Swedish model.

SAP's national popular position was consolidated during the war, because of its leading role in the National Government that managed to keep

Sweden out of World War II, and avoid Nazi occupation. The war also provided an opportunity to experiment with economic planning and an expansion of the public sector. Military mobilisation obviously necessitated an expansion of public investments and consumption. But in addition, business consented to wartime economic planning. This planning was facilitated through a number of standing public commissions, often with tripartite representation. Military mobilisation eliminated unemployment, after two decades of severe unemployment problems.

The social engineers and cadres of the labour movement approached the end of the war with the premise that it must be possible to sustain full employment in peacetime too.[1] They saw the wartime experience as a validation of the thesis that this required more public intervention in the economy than had been the case in the 1930s. They also interpreted the wartime experience as evidence that it would be possible to legitimate higher levels of public consumption and taxation. This could, in turn, facilitate an ambitious build-up of public social insurance and welfare services. These premises informed the Post-war Programme of 1944, whose chief author was Minister of Finance, Ernst Wigforss. The Programme called for an increased degree of planning (*planmässighet*) through tripartite branch councils, and a nationalisation of industries, if there was evidence that nationalisation would be likely to create better provisions for social needs. The decision as to whether an industry should be nationalised would be determined by special public commissions, and above all by the Post-war Planning Commission, the 'Myrdal Commission'. The programme also called for an extensive build-up of the welfare sector, for which Gustav Möller would be responsible.

The ambitions of the Post-war Programme in the social policy area were realised quite readily. Most of the Möller reforms were already implemented by 1948. Political discourse had shifted significantly in favour of expanded public social consumption during the war and as a result of the diffusion of Keynesian ideas. The Liberal Party converted to Keynesianism in the post-war period, and the distinguished Keynesian professor Bertil Ohlin became their party leader. In this climate, when the levels of public consumption advocated by the SAP were no longer particularly controversial,[2] Möller managed to implement programmes consistent with his ideas as well as with the norms of the social democratic welfare policy regime type (see the previous two chapters). A set of major flat rate welfare reforms was implemented. This included universal pension and child allowance reforms, and extensive public housing programmes. As a result of these reforms, the residual poor relief component of social policy was reduced from 15 to 3 per cent between 1940 and 1950 (in 1930 it was 23 per cent). As the fiscal effects of the reforms kicked in, social expenditure over GDP increased from 8 in 1945 to 12 per cent at the end of the 1950s (Olsson 1987: 5–6, 13). In 1948 the National Labour Market Board (AMS) was nationalised and consolidated local employment offices, reflecting the government's post-war commitment to full employment (ibid: 5–10).

The latter reform was an indication of the social democratic government's commitment to '*planmässighet*' in the economy. But in this area, Swedish capital and the bourgeois parties were not willing to accept the principles of SAP's Post-war Programme. This was in contrast to social policy, and in contrast to the exceptional circumstances of war. Swedish business mobilised in the popular and electoral arenas to defend their prerogatives, and the strategic orientation shifted once again in favour of the confrontation strategy of the 'Director's Club' (Söderpalm 1976: 108–43). Ample funds were provided for the Conservative and Liberal Parties to articulate a more market oriented 'social-liberal' alternative to the Post-war Programme in the elections of 1946 and 1948, and to discredit 'socialist planning'. Although SAP remained in power, they lost significant support and were forced onto the defensive on economic policy. They were blamed for miscalculating economic trends after the war (which they did). They had predicted a recession rather than the boom that followed the war, and as a result inflation increased. In 1948, the Czech insurrection also served to bolster the anti-socialist campaign. SAP's strategy also presupposed the cooperation of business, which managed to marginalise the more radical discussions of the Myrdal Commission. A commission of branch councils was never formed, because business refused to participate.

Given the post-war boom that commenced in the late 1940s, it was difficult for SAP to articulate concrete reasons for the need for increased '*planmässighet*'. Their strategy was premised on the incapacity of markets to provide for full employment and social policy. Social democrats were also increasingly satisfied with the present state–market mix. Their paradigm was based on empiricism and experimentation that seemed to refute their initial post-war thesis. Full employment and welfare provisions could be rendered compatible within the terms set in the 1930s. The terms of the class compromise as forged in the 1930s were thus confirmed as SAP backed down from an ambitious nationalisation platform and meso-level economic regulation.

Within these terms of compromise, and these state–market boundaries, one salient issue remained unresolved. This was the issue of inflation, and how wage developments should be regulated in a full employment economy. In this area, the bourgeois parties argued that the government's full employment commitment was too ambitious. But in addition, the question of incomes policy, which was raised particularly by Beveridge at the end of the forties, was thus on the agenda. Officials in the Ministry of Finance at the time supported incomes policy, and the idea that unions should accept macroeconomic responsibility in their incomes policy. This, however, became a very delicate question that struck at the heart of regulation and representation of workers, and the relationship between SAP and LO. It was not reasonably resolved until 1955, when the government converted to the principles of the Rehn–Meidner model, advocated by the LO since 1951.

The Rehn–Meidner model

LO economists Gösta Rehn and Rudolf Meidner began to formulate their ideas in the late 1940s. Rehn and Meidner's position expressed the reluctance of unions to accept macroeconomic responsibility for price stability. While Rehn and Meidner accepted the premise that the full employment economy created inflationary problems that required a reform in wage relations, they argued that such a reform should not contravene the basic task of unions to represent their members in wage bargaining, as explicit incomes policy would. They argued that it would be impossible for unions to contain wages if the full employment economy generated an excess demand for labour power. Incomes policies would be particularly dangerous for union legitimacy, since in this context significant portions of workers would be offered higher wages by market demand than the unions would demand in negotiations. Why would workers belong to unions if they were given wages lower than they otherwise would obtain (Rehn 1948; Meidner 1948)? Rehn and Meidner's alternative reform of wage relations was presented in a Report to the LO Congress of 1951. The Congress endorsed the Report, and thus the Rehn–Meidner model became official LO policy (LO 1951).[3]

The policy elements contained in Rehn and Meidner's recommendations were not new.[4] Rather, the Rehn–Meidner model's novelty was that it rearticulated them and presented them as a set of internally coherent and mutually supportive measures with an overall macroeconomic and political rationale. The prescriptions of the Rehn–Meidner model can be summarised briefly in the following manner: LO was to coordinate wage demands and negotiations of all its constituent member unions in order to set a general wage norm for its entire constituency. The principal aim was to achieve a wage level high enough to provide wage increases and equality, but not so high as to endanger full employment. The key point of the model was that this wage rate was not to be set according to the ability of the individual firm to pay, but according to what was articulated as a 'just' wage (the ideal that was never quite achieved was 'equal pay for equal work'). In this sense, the relationship between a firm's profitability and the wage level was attenuated. This implied that inefficient firms with low productivity, which could not pay labour at the going rate, would go out of business. But the profitability of efficient and highly productive firms would be enhanced. These firms would enjoy quasi-economic rents and would be provided with an ample labour supply, released from the firms that had gone out of business. This created incentives for expansion in the dynamic sectors of the economy. Thus aggregate productivity was enhanced and higher wage levels became compatible with full employment. As such, the Rehn–Meidner model constituted a policy paradigm for the regulation of the 'disarticulated Fordist' growth model discussed in the previous chapter.

It was important that the right wage level was obtained. If the wage rate was set too high, it meant that too many firms were crowded out and full employment could not be ensured. Similarly, an overly high rate would lead to inflation, undermining the competitiveness of the Swedish economy, and thus undermining employment. However, if wages were set too low, not enough labour would be supplied to dynamic industries through lay-offs in the declining sectors. It would also mean that excess profits were reaped in some sectors with an excess demand for labour. This would make these firms inclined to increase wages beyond what had been negotiated – this is known as 'wage drift'.[5] Wage drift fuels inflation, increases inequality and undermines real wage gains in sectors of the economy without wage drift. Inequality and the undermining of real wages for some may undermine solidarity within the labour movement; moreover, inflation undermines competitiveness in the economy as a whole. In sum, both too high profits (leading to wage drift and structural rigidity) and too low profits (leading to unemployment and also structural rigidity) were bad for the economy from the perspective of the labour movement. Wage determination became the key mechanism regulating the balance that ensured dynamic accumulation and distribution.

The role of the government in this strategy would be threefold. Firstly, the Ministry of Finance, rather than the unions, would retain the main responsibility for containing inflation while ensuring full employment. Fiscal and monetary policy had to be counter-cyclical (restrictive to moderately expansionary), preventing both demand-determined unemployment and demand-pull inflation. Apart from providing price stability, keeping demand-pull inflation in check would enforce the squeeze on profits by preventing companies from passing the burden of wage increases on to the domestic consumer.

Secondly, it was realised from the outset that demand management alone could not sustain full employment, as supply bottlenecks would appear. As a remedy – thirty years before Reaganomics – LO suggested the government pursue a strategy of supply-side economics (although this variety was highly interventionist). A selective labour market policy was to ensure that labour power was channelled from stagnant sectors into dynamic sectors, by providing education, information, generous grants for families to move, and so forth. The idea was that the incidence of structural change was to be shifted from the individual affected to the society as a whole. Labour market policy, in a sense, replaced the price mechanism as the chief determinant clearing the labour market, as solidaristic wage policy severed the relationship between wage rates and marginal productivity at the level of the firm.

The third dimension of government policy in the Rehn–Meidner model emanated from a fundamental tension in the wage–profit relation, and the objectives of maintaining full employment and preventing wage drift. There is no guarantee that there is an ideal 'happy medium' profit level that ensures capital accumulation consistent with full employment, without generating wage drift. The profit squeeze required to contain wage drift may translate into a lower propensity to save, invest and employ, and lead to unemployment. This was not, for Rehn and Meidner, a reason for unions to moderate their wage claims. Rather, they suggested that public savings should be made readily available for productive investments at a low rate of interest. Hence public savings and investment would substitute for foregone private investments in the context of the profit squeeze (Pontusson 1992: 61, cf. Rehn 1952: 30–54)

The Rehn–Meidner model was not immediately accepted by the Social Democratic Government and SAP as the appropriate paradigm of economic policy. Throughout the early 1950s, the relative pros and cons of incomes policy versus profit squeeze and selective labour market policy was debated.[6] But the decisive turning point came, then, at an extraordinary joint LO–SAP congress in 1955, which was called to resolve mounting tensions over economic and wage policy, when Prime Minister Tage Erlander declared that he had been converted to the LO (Rehn–Meidner) position. This was soon followed by the appointment of Gunnar Sträng, a former trade unionist, as Minister of Finance who was to hold this post until 1976. Per Åsbrink, an active Social Democrat who had commented favourably upon the Rehn–Meidner model in *Tiden*, was appointed Governor of the Central Bank. In 1957–58, the government dealt with the recession, not primarily through pump-priming, but through expansion of selective labour market policy, as prescribed by the Rehn–Meidner mode (Pontusson 1992: 65). The labour movement had found a paradigm that allowed it to ensure that its internal terms of legitimacy corresponded to the terms of capital accumulation and the historic compromise. The Swedish model and social democratic regulation reached its zenith in the decade that followed: full employment was maintained, inflation was low, macroeconomic balance was ensured and economic growth, including productivity growth, was high. At the same time, real wages increased and were even levelled out.

The following indicators illustrate this state of affairs. The average annual rate of productivity growth in the manufacturing sector was 5.8 per cent in 1957–62 and 1969–74, and 8 per cent in 1963–68 (IUI *et al.* 1984: 367–70; Erixon 1991: 245). The latter rate was exceptional, including against comparative OECD standards, and this productivity rate coincided with a comparatively low profit-rate and high wage equalization (ibid: Erixon 1994: 31). Sweden's rate of unemployment was between 1 and 2 per cent throughout the post-war period, and this was combined with a comparatively very favourable 'Phillips curve' relation in the 1950s and 1960s. A particularly good indication that stabilisation policy was successful in regulating Sweden's disarticulated Fordist growth is the fact that the difference in variation of export and GDP growth was comparatively large in Sweden (ibid.). Sweden's record in reducing private and social wage differentials and eliminating poverty is often cited. See, for example, Åberg (1984) and Olsson (1987: 56–62).

The broader significance of the Rehn–Meidner model for the social democratic welfare state

The importance of the Rehn–Meidner model for post-war social democratic regulation in Sweden cannot be underestimated. It was the paradigm that informed the regulatory practices that rendered the universal welfare state compatible with the reproduction of the national capitalist economy; that is, the policy routines of wage determination, labour market policy, and macroeconomic policy. These can be said to constitute the core of Sweden's Fordist mode of regulation.

This study focuses on these sets of policy routines, because they serve as a strategic vantage point from which to analyse the Swedish welfare state as a whole. Their integrative centrality makes them critical for an analysis of the tensions between accumulation and legitimation imperatives. One would expect the tensions between the social citizenship norms of universalism and de-commodification on the one hand, and the requirement to ensure the overall functioning of the capitalist circuit of accumulation on the other, to be particularly acute in the practices and state apparatuses of this policy-routine ensemble. This can be construed in terms of a dialectic of regulation, with tendencies and counter-tendencies, where contradictions between the commodity form of capitalist accumulation and the de-commodification norms of social citizenship need to be mediated by these institutionalised policy routines.

Because of the integrative centrality of this ensemble, it also provides a good vantage point for tracing the terms of representation of social forces within the Swedish state. By studying the nature of representation (which includes identifying those who are not represented) in this central set of state apparatuses, one can get a sense of the hierarchy of representation in the Swedish welfare state as a whole.

When power-mobilisation theorists discuss de-commodified distribution they tend to emphasise social policy based on citizenship entitlement. However, the Rehn–Meidner model was perhaps even more critical in facilitating de-commodification. While solidaristic wage policy did not, of course, eliminate altogether commodification as an active force on the labour market, its force was nevertheless significantly mitigated. The relationship between the marginal productivity of individual firms and their wage rates was attenuated. Furthermore, unemployment ('the reserve army of labour') was eliminated as a disciplinary stick to a large extent. Moreover, full employment and solidaristic wage distribution also prevented a fiscal overload on social policy programmes such as unemployment insurance, and thus ensured that social benefits based on the de-commodification principle were rendered compatible with capital accumulation.

But the Rehn–Meidner model also made relatively de-commodified distribution compatible with the reproduction of the overall circuit of capitalist accumulation. Since solidaristic wage policy implied a relative restriction of wage increases in the more dynamic sectors of the economy, it ensured that Sweden's export sector remained competitive. Moreover, since stagnating firms were overly 'punished' (by the enforcement of higher wages than these could afford), the Rehn–Meidner model released capital and labour (through the selective labour market policy) to facilitate the expansion of these sectors.

The Rehn–Meidner model operated as a Fordist mode of regulation in the sense that it set wages according to the principle of *ex ante* integration, and it deliberately promoted relative surplus augmentation through technological innovation of the Taylorist labour process. But such innovation was not primarily ensured through an expansion of domestic aggregate demand. Rather, it was ensured through the 'transformation pressure' that the Rehn–Meidner model exerted on the Swedish economy, and by the demand-pull of the international economy.[7] This is not to imply that the expansion of private and public mass consumption was not important for Fordist accumulation in Sweden, but the balance of payments constraint was comparatively severe in Sweden's disarticulated Fordist growth model.

Paradigm versus practice

The SAP adopted the Rehn–Meidner model in 1955 and the government assumed a policy stance that can be interpreted as consistent with the model in the recession of 1957–58. One should not, however, conflate the official endorsement of a model of economic policy with actual institutionalised practice. To what extent are the prescriptions of the Rehn–Meidner model actually reflected in such practice in the post-war period?

First, one might raise the question; to what extent were trade unions able to translate their subscribed norms of solidaristic wage policy into concrete practice? The Rehn–Meidner model prescribed a form of 'objective work evaluation' to ensure equal pay for equal work. Thus far such norms have not proved possible to formulate, let alone implement. Such norms run up against two difficulties. Firstly, it is extremely difficult to parsimoniously formulate such norms because of disagreements and distributive rivalries within the union movement, both within the LO area and particularly in relation to the outlook and demands of the unions of the white-collar confederations TCO (*Tjänstemännens centralorganisation*) and SACO (*Sveriges akademikers centralorganisation*). Secondly, obviously wages are not set by unions but generated in negotiations with employers that do not subscribe to solidaristic wage policy. Thus, even if a moral economy of solidaristic wage policy can be formulated, it has to contend with the competing norms of employers in negotiations, interested in cheap but readily available labour power. SAF, for example, certainly did not subscribe to the profits squeeze principle of the Rehn–Meidner model.

In practice LO's solidaristic wage policy evolved as a result of complex internal negotiations between the respective member unions and the federation, that then set the framework for external central and industry-level negotiations with employers. In addition, particularly in the preparatory stages of negotiation rounds, SAF and LO discussed the interrelationship between wage developments, economic policy, and trends in the economy. In the absence of work evaluation, LO developed a policy of coordinated wage bargaining with norms-governed differentiation. First, a macro-economic space for 'realistic' general wage increases was set. Then negotiations ensued over norms of differentiation between different groups and sectors. At this stage negotiations also considered requests by individual unions to be exempted from the norm and to be supported in bargaining for higher wage increases. Demands for such exemptions tended to arise for a number of predictable reasons. Often they were motivated by the desire to take advantage of excess demand in a particular sector. At other times they were motivated in terms of compensation for wages that had lagged behind the general trend of wage increases. Finally, exemption requests on behalf of low-wage workers invoked working class solidarity and the ideology of equality. Sometimes these 'exemptions' were formulated as a *quid pro quo* for participation in centralised negotiation in the first place (Meidner 1973: 30–37). It should be pointed out, however, that LO held a trump card in this context. In the 1930s, in the wake of the Saltsjöbaden Accord, member unions had ceded the decision-making power over their strike funds to LO as the 'representative of the working class as a whole'. Although LO has never denied unions requests to use their strike funds, it did give LO definite capabilities to deter any defections from coordinated bargaining.

Solidaristic wage policy implied in practice an acceptance of the latter kind of appeal (on the grounds of promoting equality) and an attempt to resist the two former forms of appeal as far as possible. ('The limits of the possible' in this context should be understood in terms of the need to maintain the legitimacy of the system in the eyes of members in the sectors experiencing excess demand or a long-term lag in relative wage growth.) Hence, LO tended to devise formulae in their wage demands that led to general wage increases within the space provided by general productivity growth, combined with further wage growth for disadvantaged groups (ibid: 35–46; see also Kugelberg 1985: 44–103).[8] It has not always been possible to resist other forms of exemptions, and insofar as wage drift has been a factor, compensation for lagging wages has also been accepted. In this context, LO has had to resolve internal distributive tensions with demands that exceed productivity developments. But, it was precisely to ensure that these forms of demands did not arise and 'overload' coordinated and solidaristic wage bargaining, that unions required the Social Democratic Government to play its part in the Rehn–Meidner scheme. That is, to pursue an economic policy that sustained full employment at the same time as holding back the tendencies towards wage drift. This leads to the question, to what extent was economic policy consistent with the Rehn–Meidner model and therefore facilitated solidaristic wage policy?

According to Lennart Erixon, there was an effective shift in 1957–58 in the macroeconomic stance that suggests that the practice of economic policy was actually consistent with the nominal commitment to the Rehn–Meidner model. As of 1957, fiscal policy was no longer heavily expansionary, which it had been in the late 1940s and 1950s and the tendencies towards inflation and balance of payments deficits were reduced, despite the elimination of wartime price controls. Rather, fiscal policy tended to vary between being restrictive and weakly expansionary over the business cycle. There was also a shift away from a 'passive' monetary policy with low interest rates (as prescribed by Keynes), to counter-cyclical monetary policy (Erixon 1988).

But Erixon does not go so far as to suggest that fiscal and monetary policy is the *result* of a straightforward and coordinated application of the Rehn–Meidner model. Indeed, he makes the point that this is not the case. Although the macroeconomic policy stance in the 1966–68 and 1970–72 recessions were sufficiently restrictive to be in line with the Rehn–Meidner model, he suggests that the fiscal policy stance in the previous peaks were too expansionary to be consistent with the model (ibid; Erixon 1994: 30). To this one might add that Sweden's devaluation in 1949, when Sweden together with many other Western European countries followed Britain's lead (to be discussed below), probably went beyond an adjustment of an overvalued currency (Lindbeck 1975: 82).

The monetary policy stance was ambiguous in its support of the Rehn–Meidner model. While it had been counter-cyclical since the late 1950s, as the model prescribed, it also tended to lead to somewhat higher interest rates (ibid: 125–28), which the model did not favour. A reasonable interpretation is that interest rate policy came to compensate for an overly expansive fiscal policy, an undervalued currency, and other tendencies towards overheating. Åsbrink, the governor of the Central Bank, identified excessive wage increases, especially increases to compensate for inflation and wage drift, as his motive when he increased the nominal discount rate from 3.5 to 5.5 per cent in 1955 (Kugelberg 1985: 52–53). This increase set the precedent for subsequent monetary policy (Kock 1962: 418–76). Hence the tendency towards higher interest rates in the late 1950s might express tensions in the mode of regulation. One should put this ambiguity in perspective however; the interest rate remained at a historically low level throughout the entire period 1945–73 (especially if one considers real net interest payments after tax-deductions).[9] This is not least because of quantitative controls, which were consistent with the model (see p. 91).

Erixon (as well as Mjøset) ends his account by pointing out the discrepancy between Rehn–Meidner's prescriptions and actual macroeconomic practice. I believe one can further illuminate the situation by adding a political dimension to the analysis. One can make sense of this alleged discrepancy with reference to the understanding reached between the government and LO, as well as with reference to the broader capital–labour accord.

As was pointed out above, there is an ambiguity in the Rehn–Meidner model in the sense that there is no guarantee that there was a 'happy-medium average profit rate' that would sustain capital accumulation at the level of full employment, without generating wage drift. If the two policy objectives clashed, unions would not hold back on their negotiated wage demands (the whole point of the Rehn–Meidner model was that unions would not assume macroeconomic responsibility *qua* incomes policy), but rather demand that the problem was redressed by public savings and selective policies. The government, however, would not necessarily consider itself as having sufficient tools at its disposal (given, among other things the limits imposed on investment politics by the political outcome of the 'planning issue' in the 1940s). Moreover, since it is difficult to quantify exactly what a 'just' negotiated wage level is, the government would also tend to put pressure on labour to contain wage demands. In this context, the Ministry of Finance would mediate between unions' demands, the interest of capital in augmenting high profits, and the 'general interest' of a full employment economy. This argument will be spelt out in detail in the subsequent section of this chapter.[10]

The government's commitment to the broader principles of the Rehn–Meidner model is nevertheless reflected in the development of a number of institutions, policies, and economic–political instruments. Above all this commitment is reflected in the development of a selective labour market policy. From the recession of 1957–58 onwards, the Swedish government addressed tendencies towards increased unemployment mainly through selective labour market policy, as prescribed by the model. While the idea of selective labour market policy was not new at the time, its prominence grew progressively after 1956. In 1973 Sweden spent 2.3 per cent of its GDP (about 7 per cent of the government budget) on selective labour market policy, which is far more than other OECD countries. It is doubtful that this expansion would have taken place without the supply-side oriented macroeconomic rationale provided by the Rehn–Meidner model (Pontusson 1992: 65; Erixon 1994: 28, 30).

The post-war corporate tax system is also consistent with the counter-cyclical prescriptions and the prescriptions of investment- and productivity growth-promotion of the Rehn–Meidner model. The most prominent aspect of post-war corporate taxation, however, was the so-called investment fund (IF) system, which bolstered the capacity of the state to pursue a counter-cyclical policy. The investment fund system, implemented in 1955, let corporations exempt up to 40 per cent of their profits from taxation by setting them aside in an investment fund.[11] However, 46 per cent of these funds had to be deposited in a blocked, interest free account in the Central Bank. The funds deposited in the Central Bank could then be released by the government in recessions, and at business cycle peaks they served as a means of curtailing liquidity. In order to make the scheme sufficiently attractive, the government let corporations deduct from tax 10 per cent of any investment financed by the funds. It also let corporations draw freely from 30 per cent of funds that had been set aside for more than five years. The attractiveness of the IF-system was also enhanced by a tightening of depreciation allowances. These allowances nevertheless remained relatively favourable for business fixed investments, and thus favoured productivity growth (Pontusson 1992: 70–73).[12]

The 1959 supplementary pension reform (ATP) was designed to integrate distributive norms and economic regulation. Following the principle of de-commodification, it was based on a 'pay-as-you-go principle' rather than the actuarian 'premium reserve principle', where those presently employed actually funded the pensions of those presently retired. At the same time, the Social Democratic Government decided that the premiums should generate a savings surplus. This fund would buffer any sudden increase in pension fees. More significantly, *qua* the Rehn–Meidner model, it would counteract wage drift and provide a pool of low interest investment funds. Indeed, in order to fund future pensions, the system assumed that productivity growth would be sustained, and that the investments released would help ensure such productivity growth. (Productivity increases would sustain high wage rate increases and hence a high rate of inflow into the pension funds.) (ibid: 79–80).

Thus, the ATP system became a significant source of public savings, which the Rehn–Meidner model called for, while its emphasis on employers' contributions also was consistent with wage-drift inhibiting profits squeeze (ibid: 80; Martin 1984: 213–17). In particular, the ATP system became a source of finance for public housing construction, a social policy programme that was thus intimately integrated with fiscal and monetary policy.

The ATP system also played a broader socio-political role. The Agrarian Party (then the Centre Party) left the government on the issue and it signalled the end of the 'red–green coalition'. But from the resolution of the ATP issue onwards, the Social Democrats increased their political appeal among the white-collar workers and hence 'the extended working class' (Marklund 1988).

Credit policy, housing policy and the ATP system were articulated into an important subsystem in the mode of regulation. This subsystem also exemplifies how social-citizenship, de-commodified, forms of integration nevertheless can serve a reproductive function for capital accumulation. The ATP system raised funds through employers' contributions that also facilitated a wage-drift inhibiting profits squeeze. These financial resources, mobilized into 'AP funds' provided low-interest loan capital,[13] in particular for public housing construction. In other words, dwellings were distributed according to the social citizenship principle (subsidised housing) to working class families, that moved to the growth poles of the economy (ibid: 84; Esping-Andersen 1985b: 187–90). Credit regulation and monetary policy were synchronised with pensions and housing policy. The legal institutional framework of the AP funds ensured that their main area of operation was the bond market, which in turn was the financial market most directly and fully subject to Central Bank regulation. As a result, the AP funds were compelled to invest in government bonds at a low rate of interest, that in turn financed housing. In the period 1960–65, 42.4 per cent of AP-fund net lending went to public housing. In 1966–71, the figure increased to 50.7 per cent (Pontusson 1992: 84–87).

Instruments of quantitative credit rationing played an important role in counter-cyclical policy and welfare state expansion. The overall objective was to ensure that a countercyclical policy was made consistent with low interest rates, which would facilitate welfare policy. This objective was, of course, also consistent with the Rehn–Meidner model. The credit supply was controlled through four administrative mechanisms: the Central Bank control on bonds emissions, bank reserve ratios, and voluntary agreements by financial institutions to buy a set quota of bonds favoured by the Central Bank. The latter agreements were realised against the backdrop of the latent threat of FIAT legislation on interest rates. Foreign exchange controls ensured that Swedish interest rates could diverge from international rates at fixed exchange rates, without leading to capital flight (Mjöset *et al.* 1986: 131; Notermans 1993: 140–41).[14]

The fixed exchange rate, a low yet counter-cyclically managed discount interest rate and joint-central wage bargaining created a set of relatively stable and predictive parameters for economic regulation. For example, it enabled SAF and LO to calculate their negotiating strategies, based on cost and productivity developments. Another factor in price-anchoring, held up as central in trade union circles, was the role played by the cooperative sector, which priced their products according to the self cost principle, and thereby held back price-setting on oligopolistic markets, and made production costs the chief determinant of consumer price developments.[15]

State–civil society relations: forms of corporatist representation and social regulation

How were social forces represented by this mode of regulation? An adequate treatment of this question requires a specification of the procedural dynamics – that is 'the form' – within the state and of the institutional separation between the state and civil society. This is to be understood as a further refinement of the concept of 'historic bloc'. Here two concepts of neo-Marxist state theory are particularly useful; 'unequal representation' and 'tripartism' (Mahon 1977: 165–98; Jessop 1979: 185–212).

The representative patterns of the mode of regulation of the Swedish model can be defined as tripartite.[16] Tripartism implies a dual mode of representation. Forces of civil society are indirectly represented in two ways. Firstly, individual citizens (abstracted from social stratification as determined by the essential class division in the capitalist model of production) (Poulantzas 1978: 54–74) are represented through political parties in Parliament.

Secondly, functional interest representation is granted to the peak organisations of labour and capital. The latter have been bestowed with direct representation in the policy process, in exchange for not pursuing their individual interests in a manner that disregards the socially constructed 'general interest'. The interest groups 'assume social responsibility' (*tar samhällsansvar*). Moreover, different branches of the formal legal state represent different social groups through their function in the policy process.

This definition of the institutional forms of tripartism is intended to clarify the nature of the separation and connection between the state and civil society in the process of social regulation. Political discourse in civil society and the power resources of social subjects create general political constraints of legitimacy for state action (that is, the configuration of social hegemony). However, those constraints are channelled to the state, by which regulatory policies are executed, through the available modes of representation. This creates a 'relatively autonomous' space for policy discourse and paradigms (informed by economic theory, for example) and policy making (which occurs through specific steering media such as money and law) (Offe 1985). Autonomy implies that policy discourse is not identical in form and substance with the 'national popular' discourse of civil society. Relativity of autonomy implies that policy outcomes cannot contradict the national popular discourse in the long run, without a crisis of legitimacy and representation. The forces of civil society can 'censure' 'illegitimate' policy through the election process and the party system, as well as through the peak associations of their interest groups. Capital can also 'censure' policy through capital flight, a special privilege that is bestowed on capital as a result of one essential structural feature of the capitalist mode of production: the formal separation of politics and economics through the institution of private property. In instances of political crisis, social forces may also oppose policy through illegal means, such as wildcat strikes. Indeed, such opposition is an indication of organic crisis, when the configuration of structures and superstructures is essentially contested, not only in content but also in form. At the same time, modes of regulation, and the state more generally, are the chief vessels through which a hegemonic power bloc is organised. The state even contributes significantly towards the construction of the very identities of social subjects as well as hegemonic social paradigms (Jenson 1989: 236–40; Jessop 1990b: 4–7).

Representation in the tripartite state is unequal (Mahon 1977: 170–74). The various state agencies are organised in a hierarchy of 'contradictory unity' for the purposes of social, political and economic mediation. The agencies at the apex of the hierarchy serve an integrative function, and subsidiary agencies serve specialised functions. The relative degree of representation of social subjects depends upon the position of agencies within the hierarchy of the agencies to which they have access. Moreover, the degree and quality of representation depends upon the *form* of access. The state does not reflect the special interests of any one group transparently. Rather, demands in a liberal democratic state must be articulated by state agencies in terms of a policy discourse concerned with the 'general interest'. But some social forces may have access to these agencies in a less mediated manner than other social forces, and therefore can more directly define the terms of policy discourse and policy substance. The unequal structure of representation is therefore also a function of the form of access different social forces have to state agencies. In the capitalist state, the 'general interest' of 'managing the economy' serves primarily the capitalist class in general, because of its privileged position in the social relations of production. It exercises structural power. (It should be pointed out that capitalism in general is not a generic category, but a concrete and historically contingent entity that in part is the outcome of struggles and compromises between different fractions and sectors of the capitalist class itself.) (eg. van der Pijl 1984: 1–20.) Marginalised social subjects have no or little representation in the state, but rather are viewed purely as *objects* of regulation. Insofar as the state 'socialises' (*vergesellschaftet*) social subjects and their relations to one another, all social subjects are to some extent objectified by the state. But some are less objectified than others, and through less repressive means.

The boundaries and connections between the formal legal state apparatuses, tripartite modes of interest intermediation, and the private sphere of the capitalist economy were defined, in the Swedish case in the period under consideration, through the Saltsjöbaden Accord of 1938. This accord established the constitutive and procedural framework of the system of joint central regulation, in which LO and SAF would negotiate central wage norms for their constituent members in a bipartite manner (Fulcher 1991: 108–233). This agreement also set clear rules for the use of strikes and lockouts. The right of the unions to represent their members and to strike was acknowledged in exchange for the acknowledgement of management's prerogative to manage. The government formally accepted this arrangement, and extended it to the entire labour market through dispositive (procedural framework) legislation. Hence, the state was not to intervene in wage negotiation as long as the parties of the labour market 'assumed social responsibility'. The role of the formal legal state, in this context, was restricted to the pursuit of fiscal, monetary, and broader structural (labour market-, social-, agricultural-, and housing-) policy. 'Paragraph 23' served as a guarantee that capital would maintain discretionary power over the means of production within this framework. The absolute nature of this prerogative was challenged by the Post-war Programme of SAP, but it retreated after the outcome of the 'planning debate' in the 1940s.

The Ministry of Finance was located at the apex of this mode of regulation. Its ability to pursue an active macroeconomic policy was ensured through a stable party system, with the SAP as the 'natural party of government'. There was also a common economic policy discourse, based on the theories of the Stockholm School, that expanded beyond the party boundaries.[18] As we saw in the previous chapter, a common concern with 'rationalisation' provided a common intersubjective framework at a higher level of abstraction. Effective control over the Central Bank, and a 'special relationship' in cabinet between the Prime Minister and the Minister of Finance, were also crucial in ensuring the pivotal position of the Ministry of Finance and its capacity to serve its Keynesian functions.[19]

In capitalist states, subjects associated with the dominant fractions of capital typically have privileged and more direct access to the Ministry of Finance. In post-war Sweden, this was countered by the exceedingly strong role of LO in the definition of the paradigm of economic regulation (the Rehn–Meidner model). Hence, the union federation (LO) and the employers' federation (SAF) seem to have had indirect access on relatively equal terms, through informal deliberation at Harpsund and in the Thursday Club, as well as through formal representation in public commissions. In tripartism, capital maintained a privileged position in terms of structural power (Offe and Wiesenthal 1985: 170–220), but this was balanced by the fact that trade union officials participated in the formulation of policy through the channels of the Social Democratic Party (Åmark 1988: 57–59, 64–72, 79–80). Other important agencies of social representation were the Ministry of Social Affairs which was charged with the creation of an institutional and universal welfare state, and the Labour Market Ministry and the tripartite Labour Market Board (AMS). These agencies provided intra-state channels of representation that constrained the Department of Finance. But at the same time, they were disciplined by the Department of Finance above all through the budget bargaining process, where economic parameters were regulated by the Ministry of Finance.[20] Cabinet meetings and the budget negotiation process constituted the main channels of communication between the agencies in question.

'Representation of labour' begs the question 'which labour?'. In the golden age of the Swedish model the answer was clearly the Fordist/Taylorist worker. Implied in this was a particular interpretation of the central feature of Social Democratic ideology: 'de-proletarianisation' as the cornerstone of the project of 'integral democracy' (Tilton 1988: 369–70). Within this historic bloc, integral democracy and de-proletarianisation were interpreted to mean full employment, rising real wages, basic income and welfare entitlement security, indirect representation through the liberal democratic state, and through trade unions. More participatory understandings of these terms, such as industrial democracy, were peripheralised or were abstracted to some promise for the future. Questions concerning patriarchy and the sexual division of labour were not acknowledged as questions pertaining to unequal power relations and social inequality.

The hegemonic position of the social democratic labour movement is not inconsistent with the existence of capitalist relations of production, or a capitalist 'ruling class' in the structuralist Marxist sense. Swedish capital maintained internal coherence, exercised power *vis à vis* labour, and influenced state policy through SAF. SAF can be understood as a cartel that enabled the capitalist class to pool the power resources inherent in individual capitalist firms based on control over the means of production, market control, and the structural power of capital emanating from the valorisation process (Therborn 1989: 146–49). SAF's (as well as SI's) main strategy was not to mobilise an ideology of 'national popular leadership' after 1936. Rather, it was to provide 'technical advice' through participation in public commissions, tripartite boards, and through the creation and financing of research institutes such as SNS (*studieförbundet näringsliv samhälle*) and IUI (*industriens utredningsinstitut*) (Söderpalm 1976: 43–47, 48–59, 144–53; Lewin 1967: 375–83; Browaldh 1976: 68–95).

It was possible to contain the potential tensions within this complex of state–society relations during the post-war 'golden age'. High demand for Swedish exports contained the potentially competing objectives of large real-wage increases and union unity, and a rapid expansion of the institutional welfare state on the one hand, and the maintenance of cost competitiveness and full employment on the other. Thus, relatively harmonious working conditions were ensured between the various branches of the labour movement that were in charge of respective functions (LO, and the Social Democratic state managers and personnel located in, respectively, the Labour Market Ministry, the Ministry of Social Affairs, the Ministry of Finance).[21] Consequently, the 'social citizen' welfare state could be maintained, and operate within and reinforce 'social welfare hegemony'.

However, the stability of the post-war Swedish model presupposed a set of structural–economic, institutional–political, and ideological conditions at the level of world order. These have been inadequately acknowledged in previous accounts of the Swedish model.

Pax Americana and the Swedish model

The Swedish model presupposed and coexisted with the world order of American hegemony, or Pax Americana. The norms of Pax Americana were based on 'Atlantic corporate' or 'embedded' liberalism (Ruggie 1983: van der Pijl 1984: ch. 4), which was the ideological content of the socio-political alliances associated with the 'politics of productivity.' Indeed embedded liberalism can be seen as the necessary international, or perhaps more to the point trans-Atlantic, dimension of the politics of productivity.

The world order of embedded liberalism emanated from, and was sustained by, the USA, which created multilateral institutions where peaceful inter-state bargaining could ensue (ibid: chs 5–8; Cox 1987: 211–72). These institutions not only reflected the 'national interest' of the prevailing American power bloc (based on the 'New Deal synthesis'),[22] but also were consistent with the interests of the power blocs of other western states. This consensus was partly based upon socio-political convergence (Harvey 1990: ch. 8), and partly upon American political and ideological intervention, which purged unacceptable radical elements from the other western power blocs. The discourse of the Cold War, identifying the USSR as the Schmittian 'other', was crucial in ensuring western social cohesion. This is not to say that there were important variations between the western power blocs. They ranged from the relatively market-oriented, 'residual' welfare states of the Anglo-Saxon world, to the dirigiste models of state capitalism of France and Japan, the meso-corporatist organised-capitalist German model, and to the labour inclusive Swedish model. But Pax Americana did set definite limits to possible variations.

The Bretton Woods system (based upon the capability of the USA of providing international liquidity) ensured a fixed exchange rate regime, and norms governing capital flows. It created a 'double screen' which provided a guarantee for a simultaneous balance of both international and domestic economic activity close to full employment.[23] As a result, North–North trade could flourish and ensure a mutual validation of the intensive accumulation regimes in the capitalist core. The South, despite the discourse of 'development', was maintained in a peripheral role, supplying primary commodities to the core.

How does Sweden fit into Pax Americana? Or perhaps more to the point, why is an account of the material, normative, and institutional aspects of Pax Americana relevant in explaining the cohesion of the Swedish model? After the important contribution of the 'Nordic economic policy project' (Mjöset *et al.* 1986), it is perhaps not controversial to suggest that the 'dis-articulated Fordist' economic foundation of the Swedish model presupposed the interdependent and mutual validation of Fordist production and consumption norms through North–North trade, as suggested in chapter 3. Particularly important in boosting international aggregate demand was the role played by the USA, which apart from unilaterally expanding its money supply as international trade grew, also provided large sums for reconstruction through the Marshall Plan.

Hence Swedish Fordism was dependent upon the expansion of mass consumption, despite the relatively restrictive macroeconomic policy pursued at home. It was the demand pull of an expanding international economy and the reconstruction of Europe, first bolstered by the Marshall Plan, and then by a progressive liberalisation and expansion of trade that provided for the demand of Swedish goods.[24] Expressed in another way, international demand ensured that Sweden could pursue a relatively restrictive policy (especially expressed through high taxes) to contain profit rates, wage drift, and inflationary tendencies, while nevertheless maintaining full employment. It is therefore not a contradiction that neutral and corporatist Sweden has been an enthusiastic supporter of US-sponsored multilateral trade institutions such as GATT. But the 'embedded' dimension of American hegemony, expressed in the regulation of international finance, was also important to ensure other aspects of Swedish regulation, such as a national system of credit rationing. The functional logic of the Rehn–Meidner model, then, relied on the embedded liberal institutions and norms of Pax Americana, a point that will be elaborated below.

The evolution of this Atlantic nexus of trade should not only be understood in economic terms. It was also part of a deliberate political strategy, in part driven by the need for the USA to create an international market for capital expansion. For example, the critical devaluation of the British pound in 1949 was part of an American strategy to break down the Imperial system and to increase, in the long term, the trade orientation of European economies. The USA did so by encouraging investors to get out of European currencies, and by threatening to stop Marshall aid flows if Britain did not adhere (Gill 1993: 93, cf. De Cecco 1979: 60). Twenty-five countries, including (as discussed earlier in the chapter) Sweden, followed the British devaluation. Sweden's 30 per cent devaluation in 1949 was hardly needed to 'artificially' construct an export orientation which was already in place (see Kock 1962: 367). Nevertheless this devaluation, and the problems it created for Swedish unions, was critical for the initiative to formulate the Rehn–Meidner model (Rehn 1988: 230–32). The inflationary effects of the devaluation also seriously damaged SAP's in retrospect very radical Post-war Programme to introduce more comprehensive measures of economic planning in the Swedish economy. The effect was a decisive retreat from such measures as sectoral planning and nationalisation of financial and other key sectors (Lewin 1967: 325–32).

But the political dimension of the construction of the Atlanticist nexus should not exclusively, or even primarily, be understood in inter-state terms. And certainly, the environment in which states acted cannot be grasped by the neo-realist anarchy problematique. Crucial in the formulation of the direction of Atlanticist cooperation, was the formation of a more 'organic' alliance (*pace* Gill and Law 1988: ch. 9) between social forces on an international level, with a hegemonic ideology based on anti-communism and on American New Deal principles. It was this ideological 'social purpose', not 'anarchy' that directed international state action. Kees van der Pijl (1984: 146–67, 178–88, 194–207, 212–13) has traced the forums in which this organic alliance was formed. Particularly important forums were, of course, the OECD (formerly OEEC), but also the more informal Bilderberg Conferences. International labour organisations such as the ICFTU and the ILO, in which the Gomperist[25] AFL played a leading role, moderated the political socialist and communist ambitions of European unions. In the West German case, AFL directly intervened to contain more radical strands in post-war German trade unionism.

Sweden's relationship to these more 'civil societal' and ideological aspects of the Atlanticist nexus is somewhat more subtle. There was no direct American intervention into the formation of Swedish industrial relations. However, it has been documented that the intensification of the Cold War in 1948 (in the aftermath of the Czech insurrection) was, together with the British devaluation, critical in the defeat of the SAP Post-war Programme favouring extensive economic planning. From that time on, 'planning' was no longer effectively associated with 'full employment', but rather with 'totalitarianism' (Sainsbury 1980: 48–81, 82–115). It seems then that the Directors Club (Söderpalm 1976: 119–43) and the electoral campaigns of the late 1940s, which drew on the Cold War discourse, were crucial in setting the state/market boundaries in Sweden's post-war mode of regulation. On the other hand, the New Deal discourse, dominant also among business associations of especially productive capital at the time, validated the pragmatic and co-operative strategy assumed by SAF in relation to the 'mixed economy'. But the degree and form of economic planning that could be allowed had definite limits.

Sweden should, then, be seen as belonging to this Atlanticist system. The policy of neutrality complicates the picture somewhat. But the Grotian-inspired legalist foreign policy doctrine of Östen Unden (Möller 1990: 62–71) squares the circle. As a sovereign state in an international community of states, Sweden reserved its right to an independent security policy. As a member of a community, however, Sweden had no problems rationalising participation in what it understood to be the international organisation of this community. It should be pointed out that this formal legalistic and 'intergovernmental' conception of the international community suited embedded liberalism well. International cooperation did not only imply international co-operation and co-ordination. It also implied joint recognition of sovereignty, which in the context of the 'Keynesian revolution' did not only mean joint recognition of sovereignty in an abstract sense, but also recognition of its ability to act as a Keynesian interventionist state which included the joint recognition of capital controls (Helleiner 1994; see also Burley 1993).

On the level of institutions, the 'double screen' of the Bretton Woods system was crucial in making the Rehn–Meidner model work adequately. The capability of the Swedish state effectively to pursue a counter-cyclical fiscal policy very much presupposed a multilateral fixed exchange rate regime, that acknowledged the need of states to balance full employment and the balance of payments. As we have seen, although the Rehn–Meidner model did not prescribe large deficits, it did assign a strong role to fiscal policy. Counter-cyclical fiscal policy was a critical instrument for the objective of ensuring full employment without wage drift, which, in turn, was crucial in ensuring that the potentially competing accumulation, legitimation and representation imperatives of the Swedish model were met. Moreover, the fixed exchange rate system (which served as a price anchor) combined with the internationally sanctioned instrument of quantitative capital controls were crucial for the Swedish mode of regulation. They were the necessary policy tools for a credible policy of price stability; a crucial requisite for the Rehn–Meidner model (Notermans 1993: 156–57).

5 Neo-liberal globalisation

Introduction

Chapters 3 and 4 outlined the nature of the institutions of the Swedish model and their historical and structural conditions of existence. One of the central objectives of these chapters was to substantiate the contention that was made in chapters 1 and 2, that, contrary to the claims of Giddens, 'traditional Swedish social democracy' indeed contained a sophisticated 'supply-side' as well as 'demand-side' rationality. This economic rationality was an integral part of a broader institutional ensemble that also contained an ambitious redistributive rationality based on the principle of de-commodification and the hegemonic norm of social citizenship. Together with chapter 2, chapters 3 and 4 make a case that undermines the economically based arguments for a 'modernised' neo-liberalisation of social democracy. Chapter 2 sought to refute the 'sclerosis' argument that the Swedish welfare state and labour market regulation were inherently dysfunctional, given the dynamics of capitalist transformation and restructuring.

However, the argument is not yet sufficiently advanced to make this refutation entirely convincing. It may be, as suggested in chapter 2, that there is nothing in the logic of post-Fordist socio-technological forces *per se* that is incompatible with social democratic economic rationality. But this does not preclude the possibility that contemporary social *power relations* are inherently structured so as to make it impossible to create an institutional framework – or a mode of regulation – that could provide the support that the abstract potentials of a post-Fordist de-commodification strategy would require. It may be that such welfare capitalism potentially contains an impeccable socio-economic rationality, but that the structural configuration of the socio-political context is such that it precludes the mobilisation of power resources and collective agency that could realise such a mode of regulation. Indeed, many argue that 'globalisation' indeed precludes this (eg. Scharpf 1996). By arguing that the Swedish model presupposed the public multilateral framework, which essentially was the international expression of America's Keynesian New Deal, chapter 4 tended to support rather than contradict such arguments. The Swedish model presupposed Bretton Woods – is it really relevant then in an era characterised by neo-liberal globalisation?

There is no point in denying that tendencies and developments towards transnationalisation of production and globalisation of finance have made the configuration of such a mode of regulation a lot more difficult. Indeed, chapter 2 presented an argument to that effect. The question is, however, what conclusions do we draw from such developments? This, in turn, depends on the extent to which such developments are most plausibly interpreted as intransitive 'objective' and structural changes that manifest themselves as necessities *on* social practice or whether they are in fact more transitive and contingent outcomes *of* social practices. If the former is the case, then we had better yield to them and accordingly adapt our practices in a market-conforming direction, as Giddens, Esping-Andersen and others suggest. On the other hand, if the latter is the case, then these practices can be questioned, and potentially they can be replaced by other practices that might be part and parcel of a socio-political project that seeks to institutionalise a mode of regulation to support de-commodification.

In this chapter I will analyse the character of 'globalisation' in order to discern its necessitarian and contingent aspects. I will also introduce in a pre-liminary manner my argument about what the implications of these develop-ments are for an interpretation of the crisis of the Swedish model and the constraints and prospects for its post-Fordist re-constitution (as discussed in chapter 2). These arguments will then be further elaborated and substan-tiated in chapters 6, 7 and the conclusion.

'Globalisation': some conceptual points

At present the term 'globalisation' is often used, and the 'crisis of the welfare state' is almost as often associated with it. At the same time, the term is rarely defined, or it is used in a frustratingly vague way. On a descriptive level it is generally associated with the breakdown of communication bottle-necks and a transnationalisation of economic activities, such as trade, invest-ment and production. In more systematic studies, the issue is often reduced to a quantitative one, where trans-border transactions are measured. In this context, it is often pointed out that the degree of such transactions has merely returned to the rates of the late nineteenth century. Hence, 'globalisa-tion sceptics' ask, 'what is new under the sun?', especially when present trends fall short of an abstractly postulated ideal-type of a 'truly global economy' (eg. Hirst and Thompson 1999). Globalisation enthusiasts often respond that the issue is more qualitative and has to do with the 'time–space compression' (eg. Scholte 2000)[1] of social practices. Such time–space compression has accelerated with new communication technology, which in its latter internet phase has integrated the social self into a worldwide net-work (eg. Castells 1996). In this context it is often argued that the 'flow' of 'the market' has gained in prominence over the territorially fixed and defined institution of 'the state' (eg. Stopford and Strange 1994; Ohmae 1995).

Whilst these works have generated important insights, I do not believe they pose the question in the most pertinent way with respect to the prospects of welfare capitalism and social democracy. To be sure, international trans-actions, as well as changes in social practices that can be attributed to time–space compression, are both important to the phenomenon in question. It is not that productive, however, to probe the extent to which the phenomenon is 'new' or 'old' (there is a mixture of novel and historically recurring aspects). Rather, I propose that we situate these phenomena firmly within an ontologically broader context of capitalist socio-economic and socio-political restructuring in order to ascertain exactly how they intervene in power struggles over this restructuring. This would be in order to clarify whether or not these interventions are contingent or can be attributed to objective necessities. In this context, it makes no sense to postulate 'the market' and 'the state' axiomatically against one another since the two really presuppose one another (Jessop 1997: 50–52).[2] Hence, and indeed following Jessop, I suggest that we pose the question of globalisation with reference to the manner in which:

(a) socio-economic orders become materially reproduced (or not) through the configuration of a regime of accumulation and mode of regulation;
(b) potential and tendential social conflicts are 'managed' (or not) – that is, how they are mediated, regulated and neutralised – through socially embedded authority structures;
(c) this order is (or is not) 'normalised' and stabilised through the articula-tion of the terms of legitimacy which engenders the social order with a stable 'consensual' 'mass base';
(d) questions (a), (b) and (c) interrelate to form (or not) a Gramscian historic bloc or sets of interacting historic blocs.

Hence the first part of the chapter focuses on the 'world economy' and how the world economy shapes material reproduction. The second part deals with the practices of authority structures and social regulation, and the third part deals with the construction of socio-political movements. None of these phenomena should be conceived of as isolated from one another. Rather they are all distinct aspects or 'moments' of a transnational historic bloc in formation.

For I do indeed understand neoliberal globalisation to express a *trans-national historic bloc in formation*, which is emerging on the terrain of the crisis of the embedded liberal bloc of Pax Americana (*pace* Ruggie, 1983). It involves at its economic core some highly constraining infrastructural tech-nological developments. But equally important, it also entails developments of a more contingent nature. Socio-economically this formation entails a shift away from Fordist *ex ante* integrated mass production and consumption to an emphasis on automation, flexible specialisation, internationalisation of production, a reduction of turnover time, and risk management. Socio-politically it entails the tendential developments of new constitutionalist forms of rule and a transnationally hegemonic neo-liberal social purpose. Its project is to deepen and extend commodification of social life; that is, to universalise a form of social integration that is based on the logic of self-regulating markets. Although strong forces are pulling for this formation, its institutional stability is not yet ensured. This chapter elaborates on central properties and contradictions of this world order development, and contrasts it with the preceding embedded liberal order.

Economic globalisation and post-Fordism

While American hegemony ensured the survival of capitalism after World War II, production norms and the power balance of social forces limited the scope and extent of commodification in the 'politics of productivity' of *embedded* liberalism. As discussed in chapter 2, the 'stagflation crisis' of the 1970s signalled the end of this Fordist form of accumulation. A catalyst to stagflation was the pricing strategy of OPEC, but more fundamentally it was an expression of Taylorist production norms reaching their socio-technological frontiers. Productivity growth declined, and could no longer underwrite aggregate demand expansion (Lipietz 1987).[3] Since the world recession of 1979–80, a new form of capital accumulation has been emerging, and it constitutes the 'economic core' of neo-liberal globalisation. 'Post-Fordism' entails a refraction of production relations in a number of identifiable dimensions. With the rise of a new core technology (informatics and computer technology based on the 'microchip revolution'), which facilitates the optimisation of allocation decisions, and increases productivity by breaking down information bottlenecks, the process of internationalisation of production has accelerated (Kaplinsky 1984). Cybernetics also implies a secular trend of substitution of labour for capital in production. Moreover, this core technology has radically altered the terms of the organisation of the labour process. Cybernetics can now be used to create 'general purpose' machines, that facilitate competition through 'flexible specialisation', rather than economies of scale (Piore and Sabel 1984: 194–280). These new terms for corporate strategy make the relationship between the economies of scope and scale more ambiguous. As a result, productive capital tends to perceive less of a dependence on nationally generated mass consumption.

Transnationalisation of production

The relationship between post-Fordism and globalisation is not an inherent one, however. Indeed, it was the central thesis of the pioneering work of Piore and Sabel (1984) that flexible specialisation and its attendant emphasis on economies of scope, in fact, made more local economic systems, based on small and medium sized firms, viable. A substantial body of literature illustrates this, with reference to successful industrial districts, such as Emilia-Romagna, Baden-Würtemberg, Silicon Valley, Jutland and other places (eg. Sabel 1994). These works are interesting because they point to the potential viability of some local strategies, and are important because they indicate that many alternative post-Fordist trajectories are possible. However, hyperbolic claims (that, by the way, contradict Piore and Sabel's anti-determinism) that post-Fordism ushers in the 'end of the corporation' and that the 'Fortune 500 is over' have clearly been wide of the mark. The sales by the 100 largest corporations as a proportion of GDP increased in Europe and East Asia in 1978–90 (and dropped slightly in the USA), and these as well as other corporations are increasingly organising themselves across national borders (Ruigrok and van Tulder 1995: 155). The predominant trend of post-Fordism is associated with large transnational corporations (TNCs) pursuing transnational production strategies. In response to Fordist crises, large corporations have appropriated post-Fordist technology in strategies of industrial restructuring. In this context, they have drawn on their superior capacity that scale gives them to mobilise research and development as well as marketing and sales, to shape supply chains, to raise finance, and indeed, to acquire innovative smaller competitors. In short, they have biased post-Fordist developments in their favour because of their organisational capacity to shape industrial complexes and their transformation (ibid.). Conversely, competition in the context of profound socio-technological restructuring has to a large extent been defined in terms of the capacity to control these networks, which has increased the incentive to mobilise these capacities through, for example, mergers and acquistitions. The increased importance of transnational corporations is indicated in dramatic increases in foreign direct investments (FDI) since the early 1980s (Figure 5.1). Furthermore, in these decades, when international trade has grown faster than GDP, it should be pointed out that 70 per cent of such trade is directly or indirectly controlled by these corporations (through, for example, intra-firm trade) (Harrod 1998).

It is important, however, to pinpoint the many nuances of transnational production and to dispel some of the myths that circulate about the phenomenon. Whilst the phenomenon is intimately related to the reductions in communication costs, and increased scope for corporations to optimise their operations geographically, this does not mean that corporations have become 'footloose'. It most certainly does not mean that investment decisions can be reduced to a search for the lowest possible labour costs, ushering in a new division of labour where capital is diffused to the periphery (as Fröbel *et al.* (1980) predicted). In fact, whilst a number of export-processing zones have grown up in the wake of the process as important semi-peripheral appendices in the division of labour, the evidence shows that foreign direct investments cluster in the three core regions of the world economy (North America, Europe and East Asia). Spatially FDI flows are fixed primarily

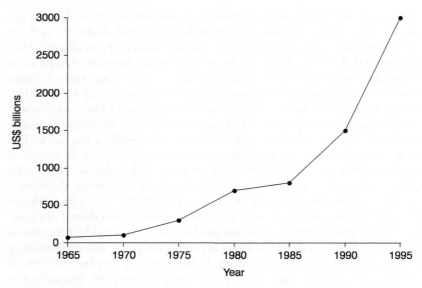

Figure 5.1 Growth of foreign direct investment (flows).

Source: Dicken (1998, cf. UNCTAD *World Investment Report* (various years). New York and Geneva: UN).

within these regions, and secondarily between them (for an overview, see Dicken 1998: ch. 2). Hence, with regard to production, it probably makes more sense to talk about 'continentalisation' and 'triadisation' as opposed to 'globalisation'.

This begs the question, what determines the 'geography of production'? To be sure, the development of areas such as the Macquiladoras indicates that factor prices is one determinant. But a more important economy is customer and market proximity, that is 'Marshallian' agglomeration economies. According to Dicken (ibid: 76), this is *'the* most important single factor in helping to explain the geography of economic activity' today. This dovetails with the importance of 'just in time' delivery in flexibilised production processes, where storage costs are minimised and where small-batch production is produced and delivered as specified by customer demand. Another important factor continues to be economies of scale, although this works differently from the way it did in the Fordist period. According to Castells (1996), the new production paradigm differs from previous ones in that product innovation is to a larger extent an aspect of the standard operation of the paradigm itself, as opposed to the shift from one paradigm to another. This is because the life-cycle of a certain commodity is shorter than before, requiring constant intervention in research and development and marketing to ensure continuous realisation of the product. Hence, R&D and marketing are pooled to particular locations with the infrastructure and appropriate factor endowments. One can argue that this economy of scale is a response the large corporation (as opposed to the small producer) can make in response to market uncertainty. Other such responses include more 'traditional' ones such as mergers and acquisitions geared towards maintaining market shares and price-setting privileges (ibid: 77–78; 190–93), as well as outsourcing and the deployment of more 'flexible' practices of work-time distribution and/ or wage setting within the corporation (eg. Ruigrok and van Tulder 1995: 179–99).

Transnationalisation of production, then, does not imply 'footlooseness' or an 'end to geography', and this has led globalisation sceptics to question whether these are truly transnational firms. Hirst and Thompson (1999), prefer the old term *multi*national firm, to underline the point that these corporations indeed continue to pursue their strategies from within a single national (or, they allow, continental) centre and 'home base'. As supporting evidence, they show that about 60 to 75 per cent of manufacturing and sales tend to be centred around the home country/region, and the asset/ ownership concentration is even higher (ibid: 80–84). Ruigrok and van Tulder (1995: ch. 7) affirm this view by showing that share ownership, and also to a large extent R&D and employment, not to mention the nationality of the members of the board of directors, are indicators that show a signifi-cant home-nation concentration. As nationally centred operators, they are also pursuing, according to Ruigrok and van Tulder, nationally distinct post-Fordist restructuring strategies. With reference to categories already introduced in chapter 2, American corporations pursue a more conservative neo-Taylorist strategy, whereas Japanese corporations internalise flexible specialisation within corporately controlled and monopsonistic supplier and sales networks ('Toyotism'). In Europe, a hybrid of tendencies is discernible. I shall return to the implication of this analysis for globalisation as a whole below.

Drawing on the theme of national variations, a number of specific points can be made with regard to Swedish corporations. The importance of the transnationalisation of production for Sweden can hardly be exaggerated. In sheer quantitative terms these corporations pursued an aggressive continentalisation strategy in the late 1980s and early 1990s, through which Sweden experienced a huge deficit in foreign direct investment flows (Figure 5.2), which amounted to about 18 per cent of gross domestic capital formation in 1987–92 (UNCTAD 1999: Table B.5). In terms of stock, Swedish outward direct investment equalled 30 per cent of GDP by 1995, well above the world trend (Figure 5.3). In *absolute terms* Sweden had the second largest net outflows of FDI 1987–91 in Western Europe (below Germany and slightly above France) (Thomsen and Woolcock 1993: 20). These were investments that Swedish TNC could engage in with the assistance of the finance houses at the epicentre of the 'capital sphere' to which they belonged (Ruigrok and van Tulder 1995: 161).[4]

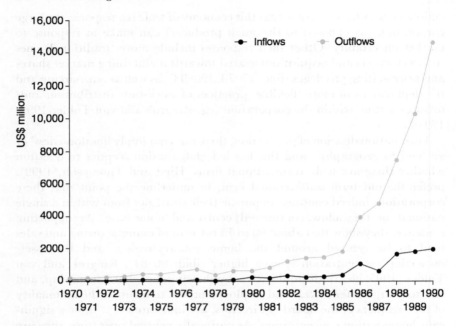

Figure 5.2 Foreign direct investment flows: Sweden 1970–90.
Source: IMF (1999) *International Financial Statistics Yearbook*. Washington DC: IMF.

Ruigrok and van Tulder conclude from this concentration of financial power that Swedish TNCs also remained nation-centred. This is highly dubious. It is probably more accurate to say that these owners assumed an increasing transnational outlook and hence do not fit Hirst and Thompson's MNC mould. This is because in *organisational* terms, Swedish corporations have become fully transnational corporations to a much larger extent. This is not insignificant for the question of social democracy, since most states with highly developed social democratic institutions in fact are small states (and hence one must be careful to generalise from the experience of G7 economies). As Ruigrok and van Tulder indeed concede, Swedish corporations show a very high proportion of employment abroad. The same goes for sales outside the home country.[5] Swedish corporations, especially those in the engineering input sector, have pursued what the aforementioned authors call 'multi-domestic strategies'. Chiefly motivated by economies of customer proximity, they expanded mainly through horizontal integration, wherein they sought to dominate production in many domestic markets. Initially, this was due to a small home market, but the strategy has become even more prevalent given the general importance of economies of customer proximity. In organisational terms, this has led to a rather loose 'confederal' corporate structure, where the divisions act rather autonomously in their

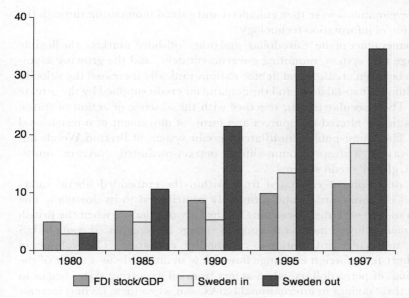

Figure 5.3 Inward and outward stock of foreign direct investment as percentage of GDP.
Source: UNCTAD *World Investment Report*, Annex Table B.6. New York and Geneva: UN.

respective local industrial systems of operation. The executive board attempts to maintain strategic control. However, in this process it must also concede bargaining power to the local divisions in order to maintain control and tap the knowledge of local conditions (Forsgren 1989). Hence, though the TNC might be questionable as a term for corporations domiciled in the G7 states, it certainly is not for those domiciled in Sweden and hence for an assessment of the Swedish model.

Globalisation of finance

A more spectacular aspect of economic globalisation than the transnationalisation of production is the transformation of international monetary institutions and global financial markets. This was in part due to the maturation and crisis of Fordism, leading to an expansion of international commerce as well as demand for credit in its crisis phase (due to the 'fiscal crises' of states). This was given a decisive catalyst by the re-channeling of savings and credit caused by the OPEC increases in oil prices ('the recycling of petro-dollars'). Another important impetus associated with the breakdown of the Bretton Woods system was the change to flexible exchange rates, which increased the importance of futures markets and hedge funds. But these developments were then enhanced and gained momentum through the revolution of information technology.

The emergence of the 'Eurodollar' and other 'offshore' markets, the flexible exchange rate system, mounting government debt, and the growing asymmetries between creditor and debtor nations radically increased the velocity and volume of capital flows and the demand for credit supplied by the private sector. These secular trends, together with the absence of action of states, have radically altered the sources and forms of movement of international credit. The 'quasi-public' multilateral credit system of Bretton Woods has given way to a deeply commodified, market-mediated, 'private, multi-centred, global' credit system.

This development emanated from within the embedded liberal international economic order, and ultimately contributed to its downfall. The process started with the 're-opening' of the City of London, when the British government allowed merchant banks to engage in deregulated trade in US dollars to finance international commodity exchange. The volume of these short-term foreign exchange flows grew significantly as a result of the 'recycling' of petro-dollars, when actors from oil exporting states began to deposit their savings in international banks, and when these savings increasingly became the source of finance for balance of payments deficits. A further impetus behind the increased importance of these 'offshore' merchant bank exchanges was the shift from the Bretton Woods fixed exchange regime to a floating exchange rate regime. This increased speculative pressure on the value of currencies. Crucial in this context was the *modus operandi* of the foreign exchange futures markets. Hence, short-term flows increased and became even more volatile, which, ironically increased the demand for the financial services of hedge fund managers even more (Strange 1989; 1998; see also Thrift 1987).[6] In recent years the privatisation of pensions savings, and the deregulaiton of equity markets have added further impetus to these global short-term financial flows. Mutual fund pension managers are notorious for following the hedge funds in their investment decisions (Harmes 1998). This is an important point with reference to the argument advanced against Giddens in chapter 1. He favours the development of private insurance. However, the speculative movements on the global financial markets that it implies have devastating effects on the kind of post-Fordist development that 'no authority without democracy' requires.

The provision of international liquidity, then, is no longer the public multilateral affair that it was during the Bretton Woods, but rather a process that takes place through deregulated and short-term inter-bank markets (Aglietta 1985). Consequently, high finance has become so powerful in the allocation of economic resources that it has been described as the pivotal agent in the formation of the emerging global hegemony (Cox 1987: 267). Economically, this reflects a subsumption of productive forms of capital to circulation forms of capital. Rentier profit has increased in importance relative to profit from production, and increasingly, accumulation is sustained through a decrease in turnover time,[7] and the reduction of labour costs, rather than through productivity increases and mass consumption (van der Pijl 1984: 265–86; 1998; Harvey 1990: chs 10 and 11).

This, incidentally, also has implications for the manner in which we conceptualise the much more limited process of transnationalisation of production. This is because these corporations, in their exchanges as well as in their savings and lending decisions, operate through these markets, and are hence constrained, enabled and shaped through them. According to Castells (1996: 474):

> Thus, above the diversity of human-flesh capitalists and capitalist groups, there is a faceless collective capitalist, made up of financial flows operated by electronic networks . . . This network of networks of capital both unifies and commands specific centers of capitalist accumulation, structuring the behaviour of capitalists around their submission to the global network. They play their competing, or converging, strategies by and through the circuits of this global network, and so they are ultimately dependent upon the nonhuman capitalist logic of an electronically operated, random processing of information.

As discussed already in chapter 2, the discipline of these global short-term money and capital markets have biased the pattern of post-Fordist restructuring. The volatility they engender on aggregate demand enforces the imperatives of numerical flexibility and reduces time horizons. At the same time, paradoxically, they further bias post-Fordist restructuring in favour of corporations that can mobilise economies of scale so as to manage the volatility. As Dicken points out, it is the corporate form, in the context of market instability, that can absorb the costs of research and development that can mobilise marketing networks and that can access finance.

This changing form of capital accumulation has certainly changed the cost–benefit structure of capitalists in relation to the welfare state. But not only have the interests of capital changed in favour of deeper commodification, individuation, and market clearing; and against public welfare provision and collective bargaining. The *structural power of capital* to realise its preferred forms of accumulation and regulation has increased as a result of an emerging *territorial non-correspondence* (*pace* Murray 1971) between markets and states (Gill and Law 1989). Through transnational mobility, capital can counter attempts at regulation by states – which in this context are in competition for scarce investment resources – and make the essence of the *raison d'État* to court this structural power. 'Business confidence', now more than ever, determines the direction of capital flows, the availability of finance, and future investments, upon which future production, employment, and tax revenue depends.

These developments are of great significance for the Swedish model. As we saw in the previous chapter, the Rehn–Meidner model required a policy of counter-cyclical fine tuning with low rates of interest, as well as an evenly expanding world economy. Jonathon Moses (1994: 132–35, 138–40) has clarified how the shift from the Bretton Woods system to the globalisation of finance has served to undermine these relationships. He argues that the capacity to exercise foreign exchange and capital controls was crucial to the Rehn–Meidner model. Otherwise, in small open economies, monetary policy tools need to be geared towards defending the balance of payments (an especially acute imperative for small economies with limited scope and reserves for maintaining prolonged deficits or surpluses). Once evasive currency swaps of transnational economic actors (such as transnational corporations, banks, and other financial institutions) rendered capital controls ineffective, the state ran out of a number of policy tools required to defend the Rehn–Meidner model, at least in a context where public debt accumulated as a result of an attempt to manage Fordist crisis (to be discussed in the next chapter). Globalisation of finance implied that it became impossible to politically control both the exchange and interest rate, since creditors always would have the option of 'exiting' from debt denominated in Swedish crowns. This made it exceedingly difficult for the state to continue to navigate between the Scylla of unemployment and the Charbydis of wage drift, inflation and insufficient transformation pressure. As we shall see, in the first part of the 1990s, Swedish policy-makers navigated into the arms of both monsters.

'New constitutionalism' and the 'G7 nexus': the practices and socio-political basis of neo-liberal transnational hegemony

Some would argue that the term 'globalisation' expresses nothing more than the bourgeois ideological obfuscation of the aforementioned change in the spatial fix of capital accumulation, territorial non-correspondence, and its attendant effects on social power relations (Harvey 1997). There is much to be said for this, as an antidote against cliché-ridden phrases on the 'need to adjust to the global market-place'. But one must not forget that ideology is part of the reality that needs to be explained. Particular forms of capital accumulation depend on particular forms of regulation. These are only adequately analysed with reference not only to economic, but to also political and ideological factors.

There is nothing inherently neo-liberal in the technology of the new forces of production as such. It is true that technology does have certain imperatives, but also that these necessities have their contingencies as the discussion on post-Fordist possbilities in chapter 2 showed. Indeed, general-purpose machines may be more efficiently appropriated in more collectivist production paradigms emphasising functional flexibility through co-determination, and the public goods of training and R&D.

Moreover, global finance has not re-emerged as a consequence or dimension of post-Fordism. IPE literature has long since persuasively argued that the breakdown of Bretton Woods depended decisively on more strictly political factors (eg. Block 1977: 139–225; Strange 1989; Helleiner 1994). The early initiatives of financial deregulation did not so much reflect a neo-liberal hegemonic strategy as short-sightedness – actions informed by state interest without the 'ethico-political' resolve to sustain the embedded liberal monetary regime (expressing hegemonic crisis).[8] But since the 'Volcker shock' in 1979, monetarist policy coordination and capital deregulation has increasingly been driven by a hegemonic neoliberal strategy (ibid: 123–68). The emerging neoliberal form of rule and transnational macroeconomic regulation is based on what Stephen Gill (1991a, 1992, 1993) has called a 'new constitutionalism'.

New constitutionalism contrasts sharply with the 'double screen' of the Bretton Woods system. The latter was sustained by the dollar-based fixed exchange rate regime, and public multilateral norms governing capital controls and flows. The purpose of the double screen was to facilitate a simultaneous balance of both international and domestic economic activity close to full employment.[9] Expansionist policies in the USA, and American foreign direct investment became especially important to ensure sustained aggregate demand, and to facilitate expansionary policies in West European economies and their Fordist growth models.[10] The double screen, however, broke down in the 1970s as the 'Triffin's dilemma'[11] became increasingly acute, and as the USA vetoed a public multilateral reform of the monetary regime, based on Special Drawing Rights.

Whereas the double screen ensured the capacity of states to manage aggregate demand and to mitigate market-generated social disruption, new constitutionalism deliberately reshapes state–market boundaries so as to maximise the exposure of states to international capital markets. New constitutionalism implies a deliberate abdication from discretionary state action that violates market norms (the metaphor of Ulysses tying himself to the mast is often invoked). Thereby the classical liberal separation between state and economic forms is *politically* enforced. The purpose is to create a buffer against demands for protection against market effects, and to discipline social actors to conform to market constraints and criteria.[12] Globalisation, then, is not only a matter of the structural power of capital constraining states. State actors deliberately mobilise the structural power of global capital in a neo-liberal strategy (Panitch 1994). This is the political *raison d'être* behind the increased emphasis on Central Bank autonomy, and capital and currency deregulation. An important effect of this is that a neo-liberal variant of post-Fordism is promoted, as, for example, unemployment generated by austerity policies reduces the bargaining power of organised labour on the shopfloor.

This political dimension to financial globalisation applies to Sweden as well and as a result the highly structuralist account of Moses, cited above, needs to be modified. Of course, this is in part because financial globalisation is itself to a large extent a political artifact and has decisive transitive dimensions. However, it is also because, as Notermans (1994) points out, Moses' account does not provide a sufficient explanation for the disciplinary neo-liberal policy shift in Sweden (and Norway). Moses argues that the full employment commitment became impossible to attain because of the loss of control of the interest rate. But this argument only holds in the context of a fixed exchange-rate policy. Moses, however, fails to explain why a fixed exchange, rate policy was pursued. Notermans (1993) argues that the configuration of a fixed exchange, rate with capital mobility was a deliberate move to make the interest rate operate as a disciplinary device according to the principle that we have here called 'new constitutionalism'. This radical reconfiguration of policy, according to Notermans, had the explicit intention of curbing inflation. Notermans' argument is given further credibility by the fact that deregulation of capital markets went hand in hand with a 'sterilization policy' whereby financial flows were deliberately 'purified' from any other motives than market motives. In principle, Swedish policy-makers could have mitigated the power that global financial markets had on Swedish interest rates through a proactive state policy of foreign borrowing. However, as Sweden deregulated capital markets in 1985, the Central Bank and the Ministry of Finance also asserted a 'borrowing norm' whereby they vowed that the state would not cover payments deficits through state borrowing.[13] The record shows that indeed this was the deliberate intention (Sweden. Ministry of Finance 1985c; Hörngren 1993).

It is a misunderstanding, then, to argue that globalisation equals the end of the nation state. National agencies and instruments of economic policy, and by extension the inter-state system, have remained central to new constitutionalism. The territorial non-correspondence between the operation of markets and states has been important to ensure the 'exit option' of capital (there has to be something from which to exit). Consequently, positive international economic policy, for example coordination monetary and exchange rate policy, takes place through loose, *ad hoc* 'inter-governmental' arrangements, within general constitutive framework-arrangements like free trade treaties. As in the embedded liberal system, this allows for a privileged role for the predominant state, what neo-realists call 'the hegemon', to shape intergovernmentalism and to reap certain exclusive benefits. Despite a relative decline, the USA has retained this position (Strange 1987). But apart from the change from an embedded to a neo-liberal social purpose, the USA has also pursued a more 'minimalist' hegemony since the Reagan presidency (Cafruny 1989). This implies that the USA has used its unique structural power, emanating for example from its 'seignorage' position of providing the world currency, to pursue a narrow self-interested policy to sustain domestic economic growth at the expense of the world economy as a whole (eg. Davis 1984; Lipietz 1989).[14] Most significantly perhaps was the American macroeconomic policy stance in the 1980s. The combination of an expansionary fiscal policy (due to military expenditure and tax cuts) and tight monetary policy drained liquidity and finance from international markets. This is, of course, in sharp contrast to the role played by the USA as a supplier of liquidity and finance in the Bretton Woods system.

This loose articulation of formal policy mechanisms is accompanied by a tighter articulation of a common substantive hegemonic strategy of a transnational power bloc, that can aptly be labelled the 'G7 nexus' (Gill 1993, 1994). Its cohesion is articulated through private informal fora (such as the Trilateral Commission, the Bilderberg Group and the Pinay Circle), as well as public formal fora (such as the OECD, IMF and the Bank of International Settlements) (Gill 1990, 1994; van der Pijl 1984, 1998).[15] It also permeates key branches of state structures, such as ministries of finance and central banks, in part through their connection to these transnational fora. Apart from its neo-liberal ideology, this power bloc differs from the embedded liberal bloc in its exclusion of organised labour, and in its lack of tolerance of autonomy of the technocratic managerial strata (who were instrumental in forging the policy of class compromise in the Fordist period) from business interests, and the subordination of productive capital to financial capital. Indeed, van der Pijl characterises the strategy in terms of an 'owner's revolt' (ibid.).

In order to trace this socio-political dimension of neo-liberal globalization, one needs to go back to consider the reaction of elites against the international radicalisation wave of the early 1970s, that was interpreted by Huntington *et al.* (1975) in a Trialteral Commission report as 'a crisis of governability' and 'excess democracy' (Gill 1990: 238). This highlights how conditional the 'embedded' dimension of Pax Americana actually was. The welfarist material concessions after World War II need to be considered in the context of the Cold War, and the need to integrate the highly organised European working class, with socialist propensities. Union cadres served an important function in producing mass consent to American hegemony (van der Pijl 1984). But the material concessions had to be consistent with capital accumulation and American geo-political strategy. Social democrats, organised labour, and even left-wing liberals broke with these terms when they attempted to co-opt, but also accommodate, peace activists, Third World advocates, feminists, and rank-and-file militants reacting against the discrepancy of the myth and reality of 'the affluent society'. But these political expressions of a legitimation crisis did not form into a coherent counterhegemonic force. Moreover, the attendant extension of welfare reform and the new international economic order that were nevertheless attempted conflicted with business interests. It was in the context of this failed radicalisation wave, the economic problems of stagflation, and what was considered the potentially subversive effects of inflationary Keynesianism, that business and economic policy elites successfully took an increasingly antagonistic stance towards unions, economic regulation, and the welfare state. The US victory in what Halliday (1986) has called the 'Second Cold War' enhanced this tendency.

Again, the next chapter will relate these developments to a more detailed discussion of the Swedish context. Therein, it will be argued that changes in Swedish socio-economic governance conforms to this political pendulum movement from radicalisation to neo-liberalism. Swedish social democracy initially underwent radicalisation as a result of the tensions and contradictions emanating from the Fordist crisis and the crisis of Pax Americana. Given labour movement hegemony, the radicalisation wave was particularly strong in Sweden and permeated state structures through the Social Democratic Party. Sweden's radicalisation wave culminated in the so-called wage-earner funds, that would have represented a much more dramatic intervention in the capitalist economy, in order to ensure that it maintained and expanded its redistributive function. The Swedish business community then began rather successfully to mobilise a neo-liberal counter-strategy. By the mid-1980s, neo-liberal norms had also permeated social democratic state-management circles, especially in the Ministry of Finance and the Central Bank. In 1985, they changed the configuration of economic policy in a new constitutionalist and neo-liberal direction. This strategy went very much beyond what the structural imperatives of global financial markets required, as the intent and actual practice was to mobilise the power of these markets to restructure Swedish society in a more market-oriented direction. This change, I will argue, was at heart of the crisis in Sweden in the early 1990s, which was not only an economic crisis, but also a broader political and politico-cultural 'organic crisis' in the Gramscian sense. At the same time, in the Swedish case at least, I will argue that the causal power attributed to elite fora for the neo-liberal convergence is overstated and is an insufficient explanation. Rather, *pace* Nicos Poulantzas, I will emphasise the manner in which the institutional forms of policy making in the capitalist state biased development in this direction.

Tensions and contradictions

The prospects of success of the emerging transnational power bloc should not be underestimated. Many, notably neo-realists, have pointed to the absence of a single dominating state to provide the international public goods for global cooperation. However, in the new era, with a structurally different relationship between markets and states, a transnational power bloc may not need such a realist 'hegemon'. According to Helleiner (1990), hyper-liberal financial and monetary regimes (as opposed to Keynesian ones), based on private multi-centric finance, can function without a dominant state.[16] Since accumulation is ensured through decreased turnover time, cost-cutting, and labour shedding, rather than through an articulation of mass consumption and mass production, the deflationary effects of neo-liberalism may not be as detrimental to capital accumulation as they would have been in the Fordist era (Harvey 1990). In a nutshell, neo-liberalism may be viable because the ability of transnational capital to regulate itself has increased. At the same time, the capacity of the nation state to pursue market-inhibiting regulation has decreased, and the social forces which stand to benefit from such regulation find it increasingly difficult to organise the relational power necessary to make politically effective demands.

In the late 1990s, there was much that spoke for such a stabilisation of the world economic order. In 1997–98, the Asian financial crisis was contained, and the USA experienced quite a remarkable economic recovery which seemed to indicate the creation of a 'new economy', which we have discussed in terms of a neo-liberal variant of post-Fordism. The orientation of Third Way social democratic governments in Europe in the late 1990s was4 also an indication of such stabilisation. Where conservative and christian democratic governments had run into legitimation problems in their neo-liberal reform programmes, Third Way governments had, at least in the short run, consolidated the neo-liberal turn by continuing the route of welfare state retrenchment and re-commodification of labour markets. On the other hand, a global neo-liberal order is not predestined to sustain itself. After the 'Reagan boom', an increasingly self-regulating capitalism has periodically been associated by deep recessions and extremely sluggish recoveries that have put the fledgling institutions of disciplinary neo-liberalism under strain. In this context, the problem of debt remains a latent problem that tends to threaten the validation of the circuit of credit and/or generate social and political instabilities that at times generate geo-political tensions.[17] In this it is also important to re-state that deregulation of labour markets may not provide for the most efficient adaptation of 'post-Fordist' flexible specialisation. Thus, it may be that the capitalist accumulation process has not freed itself from the imperative of returns to scale (Boyer 1987: 10–16; 1991; 1997; Boyer and Petit 1991). On the socio-political level, the increased inequalities, implied in the dismantling of the welfare state, mass unemployment, the polarisation of the labour market, as well as the failure of the neo-liberal regime to manage environmental crises, generate antagonisms and social forces which may yet challenge the order. It is in this context that we need to consider the recurring 'anti-capitalist' manifestations that after the World Trade Organisation summit in Seattle caught the public eye but that really started to gain momentum in the French protests against the Maastricht convergence criteria at the end of 1995. The Gordian knot for such social forces, however, is to mobilise and link sufficient power on the local, national, and global level to challenge the structural power of capital.

Furthermore, while they have, on the whole, been neutralised and managed, antagonisms at the core of the G7 nexus pop up at times as a result of these tensions and different ideas on how to deal with them. Although the pivotal globalising elite-stratum is in agreement on the need to exert monetarist discipline, and reduce social public consumption, there are often significant differences in outlook on how to regulate the world economy. The principal division has tended to run between financial consortia and states of the Anglo-Saxon heartland, and those of continental Europe ('Rhineland capitalism') and Japan (van der Pijl 1998). In the latter regions there are strong state capitalist traditions, productive capital is still relatively prominent and social democracy and/or traditional conservatism are relatively strong as political movements. Here one tends to find support for 'compensatory liberalism' (Gill 1994). The ideology of compensatory liberalism differs from Thatcherite/Reaganite hyper-liberalism in that in certain instances it pragmatically promotes the displacement of market mechanisms in favour of public norms, for the purpose of ensuring consistency and disciplining certain collective actors so they will act according to market rationality (eg. fixed exchange-rate norms rather than floating exchange rates, and public targets for borrowing and inflation rates). Compensatory liberalism may come into conflict with hyper-liberalism on a transnational level, where the former ideology may promote 'strong' transnational regimes of constitutionalist regulation, while the latter would rather abstain from such regulation and 'leave things to the market'. The conflict between the United Kingdom and the 'Euro 12' countries on issues such as the EMU and tax harmonisation are instances of this.

One moment at which these antagonisms seemed to have a fundamental effect on the order was at the end of 1998. That is when the Minister of Finance of the newly elected government of Germany, Oskar Lafontaine, together with his French colleague, Oliver Strauss-Khan, began to propose a whole host of Keynesian and regulatory initiatives in Europe as well as in the trans-Atlantic arena. Conversions within the dominant fractions of the German Social Democratic Party to a Blairite Third Way ensured that this movement was swiftly neutralised, however. Nevertheless, concerns about foreign takeovers of German corporations (eg. the Vodafone–Mannesmann affair) and the questioning of the subsidising practices of regional German banks (which is part of German meso-level industrial policy), as well as concerns over the unilateralism of the new US administration (with regard to the Kyoto Protocol and a nuclear defence shield), are examples of instances that continue to generate tensions.

The hyper-liberal/compensatory liberal divide is also significant in relation to the forging of popular consent. While it predominates in policy discourse, neo-liberalism has not been diffused adequately to the popular strata in the Rhineland capitalist areas. Social democratic and christian democratic parties may have adopted neo-liberal policies, but in the popular arena these policies tend to make them vulnerable where their consent from the mass base still depends on a welfarist ethos. This is in sharp contrast, of course, with the populism of Thatcher and Reagan, who also managed to restructure the 'common sense' of civil society (Hall 1988). This lack of a fusion between policy and a positive popular project makes 'compensatory liberalism' politically unstable and vulnerable. At the same time it explains the attraction of the notion of a 'third way' which, it is hoped, would provide a way to fuse market liberalism with the norms of the 'social market'.

The conflict between compensatory- and hyper-liberals is related to the basic paradox of capitalist socialisation, that the private realm must be politically constituted: '*Laissez faire* is planned' (Polanyi 1944). While capitalism is essentially based on self-regulation, such regulation can only take place within the framework of law (especially contract law) and order, when certain common standards are set, and when certain 'public goods' are provided. This need for social regulation is experienced more acutely by productive capital-fractions than circulation-fractions, since they are confronted with more concrete problems in the process of realising profit (for example, the need for stable labour conditions, technical standardisation and innovation, and the assurance of a stable capital-value for machinery.) This paradox of *laissez faire* actually points to its limits, and opens space for resistance, compromise, and the undermining of the logic of commodification, and counter-hegemonic projects. Capital is dependent upon the public realm, which in turn depends on legitimation and mass loyalty, subject to popular mobilisation. The territorial non-correspondence of globalisation blunts the force of these counter-tendencies. But they are re-emerging on macroregional terrains. Regional economic integration requires standards for goods, patents, dispute-settlement mechanisms, and currency stability. This requirement for capital has a tendency to contradict territorial non-correspondence, and provides a site on which questions beyond, and even against, the interests of capital can be brought onto the agenda. Hence the formation of macroeconomic blocs become important in the search for alternatives to neo-liberalism.

Consider, for example, the process behind 'Europe 1992'. It reflected the global developments outlined above (eg. Holman 1992). The creation of the single market, as laid out in Lord Cockfield's White Paper is quite consistent with the neo-liberal strategy on a global scale. The principles of 'subsidiarity' and 'mutual recognition' ensure simultaneously sufficient common norms, while ensuring the territorial non-correspondence of new constitutionalism (see Grahl and Teague 1989). However, behind the consensus over the single market one can discern the attempt to assert a competing accumulation strategy. The Social Democratic federalist ex-President of the Commission, Jacques Delors, envisioned a transnational 'neo-Fordist' Europe, where regimes of social and environmental standards, transnational macroeconomic policy regimes, and a Community-wide industrial policy would not only sustain welfare capitalism, but also diffuse it to the periphery. Delors advanced this agenda by pursuing a 'Russian doll' strategy, where at every stage of integration, he managed to secure vague commitments from member states for further regulation, which he then vigorously pursued at timely moments (Ross 1992).

However, this vision has been hampered not only by the political weakness of the European labour movement and a social democracy which is increasingly adopting a neo-liberal policy stance. It has also been rendered improbable by the daunting task of creating the required new transnational institutions. Unanimity is required to make the Social Charter binding. At present it is merely a diluted statement of principles, a dilution that reflects the compromises necessary to make it exist at all. Moreover, by using the 'exit' option, and tactical alliances with various other members, Britain has managed to stall any real progress on 'social Europe' (Rhodes 1991). The compromises of the Maastricht Accord has had the effect of creating a European Union consistent with compensatory liberalism, with Thatcherite hyper-liberal and social democratic forces cancelling each other out. There is no legal clout in the social commitments of Maastricht. The politics of the Third Way really represents a consolidation of this tendency.

There is, however, a commitment to a transnational macroeconomic policy implied in the Monetary Union. But the institutional design of the EMU is an expression of new constitutionalism. It is important to emphasise, though, that Maastricht may not signify a stable crystallisation of EU institutions. The 'Maastricht convergence programmes', demanding budgetary cutbacks that further enforce austerity tendencies and unemployment rates, proved unpopular in many countries, including Germany which was pivotal to the whole project. Germany had serious difficulties in meeting the criteria, and it was against the background of the discontent of the attendant cutbacks that the aforementioned 'moment of Lafontaine' emerged. Thus far the SPD (Social Democratic Party of Germany) has been lucky that it has not suffered an electoral fallout as a result of the abandonment of the Lafontaine position.[18] This can be explained by the corruption scandal that has hit the CDU (Christian Democratic Union) as well as the temporary depreciation of the Euro and the strength of the American economy that has generated growth in the European economy. Nevertheless latent pressures remain, not the least of which is mass unemployment in the former GDR. In other words, at least in Europe, a stable order has not yet crystallised, and again as the 'Lafontainian moment' suggests, in the longer term the actual content of monetary and economic union might be open for contest. As a result, rather than being an instrument to enforce new constitutionalism, the EMU might become an instrument that undermines it.

Ultimately, however, any alternative to neo-liberalism emanating from official political society will be limited unless it is based on coherent popular mobilisation. In the end, while the immediate causes of Lafontaine's resignation are shrouded in some mystery, it is clear that the initiatives were fragile because of his weakness and that of his allies in German civil society. His rival and champion of a Third Way, Schröder however, exemplifies what Jenson and Ross (1986) discuss in terms of 'socialism without the workers' (and with some modifications one could apply the same analysis to Joschka

Fischer and the German Green Party). By this they mean that leaders of left-wing parties are increasingly becoming autonomous from the organisational base of 'their' movement because, through their mass media appeal, they are seen as the ones that can mobilise electoral majorities by broadening the appeal of the party. These leaders can also assume a free hand in 'pragmatic' reformulation of policies, according to what is considered expedient in the realm of electoral politics and what is considered 'realistic' in policy circles. This is an expression of social movement weakness.

It is important to note, then, that the salience of neo-liberalism in part is the outcome of the failure of the radicalisation wave of the 1960s and the 1970s to forge a coherent counter-hegemonic bloc. Although some of the issues raised by these groups, such as sustainable development, gender equality, and racial equality, have remained in the limelight, the praxis of these groups tends to be restricted to fragmented pressure politics, or they are effectively marginalised.[19]

The prevailing sense of leading sociologists is that such fragmentation of social agency is an outcome of changes of social structures and this fragmentation defines the limits of the possible. In my view, the least convincing of these accounts are those that consider this an inherent part of the process of globalisation. The argument in this context is that the breakdown of information-bottlenecks has changed the spatial fix of communicative interaction to such an extent that cohesive nationally based forms of social mobilisation have been undermined (eg. Giddens 1991; Castells 1997; see also Scholte 2000). According to Giddens, global influences undermine the traditional normative substructure upon which these institutions of mass mobilisation were based, forcing people to reflexively negotiate global and local influences in their lifestyle choices. We encountered this argument in chapter 1, where Giddens connected this analysis to his optimistic assessment of the emancipatory potential of this development through the Third Way. Castells is more pessimistic, arguing that the disjuncture of these time–space frames in the emerging 'network society' makes it impossible for people to engage in 'reflexive life-planning', apart from the globalising elites with access to strategic nodes of coordination in the global political economy. Castells argues rather more pessimistically that this state of affairs is likely to engender a hyper-local, defensive, narcissistic and often reactionary type of identity politics and he situates the rise of ethnic nationalism and religious fundamentalism in this context.

It is true, of course, that significant segments of the world's population, at least in advanced capitalist societies, now communicate, or are subject to global communication, to a much larger extent than before (through the internet and satellite television, for example). This makes everyday life very different from the late nineteenth century (which as we recall some argue was more globalised than the present, when mass populations still lived and acted mainly in local quasi-autarkic, traditional, rural communities).[20] On the other hand, there is very little evidence that it is this that affects the manner in which people organise themselves so as to act collectively and make collectively binding decisions (through interest groups, unions and parties). Indeed, it seems that the aforementioned literature is too keen to leap from correspondence through the internet to social mobilisation with very little evidence. Parties and other organisations of collective action remain on the whole locally and nationally organised.

A more convincing part of the literature focuses on socio-cultural trans-formations from modern to 'post-modern' or 'late modern' society, but does not reduce this to an outcome of 'globalisation'.[21] Lash and Urry's *The End of Organized Capitalism* (1987: esp. ch. 9) remains as an exemplary work in this context. They argue that the power mobilisation of labour, which lay behind the Fordist compromise, was mediated culturally and presupposed a particular form of identity construction generated in working-class commu-nities that now have been undermined. The result of this is a much more decentred, short-termist and heterogeneous social structure, which indeed has been engendered by a socio-cultural dialectic associated with Fordist developments themselves. First, Fordism changed the mode of consumption of the working class, which in turn undermined its cohesive solidaristic 'communities in struggle'. Important in this context was the retreat of the mass consuming worker to a nuclear family sphere where, for example, sub-urbanisation and television entertainment played a crucial role. With the attendant increased influence of advertisements through the mass media, the 'semiotics of everyday life' became much more based on subliminal communication based on the manipulation of instincts as opposed to rational discourse. This went hand in hand with a bureaucratisation of representative structures such as trade unions that tended to alienate the relationship between leadership and management. The change of the semiotics of every-day life went hand in hand with an ascending 'service class', employed in mass consumption markets, the welfare state, and in administrative super-structures. This development, together with the numerical decline of the blue-collar working class, engendered by the increased capital intensity of production, fragmented the wage-earning strata of the social structure. It is against this background, Lash and Urry argue, that one must understand the difficulty in generating a cohesive counter-hegemonic bloc that might challenge neo-liberalism. Offe (1996) has recently argued that the agenda becomes even more daunting, when one considers that unity not only has to be achieved, but that this unity must generate a functionally viable set of alternative policies.

The importance of these arguments must not be underestimated. On the other hand, one wonders if they are not overly determinist projections of what in fact are institutionally contingent outcomes in Anglo-Saxon as well as christian democratic forms of welfare capitalism. To what extent do insti-tutions, where social democracy has been hegemonic, have the potential to counteract these fragmentary tendencies? Lash and Urry, to their credit, support their argument through a careful empirical and comparative study which includes the USA, the UK, Germany, France and Sweden. Also they concede that the development is uneven and that the fragmentary tendencies are the least developed in Sweden, but they argue that the tendencies are apparent there too and they point to the fragmentation of collective bargaining and the reduction of unionisation rates in Sweden in the late 1980s (ibid: 236–52). But this is probably the least convincing part of the whole book. Unionisation rates subsequently rose in Sweden in the 1990s and it is far from certain, as I will show in the next chapter, that the fragmentation in question expressed a structural shift as much as an institutional unravelling that was the result of strategic choices and miscalculations by political elites. In other words, returning to the theme raised at the end of chapter 1, the institutional mediations and strategy may still be important determinants that may hold out some hope for counter-hegemonic mobilisation that is more potent than the rather lame Third Way.

Summary and conclusion

This chapter has used the Gramscian concept of 'historic bloc' to organise its discussion about the nature and meaning of 'globalisation'. It has pointed to the central importance of disciplinary neo-liberalism as a practice of social regulation, which has the intended effect of deepening the commodification of social life. This practice has become the prevailing response in an emerging global political economy engendered by economic and political aspects of the crisis of Fordism. Central in this regard is the mobilisation of the structural power of capital that emanates from the territorial non-correspondence of transnational capital accumulation and the formal national and inter-governmental organisation of economic and social policy. The effect of this practice is that it favours a neo-liberal variant of post-Fordism.

The chapter has pointed to the contingent, transitive and political dimensions of the formation of this historic bloc. It has done so, however, without ignoring important structural shifts. Transnationalisation of production and globalisation of finance do have important objective dimensions, connected to the breakdown of communication bottlenecks. The most determinate of these dimensions is transnationalisation of production, although the footloosedness of TNCs has been highly exaggerated (but for small states, like Sweden, they appear more footloose). Global financial markets are more global and footloose in their operation, but on the other hand this globalisation is in the last instance more a product of contingent factors than an essential element of post-Fordism.

Socio-politically, the chapter has emphasised the diffusion of neo-liberal norms in global governance. On the other hand, scepticism has been expressed with regard to the argument that sociological globalisation is the force that is undermining nationally based organisations of mass mobilisation. A distinction needs to be made between globalisation and post-modernisation in this respect. But even considering this, one should not rule out the prospect of specific institutions associated with the social democratic welfare state reproducing collective agency in the form of trade unions, for example. In the next two chapters these arguments will be substantiated with a detailed empirical account of developments in Sweden since the late 1960s.

6 The organic crisis of the Swedish model

Introduction

The previous chapter showed how the embedded liberal world order, which was ultimately underpinned by the hegemony of the American New Deal state, has given way to a transnational neo-liberal hegemony. The transition from one world order to another was marked by a crisis of capital accumulation as well as legitimacy. It was acknowledged that phenomena such as globalisation of finance and transnationalisation of production structurally underpin transnational neo-liberalism. But the chapter rejected determinist interpretations that this configuration was itself the 'inevitable' outcome of structural forces. To be sure some kind of shift was inevitable, but not the particular shift that prevailed. Rather, the chapter emphasised that the breakdown of the embedded liberal system was part of a broader socio-political crisis, that in fact initially triggered a left-wing response, which pointed to the contradictions between the ideals of democracy, equality and affluence, and concrete reality. Neo-liberalism was interpreted as a political reaction against this, which then shaped an environment which was conducive to a transnationalisation of production and globalisation of finance.

It is in fact in the context of this aborted left-wing challenge to embedded liberalism that the democratic critique of the welfare state that Giddens invokes in his discussion of 'no authority without democracy' first emerged. Swedish developments in the 1970s and the early 1980s are very interesting in this regard, because the social democratic political establishment initially responded to this challenge by trying to incorporate some of the demands of the left into a project of social reform that pointed towards a democratic socialism. Hence, the rationale was, social democracy would respond to this crisis of representation and consolidate its hegemony. This could in fact be interpreted in Second Internationalist terms as moving from the stage of 'social democracy' to 'economic democracy' and the social democratic leaders and Prime Ministers of the time, first Tage Erlander and then Olof Palme, explicitly invoked this language themselves (Erlander 1979; Palme 1987). These reforms were in fact also understood in terms of a Third Way, but contrary to the Third Way of the 1990s, this was not a neo-liberal Third

Way between social democracy and neo-conservatism, but a socialist one between capitalism and Soviet communism.

In this chapter I will describe the development of this reform movement and its defeat as the political pendulum shifted to the right. My purpose in doing so is to underline the distinctly political and contingent nature of its defeat. Hence, I will seek to empirically substantiate my claim made in earlier chapters that the crisis of the Swedish model was not due to micro-economic dysfunctions, nor can it be reduced to structural causes of 'globalisation' that are beyond political control.

The chapter is divided into two main parts. The first part traces the forces that compelled Swedish social democrats to radicalise their political agenda, outlines the component parts of the reforms – co-determination, industrial policy, and interventionist investment politics based on the wage-earner funds – and assesses the legacy of these reforms. The second part of the chapter accounts for the pendulum movement to the right and towards neo-liberalism. This movement was initially directed by an increasingly politicised business community through the employers' federation, SAF, but has since the mid-1980s also permeated critical elements of the Swedish social democratic elite, which has consolidated compensatory neo-liberalism in Sweden.

A brief narrative of electoral politics

The period that I am about to cover is rather turbulent in terms of events. Swedish electoral politics in particular became more turbulent compared to the period 1932–69. It is not my purpose to narrate these events in detail but to account for the more fundamental socio-political developments behind the events. The period starts with the so-called 'red wave', charac-terised by the rise of the New Left, wildcat strikes, and a general radicalisa-tion of Swedish politics. This was also a period where the social democratic establishment sought to respond and accommodate this leftward shift with a number of reform initiatives. These included more labour-oriented labour legislation including the co-determination act (MBL), increased social consumption, a more active industrial policy and, most controversially of all, the wage-earner funds. In this context, the third way is invoked as a term to describe a path between capitalism and state socialism. It should be noted that the reform agenda was not only carried by the SAP and the Com-munist Party, which explicitly defined itself as a New Left Euro-Communist party. The Liberal Party and the Centre Party also sought niches in the reform agenda to outflank SAP. (The Centre Party championed decentrali-sation and environmentalism and the Liberals were actually the first party to raise the topic of wage-earner funds.) Also in this period the Conservative Party increasingly distanced themselves from their social authoritarian past and, under their new name ('the Moderates') increasingly defined them-selves as the champion of the market-economic principle.

The year 1976 marked a turning point in Swedish politics when this 'red wave' abated, and for the remainder of the 1970s Swedish political society was divided between two evenly balanced blocs (the 'socialist' and 'bourgeois' blocs). In 1976, the Social Democrats lost control of the Riksdag for the first time since 1932. A rather fragile 'bourgeois' coalition of the Moderates, the Liberal Party, and the Centre Party assumed office, with the leader of the latter party, Thorbjörn Fälldin, as Prime Minister. This coalition managed to defeat the SAP through a broad-based attack that included the themes of decentralisation and environmentalism (the Centre Party), civic rights and freedom of choice (the Liberals) and freedom of choice and free enterprise. Whilst effective as a broad front in opposition, this would prove to result in irreconcilable policy positions in government. The coalition parties were continuously at odds over energy policy and the government collapsed in 1978 over the issue of nuclear power. It gave way to a Liberal minority government which, with only just over 10 per cent of the seats in the Riksdag, in fact operated as a mediator between the blocs. The bourgeois coalition was re-elected and re-formed after the election of 1979 (when they managed to obtain one more seat in the Riksdag than the socialists). This coalition faltered in 1981 when the Moderates left the government after its partners had made a deal with SAP over tax reforms. This spoke to a second tension in this coalition, which was the position taken on the welfare state. Whilst the Liberals had since long abandoned wage-earner funds and had demonised them just as much as its coalition partners, the Centre Party and the Liberals were pro-welfare state, whereas the Moderates were increasingly defining themselves as a neo-liberal party. SAF played an instrumental role in the neo-liberal ideological shift of the Moderates through its sponsorship of a number of ambitious young politicians that included Carl Bildt. SAF was also successful in its attempt to shape the overall political climate. Overall, and especially after 1979, the bourgeois coalition government shifted increasingly towards neo-liberal policies. The bourgeois reign coincided with increased economic imbalances in Sweden, a 'structural crisis' in the export sector, stagflation, and budget and payments imbalances (though unemployment was kept on a low level), that at a number of times were adjusted through devaluations.

The SAP was re-elected in 1982 on a traditional social democratic platform, which promised to consolidate the Swedish economy without welfare state cutbacks. Co-determination and social programmes implemented in the 1970s were maintained, but active investment politics in the form of industrial policy was very much toned down and the wage-earner funds scheme was essentially shelved. (A symbolic wage-earner fund scheme, without much relevance for economic policy was introduced in 1983.) Instead the government based its policy stance on export-led recovery through a 'final' devaluation and incomes policy. Again, the Third Way was invoked as a political term to describe policy, but this time it was understood as a path between Thatcherism and Keynesianism as in the first years of

Mitterand's presidency in France. After the mid-1980s, however, it is no longer possible to talk about 'traditional' social democracy, as government macroeconomic policy became deliberately compensatory neo-liberal. In this context, the policy of the Third Way, at least in macroeconomic terms, in fact resembled that advocated by European social democrats at the end of the 1990s. Initially, the policy was successful and restored macroeconomic balance. In 1990, however, underlying tensions manifested themselves dramatically in the form of strikes, leap-frog wage bargaining and capital flights, and a plummeting of support for SAP. In 1991, the economics of 1976 was replayed as Sweden entered a severe recession coupled with structural problems (as discussed in chapter 2) and it was in this context that the Swedish model definitely lost its appeal as a paradigm for social democrats world-wide. One notable difference between the economic crises of the 1970s and the 1990s is, however, that unemployment was kept low in the former period but increased rapidly in the latter period.

The year 1991 was also a political replay of 1976. The elections of that year brought a decisive bourgeois majority, with a clear mandate to govern according to neo-liberal norms. The Conservatives under Carl Bildt were definitely the leading force of this government, and New Democracy, a right-wing populist party, too xenophobic to be in the cabinet, lent its support for neo-liberal reform in Parliament. This ushered in a phase of significant welfare state retrenchment, which was continued and consolidated under social democratic governments from 1994 onwards. The almost instantaneous collapse of the political appeal of the Moderate-led coalition when the economic imbalances became more acute, however, halted a trend towards hyper-liberal Thatcherism in Sweden. Rather, there was a consolidation of compensatory neo-liberalism under the Social Democrats – a third Third Way informed by norms and analysis very similar to that described in chapter 1.

Fordist crisis in Sweden: challenges to social democratic regulation in the 1970s

The red wave

Were the first symptoms of an organic crisis of the Swedish model symptomatic of an accumulation crisis or a legitimation and representation crisis? They were, no doubt, symptoms of a legitimation and representation crisis, and they pertained to the central institutions of the mode of regulation. A crucial turning-point or formative moment occurred in Swedish political economy in late 1969, in the context of macroeconomic balance and an exceptionally favourable growth and productivity development.

On 9 December 1969, a spontaneous wildcat strike commenced in the Arctic Circle, at the Leveäniemi mine in Svappavaara which was state owned by the LKAB corporation. Within two days the strike had spread to the other mines in the corporation in Kiruna and Malmberget (Thunberg 1970: 9–17). The strike involved 4,800 workers and lasted 56 days, until the beginning of February 1970. This strike struck a serious blow to the 'Saltsjöbaden spirit' of peaceful industrial relations in Sweden, as it inaugurated a wider wave of wildcat strikes through the spring of 1970. Apart from the LKAB strike there were 250 wildcat strikes in Sweden in 1970, involving 25,000 workers. Most notably, a wildcat strike broke out at Volvo in Gothenburg in January 1970, before the LKAB strike had been resolved. Wildcat strikes at two of Sweden's most prominent export companies served to focus and intensify the debate on distributive justice, alienation, and capitalism in civil society at large. Indicators of a legitimacy deficit in existing procedures of social representation, wildcat strikes, or threats of wildcat strikes, would remain a central part of reality during the first phase of the organic crisis 1969–76. In particular, a second major wave occurred in 1974, with a total of 21,000 workers involved in strikes. (However, whereas 155,000 work days were lost in 1970, 'only' 22,000 were lost in 1974.) (Swenson 1989: 89).

One might be tempted to infer from these waves of wildcat strikes that the organic crisis was created spontaneously by manual workers on the shopfloor. The story is, however, more complex than that. There had been previous spontaneous point-strikes throughout the 1960s. Why did the one that occurred at an Arctic outpost such as Leveäniemi-Svappavaara take on a broader significance? According to labour historian Bernt Schiller, the LKAB strike gained wider significance because it occurred in the context of, and connected with, a broader radical ideological and intellectual conjuncture. Antagonisms concerning gender roles and the 'double burden' of women in house- and wage-work was reaching the SAP itself, which was confronting a new 'equality debate'. The latter was fuelled by empirical studies, including some sponsored by the state, that there were still significant inequalities in Sweden. Furthermore, antagonisms were emerging around quality of life issues and ecology, oriented against the one-sided economic growth focus of social democratic policy as well as capitalism. Not the least policies associated with what we here have called the paradigm of the Rehn–Meidner model were seen as part of the problem. Structural transformation pressure relocated economic activity increasingly to a number of urban centres and active labour market policy was ironised as *flyttlasspolitik* (moving-van policy). Then there was of course Vietnam.

It was only within this broader ideological context that the meaning expressed by that spontaneous strike in Kiruna in 1969 came to transcend its own literality to symbolise a critique and challenge to capitalism and the Swedish model. Schiller points in particular to the importance of radical journalists in the state news media, who portrayed the cause of the mineworkers in a sympathetic light. Notably, the prime-time news programme *Rapport* assigned Sara Liedman as their main reporter on the story. Liedman was an author from this northern region, who recently had written a much publicised book on the work and living conditions of the mine-workers.

The public response to the LKAB strike articulated the global intellectual critique of the New Left, that had in particular been triggered by American brutalities in the Vietnam War, together with the spontaneous resistance of workers that emanated from local antagonisms of their everyday life. Hence, the strike came to mean something more than itself: the LKAB strike took on broader connotations of distributive injustice, the core (Stockholm) oppressing the periphery (Lapland), social democratic complicity in the capitalist order, and the Vietnam War. Hence the politics of the LKAB strike had decisive 'global' and 'ideological' as well as 'local' and 'economic–corporate' dimensions. It was an expression of the crisis of Pax Americana as well as the crisis of the Swedish model (Schiller 1988: 29–32, 61–65; Schiller 1987: 35–47; Simonson 1988: 65–68).[1]

The wave of wildcat strikes expressed a legitimation crisis in the moral economy of wage determination and a representational crisis in the wage-determining institutions of joint central regulation. According to Edmund Dahlstöm *et al.* (1971) the LKAB miners were caught in the middle between the implicit incomes policy of LO's solidaristic wage policy and market-driven wage drift. As one of the LO groups with relatively high wage levels, their negotiated wage increases had been relatively modest through the late 1960s, compared to other groups. At the same time, they did not benefit from market-driven wage drift, as labour supply had been slack in the mining industry. The wage issue combined with inflated costs of reproduction (food, rent, and real estate prices) and an increased sense of alienation, generated by rationalisation and intensification of the labour process (with increased health and safety risks), and dismal urban planning of living space in Svappavaara, were the background conditions of the LKAB strike. When the centrally negotiated agreement was experienced as excessively exploitative, and when there was sense of collective power locally, the strike broke out. It was particularly the agreement on piece-rates that caused a grievance that triggered the strike. It did not conform to rank-and-file expectations, despite the company's excessive profits.

Thus, a central component of the story was the sense of alienation within the union collective. Local union members could do little by legal means to influence their situation, since the central union controlled the strike weapon. The system of joint central regulation had increasingly removed any meaningful union decision-making away from the shopfloor to the peak level (Dahlström 1971: 203–09; Thunberg 1970).

However, according to Peter Swenson (1989: 87–88), the dynamics of the wildcat strike wave cannot be simply reduced to a reaction of the rank and file against unresponsive union institutions and elites, which had been co-opted by capital. Miners were not against the centralised solidaristic wage policy exercised by LO. Rather, the strongest incitement to rebellion was the fact that wage and relative benefit levels lagged behind those of white-collar employees organised, not by LO, but by the TCO-affiliate, SIF. White-collar employees at LKAB tended to have the highest salaries in industry, and they did not conform to the norms of solidaristic wage policy. Employees who belonged to SIF received compensatory wage increases that corresponded to the aggregate average wage increases in the LO area. These were consequently much higher than those the miners received, since the miners' increases were held back by solidaristic wage policy. According to Swenson, then, the miners acted within a moral framework set by the LO President himself, Arne Geijer. At the 1967 SAP Party Congress, Geijer had made a much publicised speech where he attacked TCO wage policy. Affiliates of TCO should contribute to solidaristic wage policy, Geijer argued, and they should confine their wage demands so they did not exceed those demanded by the higher paid groups of the LO collective. Otherwise, he warned, LO's affiliates could not reasonably be expected to hold back their wage demands (Swenson 1989: 87–88).

There was, however, also another dimension to the wildcat-generating distributive tensions that pertained to the capital/labour nexus, as opposed to the white-collar/blue-collar nexus. First, whereas on a central level union leaders assert the need to promote the wage share of value added in relation to profit, they are silent about this issue on a local level, where, following the logic of solidaristic wage policy and the Rehn–Meidner model, profits are higher than average in expanding sectors and firms. This creates a space for autonomous local union forces to generate moral economic norms regarding wage/profit proportions. This also applies to questions of local production design and work rules. Centralised unions tend not to intervene to contradict these notions, but actually tend to encourage local expectations as part of their negotiating strategy, and at a rhetorical level promote the idea of workers' control. Hence in firms with high profits, it becomes difficult to render compatible moral economic norms, with the macroeconomic concerns of wage-levelling and structural transformation, even when, as was the case with the wildcats, local workers acted within the norms as constructed by the leadership itself (ibid: 90–91).[2]

Finally, a significant cause of the wildcat strikes was the increased scope of time and motion work, monotony, repetition, and the increased size of firms. In other words, alienation associated with the further development of Taylorist production techniques (Simonson 1988: 66, cf. S. O. Andersson 1969: 158).

The organic crisis of the Swedish model, then, began as a distributive crisis in the moral economy and a crisis of representation and democracy. These two dimensions of the crisis had, in turn, two sub-dimensions. The distributive crisis was in part a question of distributive conflict between capital and labour – profit and wages. But it was also a question of inter-union rivalry and distributive conflict between blue-collar and white-collar workers. The crisis of democracy and representation was in part a re-emergence of politicisation of the shopfloor – a rank-and-file rebellion against Taylorism and the prerogative of management to manage; industrial democracy was brought back to the agenda by the wildcat strikes. But the crisis of democracy also pertained to representation and accountability within the increasingly centralised union structures. It should be emphasised that this challenge to the Swedish model was not anti-social democratic. Rather, it pointed towards contradictions between social democratic ideals, such as solidaristic distribution and indeed the aspiration to democratise all aspects of life, and actual practices.

While the organic crisis was initially one of distribution and representation, not one of accumulation, it was profoundly conditioned by cumulative changes generated by the logic of Fordist transition. The extension of Taylorist norms, for example, was a component part of the labour process innovation and production norms that this intensive regime of accumulation presupposed. Furthermore, increased centralisation of wage determination was the consequence of a consistent application of solidaristic wage policy and the Rehn–Meidner model. The excess profits that emerged in business upturns in companies such as Volvo, that triggered wildcat strikes, was a logical consequence of the success of the wage levelling of the Rehn–Meidner model.

As a result of changes on the labour market, the macroeconomic significance of inter-union rivalry between LO and TCO affiliates increased, and thereby started to strain the system of joint central wage regulation. This fragmentation can also be explained with reference to Fordist transition and welfare state growth. As the welfare state expanded, and as the Taylorist logic of separation between conception and execution in the labour process unfolded, a significant stratum of white-collar wage-earners emerged. Whereas wage increases of the salaried strata could previously be ignored in macroeconomic deliberations, this was no longer the case as its size relative to the overall labour force grew.[3]

A significant aspect of this structural change in the labour force was that it comprised a feminisation of the labour force, as it was particularly part-time employed women who were recruited to these jobs. This represented a cumulative change in the distributive norms of the social relations of reproduction. Reproductive work was increasingly moved from the family to the state, where women acquired unionised jobs and had their wages determined through bipartite or tripartite deliberations (Baude 1979: 145–75). The feminisation of the workforce, therefore, contributed to the increasing difficulties of solidaristically co-ordinating wage bargaining, since women were employed in sectors organised mostly by TCO, not LO, unions.[4] This white-collar–blue-collar divide did also to a large extent divide collective bargaining into one process of bargaining for the export-oriented sector and one for the domestic sector.

The feminisation of the workforce, then, contributed to the fragmentation of joint central regulation of collective bargaining. On the other hand, though, the feminisation of the TCO union members, who enjoyed less of the elite position of the older type TCO members, served as a catalyst to a process of convergence in the outlook of TCO and LO that was on the way in any case. Eventually, in the 1970s TCO officially endorsed the principle of solidaristic wage policy (Nilsson 1985: esp ch. 13).[5] This, in other words, with TCO's unionisation rate equalling that of LO (the total rate of union-isation in Sweden was about 80 per cent from this period up to the present), provided the potential for a reformulation of solidaristic joint central regula-tion. Hence, whilst fragmentation of bargaining posed great difficulties, on the level of principles, obstacles to a generalisation of solidaristic wage policy had been removed.

Overall, these developments made it increasingly difficult for the existing tripartite structures to represent labour adequately, because it became inadequate in reproducing the 'moral economy' as understood by labour. In part this was because the meaning of the moral economy was being redefined to include gender equality, increased democracy in the workplace and regional economic balance. But it was also in part because it had become more difficult to pursue solidaristic wage policy when bargaining was fragmented into three, as opposed to one, major bargaining rounds.[6] Importantly, these developments also put a strain on the capacity of the tripartite structure to ensure the competitiveness of the Swedish export sector in the context of the fixed exchange-rate system, since fragmentation encouraged leap-frog bargaining which in turn tended to result in increased wage-push inflation. At the same time, the agreement between TCO and LO on abstract principles also created abstract potentials.

The economic crisis of the 1970s

Initially these strains on the economy were not acute, but this changed when the economic crisis of the Fordist world order reached Sweden in 1976 and deepened the internal organic crisis discussed above. Recalling chapter 5, this economic crisis of Fordism found its empirical expression in stagflation, and was essentially determined by overaccumulation and declining produc-tivity growth, which then was exacerbated by the oil crisis. This crisis reached Sweden after some delay, because Sweden initially benefited from the raw materials boom of 1974–76. But after this boom had abated, Sweden would in comparative terms experience the most severe structural economic crisis in the OECD during the second half of the 1970s.[7] This exceptionally severe structural crisis can be explained with reference to the particular composition of the Swedish export sector (in what chapter 3 referred to as the disarticulated Fordist growth model), dominated by firms producing in a late phase of the product cycle. These firms increasingly faced price competition. Moreover, the relatively important role played by special steel exports, experiencing particularly intense price competition, contributed to the deterioration of Sweden's export performance (Erixon 1984: 115–16, 123–24).[8]

In this context, the increased consumptive and distributive pressures generated by the first phase of the organic crisis clashed with narrowing scope for underwriting such pressures through export earnings. As the non-socialist government that took office in 1976 tried to maintain full employment and social welfare services and entitlements, Sweden accumulated substantial budget and payments deficits and a foreign debt during the period 1976–82. Inflation soared, profit rates declined, as did savings, investments and capital formation (Ryner 1994: 247–50).[9]

The economic policy stance of the non-socialist governments of 1976–82 is often described as more social democratic than that of the Social Democrats. This, however, is a very superficial interpretation. As indicated above, the Social Democrats had always carefully avoided the formation of budget deficits. Their Keynesianism had always, as shown in chapter 3, been more Kaleckian, appreciating the problems of regulating a capitalist economy at full employment merely through deficit spending. The non-socialists, on the other hand, had consistently demanded a deficit financing of welfare state expansion, and lower taxes. It is in fact more to the point to describe the attempt by the Palme government to 'bridge' the recession in 1974 through deficit-financed expansion, as an application of non-socialist, 'vulgar Keynesian', economic policy (Erixon 1984). Be that as it may, both the economic policy of the SAP in 1974–76 and the policy of the non-socialists were expressions of the increased tensions and contradictions of the Swedish model.

Responding to the crisis: the social democratic reform agenda of the 1970s

The increased demand for social goods and services, emanating from the grievances of the first phase of the organic crisis, in conjunction with the structural economic crisis, implied that the old state–market boundaries of the Swedish model would have to be altered. Politically, this need may be expressed in terms of a Gramscian 'war of position' between the left and the right. In short, social democracy tried to turn the crisis of representation into an opportunity to consolidate their hegemonic position. Tage Erlander, the outgoing Prime Minister in 1969, used this as the opportunity to turn against the 'end of ideology' thesis that had become popular in bourgeois circles, because it suggested that as the affluent society spread, the working class would abandon their class-based politics and behave like liberal middle-class individuals. Erlander countered this with the thesis that increased affluence would lead to ever higher expectations that would require further class struggle in the context of more advanced productive forces (Erlander 1979).

First there were a number of reforms that continued on the post-war path of expansion of social programmes, but that were intended to address the newly articulated needs. More resources were allocated to regional support and labour market policy. Notably, reflecting an increased consciousness of gender equality, an ambitious parental insurance was introduced in 1974 and a public investment programme in daycare was implemented. The latter developments reflect a continuation of the secular trend in substituting the welfare state for the nuclear family as a site for reproduction of the labour force. In addition, in the same year, replacement rates for health insurance were increased to 90 per cent. Overall social expenditure increased from about SEK 40 billion per year (1975 prices) in 1967 (just under 20 per cent/ GDP) to about 100 billion (30 per cent/GDP) in the late 1970s (S. E. Olsson 1993: 120–21).

In addition there were a number of other institutional reforms that implied qualitative shifts from the post-war Swedish model.

Co-determination

LO was not oblivious to the problems behind Kiruna of 1969. Indeed in 1966, a report was tabled at the LO Congress – *Trade Unions and Technological Change 1966* – which on the basis of workplace surveys pointed to the social costs of technological change born by workers, and in terms similar to Bauer's notion of misrationalisation it sought ways of making technological change compatible with an elimination of these social costs. Apart from pointing to the need to expand labour market policy, it also pointed towards the need for co-determination, and a need to limit the managerial prerogatives through procedural regulation of management practices. However, the caution with which the party and the union leadership approached these reports were only overcome by subsequent events (Martin 1984: 227–29).

After Kiruna, the unions returned to the themes of this report in their attempts to respond to the grievances of the rank and file. The strategy of LO was to maintain centralised control over wage bargaining. The demand for local union democracy would be satisfied by assigning local union representatives with the task of negotiating improvements in the workplace and addressing the issues of alienation, stress in the work environment and health and safety raised during the events of 1969 and acknowledged in the 1966 report. This, however, required an all-out challenge to one of the pillars of the Fordist compromise: the right of management to manage as codified in the famous Paragraph 32 (formerly 23). Consequently the theme of 'industrial democracy', which had been displaced from the social democratic agenda after the post-war settlement, came to define the proceedings of the LO Congress of 1971. The Congress called on the government to introduce legislation that would attenuate this managerial prerogative and replace it with a legal procedural framework where local unions could represent their members' concern on these issues. Quite remarkably, such a forward assault on the Saltsjöbaden Accord of 1938 (not only because of its challenge to the managerial prerogative but also because its break with the principle of solving issues in a bipartite context as opposed through state legislation) was possible after 1969. On this issue, TCO was in agreement with LO as it reached similar conclusions and articulated similar demands itself. Moreover, the Liberal and Centre Parties would not allow SAP to become the champion of industrial democracy, but proclaimed their support for such legislation as well.

Hence, progressively in the period 1971–76 the following laws were introduced. First, the new Work Safety Law of 1973 expanded the scope and application of health and safety regulation in the workplace. Most notably it gave the compulsory union safety official the authority to immediately halt any part of the production process s/he considers to be in contravention of these regulations. Hence it moved the burden of proof to management to show that the process was compliant with the regulation in the Labour Court. Until this was proved, the union view would prevail. The law also stipulated that safety officials must be given all information about planned changes to the workplace in advance, and that these changes could be held back by the official on health and safety regulation grounds. Second, the Security of Employment Act made unreasonable dismissal illegal, with unreasonableness so broadly defined so as to make any firing beyond redundancies extremely difficult. Again, if the parties disagreed on the 'reasonableness' of the dismissal, the union view prevailed. This law also required the employer to give notice of dismissals and redundancies ranging between one and six months in advance depending on the circumstances. Third, a set of laws gave the unions right to select two members to serve as regular members of the board of corporations with more than 25 employees. Finally, the Co-Determination Act (MBL) of 1976 essentially set a dispositive constitutional framework for industrial relations. Most significantly, it set an enabling framework for the unions and the employers to negotiate on all matters of work organisation and management. It also gave the unions a 'residual right to strike' on such issues even if a collective wage agreement was in force at the time. Nevertheless MBL set certain minimum substantive conditions. For example, management had to initiate negotiation in advance of any important change in operations, and was obliged to negotiate in good faith if called on to do so by the union. With MBL, the 'presumption of the union view' prior to Labour Court arbitration, was generalised to all areas of workplace co-determination.

This was a challenge to management prerogatives and it was taken as such. Below we will discuss how this was one of the central factors that provoked SAF to assume a more confrontational stance. At the same time, it should also be noted that employers also realised that they needed to respond to grievances in the workplace, and they began to develop concepts and experiments with 'new factories', emphasising human relations and non-alienating work as a productivity strategy that nevertheless maintained management prerogatives. Notable examples were the experiments at Saab and Volvo, the latter leading to the famous Kalmar plant.

The EFO model

A second initiative came from technocrats and cadres within SAF, reflecting their concern about the inflationary and attendant competitiveness effects for Swedish industry arising from inter-union wage rivalry which became abundantly clear by the agreements of 1966. In 1967, SAF proposed that they, together with LO and TCO, explore the possibility of increased co-ordination of wage bargaining so as to make it consistent with macro-economic stability and long-term competitiveness. They proposed a highly structured procedure of simultaneous negotiations, wherein a committee of experts would determine the room for wage increases in the different sectors. The committee of experts would consist of representatives from the interested parties as well as a number of independent experts, who would estimated the scope for economically viable wage increases in the LO and TCO sectors. In this context they would in particular consider projected productivity growth, the profit rate required for adequate investments and the require-ment for balance of payments equilibrium. If the experts failed to agree, an arbitration board would decide on a binding estimate. LO and TCO rejected the concrete proposal arguing that this assumed that wage determination was merely a technical matter and denied the conflict of interests between the parties. Nevertheless, they agreed that it was a good idea to have within collective bargaining an explicit and shared reference point that reflected upon the long-term macroeconomic stability of wage negotiations, whilst being realistic with regard to the inherent conflict of interest of the parties.

The result of the ensuing deliberations was the 'EFO model', named after the chief economists of TCO, SAF and LO (Edgren, Faxén, Odhner), who were responsible for its formulation. Taking its inspiration from a Norwegian public commission headed by Aukrust, the EFO model divided the economy conceptually into an export-oriented, or import-competing, sector subject to world market constraints (the 'C-sector') and a 'sheltered' domestic sector (the 'S-sector'). The main difference in assumptions between the two sectors of the model pertained to price formation and productivity growth. It was assumed that mark-up pricing was the norm only in the S-sector and that this sector had low productivity growth, whereas the C-sector pricing was subject to market constraints ('price-taking') but had a high rate of productivity growth. The model acknowledged LO's solidaristic wage policy insofar as it assumed that wage growth would be the same in the two sectors and that the C-sector would be the 'wage leader' (i.e determine the scope of wage increases). Since productivity growth was lower in the S-sector, it was assumed that it could only sustain such increases by increasing prices that would translate into higher inflation which, it was predicted, would result in inflation rates that were higher than abroad. This was considered acceptable as long as the long-term competitiveness of the C-sector was sustained. This, it was argued, implied that the 'room' for wage increases was determined by the profit rates necessary to engender the rates of investment required to maintain this competitiveness which, it was assumed, would be determined primarily by technological change. The ultimate constraint was formulated in these terms: 'we are not free to choose our own rate of technological development' (Martin 1984: 243, cf. Edgren *et al.* 1970).

It is important to underline that the EFO model was exactly what it purported to be – a rationalistic inter-subjective reference point determined from a set of agreed premises. It did not resolve the conflicts between the parties. As we shall see, the determination of the 'walls' between the 'corridors' of wage rates and profit rates was by no means straightforward. In particular, LO and SAF developed explosively different conceptions of the complex relationship between profits and investments that were based on fundamentally different conceptions of the appropriate form of credit institutions that would finance the investments. Considering the requirements for profits squeeze in solidaristic wage policy, LO argued that profit rates need not be as high as SAF assumed, because of the existence of collective savings, in the form of, for example, the ATP pension funds (the AP funds). SAF, however, refused in principle to accept such collective savings as a legitimate source of financing (Martin 1984: 246). The situation has hardly been clarified by post-Fordist restructuring and globalisation which has made the profit–investment (and indeed employment) relationship even more complex and contentious (see Ryner 1994: 268–77).

The EFO model was followed by the 'FOS model' in the 1998, which was the product of another tripartite report commissioned to modify the EFO model on the basis of economic changes (Faxén *et al.* 1989). The main difference in this report is, firstly, that it is based on a three-sector division (the S-sector is divided into a public and private sector). Secondly, it is primarily concerned with devising methodological procedures of wage determination that translate macro-agreements between the parties into local agreements. The intention is to reduce inflationary wage drift whilst encouraging wage differentials that favour employment in growth niches. Notably, it advocates procedures to contain short-term market movements of wages and prices (which it sees as inflation-inducing *sui generis*) both in wage determination and economic policy. Finally, rather than considering productivity growth as an exogenous variable, it invokes Verdoorn and points to the positive relation between demand expansion and productivity via investment levels, technological innovation and capacity utilisation. Overall the model is concerned with methods of wage negotiation that can support non-inflationary productivity growth at high levels of aggregate demand in the K-sector, whilst sustaining corresponding wage increases in the other sectors (see also Standing 1988: 126–27).

Industrial policy

We have pointed to the problems in order to underwrite the social reforms of the 1970s within the context of the Fordist crisis. It should be pointed out in this context that the vulnerability of the Swedish model to changing international economic fortunes was not new to, particularly, LO and some factions of social democratic state-management, especially associated with the future Minister of Industry, Krister Wickman. Notably, back in 1961, LO had presented a report to its Congress, entitled *Coordinated Industrial Policy (Samordnad industripolitik)* (Martin 1984: 219–23, cf. LO 1961). The main theme of this report anticipated future problems in managing the Rehn–Meidner balance between solidaristic wage policy and structural transformation. Increased international competition through what in later terminology would be called 'social dumping' was seen as the main threat, from countries in the developing world but also from OECD countries with lower ambitions with regard to the welfare state and full employment. The report pointed to the need to increase the (national) mobility of capital so as to further facilitate the transition from stagnant firms and sectors to expanding and dynamic ones. The instruments that the report proposed were compatible with the profits-squeeze objective of the Rehn–Meidner model: self-financing of corporations was to be discouraged and profits should instead be channelled to the capital market, from where it would be allocated to the high productivity sectors. For this purpose the report pointed to the need to increase competition on the credit market, where they seemed to have in mind the need to challenge the monopoly of the SHB and SEB spheres. First, the report advocated that the AP funds should be allowed to purchase shares in order to ensure that pensions savings would be channelled to productive investments. But the report points to the need for an overall strategic coordination of investments through the formation of a Ministry of Industry through indicative planning. Most notably, however, with explicit reference to the problem of solidaristic wage policy, the report proposed bipartite 'branch rationalisation funds', which, invoking a term of Wigforss, they called 'social enterprises without owners'. The idea was that trade unions would agree to relative wage restraint in exchange for allocation of 'excess profits' to bipartite credit institutes organised at the branch level and these would then lend money to enterprises in the expanding and innovative niches. This arrangement would make the wage restraint required for structural investments acceptable to the unions because it would reduce the capacity of firms to finance wage drift and would not be seen as a distributive issue where capital gained at the expense of labour. Instead, the finance could be secured for future overall wage increases across the board. This report was written at the height of the golden age, when there was little immediate need for such reforms, but the theme of creating bipartite and tripartite credit institutions to mediate the imperatives of solidaristic wage policy, macroeconomic balance and structural transformation would recur through the period of crisis in the late 1960s and throughout the 1970s. The discussions focused on the accumulated pension (AP funds), which in terms of quantitative credit potential would equal that of all the investment banks and insurance companies combined.

In 1967 the SAP, very suddenly, in response to a poor performance in local elections, launched a new industrial policy, with the intention of channelling collective savings into industry. Central to this was the setting up of a State Investment Bank, which was given the mandate to borrow five times its assets (provided via the budget) and rechannel these investments to industry. In 1968, a Ministry of Industry was set up with the mandate of formulating an industrial policy strategy. This strategy was to be based on careful analysis of structural change in different branches of industry and the work of consultative councils representing firms, public as well as private credit institutions and unions. The Ministry of Industry was also to give proactive support to Research and Development.

These measures were given a rationale in a joint LO–SAP report, which to a large extent restated the rationale of the 1961 LO report, though it was cast in 'broader ideological terms and with greater urgency' (Martin 1984: 231) as it anticipated that the 'very favourable conditions' of the post-war years could come to an end. The theme of the need to make international competitiveness compatible with the principles of equality, social security and solidarity, and the need to counter concentration of ownership, are hence connected with the rationale to promote 'economic democracy' as the next stage of the social democratic historical project (ibid).

'Fund-socialism': the fourth AP fund, the wage-earner funds, and renewal funds

The final and politically most controversial set of reform proposals that were formulated in response to the red wave pertained to collective capital formation. Politically the most explosive of these were the wage-earner funds. These initiatives all addressed the problem formulated in the *Coordinated Industrial Policy* document of 1961: how to make the profits squeeze that solidaristic wage policy required compatible with adequate investment levels. Although it was the left wing of the Liberal Party that first articulated the issue of wage-earner funds (in an effort to outflank the SAP to the left in the wake of the events of 1969) and had managed to make the issue the subject of a public commission in 1974, it was the LO that took the lead also on the issue of collective capital formation. The issue was tabled at the 1971 LO Congress in the form of a motion of the Metalworkers Union (LO 1972).

The metalworkers' motion was introduced against the background of the wage round of 1970 when the LO had managed to hold its own in white-collar union deals at the same time as the government had enforced a restrictive macroeconomic policy. This had led to plummeting profit rates that the *Long Term Economic Survey* of the government had identified as a threat to future investments due to a shortage of equity capital. The LO motion addressed this survey explicitly by referring to themes from the 1961 LO Report. The issue was, according to the motion, how one would raise sufficient equity capital without creating negative consequences for the distribution of wealth. It rejected the idea of private savings as a source for such investments due to its distributive implication and also because a high degree of self-financing of corporations makes them insensitive to macro-economic stabilisation policy. The motion also argued that only long-term investment planning could ensure competitiveness, and although corporations understood this, invoking the theme of misrationalisation, it was argued that public participation was needed to ensure that not only private but broader social considerations were taken into account. Instead it was argued that, since the survey accepted that Sweden had an abundant source of loan capital in the form of the AP funds, but a shortage of equity capital, the logical conclusion would be to allow the AP funds to be invested in equity capital. The government would comply to this demand to some extent in 1974 by allowing some of the pensions savings (the 'fourth AP fund') to purchase shares for 5 per cent of the fees paid into the system in that year alone. In 1979 that amount was increased, but in exchange it was stipulated that AP funds could only hold a maximum of 10 per cent of the shares in any one company. More controversially the Metalworkers' motion also returned to the themes of 'enterprises without owners' and 'branch rationalisation funds' of the 1961 Report. As a consequence of this, Rudolf Meidner was asked to look into the subject and provide a more concrete proposal for the 1976 Congress (Martin 1984: 269–71).

The participants of the Meidner Committee states that they opted to consider the 'big solution' to the questions that had been assigned (Interviewees 11 and 14), and the Meidner Plan certainly had that intention. In essence, it looked for an institutional mechanism that would resolve the tensions that it was apparent by the early 1970s that the Rehn–Meidner model had provoked. Hence it proposed a system of collective capital formation that would (a) provide solidaristic wage policy with the mechanism it needed to operate without redistributing income from labour to capital in high profit firms (as is implied in their relative wage restraint as they conform to the general wage norm), (b) counteract the concentration of wealth and power implied in self-financing of investment as implied in high profit rates, and (c) provide a power resource for labour to make the co-determination, and hence industrial democracy, effective (ibid: 273–74). The basic idea of the Meidner Plan was that the wage restraint that unions exercised in high-profit enterprises should be awarded with a corresponding emission of shares to be held by the unions in wage-earner funds as the representatives of labour. Such emission was to be compulsory and stipulated in law (the Plan suggested 20 per cent of pre-tax profits in all enterprises with more than 50 employees). These funds would constitute new equity capital at the disposal of the individual companies in question. The capital and the dividend would not be allocated to individual workers but would be held by the funds. Workers from individual enterprises would, however, obtain the corporate decision-making power that the shares implied and they would elect their representatives democratically (cf. Meidner *et al.* 1976). In due course, depending on the rates of profit, the scheme would imply a gradual socialisation of the means of production.

Meidner and his colleagues insisted that the scheme was neutral with regard to capital formation. However, as Martin (1984: 273) points out, this is not correct insofar as the scheme was intended to make wage restraint acceptable and to pre-empt the vicious cycle of wage drift and compensatory bargaining at the rates of profit which were now considered necessary for adequate future investments. In other words, it provided a way to make solidaristic wage policy compatible with higher rates of capital solidity.

Needless to say, the Meidner Plan was, to understate matters, highly controversial, and was the substance of much of the politics discussed below. It was not accepted by the SAP, but became the basis for deliberations of joint SAP–LO proposals, the last of which was approved in 1981 for the 1982 elections. In this proposal, the extremely radical mechanism of compulsory emissions of shares from profits was removed. Instead it would be financed by a 1 per cent increase of the payroll tax used to finance the AP system. In addition, 20 per cent of 'surplus-profits' above a specified 'normal' profit rate would also be taxed and allocated to the funds. The funds would then purchase shares on the stock market, seeking high returns just like any other investment company. The return would go to the pension system. This scheme was clearly much less radical than the Meidner Plan and in many respects it resembled a more potent version of the fourth AP fund. It could be argued that it differed from the fourth fund qualitatively in two ways. First, the excess profit tax is clearly an instrument intended to make wage restraint more compatible with solidaristic wage policy. This is because the wage drift effect and the redistributive effect in favour of capital could be considered to be mitigated by the tax. Second, union participation in the funds and the corporate voting rights would operate as in the Meidner Plan but naturally with a much lower share of the vote. With regard to stated aims, they were the same as in the case of the Meidner Plan, except now the contribution to capital formation was also an explicit aim (Martin 1984: 330–31).

A final 'fund socialist' initiative that is worth mentioning is the so-called 'Renewal Funds'. They were actually formulated and passed into law in 1984, long after the period of reform discussed. Nevertheless, they are an interesting initiative that relates to the general orientation of the thinking of the 1970s. The Renewal Funds were implemented as a *quid pro quo* by the government for union wage restraint in 1984. It stipulated that 10 per cent of corporate profits in 1985 would be put into non-interest bearing accounts at the Central Bank for five years. Companies could apply to use these funds before five years for purposes of research and development, retraining of the workforce, and innovation. One stipulation for approval was that the local union authorities should approve of the application. The idea with the Renewal Funds was to bolster co-determination and labour market policy in structural renewal (Eriksson *et al.* 1991).

The reforms of the 1970s: an appraisal

Together the aforementioned reforms added up to a comprehensive response to the crises of accumulation and legitimacy in the 1970s. The co-determination reforms together with a set of decentralisation and participation-oriented initiatives in the public sector in the early 1980s (to be discussed below) potentially opened up space for less alienating practices, more democracy and control in spheres where people live their daily lives. Ultimately, co-determination has not quite lived up to its promise to provide industrial democracy, but legislation has been implemented, and collective agreements on the basis of this legislation have been struck. This has, at least to some degree, increased the inclusion of workers in the determination of the labour process. It (along with the Work Environment and Employment Protection Laws (LAS) that were also passed in the 1970s) has, as discussed in chapter 2, shown promise as an institutional form to facilitate functional flexibility in post-Fordist production processes, applying cybernetic automation and general purpose machines (Standing 1988: 93–94). Thus, it could be argued that it could provide the microeconomic foundations of a progressive post-Fordist trajectory based on what Leborgne and Lipietz call 'negotiated involvement'.

Negotiated involvement, however, would require a macroeconomic framework. In this respect, the co-determination reforms would have required that the solidaristic wage relation could have been appropriately reformulated in a manner that took into account changes in the labour market, such as the increased importance of the service sector. Reforms along the lines of the EFO and FOS models would have been desirable in that respect. Such reforms were not firmly established, however, despite the fact that LO and TCO unions moved closer on the issue of solidaristic wage policy in the course of the 1970s and early 1980s. The EFO model provided a useful analytical reference point for understanding Sweden's negotiated labour market, but it would never constitute a solid norm for coordinated bargaining. Most importantly, the SAF and LO could not agree upon the quantitative relationship between the rate of profits and the general wage rate because of their diverging interests, and because they developed a fundamental ideological disagreement on the role of collective versus private savings and finance in the economy. In the absence of an effectively encoded central wage norm, wage-push inflation continued to be a recurrent problem in the Swedish economy at levels approaching full employment (Martin 1984: 248; Fulcher 1991: 204–14).

Increased social programmes and entitlements in the 1970s provided progressive improvements for social citizenship. But it is questionable whether this expansion of the welfare state is compatible with the changing requirements of capital accumulation. At the same time, it should be underlined that in many respects LO Reports from the *Coordinated Industrial Policy* of 1961 to the Metalworkers' motion of 1971 (and perhaps less surprising, the FOS Report of 1989) show remarkable lucidity with regard to some of the central problems that lay ahead. That is, in terms of adequate investment levels, over-liquidisation in the national economy and even the macro-economic steering problems associated with globalisation. This raises the question, to what extent were the proposed remedies, co-ordinated industrial policy, the AP funds, and wage-earner funds, viable and effective as com-plements to counter-cyclical macroeconomic policy? The historical record shows that they were not effective. But was this failure due to an inherent functional inappropriateness or was it because politically these proposals were never seriously pursued?

Industrial policy gained prominence in the SAP's platform, and it pro-vided the basis for an exceptionally successful election campaign in 1970, but the implementation of the industrial policy programme must be con-sidered a failure. Rather than promoting transformation pressure, industrial policy was institutionalised so as to subsidise bankrupt corporations, and to retard such pressure. According to Pontusson (1992: 151–58), this was because the initial design of industrial policy institutions was flawed. Tripartite bargaining on the general terms of industrial restructuring was never successfully implemented, and in contrast to the case of the labour market board, they acted as 'buffers' against policy control rather than as channels of control. Moreover, in contrast to Japan and France, the capital of the Swedish investment bank was too small to have sufficient capacity to effectively intervene in capital markets. As a result, industrial policy tended to become a process based on *ad hoc* case by case bargaining, of which corpo-rate managers who needed the resources could take advantage. In addition, a coherent substantive *strategy* of development was never created either. As a result, industrial policy became based on an implicit alliance between labour and stagnant industry, as opposed to advancing industries. It became a bail-out mechanism for stagnant industry, and therefore industrial policy was abandoned in the 1980s by SAP. According to Pontusson, the reasons for this policy failure are political. The chief intellectuals in the Ministry of Finance were always sceptical about Wickman's ideas, and they only gained prominence because of the prospect of electoral defeat in the late 1960s. These intellectuals were also the first in the 1980s to draw the conclusion that industrial policy *in general* was a failure, whereas other agencies, such as LO, argued that the AP funds and particularly wage-earner funds could provide more effective steering and a better industrial policy.

Comparative political economy has, of course, argued that industrial policy presupposes a bank- and loan-capital based structure (eg. Zysman 1983) that is rendered increasingly problematic as transnational corpora-tions crave equity capital to finance their restructuring strategies. In addition, the growth of the volume of capital flows has made such steering as well as macroeconomic steering increasingly problematic, as we saw in chapter 5. What is notable about the wage-earner funds as well as LO's proposal for the AP funds is that they were based on steering through equity capital, and that they were to counter the structural power of capital at the level of profit augmentation. Given the quantity of the sums involved in these plans, and given that they were supposed to support co-determined labour process restructuring *à la* negotiated involvement, it is far from self-evident that these instruments would not have been effective. Furthermore, it should be pointed out that wage-earner funds could have served a stabilising macro-economic function when the economy tended towards overheating as it would have removed liquidity from the economy and countered leap-frog bargaining and inflationary tendencies. Considering the importance of infla-tion for the subsequent unravelling of the Swedish model and the movement towards neo-liberalism (Notermans 1993), the political pre-empting of this as a possible policy response is very significant indeed. Finally, wage-earner funds would obviously have served as a balance for Swedish labour *vis à vis* the multi-domestic transnational strategy subsequently pursued by Swedish corporations.

The point is, though, that in the end no meaningful wage-earner fund programme was ever implemented. A rather symbolic and watered down variant of the 1981 proposal was implemented in 1983, where the payroll tax was reduced to 0.02 per cent and where the build-up of the funds was restricted to seven years. Moreover, 3 per cent of the value of the amount received from the AP funds had to be repaid. In the end, the non-socialist government dismantled the funds after coming to power in 1991 and re-allocated the money to funds for academic research. It should be pointed out, though, that the fourth AP fund as well as the wage-earner funds have a good, albeit limited, record in facilitating industrial renewal in Sweden (Pontusson 1992: 201–09).

To address the prospective viability of the overall reform effort of the 1970s must inevitably be a speculative exercise. Nevertheless, there can be no doubt that the effective determinants behind its failure are political. Critical elements of the reform package were never implemented as operative policy. Their institutionalisation was pre-empted by social forces that did not share the principles that underlined the effort. The failed attempt of the left to change the state–market boundaries of regulation was succeeded by an attempt by the right to change these boundaries. The second phase of the organic crisis entailed a political pendulum movement, where the red wave was contained, and a 'blue wave' began to gain momentum. Swedish capital was subjected to what it perceived as severe political and economic pressures: the profit squeeze, increased employers' contributions to finance social consumption, juridification of the labour process, and an outright challenge to private ownership of the means of production. This triggered a change in the ideological and strategic orientation of SAF, behind which lay a shift in the balance of power within SAF. Small entrepreneurs had long had grievances against the policies of tripartite accommodation. Their increased activism, and SAF's setbacks in the 1970s, which above all disillusioned representatives of the corporations in the export sector, politicised the SE Bank/Wallenberg sphere, which now would take on a leadership role within SAF, at the expense of the Handelsbank sphere. It should be recalled that the Wallenbergs had always had a more liberal orientation than the SHB sphere, in which one finds the champions of the Swedish model (Schiller 1987: 124–28, 135–38). In addition to this, Volvo emerged as an independent force on the stage, represented by its CEO, Gyllenhammar. Gyllenhammar was a pragmatist on questions about industrial policy,[10] but he also played a leading role when SAF's member affiliate for the manufacturing corporations, VF (*verstadsindustriförbundet*), took the initiative to decentralise wage bargaining (Elvander 1988: 84).

The pendulum shifts to the right: neo-liberalism in Sweden

SAF's 'free enterprise' campaign

A turning point for the SAF was the appointment of Curt Nicolin, formerly CEO of ASEA, a Wallenberg sphere company, as Chairman in 1976. This appointment was described as a 'culture shock' by a number of senior officials in the organization (Schiller 1987: 137–38; Ehrencrona 1991: 257). The change of orientation was ensured by the appointment of Olof Ljunggren as Director General in 1978. At this juncture, the SAF assumed a position of total non-accommodation in the public commission responsible for ironing out a compromise on wage-earner funds. Prior to this SAF had in fact prepared an alternative proposal for collective capital formation. But the so-called 'Waldenström Report' (SAF and SI 1976) was now shelved. From this point onwards SAF's policy and ideological orientation becomes increasingly uncompromisingly hyper-liberal – that is, an ideological orientation that advocates market relations in all aspects of social life.

But SAF changed in more respects than its policy substance. More importantly, perhaps, it changed the nature of its activities. In contrast to the non-hegemonic orientation in the accumulation strategies of Swedish capital in the past (chapter 3), it started to take on the role of an aspiring hegemonic *party*. That is, SAF attempted to assume leadership in defining the terms of political discourse, not only at the level of policy, but also at the level of popular culture (Clement 1992). The origins of this strategy can be traced to a pilot project which was launched by SAF in the early 1970s in reaction to the red wave. It was felt that SAF had lagged behind LO in defining the terms of politics, and had therefore been forced into a defensive posture. In a report to the SAF Directorate, Sture Eskilsson, responsible for this project, emphasised 'the strategic role of theoretical debate' from which an 'ideology of business' could emerge. A more systematic policy was formulated in 1978, and Eskilsson was given the mandate and resources to create and manage an ideological apparatus that included a publishing house, advertising agencies, and a permanent infrastructure for organising seminars and workshops (Schiller 1987: 46–47, 148–49). This apparatus was definitely decisive in halting the wage-earner fund initiative. From 1978, the terms of discourse in Sweden also swung to the right, most notable in the relative rise of the Moderate Party since the 1979 election when also the Liberal Party returned to a market-oriented posture in economic policy, and in the marginalisation of radical discourse.

The wage-earner fund question was the catalyst that thrust the SAF into its new role. But since the 1980s up to and including the present, this ideological apparatus has been used for offensive purposes in the battle for position. Solidaristic wage policy, corporatism and the welfare state thus became the targets in SAF's new policy programme, *Marknad och mångfald (Free Markets and Free Choice)*. This policy statement calls for 'free enterprise, personal ownership and responsibility'; 'pay formation based on the free market'; 'focus on the employee – a stimulating job in a sound environment'; 'an efficient labour market, requiring reduced taxes and employers' social insurance contributions and reduced public social insurance benefits' (SAF 1990). In the 1980s SAF also became increasingly vocal in their call for Swedish entry into the EC.

In relation to the state, SAF began to aspire to a less mediated form of representation than the tripartite form (Ahrne and Clement 1994: 223–44), which tends to coopt and mitigate special interest articulation (Rothstein 1991: ch. 17). In neo-Marxist terms, this can be understood as a demand for less state autonomy in relation to the structural power of capital. In January 1992, SAF finally withdrew all their representatives from government boards, with the explanation that their institutional frameworks made SAF representatives 'hostages' of the boards (Ahrne and Clement 1994: 224–25, cf. SAF 1991: esp. 9–18). This drive for more transparent representation was also reflected in organisational changes within SAF itself. In the old structure as shaped after the Saltsjöbaden Accord, the central wage negotiators enjoyed a significant degree of discretion and autonomy. This autonomy was been significantly reduced, culminating in the abolition of the central bargaining directorate in 1990. SAF's activities, on a confederal level, have become increasingly geared towards propaganda, research services and the like, whereas the member associations, organised according to branches, have become responsible for wage bargaining. SAF's ultimate aim is to emphasise wage setting on the level of the firm, where it can become a management tool.

As argued above, SAF's changed orientation coincided with increased activism in the Wallenberg sphere in the organisation. It is, however, not sufficient to end the analysis there. It is important to contextualise, especially the more 'offensive' posture of the 1980s, with reference to profound changes in the social relations of production. SAF's new policies reflected the new orientation of the export manufacturing sector, especially the engineering sector, and it was their branch association, VF, that at the owners' demand, spearheaded the change. As a result of the crisis of the 1970s, they pursued a radical restructuring of the labour process (Elvander 1988: 94–98), introducing automation and general purpose machines (flexible specialisation). They also pursued a strategy of internationalisation of production. This was a very significant shift: Swedish capital was always export oriented, but production tended to be based in Sweden. The process of internationalisation of production commenced in the late 1960s, but took on more significant proportions in the 1980s when production was increasingly relocated abroad (Larsson 1980: 92–93; Ryner 1994: 271–73) (Figures 5.2 and 5.3).

Firms in the engineering sector, then, abandoned the tripartite, joint central strategy of wage formation in favour of what we called in chapter 2 a 'flexible neo-liberal' post-Fordism, where wage flexibility became a corporate instrument for management in individual firms (Pontusson and Swenson 1993: 37–66; Mahon 1994: 357–62). They became increasingly interested in creating a skilled core workforce, loyal to the corporation, employing general-purpose machinery, and a cheaper peripheral workforce for low-end jobs. Hence, centralised bargaining and the setting of general wage norms came to be perceived as an obstacle, especially since unions were able to enforce high wage increases in the 1970s. Excessive wage increases were in this context addressed by offering core-labour individualised profit-sharing schemes, which proliferated in the 1980s (eg. Sköldebrand 1989).

Internationalisation of production enforced this trend towards a hyper-liberal strategy. As Sweden diminished in importance as a base of product development for export-oriented corporations, it became less important for these corporations to ensure a mode of regulation that combined a sustained domestic effective demand with price stability. It became rather more important (and possible) to insist on high profits to ensure a high solidity (a low debt to equity ratio to sustain increased firm-specific R&D expenditure) (Erixon 1984: 137–41). Moreover, internationalisation of production relieved the shortage of supply of labour (as capital could expand in high unemployment areas).

A threat to this strategy was of course the capacity of a highly unionised workforce in low productivity sectors to demand compensation. But the failure of the EFO model in the 1970s led to a loss of interest in incomes policy among employers in the export sector, because they no longer saw it as a remedy to that threat (De Geer 1989: Ch. 7). While the full employment economy was retained, the occasional devaluation was probably seen as a better last resort to defend competitiveness than incomes policy (Erixon 1984: 141). This was especially because the corporations had increased options to pre-emptively swap currencies. Subsequently SAF set its sights on re-introducing unemployment as a stick, by demanding a macroeconomic policy that did not accommodate full employment.

This leads to another dimension of the restructuring of Swedish capital. Not only did production relations change, but so did the articulation of productive and financial capital. The Wallenberg/SE sphere and the SHB sphere remained the two largest clusters of control. But also three other spheres emerged, centred around productive corporations that had achieved a degree of independence after the collapse of the Skandinaviska Bank in the early 1970s. These were the spheres of Skanska, Volvo, and Boliden.[11] The emergence of the latter spheres signifies the development of significant financial activities within productive capital, which in turn may lead to more short-term investment horizons, as corporations yield a significant proportion of their profits through the buying and selling of firms and through stock market speculation. In general, the Swedish financial system became relatively more market-mediated in the 1980s. In part this was expressed by the growth of a 'grey' bond and money market that resulted from inflation and debt (discussed in more detail below). But it is also indicated in the rapid growth of the stock market, which had been stagnant in the inter- as well as post-war period, despite Sweden's economic development (Figure 6.1). The increased emphasis on financial transactions in corporations, and an increasingly market-mediated financial system, are likely to lead to a more market-oriented outlook of capital. This corroborates with the changed orientations of SAF. It may also lead to less emphasis on long-term investments in productive capital on behalf of the banks.

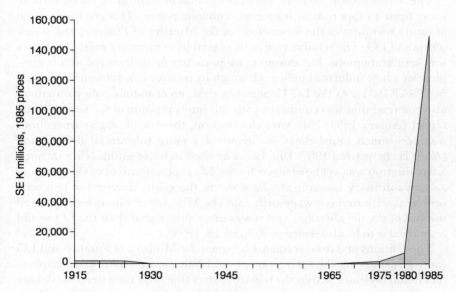

Figure 6.1 Annual turnover on the Stockholm Bourse.
Source: Erixon (1991, cf. *Affärsvärlden* 1991).

Social Democratic retreat and the new neo-liberal direction: the 'economic policy of the Third Way'

The shift of SAF towards an explicit anti-welfarist and anti-corporatist posture in the 1980s constitutes a third phase of the organic crisis. A second dimension of this third phase is the 'economic policy of the Third Way' which the Social Democratic government of 1982–91 implemented. This policy package was initially construed as a return to traditional Social Democratic politics, after the radical wave of the 1970s. As it turned out, however, a significant compensatory neo-liberal component was introduced by stealth in the critical year of 1985.

When the Social Democrats returned to office, they inherited the legacy of structural crisis from the 1970s: an uncompetitive export industry, lack of investment, a structural budget deficit, and rapidly increasing foreign debt. The new government intended to create a substitution effect within the institutional form of the old tripartite system. It favoured private investment in the export sector over public and private consumption. The aim was to restore economic balance and sustainable growth and productivity, without giving up the commitment to full employment and welfare state universalism. The cornerstone of the plan was a 20 per cent devaluation, and a conservative stance on fiscal policy and domestic monetary policy. It was hoped that increased profitability, operating in combination with co-ordinated wage determination and labour market policy would realise this substitution effect (Ryner 1994: 251).

The 'Crisis Group' of 1981 was instrumental in facilitating this transition away from a more radical stance on economic policy. This group consisted of future members of the inner circle of the Ministry of Finance, and senior officials of LO. The relative role to be played by component policy measures was kept ambiguous. For example, wage-earner funds featured as a centrepiece of a new industrial policy, although its relative role remained unspecified (SAP 1981). At the LO Congress of 1981, an economic policy statement also emerged that was consistent with this interpretation of the Crisis Group report (Åmark 1988: 76). After the election, the role of wage-earner funds was very much toned down in favour of a more substantial devaluation (*Ibid.*; H. Bergström 1987: 109–12). The need to boost profitability through a devaluation was acknowledged by the LO representatives of the group as an extraordinary measure in the wake of the crisis, despite the potential problems with divisive wage drift. But the Ministry of Finance determined the size of the devaluation, and it was more substantial than the LO would have liked it to be (Interviewee 6, April 16, 1993).

The tensions and disagreements between the Ministry of Finance and LO (and TCO) during the early years of the 1980s can be explained in terms of functional divisions within the tripartite structure, and the attendant debate over the extent to which unions can hold back on wage demands without endangering solidaristic wage policy. But in 1985 a major shift occurred that can only be described as an attempt by the Ministry of Finance and the Central Bank to redefine the terms of the tripartite state. An ideological rift developed, and what has been called the 'War of the Roses' started in earnest between the government and the unions, as a result of a change in money and credit (debit) policy.

In 1985, the government deregulated capital and foreign exchange markets. Moreover, the strategy in managing the public debt changed. The government declared it would no longer borrow abroad directly to finance the debt, but instead would only borrow on the domestic market (i.e. only issue bonds in Swedish crowns). This meant that in order to maintain the balance of payments, the Swedish interest rate would have to increase to a level where private agents would hold bonds or other debt in Swedish crowns, despite the devaluation risk (V. Bergström 1993: 159–60). The broader purpose was to implement a so-called 'norms based' monetary policy, which was intended to contain inflation by exerting market discipline on collective actors, such as unions and social service ministries, in wage and budget bargaining. The increased dependence of the Swedish national economy on short-term liabilities that resulted is illustrated in Figure 6.2.

The immediate reason behind this shift in monetary policy can be explained in terms of the cumulative effects of enduring inflation and budget deficits that had eroded the institutional capacity of the Central

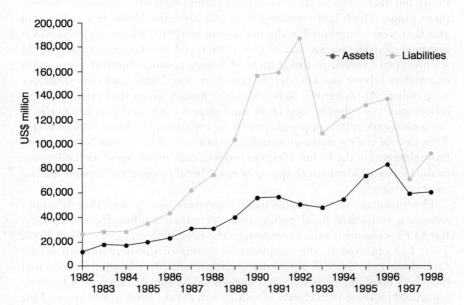

Figure 6.2 Other international investments (than direct and portfolio) in the private sector in Sweden.

Source: IMF (1999) *International Financial Statistics Yearbook.* Washington DC: IMF.

Bank to ration credit and control the money supply. It became impossible for the Central Bank to ration credit, given the excess demand for credit that was generated by the combined effect of high inflation and low interest rates. A 'grey' non-bank credit market of 'finance houses' emerged and grew through the late 1970s and the early 1980s, which undermined the capacity of the Central Bank to control the money supply. Initially, through the period of 1980–84, the Central Bank attempted to respond through an extension of its credit-rationing regulation. But further financial innovation rendering such regulation ineffective, and pressure from the powerful established banks, put pressure on the Central Bank to deregulate. In this context, internationally determined interest rates, enforcing a discipline through the balance of payments constraint, were seen by the Central Bank as the only effective means of controlling inflation (Notermans 1993: 142–43, 145–46). The Central Bank in turn put pressure on the Minister of Finance, who pressured the Prime Minister to allow such deregulation (Feldt 1991: 282).

Notermans' account of the immediate causes of this shift in monetary policy is reasonable. But his account does not adequately explain why *deregulation* was deemed to be a remedy. It is not self-evident that deregulation was the optimal or even a rational way to address the inflation and deficit problems. Why were other remedies disregarded, such as administrative controls at the level of profit augmentation (for example, wage-earner funds, but also less radical forms of intervention, such a build-up of the investment funds, which had remained dormant since the 1970s as a policy tool and that were abandoned in the tax reform of 1990)? Moreover, why was it assumed that the imposition of global financial market constraints would stabilise price levels, in the context of falling nominal interest rates and a negotiated labour market characterised by wage drift and compensatory bargaining? Applying the Rehn–Meidner model, given that credit deregulation took place in the upturn of the business cycle and was pro-cyclical, one would expect this supposed remedy for inflation to be highly inflationary. This case of policy selectivity and institutional amnesia (the forgetting of basic elements of the Rehn–Meidner model), only makes sense with reference to the increased ideological appeal of neo-liberal economic discourse among state managers.

The rationale of the norms-based monetary policy was that it would enforce a restrictive fiscal policy, and strengthen implicit incomes policy. But LO's economists took exception to the new monetary policy (LO 1986: 5–7). LO objected to the conjunctural effects of the deregulation of the capital markets. Since financial deregulation took place in what in 1985 had become a booming economy, they argued that a spiral of increased borrowing would increase the velocity of money and overheating would ensue. This would lead to severe inflationary pressure and it would be impossible for LO to restrict compensatory nominal wage demands. But more importantly, the LO economists argued, deregulation of the financial markets and the new borrowing policy of the state necessarily implied that when the government was subsequently forced to cool the economy, it could only do so at the expense of union members. Either a state-sanctioned wage freeze or an abandonment of the full employment commitment would be required. The increase of interest rates would also increase the demand for high profits, and thereby further undermine the prospects for solidaristic wage policy, which were already strained because of SAF's (or to be more specific VF's) deliberate policy of decentralisation of wage determination. Not only did deregulation lead to a wage-drift generating overheated economy, it also divested the government of all stabilising instruments, *except instruments designed to exert labour discipline*. This reshaping of the ensemble of regulation effectively marginalised labour representation, and increased the degree of discipline on labour, since wage restraint had become the only available means to stabilise the economy. This new ensemble also favoured the representation of capital, because of the pivotal role given to the central bank in managing interest rates.

In the medium term, SAP's economic policy was quite successful in balancing budget and payments deficits, and in boosting profitability and investment, while maintaining full employment. This is not without significance, because by the mid-1980s the SAP Government had demonstrated that the vast expansion of the public sector in the 1970s could be made compatible with fiscal balance.[12] But GDP and productivity growth was not enhanced (Sweden. Ministry of Finance 1990: 4).

The Achilles' heel of the strategy was that the problem of wage determination was not resolved but exacerbated. The strategy presupposed that the trade unions in the LO and TCO areas would exercise wage restraint in exchange for full employment. Given the convergence of the two confederations towards solidaristic wage policy and the intellectual framework of the EFO and later FOS model, this strategy was not without substance. But the devaluation, combined with VF's new strategy of wage decentralisation, posed threats to this strategy. After all, increased profit rates without productivity growth were a recipe for wage drift and inter-union rivalry, and the pro-cyclical deregulation of the credit market and the marketisation of interest rate determination wrought havoc on the fragile tendencies toward a new joint-central wage determination system. VF enticed Metall out of central negotiations as early as 1983. With the exception of a calm wage negotiation round concluded in 1986, wage drift, bargaining fragmentation, strikes and compensatory bargaining would characterise the rest of the decade. It is important to note that, as argued in chapter 2, this cannot be interpreted in terms of 'sclerosis' on the labour market. A more reasonable interpretation is that by violating the terms of solidaristic wage policy, economic policy, especially after 1985, fuelled inflation despite its intention to curb inflation (Ryner 1994, cf. Elvander 1988 and Ahlén 1989).[13] In particular, the strategy created an uneven pattern in wage determination. Wage increases were granted in the export sector through wage drift, while great efforts were made by the government to contain compensatory wage increases in the sheltered sector. A final problem was that the strategy was not conducive towards increased productivity growth (Erixon 1989), which could have relieved the inflationary pressure.

Together, these contradictions translated into a devastating political fall-out for the Social Democratic Party in the early 1990s. Firstly, the fragmentary tendencies in collective bargaining were encouraged rather than mitigated. Secondly, the increased reliance on instruments of imposition (i.e. explicit incomes policy) provoked a counter-reaction from a labour constituency that since the late 1960s had demanded more, not less, representation of their interests. These two developments played into the hands of a third development, namely SAF's neo-liberal strategy, particularly its ambition to decentralise such bargaining and to individuate the identity of its employees. As a consequence, SAF also made headway in breaking the wage-earner alliance, and particularly the ideological affinity to the welfare state of the predominantly male workers in the export sector (Jenson and Mahon 1993: 91–95). Moreover, the efforts of the government to impose wage restraint served to validate neo-liberal discourse about an oppressive welfare state, and it posed a serious threat to the legitimacy of unions as representatives of their members (Ryner 1994: 262–64). I would suggest that it is against these factors that we view the electoral defeat of SAP in 1991.

The effects of the monetary policy deserve special treatment. Credit deregulation had disastrous consequences for the Swedish economy. Since it was pursued in the middle of a booming economy, it created a massive credit bubble of speculation in real estate, that burst as the recession hit in 1991. This led to a virtual meltdown of the Swedish banking system, and for a while even the mighty SE bank faced bankruptcy.[14] The banking system as a whole only survived through a transfusion of liquidity from the state that dwarfed most social expenditure programmes in its magnitude. The 1992/93 state bail-out of Nordbanken, Götabanken and Första Sparbanken cost SEK 67.5 billion (Brown-Humes 1993). This equals the total 1991/92 budgets for the Labour Market *and* Defence Ministries. Sweden's generous employee health insurance system, with 100 per cent coverage from the first day of illness, which was the focus of SAF's crusade against the unreasonable extravagant decadence of the welfare state in the late 1980s, cost SEK 8 billion in 1991/92 (Sweden. Ministry of Finance 1991/92). These figures indicate perhaps where one should begin to look for the causes of Sweden's then rapidly increasing budget deficit and public debt. Another significant factor was the increased claims to unemployment insurance entitlements, emerging as a result of the shift away from a full employment regime. The main cause for the increased deficit and debt was a 135 billion SEK shortfall of revenue, resulting from tax reform (Ljunggren 1993: 17–18). The public debt increased from 45 in 1989 to close to 100 per cent of GDP in 1994 (OECD *Economic Surveys: Sweden* 1994).

One cannot but conclude that the strategy used to increase Sweden's interest rate sensitivity backfired. At best, a benign interpretation could state that the transition costs in the change from one mode of social regulation to another was immense and that the cost was born by labour and social service clients. This financial crisis also led to heavy pressure on the Swedish crown at the end of 1992 speculation (illustrated by the drop of foreign liabilities in Figure 6.2), which forced the short-term marginal rate up to 500 per cent, before the government had to give up and float the crown, which subsequently fell in value. The fall of the crown and the higher interest rates of the early 1990s are, of course, further explanations for the increased government debt.

Nevertheless one can say that recurring runs on the Swedish crown, facilitated by the sterilisation policies implied by the borrowing norm, served a political function. The rapid increases in interest rates and depreciations of the currency created a shock effect and 'crisis consciousness' that made previously politically inconceivable measures possible. The 'October Crisis' of 1990 that followed the aforementioned inflationary bargaining rounds led to the epochal abandonment of the unconditional full employment commitment, when this was subordinated to price stability. It was in the same the announcement – in a footnote! – that the Social Democrats stated their intention to apply for EC membership (V. Bergstrom 1993). The spectacular run on the crown in 1992 which led to the 500 per cent interest rates led to unprecedented multi-partisan talks between the then new Conservative-led coalition government and the Social Democrats that yielded consensus on retrenchment reforms in the social insurance system. Finally, the run on the crown that came as a result of a contagion effect of the 'Peso crisis' of 1994/95,[15] set in motion a process of budget consolidation that lasted until 1997. Especially notable outcomes of these austerity measures were the reductions in benefit levels, the introduction of waiting days, and the tightening of eligibility rules for income maintenance programmes such as the health and unemployment insurance programmes. In addition, employee contributions were introduced as a method of finance. In 1990, both health and unemployment insurance had replacement rates of 90 per cent of the income of the claimant and the entitlement came into effect on the first day of sickness/unemployment. By the end of that year, the replacement rate for the first three days of sickness was reduced to 65 per cent. In 1992, the benefit levels for the period after three days were also reduced (to 80 per cent for the first year and 70 per cent thereafter) (Olsson 1993: 361). Five waiting days were introduced for unemployment insurance in 1993 at the same time as employee contributions were increased so as to save 600 million Swedish crowns for the system. The replacement ratio was also reduced at this time to 80 per cent of the qualifying income (Anderson 1998).[16] These changes, along with the abandonment of the full employment commitment, signify a major retreat from the principle of de-commodification in labour market regulation.

The consolidation of compensatory neo-liberalism in the 1990s

The electoral defeat of the Social Democrats in 1991, and the discontent it reflected, opened the way for a deepening of the neo-liberal project in Sweden, and an opportunity to render it organic in civil society. Carl Bildt formed a coalition government with a clearly hyper-liberal agenda of privatisation, deregulation, and tax cuts formulated in the joint Conservative/Liberal programme, *Ny start för Sverige* (*A New Start for Sweden*). It was given scientific rationale and authority in the Lindbeck Public Commission. This Commission was formed in the wake of the currency crisis of 1992, and applying neo-classical economic reasoning, with great consistency it argued that Sweden's problems were caused by corporatist and welfarist regulation. The 'remedy' lay in the restoration of the Freedom of Enterprise Laws of 1846 and 1864 – privatisation, deregulation and a re-separation of the state and civil society (Sweden. SOU 1993).

But this euphoric moment of Thatcherism in Sweden proved to be short lived. Combined with the global economic downturn of the early 1990s, the steep interest rate increases that resulted from the defence of the exchange rate norm resulted in a dramatic contraction of aggregate demand. This contraction was exacerbated by the stern tightening of fiscal policy that was implied in the pro-cyclical budget consolidation. It was this collapse of aggregate demand that explains the severity of the recession in the early 1990s (OECD *Economic Surveys: Sweden* 1994: 15–16). In the wake of a rapid rise in unemployment from 1.5 per cent towards double figures in only a few years, the bourgeois government parties quickly lost popularity, and whilst the SAP really had played a major part in the events leading up to this state of affairs, they re-gained electoral ground and won the election of 1994.

The humiliating defeat of Bildt's government in 1994 indicates that abstract hyper-liberal rhetoric does not easily translate into successful institutionalisation. Above all, the ideological terrain had not been prepared against the political fallout caused by increased unemployment and welfare cutbacks. Moreover, the bankruptcies of banks hardly increased confidence in the free market. Furthermore the rapid deterioration of the budget precluded major tax reductions.[17] Finally, the need to come to a broad-based solution with the Social Democrats after the run on the crown in 1992 was bought at the price of abstaining from the more radical neo-liberal aspects of their programme, to which the Centre Party was lukewarm in any case. Together these developments decisively reduced the appeal and feasibility of the ambitious programme of privatisation and deregulation.

The return of electoral good fortune for SAP and the increase in union density, despite sky-rocketing unemployment, indicated that the organic crisis of the Swedish model did not equal a legitimation crisis *per se* of social citizenship principles. SAP, which never made compensatory-liberal discourse part of their discourse of popular appeal (as opposed to economic policy formulation) returned to power by relying on the symbols of such citizenship and, as in 1982, they promised a 'solidaristic' sharing of the debt burden, and to reduce unemployment. The SAP's popularity declined rapidly, however, as they implemented cuts to reduce the deficit, and because unemployment that remained at 8 per cent throughout the 1990s despite the business upturn. Their votes were not transferred to the bourgeois bloc. Rather, the ex-Communist Left Party and the Green Party picked up the support, and after the elections of 1998 a minority SAP administration can only govern with their active support.

To conclude this chapter, at the turn of the century a measure of institutional equilibrium seems to have been achieved in Sweden, although Sweden remains very vulnerable in the context of an increasingly transnationalised business sector and the vagaries of global financial markets.

In the latter part of the 1990s, the economy stabilised. Once 'liberated' from the imperative to defend full employment, macroeconomic policy was reconfigured. The Central Bank was granted formal autonomy and reconfigured its norm according to an explicit price stability aim (of 3 per cent). It no longer has to import stability via the exchange rate, which now floats, and monetary policy follows an inflation target of 3 per cent. As argued above, initially the defence of price stability generated an exceedingly hard-headed pro-cyclical austerity in the downturn as it coincided with a tightening of fiscal policy. This resulted in a severe contraction of aggregate demand in the early 1990s, and in the deepest recession since the 1930s. This recession resulted in further fiscal pressures because of increases in, for example, unemployment insurance claims and further shortfalls of tax revenue, but these were met through the aforementioned reforms in the social insurance system. The depreciation of the currency, along with the upturn in the economy then laid the foundations for 'jobless growth', during which time Sweden's unemployment rates converged with those of the rest of Europe. Important in this respect was a change in the tax system which, along flexible liberal lines, increased the scope of companies to meet surges in demand through overtime work as opposed to new hirings (for an overview, see OECD *Economic Surveys: Sweden* 1994: 15–16). The export-led recovery did, however, allow the government to address the fiscal deficit more rapidly than many expected. In no small measure this was because the banks it had bought and consolidated could be sold to the private sector again. In addition, the risk premium on the Swedish crown on financial markets was reduced as the Central Bank proved its resolve to fight inflation and this reduced debt payments. By the end of the decade both budget and payments balances showed surpluses.

At the very end of the decade, Sweden also enjoyed a boom driven by the IT sector, at which time also unemployment was returning to the 3 per cent level. Furthermore, foreign direct investment inflows increased and began to match the outflows (Figure 6.3). (The most likely variable that would explain this is EU membership.) The question is, however, how

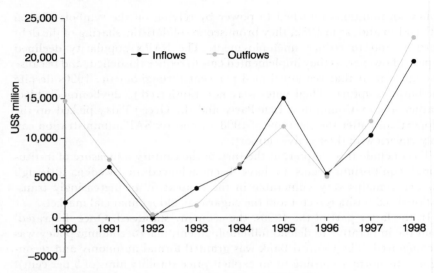

Figure 6.3 Foreign direct investment flows: Sweden 1990–98.

Source: IMF (1999) *International Financial Statistics Yearbook.* Washington DC: IMF.

vulnerable has Sweden become to the fortune of a handful of companies, such as Ericsson, that at the time of publication have began a radical labour-shedding programme in what seems to be a quickly saturating market? In addition, whilst the reduction of the Swedish deficit has made Sweden less vulnerable to short-term investment flows, the recent growth of portfolio investment in Sweden (especially in the bond market in the late 1990s) expresses continued vulnerability (Figure 6.4). Certainly, Sweden's growth model was always dependent on the export sector, but the difference is that today, after the demise of the Rehn–Meidner model, the state lacks the steering mechanisms to regulate this sector so as to ensure autocentric economic development.

In the sphere of industrial relations, the outcome has been a partial decentralisation of collective bargaining, which can be characterised as a tentative compromise between the employers and the unions. Wage negotiations are set at the level of industry. That is not on the macro-level, as solidaristic wage policy requires, but nor is it at the level of enterprise, which SAF, under the leadership of VF, advocated. In the 1990s, there have been developments of sturdier union alliances over the white-collar–blue-collar divide at the sectoral level. This, in conjunction with the need to take advantage of the devaluation effect (generated by the rapidly depreciating crown between 1992 and 1994), made employers accept encompassing branch-level agreements. If there is a silver-lining in this crisis of labour representation, then it is that it jolted white-collar and blue-collar union organisations into abandoning ossified organisational divisions (Elvander 1988) began in order to coordinate wages over the blue–white collar divide.

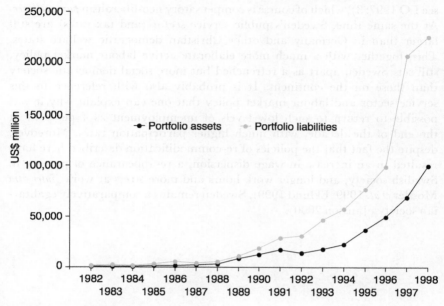

Figure 6.4 Portfolio investments.

Source: IMF (1999) *International Financial Statistics Yearbook.* Washington DC: IMF.

This generated the conditions for an export-led recovery in the late 1990s and an average increase in real wages, but one that has seen greater inequalities (Statistics Sweden 2000). At the same time, there is no doubt that low branch-level wage agreement in the 1990s, despite the depreciation, worked to the advantage of Swedish business. This has also made employers tone down their hyper-liberal rhetoric, and in 1997 the employers and LO as well as TCO unions signed a joint agreement on how to proceed in wage negotiations (Dølvik and Martin 2000). This signalled a modest return towards an agreement in principle on coordinated bargaining, including strong measures for submitting to voluntary arbitration in the case of stalemate. Clearly concerned about the inflationary effects of bargaining once the labour market tightens, the SAP Government is in the process of implementing legislation that would entail giving more power to autonomous national arbitrators (Sweden. Ministry of Industry 1999; see also Sweden SOU 1997). As an indicator of their relative weakness, LO has become the strongest advocate of this, apparently accepting a curtailment of their right to strike in exchange for a return to a higher degree of coordinated bargaining. SAF, TCO and SACO are against these moves however (*inter alia* LO 2000, TCO and SACO 1999, SAF 1998).

Together this institutionalisation of monetary policy and a more tripartite form of wage coordination with its locus on the sectoral level seems to indicate a turn towards a more 'German model' (Streeck 1994; for affirmation, see LO 1997: 3), which of course is compensatory neo-liberalism *par excellence*. At the same time, Sweden's public service sector (and tax rates) are still larger than in Germany and other Christian democratic welfare states. This, together with a much more elaborate active labour market policy, still sets Sweden apart as a retrenched but more social democratic society than those on the continent. It is probably also with reference to this service sector and labour market policy that one can explain why it was possible to return to such low levels of unemployment as 4 per cent at the end of the decade, with much higher participation rates. Moreover, despite the fact that the policies of re-commodification described here have resulted in an increase in wage dispersion, a re-appearance of poverty in Swedish society, and longer work hours and more stress at work (*inter alia* Mossler *et al.* 1999; Eklund 1999), Sweden remains a comparatively egalitarian society (Jansson 2000).

7 Why social democrats become neo-liberals

Lessons from the Swedish case

> To analytically separate the necessary from the contingent is one of the most important tasks of the social sciences.
>
> (Sayer 1992)

The central argument that runs through the previous chapters is that the neo-liberal nature of the effective capitalist restructuring that has taken place in the western world is politically and ideologically contingent. Chapters 1 and 2 challenged notions of an inherent dysfunctionality of 'post-industrial', or more to the point, post-Fordist responses that built on and extended the traditional social democratic principles of de-commodification and social citizenship. Chapter 3 challenged the notion that neo-liberal globalisation, whilst configuring structures (the structural power of capital) in order to constrain and even pre-empt such responses, was caused by an inherent structural dynamic. The structural configuration itself was seen as an outcome of contingent politico-ideological practices and struggles. The Swedish case has been used throughout as a paradigmatic case to provide empirical substantiation for the argument. The focus on this case was justified by the political strength of Swedish social democracy, both in terms of material capabilities and in terms of possessing a conscious paradigmatic rationality of social regulation, and because (consequently) the Swedish case had showed the potential to develop an alternative post-Fordist/post-industrial trajectory, maintaining and extending social citizenship norms.

What remains to be explained fully is the character of the political and ideological contingency which has favoured a neo-liberal politics of capitalist restructuring over one based on de-commodification and social citizenship. Again the Swedish case is a particularly pertinent one, because it is a case where one would have been least likely to expect neo-liberal politics to become institutionalised. Yet it was. Hence, Sweden provides a particularly fruitful context in which to sort out which factors play a particularly determining role in the politics of neo-liberal hegemony. In other words, it is plausible to treat Sweden as something approaching what Eckstein (1976) has called a 'critical case study'. Thus far, we can already rule out two determinant variables that often are associated with explanations for the 'decline of social democracy': the lack of a coherent policy concept and the incapacity to mobilise a political mass base (*pace* Przeworski 1985). With the Rehn–Meidner model and its proposed modifications of the 1970s, Swedish social democracy had a coherent alternative policy paradigm (Martin 1984) for post-Fordist restructuring. Furthermore, Swedish social democracy had managed to develop a mass political base that bridged the white-collar/blue-collar divide. Yet not only did Sweden undergo a neo-liberalisation in the 1980s and 1990s, Swedish social democracy internalised these norms and played a critical role in the neo-liberal shaping of socio-economic outcomes. Hence, there must be alternative answers to the question of why do social democrats become neo-liberals.

On the basis of the narrative provided in the previous chapter, the purpose of this chapter is to answer this question with reference to the critical case of Sweden. I will not argue against the explanations that emphasise the importance of the structural power of capital as a consequence of neo-liberal globalisation (chapter 5). I also agree that neo-liberalism is fundamentally driven by accumulation strategies of transnationally mobile capital fractions, which primarily express their interests and their conceptions of how the socio-economic future ought to look, as determined by the political process of their class formation (eg. Gill 1990; van der Pijl 1998; Holman 1992). But if we accept that the politics of hegemony is about the neutralisation of antagonisms (Laclau 1977), then this is not sufficient as an explanation of the hegemony of neo-liberalism. It does not explain, for example, why, *qua* power mobilisation theory, the reformist labour movement in Sweden did not draw on its 'political' power resources to resist this restructuring and advance its alternative restructuring project. What is particularly puzzling is that the social representatives of Swedish labour actually demobilised the power resources of labour and enhanced the power resources of capital in the 1980s. What is more, to actors at the apex of the institutions of social regulation, this seemed like the most natural thing in the world to do. Taking chapter 5 and its argument on the structural power of capital as given (and its specific manifestations in Sweden as described in chapter 6), it is this politics of 'antagonism–neutralisation' in Sweden that this chapter seeks to explain.

The significance of structural factors and the limitations of a structuralist explanation

As discussed in chapter 2, product and process technological changes implied in the semi-conductor revolution have had a profound impact on the structural context in which social democratic regulation must contend. Yet the prospects of 'negotiated involvement' imply that there is nothing inherently anti-social democratic about the productive forces unleashed by the techno-logical revolution as such. But potentials discerned at the micro-level of the labour processes in certain firms and sectors do not translate into actually realised regimes of accumulation and growth models. One can hardly avoid the conclusion that a social democratic post-Fordist growth mode was *not* realised in Sweden in the 1980s. Chapters 5 and 6 have identified and isolated a number of factors that account for this failure – the internationalisation of production, globalisation of finance and the emergence of a politics of regulation with a new constitutionalist, compensatory neo-liberal monetarist policy at its epicentre. These three factors can be synthetically labelled as effects of globalisation that increase the force of the commodity form and the structural power of capital on a social formation. Globalisation has weakened the ability of trade unions and other social groups to realise an alternative accumulation strategy based on norms of de-commodification. As a result, the dominant trend of socio-economic restructuring, although by no means successfully articulated yet as a solidified hegemonic project, corresponds to the preferred trajectory of Swedish capital: a neo-liberal post-Fordism.

It remains to be explained why this tendency became predominant despite Social Democratic managers' and intellectuals' command of the strategic levers of regulation in the 1980s in Sweden. It would be tempting to base the explanation on structural and intransitive factors. Such an explanation would suggest that these levers of regulation were not at all 'strategic' any more. Structural necessities inherent to the new social relations of production demanded that state managers and the institutions of regulation followed the predominant tendency of capitalist restructuring.

There is a lot to be said for arguments that rely on such structural factors in the sense that the space in which to steer strategies for alternative accumulation trajectories has been significantly narrowed. Capital and currency market deregulation was, as we have seen, a fatal blow to social democratic regulation. Furthermore, these markets were deregulated because the Central Bank no longer had the capacity to sustain such regulation. The rise of a grey capital market in the wake of sustained inflation, and currency swaps by Swedish multinationals, made it impossible to maintain regulations. The Central Bank and the Ministry of Finance gave up (Sweden. Bank of Sweden 1985; 1987). Feldt, the Minister of Finance, acknowledged this as a serious political defeat and the Prime Minister, Palme, clearly disliked the idea but saw no alternative. When Feldt made the case for deregulation of the financial markets (ironically, but tellingly, in connection with a meeting of the Socialist International), Palme became increasingly irritated and his body language became increasingly hostile, and just as Feldt expected him to turn down the request, Palme snapped: 'You people go ahead and do what you want, I don't understand any of that anyway!' (Feldt 1991: 260). This very uncharacteristic statement from the charismatic, intelligent and intellectually arrogant Palme, speaks volumes about the intuitive revulsion of traditional social democratic politicians to financial deregulation. It also illuminates their resignation, and deferral to a narrow group of technocrats in the Ministry of Finance and the Central Bank.

In the previous two chapters I have pointed to the difficulties that the internationalisation of production of 'Swedish' multinational corporations pose for a renewal of social democratic regulation. Their 'multi-domestic' strategies break the virtuous, autocentric circuit between wages, profits and investments that the Swedish model presupposed. Their exit options and the loss of importance of the national economy of their home-base have also reduced their incentives to rely on macro-corporatist solutions. These market tendencies contradict the imperative for relative surplus augmentation (chapter 2) and productivity growth upon which social democratic regulation relies. The market conforming economic policy of the 1980s facilitated this development and failed to address, or even conceive of, this problem (Ryner 1994).

To be fair though, as in much of the OECD world – with the exception of France and Japan – the government abandoned active industrial policy because it had failed to live up to the objectives set for such policy in the 1970s. It might not seem unreasonable for the government to conclude that there was little capacity for the state to shape markets, and the expense was unjustified, particularly given the need to deal with the structural budget deficit and debt that had been accumulated by the end of the 1970s. In fact, the dismantling of the costly industrial supports of the 1970s seemed to be one of the best ways to ensure a rapid return to fiscal balance, without cutting back on social expenditure. The conclusion of this would be that the government could do little to directly shape the product composition of the Swedish economy. This leads us back to the significance of structural factors in the crisis of the Swedish model.

It is also important to acknowledge that the government operated with a set of constraints and policy conflicts generated by the crisis of accumulation, that inhibited its capacity to facilitate restructuring compatible with the distributive and representational imperatives of the Swedish model. In particular the fiscal crisis intervened. In order to restore fiscal balance and external balance without qualitative cutbacks of social consumption and the social wage, it was necessary to accept an increase in average profit rates in the export sector in the short to medium term. If the wage restraint that in this context was necessary could not be secured because of changing orientations of the organisations on the labour market and in redistributive struggles (such as SAF's abandonment of coordinated bargaining and the decision of individual unions to agree to decentralised negotiation), there was very little the government could do. None of the Swedish union federations, nor the employers' associations, wanted direct state intervention in wage determination. And, as for example the Rehn–Meidner model used as a premise, such intervention would be futile and counterproductive. Again, had not structural changes in the labour market undermined the necessary conditions for the Swedish model?

Finally, Sweden's economy operated in an international environment, where other states had abandoned any employment commitment in their economic policy, in order to prioritise price stability above all. The Rehn–Meidner model had presupposed that demand-pull of the world economy would ensure the compatibility of a relatively restrictive macroeconomic policy with full employment and had relied on the demand-pull of the world economy to ensure sufficient effective demand. When the rest of the OECD pursued policies of competitive austerity, especially when the EC anchored its economies to the Bundesbank through the EMS, what could Sweden's government do to change this? The soft currency approach adopted in 1977 had contained unemployment, but the recurring cost crises, the emergence of the grey capital market, and the speculative run on the crown in 1992, were all results of this soft currency approach and signified its contradictions. Ultimately, such an inflationary policy breached the terms of the Rehn–Meidner model and the post-war mode of regulation.

These structural factors are of crucial significance in understanding the development of the crisis of the Swedish model, but they are not sufficient for an explanation of neo-liberal hegemony. They need to be combined with a politico-ideological account in order to reach a more compelling and complete explanation of the development of the organic crisis. A structural explanation on its own would only be adequate if one could show that social democratic elites had pursued some sort of optimal strategy to advance social democratic ends, within these structural constraints. Then one could indeed conclude: 'there was no alternative'. But contrary to this, admittedly with the benefit of hindsight, the record shows clearly that such an optimal de-commodification strategy was *not* pursued.

Considering the potential configuration of co-determination, social policy, the EFO and FOS models, industrial policy and collective capital formation as discussed in the previous chapter, I would maintain that there were alternatives. Why were these alternatives strategically selected out?

A number of things need to be explained. With respect to the politics of the 1970s, why did little come of the wage-earner funds, that were held up as a centrepiece of future labour and social democratic strategy in Sweden? The wage-earner fund issue is particularly important to consider, because they could have thrown into relief and reconfigured other policy measures that in the end did not end up having the significance they could have had, such as co-determination, or measures that ended up as failures, such as the EFO model, industrial policy and the deficits associated with social service expansion. Wage-earner funds or other forms of collective capital formation would have given workers more leverage to realise a restructuring based on negotiated involvement. They would also have served as a mechanism to contain wage drift, whilst sustaining higher profit rates and equity-based finance of industrial restructuring. They would also have provided labour with a mechanism to maintain autocentric development to counter the tendency to multi-domestic production strategies. Finally, wage-earner funds, regulating capital at the level of profit extraction, could have served as a mechanism to contain inflation-inducing credit expansion and an effective administrative, as opposed to market, method of financing deficits. (In this context one should also mention the decreased use of investment funds in favour of the bond market by the bourgeois parties to finance their deficits.)

When trade union intellectuals conceived of the wage-earner funds they were in fact quite conscious of the structural difficulties the Swedish model would face in the 1970s and 1980s. Their problem formulation and analysis show great awareness of the increased profitability requirements of inter-nationalising corporations, and collective capital formation was intended to address the ensuing problems for solidaristic and coordinated wage policy. The Metalworkers' motion to the LO Congress in 1971 saw wage-earner funds as a way to ensure an adequate domestic equity capital base, without undermining the profits squeeze requirements of solidaristic wage policy. Such an increase in the capital base was seen as particularly important as a means to ensure investments in restructuring the Taylorist labour process. Meso-level funds were also to ensure that the weakening capacities of stabili-sation policy, caused by increased economic interdependence, would be addressed, and that inflation-inducing wage drift would be avoided. Finally, the funds would, of course counteract the centralisation of ownership in the Swedish economy (LO 1972: 815–18). Hence, in this motion, wage-earner funds were the cornerstone of a strategy of industrial renewal compatible with the increased need of Swedish capital for equity capital. This dimension of the funds can be seen as an extension of the fourth AP fund. At the same time, and this was the crux of the directives, the funds would render such a strategy compatible with solidaristic wage policy, a humanisation and democratisation of the labour process, and an increase in social and workers' ownership of the means of production.

Wage-earner funds were never really implemented as intended, though they were articulated in the 1970s as the centrepiece of a strategy to address precisely the difficulties that emerged in the 1980s. It should be pointed out that since inflation and internationalisation of capital markets were major causes behind 'the necessity' of financial deregulation in 1985, these funds may have provided a meso-level alternative mode of capital control. Thus, the wage-earner fund issue remains significant for a political explanation of the crisis in the late 1980s and 1990s because of its absence. Given that it was intended to address the constraints and problems that emerged, why was the wage-earner fund response 'strategically abandoned'? That is the question for the next section of this chapter.

The defeat of the wage-earner fund initiative marked an end to attempts to radicalise the institutional mix of the Swedish mode of regulation. The implication of this was that economic policy would of necessity be increas-ingly subject to market constraints from the 1980s onwards when the Social Democrats returned to power. But if one grants that an opportunity was missed for social democracy in the 1970s, then is it not sufficient to refer to structural factors to explain the outcome in the 1980s, as for example Jonathon Moses (1994) does? Not quite, at least not in the 1980s when the neo-liberal configuration that was consolidated in the 1990s actually took place.

First, it is difficult for such an account to explain why the Ministry of Finance would pursue an inflationary policy (a pro-cyclical expansion of credit through deregulation and an interest rate policy that exacerbated distributive struggles in wage determination) to fight inflation. This suggests a particular way of conceiving inflation, and a particular way of regulating inflation that is radically different from earlier conceptions. Again, subjectivity is an indispensible part of the story. The relevant contrast is that between the Rehn–Meidner model conception of how to achieve price stability through de-commodification (counter-cyclical policy, credit market regulation, investment funds) and the post-1985 neo-classical conception based on commodification (sterilisation policy intended to increase the world market determination of the Swedish interest rate) (Sweden. Ministry of Finance 1985c; Hörngren 1993).

Second, given that another key policy component of the 1980s was to increase productive investments, it is puzzling why the government pursued a policy that encouraged capital flight that at one time led to overnight interest rates of 500 per cent, and the speculation bubble that led to a massive destruction of capital in the bank-crisis of the early 1990s. This suggests that policy makers had internalised a particular conception of how investments are best encouraged. The Social Democratic Government abandoned *dirigiste* industrial policy in favour of the 'supply-side' measures of deregulation implemented in the 1980s. The latter were justified because they would improve the 'functioning of the economy'. Although capital deregulation may have been brought about by structural necessities, it was also seen as a way to improve the functioning of capital allocation. Thus, state managers subscribed to the neo-liberal train of thought. The same line of argument was used to justify the creation of a secondary bond market in the early 1980s (Sweden. Ministry of Finance 1991). In addition, the under-financed tax reform of 1990 that was decisive to the emerging budget deficits that required the retrenchment of the 1990s, would be financed through 'dynamic effects'. This argument also betrays a particular neo-liberal conception (the neo-classical crowding-out argument and a marginalist conception of incentives) (Sweden. Ministry of Finance 1984: 15, 26–27, 35; 1987/88: 29–32; 1990: 21–22; see also Erixon 1984: 130–33). It should be pointed out that this argument is restricted to the objects of regulation of the Ministry of Finance and the Central Bank at the apex of the mode of regulation. More subordinate agencies, such as the Ministry of Labour and AMS (Sweden. AMS), stuck broadly to the Rehn–Meidner conception of labour market policy, now reconfigured and subordinated to the new macroeconomic policy.

These measures cannot be explained with reference to structural factors alone; they indicate an ideological shift among Social Democratic state managers in the Ministry of Finance towards a compensatory, disciplinary neo-liberalism. Hence, a more complete account of the crisis of the Swedish model needs to account for this ideological shift. This will be done in the third section of this chapter.

Explaining the failure of the politics of collective capital formation in the 1970s

As a result of the Metalworkers' motion, the LO Congress of 1971 appointed a working group to develop guidelines and proposals for collective capital formation.[1] In addition, the Liberal Party took the initiative on the formation of a public commission on wage-earner ownership. The Liberal Party had long advocated individual share ownership for workers, but it had been radicalised by the red wave and pressed for some form of wage-earner funds. The Social Democratic Government agreed to form this Commission in 1974, in exchange for Liberal support on economic policy.[2] While little concrete was achieved by the public commission, in 1976 the LO Congress surprisingly approved the very radical Meidner Report as official policy.

The approval of the 'Meidner Plan' surprised SAP at an unfortunate time, since preparations for the 1976 election were well under way. They went into the election without a policy on what was now LO policy on wage-earner funds and were caught flat-footed in debates on the issue. Though SAP did not lose because of the wage-earner funds, the funds became a scapegoat for the electoral loss. Subsequent negotiation also revealed substantive disagreements between party officials and LO, which would now be subject to negotiations in a joint LO/SAP working group formed to stake out a common position on the issue.

The Meidner Plan served as a catalyst in the negotiations in the public commission. Although the employers' representatives disliked the Meidner Plan, they did not rule out a compromise at hand. Wage-earner funds in a less radical form were seen by some employers as beneficial to capital formation. SAF and SI even worked out their own proposal, the so-called Waldenström Report, which in some respects was actually much more far reaching than the final Bill of 1983 (SI and SAF 1976). One decisive difference between the Waldenström Report and the LO/SAP reports was that it assigned a major role to individual share ownership, a very different principle. Nevertheless, the Waldenström Report was a pragmatic move, characteristic of the tripartite political game of social democratic regulation.

However, developments between 1977 and 1979 decisively sealed the fate of the wage-earner funds, as SAF underwent its neo-liberal shift under the leadership of Nicolin and Ljungberg. Abandoning the policy of compromise and tripartite negotiation, SAF declared that they refused to collaborate on the issue in principle. The Waldenström Report was shelved, employer and business representatives withdrew from the public commission, and began their 'free enterprise' propaganda against 'the funds'. Consequently, the non-socialist parties, including the Liberals, distanced themselves from anything that had to do with wage-earner funds, and attacked them as a means to impose 'East-bloc socialism' on Sweden.

With the wage-earner funds, the bourgeois bloc found an issue – an 'other', an enemy – around which to mobilise and forge unity. SAP and LO ironed out their differences and worked out a compromise. But the fumbling continued and the SAP Congress of 1978 did not pass the proposal. Once again the party went into an electoral campaign without a wage-earner fund policy. Facing a bourgeois electoral bloc united around the issue, benefiting from the ideological support of SAF, SAP lost the election with a narrow margin.

Finally, SAP approved a proposal in 1981, which followed the 1978 formula, but it was further watered-down and approached the suggestions of the Waldenström Report. The 1981 funds would nevertheless have made a significant contribution to collective capital formation. But at this time SAP party strategists were very unhappy with wage-earner funds. They were seen as a necessary evil needed to appease LO. The wage-earner funds were considered a liability in the elections of 1982, and the party won despite, not because of, the issue (the party's strategy was to avoid debating the funds) (Lewin 1992a: 372; H. Bergström 1987: 91–92). As discussed in chapter 6, only a symbolic scheme was introduced in 1983. LO's hopes that this might be the beginning of something more ambitious were put to rest when Palme announced that this was '*the* [only] step'.

The conventional view of the failure of the wage-earner funds initiatives of the 1970s is that they were an intellectual product emanating from trade unions circles that were exceedingly unpopular among the Swedish electorate (eg. Lewin 1992a: 368–69). The Swedish electorate embraced the consensual social welfare, mixed economy vision of Swedish Social Democracy, but did not want socialisation of the means of production. It is impossible to argue against this interpretation as it pertains to the outcome of the wage-earner funds proposal. But this thesis is both trivial and misleading as an explanation for the political process surrounding the wage-earner fund issue.

Lewin points out that the Social Democratic Party won the 1982 election despite, not because of, the wage-earner funds. The electorate voted for the Social Democrats because they were thought to be the party best suited to address the issues deemed to be the most important, to take Sweden out of the economic crisis and to ensure full employment. The commitment to introduce wage-earner funds was highly unpopular (ibid., cf. Holmberg 1982: Table 22). The most interesting implication of Holmberg's public opinion data is not that the wage-earner fund issue was unpopular as such, but that the connection was not made between wage-earner funds and the economics of full employment. It should be recalled that the wage-earner funds were intended as instruments, which were construed as absolutely necessary instruments to ensure that the goals of economic recovery and full employment could be met. Clearly, then, the labour movement failed to convince the electorate about this connection, which would have been crucial and natural to make. Why did the labour movement fail to do so?

It is tempting to explain this with reference to the hegemonic discourse of legitimation in Swedish civil society in which the 'historic compromise' between capital and labour was embedded. The historic compromise delineated clear institutional boundaries between the realm of operation of the state, the organisations of the labour market, and the capitals owning individual. The wage-earner funds represented a violation of the sphere of absolute discretion of the capital owner, and were therefore not seen as legitimate means as defined by the social welfare hegemony embodied in Swedish civil society. Thus the Social Democrats did not have an available discourse through which to justify their policy, and their adversaries, SAF and the bourgeois parties, could successfully mobilise against them just as they had in the immediate post-war period against more ambitious schemes of economic planning.

Such an explanation seems almost adequate. It is true that the required popular–ideological terrain had not been laid for the wage-earner fund proposal. But this begs the question, why had it not been prepared through a hegemonic strategy – a war of position? The ground was not unfavourable in the early 1970s. For example, anti-Americanism triggered by the Vietnam War, and rank-and-file discontent with the historic compromise, had created the feeling that capitalism was a problem that penetrated significant parts of bourgeois society. One should recall that it was actually the Liberal Party that took the initiative that led to the formation of the public commission to investigate the question of wage-earner funds. The Liberals tried to outflank SAP on the left. In addition, internal deliberations among SAF indicate a sense of resignation among the employers, and the Waldenström Report indicates that many of them were willing to grant significant concessions at this juncture (Schiller 1987: 139–41).

Hence, it is important to keep in mind that at formative moments the terms of contestability of socio-political discourse are open-ended, and the shape of its future closure depends upon political struggle. Political initiatives of the Social Democrats had been construed by the bourgeoisie as outrageously radical before, and the Social Democrats had emerged victorious. That included the struggle for universal franchise in 1917, the struggle for full employment policy with unionised wages in 1932, and the struggle for supplementary collective pensions (ATP) in 1960. An explanation of the failure of the wage-earner fund campaign must therefore account for the strategic success of the right, led by SAF, as well as the strategic failure of LO and SAP.

The strategic success of the right: SAF's free enterprise campaign

SAF's abandonment of the Waldenström Report and its successful mobilisation against the wage-earner funds is an absolutely crucial aspect of the explanation. It also served as a catalyst for a further hyper-liberal offensive through the 1980s that culminated in the Conservative victory in the 1991 election. The wage-earner fund issue constituted a decisive moment in a cumulative process of attacks on SAF's members' prerogatives and 'individual rights' that led this organisation to mobilise for ideological struggle – the proverbial straw that broke the camel's back.

As was argued in the previous chapter that the turning point happened in 1976, when the CEO of Asea – one of the flagships of the Wallenberg sphere – Curt Nicolin, became Chairman of SAF. The transition towards a more confrontational and hyper-liberal posture was assured by the appointment of Olof Ljunggren as Executive Director of SAF in 1978. Apart from indicating a more activist role by the Wallenberg sphere in SAF, the change indicated a demand for more transparent representation of the members within the organization. Notably, the initiative for creating a systematic propaganda apparatus came from the members themselves, whereas usually policy initiatives came from SAF's staff (De Geer 1989). During this time a radical reassessment of the role and purposes of SAF was also taking place, the outcome of which was an explicit emphasis on SAF's role as spokesperson for 'the free entrepreneur', as a 'moral being' (*värderingsmänniska*). For the first time SAF seriously assessed who they actually represented, and the conclusion was that it was not primarily the CEOs in the large corporations, but the 'entrepreneurs' (or entrepreneurial capital). The change in emphasis on entrepreneurship was an ideological expression of the new configuration of capitalist class formation in Sweden. This class formation was based on an alliance between transnationalising Swedish export capital, with the Wallenbergs sphere playing a decisive role, and smaller entrepeneurs. They could now unite around the conception of the independent and free entrepeneur.

It was from here on that SAF took on the role of a hegemonic party, as Clement so aptly has put it, in the sense of attempting to define both the terms of intellectual and policy debate, and the 'common sense' of the bourgeoisie as well as civil society at large (Clement 1992; Boréus 1994; Blyth 1997). The origins of this strategy can be traced to a pilot project which was launched by SAF in the early 1970s in reaction to the red wave. It was felt that SAF had lagged behind LO in defining the terms of politics, and had therefore been forced into a defensive posture. In a report to the SAF Directorate, Sture Eskilsson, who was responsible for this project, emphasised 'the strategic role of theoretical debate' from which an 'ideology of business' could emerge. He pointed to the importance of forging opinions at schools and at workplaces. Substantively, 'individualism' and 'decentralised decision-making' should be emphasised. Journalists, MPs, students, and 'the diffuse group of cultural workers' were identified as target groups (Schiller 1987: 46–47, 148–49; S. O. Hansson 1984: 23–26).

A more systematic and extensive campaign was launched in 1978 during the anti-fund campaign, and Eskilsson was given the mandate and resources to create and manage an ideological apparatus that included three publishing houses, advertising agencies, and a permanent infrastructure to organise seminars, workshops, fairs in municipalities ('Free Enterprise Days'), materials for distribution in schools, through evening newspapers, support for student and youth organizations (see chapter 6). Regional SAF offices were also set up. Particularly important was the cooperation with Liberal and Conservative student politicians, such as Carl Bildt (Gezelius 1992: 133–48).

On a national popular level in advertisements 'Meidner Funds' were connotatively linked with central planning and totalitarianism, presented in black and white images, and were juxtaposed with free enterprise, connotatively linked with freedom of choice, decentralised ownership, initiative and democracy, which were presented in colour. The material was also often targeted so as to interpellate certain groups or towns ('free enterprise – good for Växjö'; 'wage-earner funds concern us barbers too, whether we like it or not'; 'us gas-station owners too, whether we like it or not'). On an intellectual level, the publishing house Timbro published 22 books between 1978 and 1982, half of which were on free markets and wage-earner funds. The publishing house Ratio was oriented towards theoretical and philosophical debate, and also arranged seminars in philosophy and the social sciences on topics pertaining to freedom, democracy and the market. (In the process, some prominent figures of the Swedish New Left, such as Lennart Berntsson, were converted.) In addition to this, SAF and SI continued their support of the more technical think-tanks, SNS and IUI. This elaborate apparatus provided support for the bourgeois parties in the elections of 1979 and 1982, and thus the prerogatives of capital could be defended.

The initiative of this reorientation of SAF was based on domestic factors. However, Timbro, primarily, has in the process forged contacts and now belongs to a network that expanded rapidly in the 1980s. It includes the Institute of Economic Affairs in London, and the American Heritage Foundation.

The strategic defeat of the left: why did the labour movement not mobilise?

The successful mobilisation of the right is a crucial element of an explanation of the failure of the wage-earner fund initiative and the subsequent neo-liberal swing in Sweden. According to Boréus (1994 cited in Blyth 1997: 27), the wage-earner fund issue was won by SAF because it gained the 'proprietorship of the [definition of] ideological concepts' and hence gained the 'high ground' in the definition of ethical concepts such as 'freedom'. This marked a striking departure from the defensive posture that representatives of Swedish capital had really had since 1917.

No doubt, then, the power of capitalist agency in hegemonic struggle was decisive for the outcome. But this does not explain why the labour movement did not mobilise the kind of counter-campaign that had been successful before. The labour movement had been subject to ideological challenges before, and had consolidated its hegemonic position by engaging in ethico-ideological struggle. That was the case with universal suffrage, the new economic policy in the 1930s, and the issue of ATP, for example. What is striking with the wage-earner fund issue is that the labour movement never really mobilised and engaged in an ideological struggle with SAF. Why not?

As indicated above, it is often contended that the wage-earner fund initiative was an intellectual product without much support from the rank and file. This is an assessment which requires some significant qualification. It is true that the Metalworkers' motion of the 1971 Congress – in contrast to the industrial democracy initiatives – emerged due to technical issues pertaining to solidaristic wage policy and economic regulation, conceived by the Metalworkers' research department, that caught very little attention at the 1971 LO congress. It is also true that the labour movement failed to mobilise adequate commitment from the rank and file of the party, to work for the proposal, and they also failed to sufficiently convince even all their core voters. However, it is fair to characterise the emergence of the wage-earner proposal as caused by pressure from below. The main impetus behind the initiative was that, in the wake of the 1969 wildcat strike wave, it became acutely necessary for the unions to do something about the excess profits that solidaristic wage policy generated in the most profitable sectors of industry (Meidner *et al.* 1976: 13–15; Swenson 1989: 85–95). Moreover, the radical version passed at the LO Congress of 1976 would not have become official union policy had it not been due to pressure from below.

The working group that was appointed after the 1971 congress, led by Rudolf Meidner, worked with two potential solutions to the solidaristic wage policy dilemma: 'the small solution' and 'the big solution'. The 'small solution' was a scheme based on the fourth AP fund. 'Excess profits' would be taxed and transferred to a union-controlled equity fund. The 'big solution' was derived from the consistent and logical consideration of the problems that solidaristic wage policy created for the mediation of the full employment and distributive justice criteria in the most productive branches of the economy. How would the unions get at the profits, at a microeconomic level, in the most productive firms, which they could have obtained in firm level bargaining? The big solution led to a recommendation of compulsory share-emissions that in the long run would imply that labour as a collective would achieve a majority share of the ownership of the means of production. Meidner and his co-workers (Anna Hedborg and Gunnar Fond) originally intended the 'big solution' to be a discussion piece. However, they decided to present the ideas in seminar groups with shop stewards and other rank-and-file union activists. It was the overwhelmingly enthusiastic reception of the proposal at this level, and in a survey distributed to the membership, that ensured that the 'big solution' would be presented at the LO Congress of 1976. There it was subsequently passed, and after the passing of the proposal the congress members sang in unison, for the first and last time, the Internationale (Interviewees 11 (March 1993) and 14; see also Pontusson 1987: 13; on the surveys, see Meidner *et al.* 1978).

At the level of rank-and-file activists within the blue-collar union federation – the industrial workers – there was initially quite overwhelming and intensive support for the proposed 'big solution'. If anything the intellectuals tried to strike a cautionary note. Meidner obviously did not back down from his report, but he made a speech to the effect that the delegates should think carefully whether they were prepared to face the political implications of such a radical proposal. The Presidents of LO and the Metalworkers' Union, Gunnar Nilsson and Bert Lundin, while they endorsed the proposal in principle, nevertheless distanced themselves from a commitment to compulsory share emissions (Interviewee 14). The Congress nevertheless passed the Meidner Plan, and even extended its scope to include all firms with over 50 employees, not 500.

Hence, it is very misleading to suggest that the Meidner Plan was devoid of any rank-and-file support. It also had the principal support of LO's leadership. In the context of the radical ideological climate of the time, it was actually thought that the plan provided a way out of the dependency relationship labour and unionists always felt in negotiations with employers and capital owners. This was combined with an absolute mistrust of the prospects of private capital to address the economic difficulties of welfare society.[3]

In short, one can say that the wage-earner fund issue was carried through by the strong support from blue-collar union cadres. This includes both rank-and-file leaders (shop stewards) as well as union bureaucrats and intellectuals at the apex of the unions' organisational structure. However, as Pontusson points out, the labour movement failed to even attempt to mobilise its electorate through a hegemonic 'ethico-political' appeal (Pontusson 1987: 29, 31). This requires an explanation because, firstly, there is strong evidence that, while rank-and-file cadres tend to be more politicised than the average member, there tends to be a strong correlation between the views of the former and the broader membership, and it is reasonable to infer that the unions are generally good at mobilising their membership around their issues (Lewin 1979: 155–57). Secondly, LO had proved itself to be very successful in mobilising the party behind its other radical issues, such as co-determination, in the 1970s. Why did the unions not manage to mobilise their members behind the wage-earner fund issue and why did they not manage to make it a priority for the party?

There are three reasons for this failure to attempt to mobilise. First, there were some significant circumstantial reasons pertaining to the timing of the proposal that had adverse effects. In short, LO and SAP fumbled with the issue at critical junctures.[4] Second, the labour movement failed to anticipate and respond to the mobilisation of SAF. They assumed that the issue could be resolved through the normal tripartite channels of mediation and compromise.

But these can only be considered secondary explanations. Organisations like LO and SAP are run by professional cadres who do not fumble on issues that they are comfortable handling. This lends more support to a third factor. The division of roles that the institutional form of the welfare state itself assigned the different branches of the labour movement made it exceedingly difficult to devise a coherent strategy that would be pursued with vigour and energy. The intellectuals of the party, who ultimately had to make the issue one of electoral politics, were interpellated into a social policy discourse that had no intrinsic interest, or capacity, to deal with an issue pertaining to production politics. Although party intellectuals were by no means necessarily adverse to the idea of wage-earner funds as such, they found it difficult to understand what the significance of the particular technicalities was and why they could not be formulated differently to accommodate political adversaries and to make them easier to explain to the electorate. The issue was 'a strange bird in the political arena' (Interviewee 11).

This seems to confirm the view that the power resources required to mobilise for 'economic democracy' are quite different from those required for social reforms within the post-war historic compromise, as Pontusson suggests. A radical proposal such as the Meidner Plan cannot be implemented through tripartite commissions (Pontusson 1987: 31–33). This in turn points to the obstacles of the organisational form of a reformist strategy within the capitalist state. In fact, in this instance, this organisational form seems to have worked to neutralise the antagonism by demobilising the labour movement.

Politicians primarily connected to the social policy complex, in the Ministry of Social Affairs, and municipal politicians never developed an understanding of the wage-earner fund issue. A rift developed between them and the unions. As a result the issue was politically doomed, because the social service complex constituted significant portions of the political cadres necessary for mobilisation. State managers more closely associated with the Ministry of Finance, such as Feldt, were more positive to the idea of wage-earner funds (in their moderated version of 1981), because they provided a leverage for capital formation and wage restraint.[5] But a countermobilisation to that of SAF, around a radical platform, required a united alliance of trade unionists and welfare state politicians and cadres that never materialised.

Certainly, the limits of the post-war accord, or 'historic compromise', seem to have been important impediments to such an alliance forming. When the labour movement agreed to restrain their reforms to the wage-determination arena (through LO) and the social policy arena, a more integrated perspective on social transformation seems to have disappeared. Social reform was divided into two separate areas.

Paradoxically, for the social services complex it was unfortunate that no mobilisation occurred, and that not even a compromise was achieved with capital, along the lines of the compromise between the Waldenström Report and the LO/SAP proposal of 1981. This would at least have been of benefit to social insurance and service programmes. If the fourth AP fund and the limited wage-earner funds of 1983 are an indicator, such funds would have provided an impressive pool of capital for high productivity investments that would lead to taxable production that could have served to sustain the welfare state. This would have been in sharp contrast to the productive and speculative capital outflows of the 1980s.

Why the economic policy of the Third Way in the 1980s?

The wage-earner fund issue is best explained by exploring the relationship between the terms of popular discourse and the internal dynamic of the mass political parties and organisations considered as a whole. The shift towards a social democratic compensatory neo-liberalism in the mid-1980s, primarily expressed in the norms-based monetary policy of 1985, is best assessed by a more limited focus on the ideology and motivation of Social Democratic state managers in the Ministry of Finance. This is because this initiative, although it had profound effects on Swedish society, was never established as policy through the procedures of mass politics. It was exclusively an executive decision formulated and executed by a small group of senior officials in the Ministry of Finance and the Bank of Sweden. It was indicated earlier that not even the Prime Minister played a role here. He approved by deferring to the Minister of Finance ('You do what you want; I don't understand anything anyway'). While a norms-based monetary policy took effect, formulated according to a neo-liberal logic, Palme spoke about the economic policy as building on solidarity, in opposition to neo-liberal logic (Palme 1987: 102–03).

Why did this brand of neo-liberalism gain prominence as a paradigm within the Ministry of Finance and the Central Bank? It is impossible to isolate analytically any neat and clear-cut causal variables and patterns. Nevertheless it is possible to go beyond a vague identification of a set of overdetermined processes. The patterns are surely overdetermined rather than causal and linear. However, some patterns are more determining than others.

One can derive two hypotheses to explain this paradigmatic shift to neo-liberalism. First, it may be that the norms-based policy – the clearest instance of a compensatory neo-liberal policy – was formed because of the influence of transnational elite networks as discussed in chapter 5. This is a plausible hypothesis. Social Democratic state managers as well as corporate leaders are represented in the private planning bodies identified by Gill and van der Pijl.[6] They are also represented in key strategic public multilateral forums in the OECD, the IMF and perhaps most importantly in the BIS (of which the Bank of Sweden Governor, Bengt Dennis, became the Chair). Moreover Dennis, Feldt and some of the other senior officials emerged on the ladder from deputy ministerial posts in government branches with a high degree of international exposure, such as the Ministry of Trade (Webb 1989).

No doubt, then, these actors are part of a network of transnational elites, which has important socialisation effects. But one should be wary of reducing the ideological shift to this. First, these fora do not necessarily imply ideological homogeneity. Indeed, Gösta Rehn himself worked within the OECD, advocating cooperation between capital and labour in the embedded liberal era, but this did not preclude a radical expression of such cooperation as exercised in the Swedish case. Secondly, the most striking aspect of the neo-liberal conversion is not the fact that it took place, but that when it did take place it was seen as the most natural thing in the world for the officials in question. By the mid-1980s, it seemed natural for officials in the Central Bank and the Ministry of Finance to deal with the problem of inflation in the way that they did. Whilst transnational deliberation was useful and important on a technical level, participation in these fora was not experienced as a metamorphosis which changed the problem definition and broad formulation of policy. At the most such participation was experienced as validating (Interviewee 10). To conclude, then, an explanation that would attribute a decisive causality to these transnational elite fora would be hard pressed to explain why these state managers were so receptive and in tune with the compensatory neo-liberal paradigm in the first place. The fact that they were, made the neo-liberal transition, at the level of political society and the state, highly consensual and relatively devoid of antagonism – a crucial element in a process of transnational hegemonic diffusion of norms of governance.

Another thesis, advanced notably by Villy Bergström, former director of the Trade Union Institute of Economic Research, also attempts to explain the shift with reference to business sponsored agencies. But in this case the focus is on think-tanks in Sweden itself that transmitted the intellectually authoritative ideas of academic economists. He points to the particular importance of the reports of the Economic Policy Council (*konjunkturrådet*) of the business sponsored think-tank SNS (formed by Browaldh in the 1940s, see chapter 3), and seminars organised by the same organisation. These seminars, where senior figures of the state agencies in question also participated, served as a cosy forum where the intellectual shift could take place. According to Bergström, this forum served as an intellectual transmission belt of the neo-classical revolution in economic theory, as formulated by

Lucas and Friedman, for Swedish academic economists who partook in the international neo-classical revolution in their discipline in the 1970s and 1980s and used their position in the SNS to popularise its message. This seems a rather domestic and local explanation. This is not quite the case, because the function and strategy of organisations of the SNS are replicated elsewhere; SNS is part of a network that includes the British Policy Studies Institute and Institut der deutschen Wirtschaft and Institut de l'Enterprise (eg. Söderström 1989). After a time lag, according to Bergström (who must be considered a participant observer in this context), the paradigm of the SNS was then transmitted to economic policy elites. Indeed, Bergström goes so far as to suggest that the *policy* is transmitted, and he does provide empirical evidence:

> [SNS is to be congratulated on their remarkable success] in having their recommendations translated into actual economic policy. One some-times has the impression that the Ministry of Finance has read SNS's latest recommendations page by page [and copied them] . . . In 1985 SNS recommended the change that was completed in the budget [of 1991]. [SNS] introduced the concept of non-accomodating economic policy based on norms. [SNS] demanded fixed exchange rates, a deregulation of the credit market, free capital movements and a tax reform that abolished the elements of income-levelling in the taxation system. It was suggested that economic policy should prioritise price stability over full employment, though the latter had been the most important goal since 1933. . . . the reports that followed each and every one of these elements were in turn elaborated . . . in 1989 the main thesis was that Sweden should join the EC . . . I do not want to suggest that all that was recommended was wrong. However, the overall impression is that of a government that piece by piece has dismantled its own [intellectual] economic-political apparatus without coming up with anything new independently.
>
> (Bergström 1993: 160–61, my translation)

Bergström is content to leave his analysis at the level of SNS as such. The late Sven Grassman (1986) – a Keynesian economist who was once 'part of the gang' of economists but who was increasingly marginalised by his profession – infers a connection to economic interest. Mark Blyth (1997) has analysed this in greater detail in recent years and has connected it to the neo-liberal shift of Swedish business and its increasingly conscious intervention in ideological struggle. Large sums of money were offered to university departments by business foundations, to investigate questions of particular interest to business, such as profitability and inflation. According to Grassman, this created a new set of central concepts and statistical indicators that would re-shape and re-forge economic reality. This connects with the Foucauldian literature of 'governmentality' in recent years and the importance of concept formation in defining the objects to be governed and regulated, indeed in making them governable (Dean 1995).

This is very strong evidence, and again it points to the power and success of a subtle hegemonic strategy forged by Swedish business in not only halting the red wave but in neo-liberalising the intersubjective framework through which governance and regulation are formulated. In this context, the aura of academic authority that economic experts possess in Sweden has been successfully mobilised. Economists command great authority as 'independent experts' in Swedish political society. I pointed earlier to the role of the Stockholm school in the forging of post-war economic policy in Sweden. In the 1930s, it was the Social Democrats that managed to mobilise the authority of this expertise. In the 1980s SAF, understood as a hegemonic party, had managed to do the same. It should be pointed out in this context that some of the key personnel of the Ministry of Finance during the 1980s were recruited from academic circles, for example Klas Eklund. In addition, most of the senior officials of that era had been trained by academic economists at the Stockholm School of Economics and the Universities of Stockholm and Uppsala. Hence the relationship between the academic economic paradigm and the policy economic paradigm is crucial to our explanation.

Nevertheless, the problem in ending the explanation here is that it does not answer the question of *why* Swedish social democrats, with historically strong intellectual resources of economic expertise and paradigm formation (eg. the legacy of Myrdal and the Rehn–Meidner model) were by the 1980s so open to neo-liberal ideas. In other words, it does not explain the incredible degree of receptiveness that made the entire transmission in the state so smooth. The alternative economic intellectual tradition of social democracy seems to have totally disappeared as a discourse considered relevant for policy formulation in the Ministry of Finance. In this context, it is important to underline that to remain at the level of grand economic theory is to engage in reified analysis. While the state managers in question are trained economists, they do not approach their concrete policy process consciously at such a high level of theoretical abstraction. It is more appropriate to suggest that their economic training operates as a background grammar, a 'positive unconscious' (Poulantzas 1978) that shapes the manner in which they interpret economic signals and reality. What shaped this positive subconscious behind the practices of the Central Bank and more crucially the Ministry of Finance so as to generate this receptiveness?

First, it should be pointed out that substantively there is an elective affinity between the rather restrictive, but radically counter-cyclical, version of Keynesianism advocated by the Rehn–Meidner model and monetarism. This is especially so if one interprets the Rehn–Meidner model as the Ministry of Finance has done, with more emphasis on wage restraint and less emphasis on selective measures and collective savings and capital formation. From both vantage points, one would balk at the deficits and the inflation of the 1970s generated by 'vulgar Keynesianism'. Hence one could argue that there actually was an element of continuity between the restrictive policy stances of the 1980s and those of the 1950s and 1960s.[7] In this context it should be pointed out that a norm stating that the state should not borrow abroad was not new. Such a borrowing norm was a component part of the policy routines of the Swedish model. It was abandoned first in 1977, as Sweden defected from the European monetary snake, and this abandonment was much criticised by the Social Democrats, even during their 'radical phase' in the 1970s (Sweden. Riksdagens Motioner 1980/81: 1136 (Olof Palme *et al.*): 16).

However, given the structural reconfigurations associated with global financial markets, the circumstances and the effects of such a norm have completely changed. The borrowing norm as formulated in the 1950s and 1960s existed in the context of highly regulated nationally based financial markets and this makes a world of difference. It is one thing to pursue a restrictive fiscal policy in the context of a regulated money market to ensure a profits squeeze and contain wage drift. It is quite another matter to pursue a fiscal policy to assert market-determined interest rate discipline.

This brings us to the crucial determinant that explains the openness to neo-liberalism in the Ministry of Finance. What also changed was the justification for the norm and the rationality of governance that lies behind the norm. This is clearly evident in the mode of reasoning by Deputy Minister of Finance, Erik Åsbrink, in 1985. Critiquing the policy of borrowing pursued from 1977 to the early 1980s, Åsbrink states:

> When the state started to borrow abroad, it abolished the only existing *natural correction mechanism*. Deficits in the balance of payments ought to lead to an increase in the interest rate, through a foreign currency outflow, which in turn will lead to adjustments in the economy at large.
> (Sweden Ministry of Finance 1985: 58; my translation and emphasis)

The key term in the quote is, of course, 'natural correction mechanism'. Here we have explicit evidence of the Ministry of Finance invoking an image that directly opposes de-commodification. In the context of this discourse, de-commodification would be 'unnatural'.

I would argue that, whilst important for the overall explanation, the shift of academic discourse to neo-classicism, with due connection to business interests, does not explain why Social Democratic policy elites could become receptive to this discourse. The next section is devoted towards answering that question.

Why Swedish social democratic economic policy makers became neo-liberals: mutations in the form of social democratic discourse

Why did Social Democratic state managers in the Ministry of Finance become receptive to neo-classical discourse? To begin to answer this question I would like to contrast the mode of reasoning of Åsbrink in 1985 with that of the founders of the 'new economic policy' in the 1930s. I will then trace changes in the discourse that took place through time between the 1930s and the 1980s. I will suggest a focus on *the manner in which economic arguments are made in order to be considered 'serious speech acts'* that is the *form* of discourse, as opposed to the content of policy ('socialisation' versus 'Keynesianism' versus 'monetarism'). (That is, what Foucault with reference to scientific discourse calls the 'episteme' [Foucault 1970] and what the governmentality literature, following Foucault, call 'rationalities' with reference to policy-discourse [eg. Dean 1995: 560]). With such a focus it becomes clear that whilst the golden age of Fordist social democratic regulation was one of stability in the content of policy, it was nevertheless a period of profound transformation in the form of prevailing social democratic economic policy discourse (see Box 7.1). It is this change of form that enables us to explain the receptiveness of social democratic elites to compensatory neo-liberal policy in the 1980s.

Box 7.1

The Marxist rejection of Marxism and rationale for the 'new economic policy' . . .

Revisionists do not deny that the tendencies to concentration and immiseration are operative in capitalist development. But since these tendencies do not act upon dead material, but on living human beings, the latter resist, and this countertendency may be so forceful that it not only halts the original tendency, but even generates – albeit slow – improvements in the living conditions of the working class.

(Ernst Wigforss 1914 in 1971)

Nothing seems more certain than that [in the wake of the new economic policy] the old has passed, in the sense of the free market capitalist system that the old socialists saw and struggled against. It has been in transformation for a long time now, and the question is, what is the shape of the new that will be generated by this transformation. It is possible that it will be a development that is not too unlike that once predicted by Marx – with more centralism and less freedom of movement than most of us would wish. If one wants to call that Marxism, then the rescue from Marxist predictions lies in allowing the transformation to be guided by the ideas of democratic socialism that are the guiding norms of the work of Social Democracy.

(Ernst Wigforss 1949)

The well known fact that the catastrophic collapse of the capitalist system, predicted by the labour movement in its first epoch, has been continuously pushed ahead into the future is in and of itself affirmation that the prediction was faulty. But the error was not due to fauly premises and method. This crisis-theory rests on a firmer ground than many nowadays believe, insofar as it seeks the root of the problem in capital formation, as opposed to in monetary disruptions, customs-boundaries, and suchlike that rather are symptoms. The effects of the latter render matters more difficult to be sure, but they are not the root of the evil.

The old Marxian crisis theory was on the right track. Its faulty conclusions were not due to an error of judgement about the factors that were known; the errors were due to the fact that the actual course of events were affected by unknown and unforeseen factors. To the latter one should, above all, mention the labour movement itself with all its results on the trade-union and political fronts.

(Karl Fredriksson 1933)

. . . is left by the wayside by the piecemeal social engineers following the spirit of Myrdal and Popper

The discussion about Marxism should in this context not continue, but be brought to end by a contention of principle, that actually is a truism that often is forgotten. It concerns the notion that a political ideology should be scientific. A scientific theory is only true or not untrue, and never in itself political . . . Insofar as we act consciously, we follow our values and we can never say whether they are true or false . . . Therefore, a discussion about the Marxist world view becomes completely uninteresting . . . [Concerning] social science: it can show us, if it is correct, what possibilities we have to realise a political program and what tools we have at our disposal. However, it says nothing about what alternative we *should* choose.

Full employment in a society with stagnating population-growth is always subject to inflation-risks. Instruments for expansionary policy must therefore be complemented with new instruments of investment control, regional planning . . .

. . . it has been close at hand to take examples from the economic-political field to illustrate the 'new ideology' But it is not restricted to this field. Our growing knowledge in social psychology, pedagogy, and social medicine can make it possible to realise programs in ever more areas of life, where previously we only had vague and general aspirations.

(Krister Wickman and Roland Pålson 1948)

In the theory of economic policy, there is one elementary rule that says, that the number of economic political means in general must (at least) equal the number of ends. This is actually rather self-evident, and it can be illustrated through a simple analogy: A tram, which only is to move in one dimension (along the track) can in principle be steered with one lever (the accelerator). A car, on the other hand, has to move in two dimensions (the surface of the earth), and needs at least two levers (accelerator and steering wheel). An aeroplane has to be manoeuvred in three dimensions (in space) and one needs at least three levers. The three dimensional ends of the economic policy also requires the authorities to manoeuvre in 'three dimensions'; one should simultaneously steer the price-level, the employment level and the balance of payments; to suggest that one would manage this task merely through monetary policy would be as to suggest that one should fly a plane merely with an accelerator.

(Bent Hansen 1956)

. . . which in turn creates the space for the neo-classical utilitarians

In traditional socialist rhetoric, the market system has been accused for an inability to appropriately use our productive resources, and for failing to meet 'essential human needs' . . . As a description of the functioning of the capitalist system, this is probably true. However, one must observe that in a highly developed industrial society, as in the Swedish case, where the general end of economic policy cannot be specified further, than to aim for an ever increasing wealth and individual welfare, one lacks other criteria for 'essential human needs' than those that the human beings themselves express in the economic action.

That a highly developed welfare society needs a large public sector . . . that is not steered by individual free choice, ought to be a generally accepted notion.

The essential is, however, that the general principle of a maximum individually determined satisfaction of needs operates, and the means [of policy] must be an effective market allocation. A system of free relative price-formation, free competition between types of firms and production processes is to date the only known mechanism, that gives the

consumer a decent supply of goods and services that correspond to their
preferences.

(Kjell-Olof Feldt 1961)

When the state started to borrow abroad, it abolished the only *natural
correction mechanism*. Deficits in the balance of payments ought to lead
to an increase in the interest rate, through foreign currency outflow,
which in turn will lead to adjustments in the economy at large.

(Erik Åsbrink 1985; my emphasis)

To begin to explore this, consider the manner in which one would have
expected the founders of the 'new economic policy' in the 1930s to respond
to the problem of achieving non-inflationary methods to address unemployment. That is, how would one approach the problem of the 1980s from the
vantage point of the discourse of Ernst Wigforss, Gunnar Myrdal and others?

Recalling the argument in chapter 3, from the vantage point of the 1930s
one would not construe the problem as one of conforming to natural economic laws. Rather, one would construe it as a problem of capitalism as a
mode of production, which required counter-acting planning. While the
chief Social Democratic economic intellectuals of the time, Ernst Wigforss,
Karl Fredriksson, and especially Gunnar Myrdal, were critical of orthodox
Marxism as a guide for economic policy (they favoured what later would be
called 'Keynesianism'), they nevertheless subscribed to Marxian, or at least
proto-Marxian, explanations of capitalist economic contradictions and class
struggle. They construed the depression of the 1930s as a crisis of the capitalist system generated by uneven development (Wigforss and Fredriksson
in Box 7.1). In other words, the object of regulation was a productive but
contradictory and socially unjust social system whose regulation formed a
part of the strategy of the labour movement engaged in a reformist class
struggle. This is in contrast to the object of regulation in the 1980s, which is
conceived in terms of a set of interacting utility maximising individuals (see
Åsbrink quoted in Box 7.1), with which they engaged in an explicit polemic.

Wigforss, Fredriksson and others differed from Marxist doctrines of the
time (both the doctrine of the Second International and the Comintern),
because they opposed socialisation of the means of production as a grand
strategy of class struggle. Instead they believed that the working class could
and should mobilise around a pragmatic programme of economic planning
for full employment, where counter-cyclical economic policy would play an
immediate and prominent role. But *their rejection of Marxism used a Marxian
mode of reasoning*. As argued in chapter 3, their outlook was influenced by
Austro-Marxist debates, and Otto Bauer's concept of 'misrationalization'
guided their reformist strategy (eg. Sweden. SOU 1935a).

The Swedish Social Democrats of the 1930s had no inhibitions against drawing on 'bourgeois' economics as a guide for planning. Wigforss followed the English debate carefully and was especially influenced by Liberals such as Keynes and Beveridge. Domestic sources of influence included the radical liberal economist, Knut Wicksell, who had devised a theory of counter-cyclical monetary policy, and who argued for the rationality of income redistribution. Wicksell was the key mentor of the Stockholm School, to which, of course Gunnar Myrdal belonged. But the rationality of the discourse (as defined above) was still structured along Marxian lines. This Marxian–Keynesian synthesis constituted the intellectual background to the new economic policy pursued by Social Democrats since 1932 (U. Olsson 1994; Wigforss, Box 7.1). Wigforss, then, construed the 'new economic policy' as a reformist initiative that acted as a counter-tendency to uneven development as construed in Marxian crisis theory.

How can this be related to the policy shift in 1985 in a process of discursive transformation and mutation? Clearly, this Marxian–Keynesian synthesis – that could perhaps be labelled a 'labour-strategic Keynesianism' – is obviously not apparent among the state managers in 1985. Even by the late 1940s it had given way to a new articulation, which one might label the 'technocratic Keynesianism' of piecemeal social engineering. This rearticulation is the beginning of the process that made it possible for social democratic economic state managers to interpret the crisis of the 1970s and the 1980s, not as a crisis-tendency of capitalism that needed to be met with counter-vailing regulation but as the falsification of Keynesian ideas that validated the 'null hypothesis' of monetarism.[8] Bauer's conception of a rationalising but contradictory capitalist mode of production, in which the reformist labour movement engaged in a pragmatic class struggle, had been replaced by a Popperian world view, where the world is a laboratory for social engineers and an object for engineers to rationally manipulate.

It was the rise of a technocratic Keynesianism that shaped the form of policy discourse so as to make possible the articulation of social democratic neo-liberalism in 1985. There is an element of social engineering thinking in the Austro-Marxist rationality insofar as it accepts experimentation of policy-relevant ideas. But its Marxist conception of the capitalist mode of production constitutes a formidable constraint on the type of policy experimentation that is consistent with the discourse.

A definite opening to a neo-liberal discourse occurred in the 1940s when these 'problem-solving ideas' began to be articulated *in explicit opposition* not only to socialisation but also to a Marxist rationality and world view. That is, in the rearticulation from a strategic Keynesianism to a technocratic one. This rearticulation was decisively completed early in the post-war period. Indeed the passage of Wigforss, quoted in 1949, was the last version of a 'class-strategic Keynesian' text written by a senior official in *Tiden*, the theoretical-ideological journal of the Swedish labour movement. One year earlier, a young intellectual, who had just begun a brilliant career as Social

Democratic administrator and politician, would make up with the Marxist past (Wickman and Pålsson, Box 7.1). I am referring to Krister Wickman, who was encountered in the last chapter as the Minister of Industry in the early 1970s, but who held many senior posts in the Ministry of Finance and who also served a term as governor of the Bank of Sweden. His article, which dismissed the epistemology of dialectics, evoked Popper and challenged the 'metaphysics' of Marxism. In other words, whereas Myrdal's (1928) ideas had been part of a synthesis of Marxism, they now were defined in opposition to Marxism.[9]

At the same time, Wickman and Pålsson did not spare the 'metaphysics' of neo-classical economics. In this regard they invoked Myrdal's influential book, *The Political Element in the Development of Economic Theory* (1928). Following the suggested procedure of this book, Social Democratic state managers, following technocratic Keynesianism, were careful to point out that the normative dimension was external to economic theory itself. Economic theory was still a tool for political actors. But henceforth Marxism and Keynesianism were defined as opposites. Consequently the metaphors of class struggle and uneven development were replaced by economic policy 'levers', steering economies like 'trams, cars, or aeroplanes'. Classes were often replaced by individuals as the referent object of regulation (Hansen, Box 7.1).

This did not necessarily imply a conservative shift to the right in terms of the content of economic policy, which was left-institutionalist. Indeed, the content of economic policy seemed to have crystallised and assumed a definite shape. It was indeed this intellectual environment which produced the Rehn–Meidner model and it was indeed on this basis that Meidner concluded that wage-earner funds of the 1976 variety would be necessary (Meidner 1980: 343–69). But under the surface profound epistemic shifts had occurred and the new discursive form was open to neo-classical articulations.

The first (in terms of economic policy content, imperceptible) development took place in the early 1960s, when a new generation of state managers started to emerge from the ranks of the bureaucracy. Among those who would become the most prominent, one can indeed mention Kjell-Olof Feldt (Box 7.1) as well as Assar Lindbeck (1961), who had graduated from academic institutions where the teaching of economics had been standardised along the lines of neo-classical articulations of Keynesianism. Hence, what is notable with this new generation is that they invoked yet another form of discourse, another rationality, which indeed is the utilitarian one that Myrdal (1928) had criticised. Here the object of regulation is indeed utility-maximising individuals interacting on a social plane without internal contradictions and social cleavages that are constitutive to this terrain. All traces of the capitalist mode of production have disappeared.

How was it possible for such a discourse to be tolerated in the apparatuses of social democratic regulation when they contradicted Myrdal? First, it is important to note that as policy-makers this was merely a reflection of the grammar of their policy conception and action. It was quite possible for pragmatic Social Democratic ministers to appoint talented and technically capable individuals to manage the standard operational procedures of the welfare state (for a self-description, see Feldt 1994). In 1960, Feldt is also keen to justify his outlook with reference to historical stages (with echoes of 'the affluent society' in the background). During the golden age itself, these epistemic differences in the form of discourse were not decisive.

However, at the time of the crisis in 1980 the rationality of the discourse became important, because it determined the framework of interpretation when standard operational procedures had to be abandoned and replaced or reformulated. I would contend that the absence of a rationality framework *qua* Austo-Marxism and the predominance of a neo-classical framework decisively determined the openness and smoothness with which the Ministry of Finance internalised the kind of prescriptions that the SNS formulated. For by that time, the junior officials of the 1960s (such as Feldt) had risen to ministerial posts and had appointed other economists with similar training at the deputy level (such as Åsbrink) who did not even bother to reflexively situate their utilitarianism with reference to the particular historical stage of the affluent society (Åsbrink, Box 7.1). Hence, the Ministry of Finance interpreted the inflationary crisis of the 1980s as a falsification of Keynesian ideas and neoclassical monetarism was for the Ministry of Finance the only available remedy to address the problem of inflation. What is so striking about this is that the conception of the object of regulation (utilitarian individualism) was so out of step with the collective class actors (the trade unions) whose conformity to the inflation goal the strategy presupposed.

This sounds like a very idealist explanation. It is not intended to be. First, it should be noted that I am only trying to reconstruct a dynamic which has other moments (globalisation, the mobilisation of Swedish business acting on its interests) in order to explain the openness of Social Democratic economic policy to neo-liberalism. I am not claiming that this is the determining moment; it is just one moment that makes the explanation more complete. Secondly, discourse is not to be understood as 'ideas' as opposed to 'matter'. Discourses are part of concrete practices intimately connected to social reproduction, including its material aspects, in this case the paradigm of a mode of regualtion.

Can one identify any logic driving this changing epistemic framework of Social Democratic state managers? My argument will have to be somewhat speculative here. I think one can consider Göran Therborn's (1980) distinction of different modes of organisation in different state apparatuses to be relevant here. He differentiates between managerial technocracy, based on technical and scientific expertise, and cadre-organisation based on collective mass organisation. The older generation of Social Democrats that were succeeded after the war (Wigforss, Hansson, Möller, Sköld) were educated as cadres, and had already been active in 1917. The post-war generation, primarily influenced by Gunnar Myrdal, became technocratic managers – the engineers of the welfare state.[10] And it is indeed striking that the shifts of rationality in the economic policy discourse seem to stand in a co-determined relationship with the process through which social democracy is established as the agent of regulation of capitalism in Sweden. This should remind us of Poulantzas who in his argument on the 'institutional materiality' of the capitalist state emphasised the importance of the form of state ideology in biasing state action so as to favour the representation of capital.

> it is therefore not so much a question of the ideology constituted, systematised, and formulated by the organic intellectuals of the bourgeoisie – which always is a second order ideology – as it is the primary and 'spontaneous' forms of ideology that are secreted by the social division of labour and directly embodied in the state apparatuses and the practices of power.
>
> (Poulantzas 1978: 66, cited in Jessop 1985: 225)

Viewed in this way, it is also possible to find a common denominator with the failure of social democracy to mobilise around the wage-earner issue, when the 'division of labour' of social regulation between the trade unions and the social services complex precluded the development of a comprehensive hegemonic strategy.

Social democratic neo-liberalism, I think, is an apt term to describe the paradigm of social democratic economic regulation in Sweden after 1985. It should be contrasted with another strand of social democratic thought that emerged in response to the New Left bringing Marxism back on the agenda. This is the strand of thought that is reflected in the early works of power mobilisation theory, such as that of Himmestrand and Korpi. The latter was in fact employed by the Metalworkers' association to investigate the causes of the wildcat strikes of 1969 and 1974, when he began to connect with earlier strands of social democratic thought to develop his theory. With the thought of Rudolf Meidner this also connected with the more radical versions of the institutionalist tradition (1980). But this tendency towards a resurrection of the 'labour-strategic' discourse has been marginalised, initially to the trade unions, and later to sociology departments and research institutes with a subordinate role in the ensemble of social regulation. It has yet to succeed in taking advantage of the vacuum generated by the fact that social democratic neo-liberalism has failed to achieve national popular appeal, let alone full support by the party elite (in the party, trade unions, and even in subordinate state apparatuses). Yet it is on this intellectual terrain that one might begin to formulate comprehensive counter concepts of governance to those of social democratic neo-liberalism. It has been the purpose of this book to point to the continued latent potential of this legacy of the Swedish model for the European left. (It is not to be understood as a distinctly Swedish accomplishment since much of its intellectual sources were borrowed or copied from abroad). It has also been the purpose of the book to endow it with a measure of self-consciousness so as to make a modest contribution towards revitalising its energy.

Conclusion

The title of this book, *Capitalist Restructuring, Globalisation and the Third Way: lessons from the Swedish model*, may seem like an oxymoron. The discourse of the Third Way as presently articulated in social democratic modernisation discussions is premised on the irrelevance of the Swedish model. This book goes against the stream in that it asserts that the case of Swedish social democracy remains a crucial case in considerations about renewal of the European left.

The case of Swedish social democracy remains a crucial case in a positive sense, because it is not true that the institutional legacy of the universal welfare state, outlined in chapters 3 and 4, based on the norms of social citizenship and de-commodification, is *passé*. On the contrary, as argued in the theoretical discussion in chapter 1, it is crucial to hold on to that legacy if the democratisation and pluralisation of the welfare state, necessary for democratic legitimacy and governance in a post-traditional society, is to be plausible. It is also crucial to hold on to the legacy of this type of social policy regime in order to reconcile economic and distributional rationality in a post-industrial society so as to make these compatible with the democratisation advocated in chapter 1. In these chapters, I argued with the Esping-Andersen of 1990 against the Esping-Andersen of 1996 and with the Giddens of 'no authority without democracy' against the Giddens of 'no rights without responsibilities'. What allowed me to do this was regulation-theoretical analysis of Fordism and empirical works on the microeconomic dynamics of the labour market and in work organisation in Sweden in the late 1980s and early 1990s. This work was used to falsify the 'moral hazard' and 'sclerosis' thesis that has been advanced by economists in their critique of the Swedish welfare state. Against such arguments, I provided empirical evidence which supported the assertion made by Leborgne and Lipietz in 1988, that the universal welfare state and de-commodification potentially provided a viable institutional form for a socially progressive post-Fordism.

Contemporary advocates of the Third Way would probably agree with me that the Swedish model also is crucial for modernisation discussions on the left in a negative sense. The remarkably dramatic Swedish economic crisis in the early 1990s was perhaps more than anything an expression of the constraints that the contemporary global economy exerts on welfare capitalism. The crisis culminated in a speculative run on the Swedish crown that brought overnight rates up to 500 per cent at one point, expressing itself in years of negative growth and a dramatic 'convergence' of Sweden with the other mass unemployment societies of Europe. This book has underlined this by explaining how the Swedish model fundamentally presupposed the embedded liberal multilateral system of Bretton Woods (chapters 3 and 4) and by showing in chapter 6 how the forces of globalisation, as accounted for in chapter 5, intervened in Swedish socio-political and socio-economic developments to produce the outcome of the early 1990s.

But chapters 5 and 6 also constitute a critique of those who consider globalisation an intransitive and objective process to which political subjects inevitably must yield. Rather, these chapters explained how the structural power of capital which is constitutive of contemporary globalisation, was in a decisive sense itself constituted by powerful and transitive subjective forces that govern the global political economy. Following Gill, chapter 5 named the content of this governance 'disciplinary neo-liberalism'.

Chapter 6 argued that disciplinary neo-liberalism most aptly describes socio-economic governance in Sweden since the mid-1980s, which represented a profound departure from the economic paradigm that hitherto had been hegemonic in Sweden since the 1930s. This shift pre-empted the radical democratic response to Fordist crisis, which I maintain would have been necessary to realise 'no authority without democracy'. Instead it consolidated a particular type of neo-liberal restructuring in Sweden, which I have called 'compensatory neo-liberalism' and which is commensurate with the norms of the Third Way, which in turn can aptly be called 'social democratic neo-liberalism'. Disciplinary neo-liberalism assigns great importance to stability, but disciplinary neo-liberalism was anything but stable as it interacted with, re-shaped, weakened and displaced the institutions of the Swedish model.

In the short-run, this created a highly contradictory hybrid type of socio-economic regulation. It is my thesis that this hybrid was generated through disciplinary neo-liberal leadership and that it caused the economic crisis in the early 1990s. Politically though, this set the stage for further neo-liberalisation as institutions, organisations and actors, including the trade unions, succumbed and from a position of weakness were disciplined in a neo-liberal direction. It helped in this context, of course, that the 'traditional' Swedish model and the radical project of the 1970s could be blamed for the crisis (Sweden. SOU 1993) – a story which is flawed but which social democratic 'modernisers' have accepted. At the same time, the crisis halted tendencies towards a 'hyper-liberal' Thatcherite development. Hence one can talk of a consolidated compensatory neo-liberalism in Sweden, which has resulted in a relative re-commodification of social relations. In comparative terms, this is still a relatively egalitarian society because of the retrenched version of the universal welfare state that remains despite all. But it is also a very fragile constellation not least because of its vulnerability to transnational dependencies. It should also be pointed out that there is little popular enthusiasm for the constellation. The transnational business class that led the transformation has not managed to give the vision of a society of possessive individuals universal appeal in a society with relatively entrenched welfarist sentiments. The Social Democratic elites that retreated from their radical agenda, implemented and consolidated compensatory neo-liberalism, have seen their party reduced from one that enjoyed the electoral support of 45 per cent of the electorate to one that barely commands 30 per cent. The main beneficiaries of this have been populist parties to the left of social democracy. These fragilities and lack of popular appeal make further change likely, but the direction of that change is not certain.

Intellectual practice that aims to promote change in line with the spirit of the labour movement, social democracy and the left, if not with the contemporary leadership of their organisations (from which the spirit has positively flown), does indeed have to come to terms with globalisation and the transnational nature of the present (Patomäki 2000). It should come as no surprise that here I fall into line with those who consider the objectivity of globalisation to be overstated and who see it as a human artefact that can be countered with alternative politics and policy. Such policy would imply a transnational mix of supranational economic regulation and cooperation, above all to counteract the structural power of capital which depends on 'territorial non-correspondence'. It would include the political construction of boundaries to make autonomy and autocentric spaces of human self-governance and the construction of 'distributive growth coalitions' possible in specific locales (Hirst and Thompson 1999: 191–227). I will not say more than that on the issue here, except to (re-)submit in a derivative way the analytical discussion of post-Fordism in chapter 2 and the Swedish reform agenda in the 1970s, presented in chapter 6, as still relevant and fruitful sources in this endeavour. In my view, the latter was the product of the best of social democratic thinking: the synthesis of pragmatic institutionalist functionalism and historical materialist social strategic thinking.

But it is important to underline that social democracy in its present neo-liberal incarnation is part of what constrains such political aspirations and part of a problem that must be understood. After all it is social democratic governments that have consolidated neo-liberalism in Europe, not least in Sweden. It is with respect to this problem that Sweden is a crucial case study, perhaps approaching a critical case study in Eckstein's (1976) sense. One can reasonably argue that Sweden is the case where a neo-liberalisation of social democratic politics was the least likely to occur. Nevertheless a neo-liberalisation of Swedish social democracy did take place. If one can identify the determinants of this shift, in the absence of other determinants that occur in other cases, one might be well placed to gain insight into what are the more decisive factors behind neo-liberalisation of social democratic elites. It was the purpose of chapter 7 to shed light on this in order to advance our understanding of the nature of neo-liberal hegemony.

As Pontusson (1988) has argued (with reference to Przeworski), Swedish social democracy had been exceedingly successful in incorporating the white-collar electorate into its electoral bloc through the institutions of its welfare state and did not face the electoral dilemma of other parties, as the British Labour Party did. Furthermore, Swedish social democracy had played a leadership role in the shaping of economic policy and had developed a tradition and organisation for independent economic policy thinking. Not least the trade unions had been prominent in this context. This is in contrast to the case of Germany where economic policy routines and paradigmatic thinking during the *Wirtschaftswunder* was shaped by the Christian Democrats and Freiburg Liberals through Erhard. But there was nevertheless a neo-liberalisation of Swedish social democracy in the 1980s, despite the fact that these factors, often held up as explanatory variables for social-democratic rightward shifts, were absent. Why then did Swedish social democratic elites at the commanding heights of social regulation become neo-liberals?

There is no doubt that the structural power of capital and the active mobilisation of business played an important role. The structural force of capital mobility was experienced as real enough (though it was not avoided and it was deliberately enhanced). The business sponsored think-tank, SNS, through the authority of academic economists, was crucial in transmitting neo-liberal ideas to policy-makers in the Ministry of Finance. Public multi-lateral fora seem to have been more validating than determining in this process. However, the SNS was itself part of a transnational network.

But if we are to take seriously the notion that hegemony is most manifestly expressed when antagonism and the need for persuasion and conversion is notable with its absence, then these factors are not sufficient as an explanation. They do not explain why the social democratic economic policy elite, which led the 'natural party of government' since the 1930s, and that had its own independent tradition of economic policy thinking, often developed in polemic with academic economists, was so open to these ideas in the 1980s. By then, in contrast to the 1930s, the state managers in question already shared 'common sense' with the neo-classical economists. How is one to explain the emergence of this 'common sense' of the state managers?

Here I made the case for not focusing on the content of the policy paradigm, but rather looking at the form of its discourse. That is, I investigated what Poulantzas (1978) called 'the positive unconscious' of state managers, which determines what constitutes a 'serious speech act' (Foucault 1970) – the rationality – of economic policy. Here I found profound changes in the discourse during the golden age of the Swedish model itself which opened up within social democracy a flank for neo-liberal thinking. Since this change corresponds with the establishment of social democracy as the regulator of capitalism in Sweden, it suggests that Poulantzas was correct that there is something in the 'institutional materiality' in the social division between the economy and the state in capitalism that generates these effects. The internal demobilisation of social democracy in the political struggle over wage-earner funds lends further credibility to the importance of this. In this case, the formal division of labour between social policy managers and trade unionists resulted in competing conceptions and misunderstandings that prevented them from forming an alliance to put pressure on the economic managers and to counter the hyper-liberal campaign pursued by organised business.

I would suggest, in this context, that Poulantzas' insight has been neglected to the detriment of critical international political economy that seeks to understand the character of neo-liberal hegemony. Insofar as counter-hegemony also implies an engagement with regulation through the state, critical analysis and alternative policy making has to be conscious of Poulantzas' insight into the hegemonic tendencies that seem inherent in the form of capitalist public authority and cadre practice.

Appendix:
Theoretical premises and
methodology

Premises of critical theory

On what theoretical basis should one explore the problems and prospects of
the Swedish model in the contemporary context of capitalist restructuring
and globalisation? This appendix will make the case for a particular version
of 'critical theory' that assigns central importance to the thought of Antonio
Gramsci. Gramscian critical theory provides relief, where 'problem solving
theory' falls short; it can account for systemic crisis, and the implied profound
changes in social structures that define frameworks of thought and action.

This statement needs to be qualified. It does not imply that problem
solving theory has no legitimate role at all to play. Practical policy work
often requires a means–ends rationality, that heuristically assumes normative values and social power relations to be taken as given. Works based on
such a form of theory, however, ought to explicate the social purpose and
the power relations that it assumes (Myrdal 1928/1963: v–vii, 191–207).
Normative values and social power relations, however, are best explored
and determined through critical theory.

This appendix will present my understanding of the methodological and
theoretical premises of critical theory, which are based upon a historical
structural ontology and a hermeneutic epistemology (Gill 1991b: 54–72).
I seek to make explicit the type of theory and methodology I apply, and to
distinguish these from other types of theory and methodology. The criteria
for evaluating the study are then, hopefully, clarified. It can either be
judged from within its own epistemological premises, or through a more
fundamental critique explicitly grounded in philosophical debates on the
social sciences.

'Critical theory' and 'problem solving theory' should be understood in
contradistinction to one another. Problem solving theory, or 'the positivist-
evolutionary approach', provides adequate conceptual tools for the means–
ends rationality of systems management. But it is inadequate on its own as a
guide for democratic politics in the context of profound structural change.

Its aim is to make existing institutions work smoothly, and as such it provides the common epistemic framework of systems theories used by policy
makers, such as macroeconomic theory, structural-functionalist sociology,
and neo-realist international relations theory (Cox 1976: 175–96; 1981:
207–09).

Problem solving theory is universalist and empiricist. It tends to approach
problems from their empirical surface appearance, and takes the prevailing
world view, prevailing power relations, and the institutions in which they
are organised, for granted. Conceiving social reality in a manner analogous
to the atomistic physics of the Newtonian paradigm, positivist problem
solving theory holds that 'human agents and actions are to be reduced to
their outward phenomenal aspects, and science is thought of as a rationality
to be discovered in the form of regularities in the relationships among exter-
nally observed phenomena' (ibid: 178). The method is designed to advance
universally valid regularities of social reality. Concepts should be inductively
advanced through falsifiable hypotheses that are to be verified or rejected
through observation.

It is, however, impossible to separate conception from observation.
Positivist problem solving theory tends to verify tautologically its abstract-
universal, classical-liberal and utilitarian assumptions such as 'economic
man' and 'rational unitary actors' in an 'anarchic state system'. Such
a priorism becomes particularly dubious when one analyses profound structural change (and hence the very framework in which subject identity is
forged), unless one can somehow prove the existence of an essential universal
human nature that is adequately represented by such abstract universals.
This type of ontological claim is dubious in itself, because humanity is
profoundly constituted by the social context in which it exists (eg. Marx
1857: 83–100 and Polanyi 1957b: 243–48 on mainstream economics; Ashley
1986: 205–301 on neo-realist international relations theory). But furthermore, positivism often compounds the problem by totally abandoning
'metaphysical'[1] ontological questions and considerations, and by exclusively
privileging measurement and observation (empiricism).

Empiricism, equilibrium bias and *a priorism*, make problem solving theory
inadequate as a theory of structural change. In contrast, critical theory
'calls [institutions and power relations] into question by concerning itself
with their origins and how and whether they might be in the process of
changing' (Cox 1981: 208). By calling into question *a priori* assumptions
about the nature of subjects and structures, critical theory must by its very
character be absolute-historicist. It does not deny the existence of structural
and subjective fixity, but it asserts that these are transient, and bounded in
time and space – in *historical structures*.[2] The very nature of this boundedness,
the limits of given historical structures, is of central concern for critical
theory. How and why were presently existing institutions constituted, and
how might they be changing? This makes critical theory well suited for the
study of structural transformation.

Ontology of historical structures

Problem solving theory conflates social reality with an atomistic conception of natural reality *qua* Newtonian physics. This is reflected in its conception of the real concrete, and the methodology it derives from this conception. Through its distinctive type of formulation of 'falsifiable' hypotheses, it atomises and externalises social subjectivity to observable 'given' objects – 'data'. For historicist critical theory, in contrast, the social world 'is intelligible to people because it has been made by people'. Human nature and social reality cannot be abstracted from the history of its creation, 'history being but the record of interactions of manifestations of [social] substances' (Cox 1976: 213). Thus, the starting point for historicism is not 'data', constructed through falsifiable hypotheses, but 'facts', understood in terms of events created by humans in a context of interaction (Johansson and Liedman 1993: 13–106; Cox 1976: 178–79; Golding 1992: 23–28). This historicist conception of the nature of knowledge, in contradistinction to positivism and rationalism, can be traced to Giambattista Vico's critique of Descartes. In contrast to Descartes 'I think, therefore I am', Vico asserted 'The truth is what is done' (*verum ipsum factum*).

As Fernand Braudel has persuasively argued, however, the ontology of historical events is far from straightforward. Although the history of the event as such (*'l'histoire évènmentielle'*) may be important, history should not exclusively be seen as a mere succession of events. Rather history, or 'social time', should be understood in terms of 'dialectics of duration', between the history of events, conjunctural history and, *'longue durée'* (Braudel (1958) 1980: 25–62). Much of human history consists of cumulative repetitions of events (*'gestes répétés'*), signifying regularised practices that endure over shorter or longer time-spans. These give rise to structural rhythms, with relatively stable internal logics, as well as internal contradictions.

> For good or ill [the word structure] dominates the problem of the *'longue durée'*. By structure observers of social questions mean an organisation, a coherent and fairly fixed series of relationships between realities and social masses. For historians, a structure is of course a construct, an architecture, but over and above that it is a reality which time uses and abuses over long periods. Some structures, because of their long life, become stable elements for an infinite number of generations: they get in the way, hinder its flow, and in hindering it, shape it. Others wear themselves out more quickly. But all of them provide both support and hindrance. As hindrances they stand as limits . . . beyond which [humanity] and [its] experiences cannot go. Just think of the difficulties to break out of certain geographical frameworks, certain biological realities, certain limits of productivity, even particular spiritual constraints: mental frameworks too can form prisons of the *longue durée*.
>
> (ibid: 31)

The historical-structural regularities of *gestes répétés* shape and limit the parameters of the history of conjunctures and events. But these regularised practices may also break down, and in particular moments 'formative events' (for example, the French Revolution, or the Wall Street Crash) may play a crucial role in termination of an historic structure (such as feudalism or *laissez faire* capitalism).

The dialectics of duration imply a particular type of concept formation in the social sciences, based on the notion of 'historical structures'. This is the type of concept formation adopted in this study. The dialectical premise is that, on the one hand, immanent human creativity creates human structures and institutions; on the other hand, such creation takes place within a constraining framework of action constituted by a cumulative historical-structural legacy. ('[Human beings] make their own history, but they do not make it just as they please' (Marx 1885 (1976): 97). The object of historical-structural concept formation as a component of critical theory is to understand the limiting framework of action constituted by historical structures, and how they change.

Historical-structural concepts seek to represent the spatially and temporally bounded frameworks of action of social reality. They are based on a version of historical materialism that puts the subjective moment on a par with the objective moment, and that considers these moments to co-exist in an overdetermined relationship.[3] Hence, historical structures may be understood as a configuration of three interacting types of categories of force: material capabilities, ideas and institutions. Material capabilities are productive and destructive potentials unevenly available to subjects. Ideas consist of intersubjective meanings and collective images that define the framework of thought of subjects. When configurations of ideas and material capabilities converge into a coherent whole that tends to crystallise into institutional practices that stabilise, perpetuate and reproduce a particular order. Once established, institutions take on a life of their own and affect the development of ideas and material capabilities (Cox 1981: 217–20). Indeed, the Gramscian concepts of 'historic bloc' and 'organic crisis', which are thematic to this study, should be understood as such historical-structural concepts.

Critical theory, in my view, demands that historical-structural conceptualisations consider four related but distinct dimensions of social reality. Firstly, concepts must reflect the transient nature of social reality. Secondly, they must consider social reality in its synchronic and diachronic aspects. Thirdly, historical-structural analysis must move from the simple to the complex. Fourthly, concepts must have ontological depth; that is, they must be situated in an understanding of the relationship between the abstract and the concrete aspects of social reality.

Since historical-structural ontology is based on a rejection of universal and essential human nature, it follows that its concepts must be transient. Historical-structural models are context sensitive; they are designed to be applicable in certain times and places. They do not claim universal validity. Thus, the Popperian method of falsification does not apply in historical-structural analysis. The falsification of a certain model in one context does not necessarily imply that it should be universally rejected. The model may be valid in other contexts. Historical-structural hypotheses and models may be more or less historically and geographically flexible (Braudel (1958) 1980: 40–41, 45). On the other hand, transience implies that historical-structural analysis should reflect upon its historical and geographical specificity. It should also express its significance accordingly (Gill 1991b: 55).

Historical structuralism contains within itself two distinct moments of analysis: the synchronic moment and the diachronic moment. In the synchronic moment, the coherence of a particular framework of action is identified and analysed. Enduring features of an order are identified within a given time span. What is the functional, institutional logic of the order in question? Given certain ends articulated in time and space in a social formation, what are the means through which these ends are achieved? What are the particular material and ideological conditions of existence of the institutionalised order in question? By providing answers to these questions, the synchronic moment of analysis defines the functional limits, from which diachronic analysis can depart. In the diachronic moment, the objects of analysis are the contradictions and crises of an order, and the attendant social forces in historical movement and struggle over alternative projects of change and transformation (Cox 1976: 182–83; 1981: 220, 225–26; 1987: 4–5; Lipietz 1988: 13–16).

Historical-structural method implies a conceptual movement from the simple to complex. Within a temporal-spatial context, analysis reconstructs a totality of the interrelated individual moments of structure, in interrelated spheres of action. Eschewing reductionism, the premise is that their movement can only be understood with reference to the overall contextual framework of their movements. Analysis may start with an individual phenomenon or a problem (such as monetary policy in Sweden), but must then interrelate this individual moment with the broader set of interrelated forces that condition, facilitate or constrain that phenomenon (for example, the nature and structure of the state, global financial markets, international modes of monetary cooperation, and discourses that define the thought and action of central bankers) (Cox 1976: 182; 1981: 208–09, 220–21; 1987: 11).

Finally, I would suggest that a historical structures approach requires an account of ontological depth; that is an account of the interrelationship of abstract and concrete tendencies and counter-tendencies that constitute historical structures. This contention is quite consistent with a non-essentialist reading of Marx's statement on method in the *Grundrisse,* and with the view of 'critical realists' regarding 'generative structures' (Marx 1857: 100–08; Outhwaite 1987: 19–60). The premise is that the social world comprises a complex synthesis of multiple determinations that in the context of social time are to varying degrees necessitarian and contingent (Jessop 1990b: 11;

Albritton 1992: 16–21). In order to adequately grasp these tendencies and counter-tendencies and their interrelationship, 'thought experiments' are pursued at different levels of abstraction. These are not empirically 'testable' in a positivist sense. This is, firstly, because only the final resultant outcome of these interactions may be empirically available: real tendential forces may be suppressed by counter-tendencies. More profoundly, these 'thought experiments' are based on the contention that the empirical, or rather the real concrete, does not in itself express any meaningful determination available merely through observation. Rather, the real concrete (which is transient) only acquires meaning when represented through a conceptual framework.

The measure of how adequately a historical-structural model grasps onto-logical depth depends upon how its structure of concepts connects logically to produce 'in thought concrete explanations' of tendencies and counter-tendencies. Of course, in the last instance, the explanation must connect and correspond with the 'real concrete' world of events. For that reason, concepts formulated at different levels of abstraction are continuously transformed in negotiation with one another, and in the last instance, with the 'real concrete' (Gill 1991b: 59). Insofar as the historically determined real-concrete changes, the patterns of multiple determinations change. Thus, social science is a continuous, open-ended process.

The inevitable interpretative dimension

It is important to be clear about the status of the coherence of elements, events, or facts that the historical-structural models of critical theory identify. Historical structuralism is fundamentally based on a rejection of the Cartesian subject–object dualism of positivism and empiricism. This is implied in the *verum ipsum factum* premise: knowledge about social institutions is available to humanity because they have been created by humans. From this it follows necessarily that one also has to grant that social reality has an inevitable interpretative dimension (Taylor 1985).

This claim, which is raised mainly because of its epistemological implica-tions, nevertheless rests on what essentially is an ontological argument. The argument is that language – and therefore metaphor – is a limitless medium in the making of human history; in the *verum ipsum factum*. This is not to say that social reality can be reduced to language. There are 'intransitive' elements (to borrow a term from theoretical realism) that condition human existence – certain natural, geographical and other infrastructural constraints. However, such elements become socially relevant only in inter-action with linguistically mediated 'transitive' dimensions of social relations, involving active and passive dimensions of agency and structure.

The reason for pointing to the linguistic dimension of *verum ipsum factum* is to highlight that the coherence between a given set of facts may give rise to more than one meaning expressed. Hence the 'signifiers overflow the signified' (Laclau 1988: 250).[4] Creation of meaning 'has an essential place in the characterisation of human behaviour', including political behaviour. Thus the human sciences, and particularly a critical political science, must address questions concerning the creation of such meaning. In 'rare localised' phenomena there may be a single, necessitarian, meaning expressed by the relationship of facts, but it would be far too restrictive a political science that only concerned itself with such phenomena (Taylor 1985: *passim*, 21, 15).

Historical structures cannot transcend what in philosophy is known as 'the hermeneutic circle'. The totality of a structure can only be understood by the interrelation of its parts. But the parts themselves can only be understood with reference to the whole. Analysis, then, requires some form of pre-understanding of the whole, which the analyst brings to the study through his/her existence as a social being, or perhaps more specifically as a member of a research community with a socially determined set of research agendas. Thus, one cannot begin enquiry without an initial conceptualisation; a conceptualisation that cannot be self-referentially justified by the process of inquiry itself. Understanding presupposes pre-understanding (Johansson and Liedman 1993: 94–95). This is merely a slightly different way of restating that our conception of historical structures, while by no means totally relativist, is inherently subjective, and for a subject.

Since meaning, however, always is for a subject, the subjective premises of, or the subject addressed by, a given enquiry need to be explicitly stated. The object of social science in this context is to make sense of, and clarify the meaning of, a social phenomenon for a subject. This is the significance of the interpretative (or 'hermeneutic') dimension of social science. It is 'supposed to mediate between science and the "life-world"' (Outhwaite 1987: 63), that is, articulate the significance of the reality represented by a social analysis for a community.

However, the relationship between meaning and subject identity is not straightforward. The construction of meaning is not merely for a subject; the construction of subjects are also for a meaning. The political process of ideological hegemony, associated with the forging of a historic bloc, operates most profoundly exactly at the level of subject formation. Thus, the subjects for which meaning is created cannot be understood as being 'outside' or transcendentally 'above' the political historical-structural reality that is being analysed. The power-driven process of construction of meaning, with effects on subject formation, is therefore integral to the object of analysis.[5]

The complex dialectic between the construction of meaning and subject formation has in my view been most usefully conceived by Gramsci. Particularly pertinent is his understanding of the relationship between historic blocs, hegemony, organic crisis and intellectual practice. Gramsci's approach integrates a critical-realist analysis of power, particularly an analysis of ideology as power, with a firm ethical grounding of his interpretative criteria as being for a subject. Thus, he synthesises the 'is' and 'the ought' (Gramsci 1971: 125–40, 169–72). But how does one identify a subject

for whom one analyses when one explicitly acknowledges that subject formation is part of what needs to be critically analysed? How does one identify a
subject for whom one guides change and liberation, when subjectivity is
defined by the power of a given order that itself needs to be critically
analysed? Gramsci resolves what seems to be a Gordian knot by appropri-
ating his materialist conception of ideology the term 'social myth' from
Georges Sorel.

Whereas the Gramscian concepts of hegemony, organic crisis and historic
bloc are forged exactly for the end of a rigorous analysis of the subjective
and objective aspects of power relations in society, Gramsci insists that such
analysis only makes sense if it is understood to be for a purpose, for a subject.
It is possible to identify the 'progressive subject', because an order is always
to some degree contradictory, particularly in its ideological-hegemonic
aspects.

Consent of subordinate groups is ensured exactly through a hegemonic
articulation of their conception of 'common sense', rendering it compatible
with the ideology of legitimation of the power bloc. But the discourse of
common sense is not intellectually rigorous, but forged at the level of feelings,
intuition, prejudice, and unreflected opinion, hence it tends to contain
contradictory elements. Contradictions contain the potential for antagonism, especially in a hegemonic structure based on oppression, subordination,
and exploitation (Gramsci 326–43, 348–51; Mouffe 1979: 185–88, 190–92,
195–98; Hall, Lumley and Mc Lennan 1977: 46–52; Simon 1982: 58–66).
As a result identities of resistance always exist in fragmentary, contradictory
form. The role of critical/progressive intellectual practice, in this context,
becomes to render such subject identities more coherent and conscious by
explicating their condition, as well as by articulating what they can become.
This is done through a criticism ('moral and intellectual reform') engaged
at the discursive terms set by the common sense. The object of such reform is
to make the progressive elements of common sense, that may be marginal
and even incidental in the hegemonic belief structure, central in popular
consciousness.

The test of such an intellectual practice, then, becomes the degree to which
it appeals to, builds upon, and manages to render more coherent, the spontaneous common sense of right and wrong – the social myth – that such
subjectivities develop in their everyday experience with social contradictions
and antagonisms. In this regard, the rigorous analysis of power relations
constitutes a crucial contribution, because it makes such subjectivities (previously 'not in the know') aware of their own condition and how they may
change it.

The concept of social myth can be further elaborated with reference to
concrete history. Appealing to, building upon, and rendering a social myth
more coherent can also be understood as recontextualising and rearticulating
a previously existing ideological discourse, in order to make sense of new
circumstances, and to clarify which elements of the old are worth preserving,

and which ones should be discarded in the process of moral and intellectual reform. This seems to be particularly important in periods of organic crisis, when a previously articulated ideological form may have been rendered implausible. In this context, the object of intellectual practice would be to inform existing subjects of new circumstances as they attempt to reconstitute themselves and forge a modified political project.

Hence the Gramscian conception of social myth is based on a materialist and dialectical conception of ideologies. Ideology should not be seen in opposition to material processes (systems of ideas). Rather they are embodied in material modes of living. Ideologies serve the essential social function in a social formation of 'organizing human masses and creating the terrain on which [humans] move, acquire consciousness of their position, struggles . . .' (Simon 1982, cf. Gramsci 1971: 367). Ideologies are constituted by the distinct and dialectically related moments of common sense and philosophy (which also contains science). Philosophy produces a coherent conception of the world, and has the function of rendering a dominant power bloc homogeneous and coherent. Common sense is the intuitive moment, and it is dominated by the philosophical moment insofar as intuition is conditioned by a given order. On the other hand, in the last instance philosophy emerges out of the spontaneity of intuition. Moreover, the contradictory nature of common sense also implies that it contains the seed for undermining a given philosophy.

By combining the concepts of historic bloc, organic crisis and hegemony with the notion of social myth, Gramsci's analysis can be seen as being based on a particularly politically astute version of 'negative dialectics'. The latter term is associated with the Frankfurt School, and it provides the epistemological basis of critical theory.

Critical theory is based on two distinct but integral meanings of critique; 'reconstruction' and 'criticism' (Connerton 1976: 17–20). Reconstruction 'denotes reflection on the conditions of possible knowledge' (pioneered by Kant). It is concerned with the movement from 'incoherent profusion of impressions or sensations given in perception' (what Marx called 'chaotic conception' in the *Grundrisse*) to coherent understanding through systematic concept formation. Thus, reconstruction concerns itself with conceptualising the relationships of the elements/signifiers of an object of inquiry as such; the movement from arbitrary perception to systematic logical conception.

'Criticism', pioneered by Hegel in the *Phenomenology of Mind*, locates the subjective framework of critical theory in a transformative project of liberation. It 'denotes reflection on systems of constraints which are humanly produced that act as distorting pressures to which a given category of humans succumb in their process of self-formation'. These pressures are to be understood as 'coercive illusions', and the role of critical theory is to reveal these illusions, and to analyse how a given social subject can overcome them in a given context. Thus, the criterion of adequacy of critical theory is judged in terms of negation. It is judged in terms of how adequately it perceives the constraints that a given social subject faces, in its attempt to advance its aspirations.

'Criticism' relates the conceptualisation to the subjective framework of liberation to its constraints; 'reconstruction' conceptualizes the constraints to liberation. Gramsci's key concepts of historic bloc, organic crisis, and hegemony correspond to the moment of reconstruction; the concept of 'social myth' corresponds to the moment of criticism. It is in this sense that I understand these terms.

In the book the moment of criticism is defined with reference to the key concept of 'developmental democracy', which Giddens refers to in terms of 'no authority without democracy' as the nodal point of social democratic discourse of legitimation and mobilisation. It is this ethico-political notion that, for example, enabled Swedish social democrats to appeal to the common sense of Swedish civil society, and to mobilise the Swedish working class while exercising a hegemonic national-popular leadership of the social formation as a whole (Tilton 1988). It is also the inter-subjective appeal of this notion that I invoke in this study. This should by no means be seen as implying a blanket endorsement of the practices of social democracy. It does mean that I accept the general principles that this movement claims that it advocates (but not only this movement since these principles are shared by a much broader spectrum of social forces in civil society). But insofar as the practice may actually contradict norms of integrative democracy, or articulate 'the myth' of such democracy in a selective and narrow way, my framework contains the space for a critical analysis of 'actually existing' social democracy.

The moment of reconstruction relates to an analysis of the constraints of realising integrative democracy, in lieu of opposing and resisting political forces and socio-economic pressures. Central in this context is an analysis of the struggles of how the abstract principles are translated into concrete political practice, and thus how the meaning of this concept is shaped, reshaped and contested. This study is particularly concerned with the politico-economic constraints to integrative democracy, which in a capitalist market system is associated with commodification. Hence, de-commodification becomes the key concept in defining my problematic, since it mediates the moments of criticism and reconstruction; the inter-subjective principle and the constraint of realizing this principle.

Notes on research procedure

The research on the crisis of the Swedish model upon which the argument rests was conducted in 1993–95. Following the aforementioned premises of Gramscian critical theory, the problem was formulated in terms of the following problematique: how to institutionalise 'de-commodification' (the moment of 'reconsruction in the analysis) in order to advance 'developmental democracy' (the moment of 'criticism'). From this problematique,

I deduced three interrelated research aims. The central aim would be to discern the politico-economic causes of the then recent breakdown of the Swedish model. This was for the purpose of the second aim: to clarify the balance of power in Swedish society, which would clarify contemporary prospects for de-commodification strategies. These two aims presupposed a third aim: to analyse the formation and content of the post-war de-commodification strategy in Sweden, its attendant institutional arrangements and structural conditions of existence.

The approach based on the theoretical premises as just outlined was advanced through a literature review of research on the Swedish model (Ryner 1992). The central thrust of such an approach is to generate a set of internally consistent context-sensitive heuristic concepts that can serve as an initial interpretative framework. Following the model of the hermeneutic circle, their purpose is to provide the coherence and foreknowledge that is necessary as a heuristic device in order to make any research possible, without imposing preconceived answers. (Braudel (1980) characterise these models in terms of historical structural hypotheses). The model is in part deduced from concepts formulated at a higher level of abstraction, and in part from specific real-concrete circumstances. The model is then refined through concrete (empirical) enquiry. Hence, the model is refined until it becomes an explanatory model.

A strategy for empirical research was formulated on the basis of such a model, which entailed a refinement of the Gramscian concept 'historic bloc'. This model allowed for the formulation of a set of more concrete research questions. The main problem was to focus the study so as to make a macro-political case study that at the same time emphasised complexity, a manageable one-person project that nevertheless would yield the required empirical material. The problem was resolved as follows. A central set of regulatory practices of the Swedish historic bloc were identified, that served an integrative function, and thus mediated capital accumulation imperatives and legitimation imperatives for the social formation as a whole. It could be inferred from the existing literature that the institutional practices of co-ordination between wage determination and government conjunctural and structural economic policy had served such a function. This ensemble of practices was defined as the *mode of regulation*. It was argued that the existing literature had not adequately accounted for the historical-structural conditions of existence of these practices and why they had been undermined. The contribution of the project would be to specify these conditions and their transformation. The aim would be to reconstruct this interplay of structural conditions and the mode of regulation, and the attendant power struggles of political actors that ensued in this context (and possibly transformed it). The guiding model identified five interrelated dimensions of the historic bloc: mode of regulation, regime of accumulation, state, civil society and world order (Appendix Figure 1).

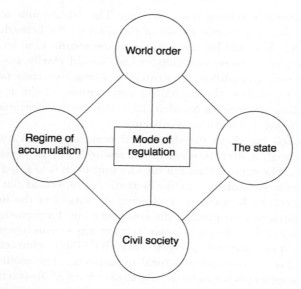

Appendix Figure 1 Representation of an historic bloc.

This framework of analysis was then related to a set of more pragmatic questions intended to guide and organise the historical research, the interviews and the archival work. The framework was elaborated in two ways in order to facilitate this. First, an explicit temporal dimension was added. The questions were posed in terms of Braudel's conception of three rhythms of socio-historical time (*longue durée*, conjunctural history, and the history of events). In this two-dimensional model areas of primary-source research and secondary-source research were defined respectively. In this scheme all aspects of the *longue durée* of Swedish socio-economic and socio-political development were understood to be in the area of secondary-source research. The history of conjuncture (the institutional dynamics of the Swedish model) would also draw primarily on secondary sources. However, the account of the conjunctures of the mode of regulation would also draw on primary sources (economic statistics and relevant government and interest organisation documents). The analysis of the history of events of the crisis of the Swedish model would consider primary sources in all spheres, except 'world order' (government/interest organisation documents, interviews, economic statistics). The historical events of formation of the Swedish model would primarily be considered through historical texts and memoirs (Appendix Table 1).

A set of more specific research questions was then formulated for the domains of primary research. In the domain 'mode of regulation/conjuncture' a set of critical economic indicators to consider were identified, drawing especially on the 'social structure of accumulation' school (see Gordon 1980;

Appendix Table 1 Domains of primary and secondary source research as set out in research design

	Longue durée	*History of conjuncture*	*History of events*
World order			
Mode of growth			X
Mode of regulation		X	X
The state			X
Civil society			X

X = domains of primary research.

Bowles, Gordon and Weisskopf 1983).[6] A set of qualitiative research questions were also formulated in this domain. For the history of events sections of formation and crisis, a set of possible critical events and turning points were identified, and a set of questions pertaining to their relative relevance for the crisis/formation were formulated.

A description of field research and the sources generated

The research was conducted under the auspices of the Graduate Programme of Political Science, York University, Toronto, 1992–95. Three field research trips to Sweden were undertaken (January-May 1993, August-September 1993 and May-June 1994). The first trip was devoted to bibliographical and secondary-source research, and the laying of the foundations for interviews and archival research (eg. conducting informant interviews).

The bibliographical research confirmed my sense of the strengths and weaknesses of Swedish social science. Twentieth century Swedish society is exceptionally well charted empirically in sociology, economics, history, historiography, economic history, ethnography and in studies of political actors and institutions. But much of the work is descriptive and empirically grounded whilst being theoretically primitive (empiricist). There are also few good synthetic works and certainly no works that systematically conceptualise the articulation of the Swedish social formation to the world order.

In terms of preparation for primary-source research, I allocated considerable time to reading about the formation and crisis of the Swedish model. The primary purpose was to clarify the narratives and to generate a list of inteviewees. Exploratory 'informant interviews' (Dexter 1970) with academic experts were also useful for the identification of officials that should be interviewed.

From this preparatory work I decided to focus the interviews on three of the candidate sets of critical events of the Swedish model in crisis. These sets of events were those pertaining to the politics of wage-earner funds (1971–83), the SAF 'free enterprise campaign' (since 1978), the SAP economic

206 Appendix: Theoretical premises and methodology

policy of the Third Way (1982–90). These sets of events were selected according to three criteria:

- the relative lack of availability of good secondary sources that were covering the narrative
- the relative centrality of the critical events for the (dis)integrative aspects of the mode of regulation
- and (related to the second point) these three events seemed to constitute the central aspects of the pendulum movement from the red wave to neoliberalism and the war of position over economic regulation that arose in the 1970s and 1980s. Ultimately, this is the question upon which the current Third Way debate on social democracy hinges.

This is not to suggest that the other candidate events are not part of the war of position (they are). But they are of less central importance and the reconstruction of these less central events was made by relying on secondary sources.

The lion's share of interviews were done during the second field trip. The ground of the narrative pertaining to the economic policy of the Third Way must be considered to have been well covered. I interviewed four of the five Deputy Ministers of Finance from the period 1982–91, the Deputy Governor of the Central Bank, as well as the Chief Economist and Chief Negotiator of LO during the period. I did not interview the Minister of Finance of the period (though one of the interviewees subsequently became Minister of Finance in the mid-1990s). But I did read his very candid memoirs (Feldt 1991), whose quality I assessed through the method of triangulation. Actors from all perspectives attest to their quality as a good source on the events witnessed by the Minister. There may be one aspect of this issue that I did not cover well. I did not interview any of the representatives of the white-collar union confederation (TCO) or its member unions. However, it is important to note that although these unions represent a large segment of the labour market, their pattern of bargaining is more internally fragmented, and thus their representation in tripartite deliberations over economic policy is weaker than that of LO. Moreover, the white-collar–government economic policy dynamics are well covered in secondary sources (eg. Elvander 1988; Ahlén 1989; Fulcher 1991; Mahon 1994c).

The interviews on the wage-earner fund issue focused on reconstructing the internal LO deliberations of the labour movement that resulted in the radicalisation and subsequent watering down of the proposal between 1971 and 1983. This is because, apart from this, the issue is very well covered in the literature (Lewin 1992; Pontusson 1987; and especially Åsard 1978; 1985). The main trade union intellectuals involved in this process were interviewed, as were other union officials indirectly involved, but heavily immersed on the issue of the connections between the wage-earner funds and the struggle over the shape of the mode of regulation (Interviewees 8 and 15). One weakness with this set of interviews is that they do not include any interviews with representatives of the SAP (However, interviewee 6 was temporarily employed by the Ministry of Finance to implement the 1983 bill that actually passed in Parliament. He is the only individual who was involved every step of the way from 1971 to 1983.) Attempts to set up interviews with SAP officials failed. This is a limitation. At the same time, one of these members is the Minister of Finance 1982–90, whose views on the wage-earner funds is well covered in his memoirs.

Of the three critical events identified for interviews, the SAF 'free enterprise campaign' is the one that is the least comprehensively explored. I have not been able to develop as extensive contacts with representatives for the employers' association as those with labour. But this is not too much of a problem, considering the mushrooming literature on the neo-liberal swing of SAF and the effect of this on Swedish political society. This literature is also good quality (Schiller 1987; De Geer 1989; S.O. Hansson from a left wing perspective; Ehrencrona 1991 from a right wing perspective; Boréus 1994; Blyth 1997). In addition, Professor Schiller, one of these authors, was one of my informant interviewees, and he helped me make strategic choices to ensure that I received a reasonably representative sense of the internal deliberations of SAF, including a sense of the internal differences according to function (propaganda or 'social information' vs policy formulation and political orientation; 'hawk' vs 'dove' (Interviewees 1, 2 and 7)).

Given my limited access to SAF and the good state of the secondary literature, I formulated my questions in terms of what I considered to be the most important factual lacunae in the secondary literature. Otherwise, I used interviews to ask open-ended questions in order to obtain material that could be subject to discursive analysis. I also used interviews for the method of triangulation in order to verify/assess the degree of subjectivity and inter-subjectivity of what other interviewees had said. Interviews were also used to identify future interviewees. Very importantly, interviews were used to identify the key documents and, more specifically, to shed light on the context of central documents. That is to situate documents, that are static statements of a certain time and place, in a process. Given the subjectivity of interviews, and especially the problem and selectivity of memory, I have used interview material very sparingly as reference for specific points. Instead, as much as possible, I have used documents for such references.

Concerning archival work, access to relevant documents did not pose a problem. Rather, the problem was one of information overload. With regard to the formation of the Swedish model, the criteria of selection of documents were set by secondary-source historiographic literature. This was also the case with 'history of conjuncture/mode of regulation', where another criteria (for the quantitiative material) also was defined by the indicators as defined by the social structure of accumulation approach. The criteria of selection for the crisis of the Swedish model were primarily set by the interviews.

Two general distinctions can be made with regard to the type of Swedish government documents that were collected. The first type of documents include the so-called 'SOU' and 'Ds'-series documents. One central aspect of corporatist state practice is the usage of the public commission process in the formulation of policy. These commissions (*Statens offentliga utredningar* (SOU)), which tend to have corporative 'expert' representation, provide thorough background research on a policy issue before a bill is formulated. Sometimes the public commission process is used to generate knowledge and information in a general policy area, without the purpose being to formulate a bill. Apart from accumulating knowledge, the public commission process has served the purpose of forging compromise and consensus among the peak interest organisations.

The SOU reports of the public commissions do not in and of themselves represent state policy. They should rather be understood as relatively open-ended explorations of a particular issue. However, the SOU documents do have a definitive discursive closure, and as such they are useful for exploring the 'universe of available discourse' (Jenson 1989) in a given policy area. Insofar as representatives of capital, labour and representatives of a particular state apparatus are willing to have their names associated with the text of a commission, one can identify their common inter-subjective understanding of an issue. Textual analysis of SOU reports, then, can facilitate the reconstruction of a hegemonic social paradigm (ibid.). Insofar as reservations are made to the findings of the majority view one can also get a sense of the terms of contestability of this paradigm as well.

The Ds document is another type of document that reflects the universe of available discourse, but not necessarily state policy. These type of documents are produced by government ministries for internal consumption and external communication. Like SOUs, Ds documents give a sense of the articulated paradigmatic discourse available to a government department. But these documents give no indications as to what extent this discourse is shared outside the department. Reports produced for interest organisations and party congresses, conversely, give a sense of the universe of available discourse for these bodies.

The relatively 'open-ended' documents are usefully juxtaposed with a second type of document that reflects state policy and the official position of interest organisations. Such documents are bills passed (Prop-series documents) and official policy statements and resolutions of organisations. By comparing the SOU and Ds documents with the prop. documents, one gets a sense not only of the discourse available, but also of the particular articulation of this discourse that has been elevated to policy. Such a juxtaposition – considered together with interviews – gives one a sense of the process of strategic selectivity (Jessop 1990b) of the state, and this contributes to the illumination of the power/knowledge relations involved in the socio-political construction of regulation.

Strategically important documents were identified, then, for the Swedish model in formation, the institutional pattern of regulation, and for the Swedish model in crisis. The main emphasis was on government documents, in part because government ministries are central to regulation, and in part because interest organisation positions are reflected in (particularly) the SOU documents.

The danger of this approach is that it tends to generate an overly 'top-down' perspective. That is, one gets no sense from these documents of the problems that organisations face in representing their constituencies. This can, however, be rectified by juxtaposing the primary research with secondary research, especially through the concept of 'structure of social representation' outlined in chapter 4.

Apart from the aforementioned documents, I collected virtually all articles written on economic policy, wage determination, and their articulation to the social democratic vision of developmental democracy and the good society, published in the theoretical and ideological journal of the Swedish social democratic labour movement, *Tiden*, from 1920 to the late 1980s. These articles give a sense of how concrete policy positions were justified in relation to general and basic values of the labour movement. They also provide important evidence of the dynamics of producing legitimacy and consent for government and trade union policy among mid-level cadres and active members in the labour movement.

As this material was processed, the questions generated by the model of hypothesis and question formulation was revised and refined, and as answers were found, it was transformed into an explanatory framework.

Evaluation of the sources generated

An adequate amount of primary and secondary sources were generated to provide an account for the formation, institutionalisation, and crisis of the Swedish model.

The primary sources, however, almost exclusively pertained to the conjunctural history and the history of events of the crisis of the mode regulation. Some of the quantitative indicators pertaining to the mode of growth were also generated (such as material on Fordist crisis and transition). No primary sources were generated that pertain to the broader structures of the state and civil society. This revised matrix on primary and secondary sources actually looks somewhat different from what was stated in the formulation of the research agenda (Appendix Table 2).

The initial research agenda was unrealistic with regards to the logistical problems of primary research. It would have been impossible to pursue any meaningful systematic primary research in the broader structural areas of the mode of growth, state and civil society. It was difficult enough to generate an adequate amount of material within the more limited areas pertaining to the mode of regualtion.

210   *Appendix: Theoretical premises and methodology*

Appendix Table 2 Primary and secondary research actually achieved

	Longue durée	*History of conjuncture*	*History of events*
World order			
Mode of growth		(X)	(X)
Mode of regulation		X	X
The state			
Civil society			

X = domains of primary research.

On the other hand, not even the most optimistic scenario would have been disappointed with the availability of good secondary sources. Good empirical work within the fields of industrial economics and work sociology was available, and thus the mode of growth can be adequately charted. The same is the case within the areas of political sociology and political science. Thus, the broader state structures and strategies could also be sufficiently charted. Finally, sources in history, ethnology and social history provided material for an adequate reconstruction of civil societal dynamics. The Swedish sources on international political economy are virtually non-existent, however. However, by drawing on the IPE literature available internationally, this research difficulty could be managed.

Notes

Introduction

1 This means that Gramsci does not consider the material base to determine the superstructure, as in orthodox Marxism rather they are seen as co-determined. Hence, drawing on Benedetto Croce's conception of immanent creativity, Gramsci's social ontology anticipates Lacan's argument that human consciousness is fundamentally formed through linguistic, that is cultural, structures as opposed to production structures (Golding 1992). Of course, for Gramsci, culture is formed with reference to economic structures and interests. For a particularly incisive yet clear exposition of Gramsci's conception on subject formation, hegemony and historic blocs, see Mouffe (1979: 178–98).

1 Recent discourse on the Third Way

1 For a more comprehensive elaboration of the Gramscian conception of ideology and its relation to philosophy and science, see Appendix, pp. 199–201.
2 'Cosmopolitan intellectual' is a term that Gramsci (1971) uses in his complex socio-historical theory of intellectual practice. Intellectual practice is the generic term Gramsci uses to describe all practices pertaining to the production and manipulation of the cognitive, subjective, and immanently creative aspects of social action. Types of intellectual practice and intellectuals are defined with reference to historically developing social functions. Different class-fractions, classes and social forces develop their own strata of 'organic intellectuals' that are specifically charged with performing intellectual functions related to the specific practice of the specific groups. Intellectuals for social classes who are involved in the forging of social hegemony – the task of assuming leadership for society as a whole, and for defining the 'general will', even the terms of 'truth' in society – assume a certain autonomy from the social forces they represent in order to render this claim to a general will plausible. In this endeavour they also bring on board 'traditional intellectuals', eg. academics, bureaucrats and even priests, whose practices are a legacy of sedimented social forms, that nevertheless remain central to the general governing of a social formation. 'Cosmopolitan intellectuals' belong to this category. Emanating from the social functions performed by clerical scholars of the Catholic church of the Middle Ages (or even further back in the Roman Empire by, for example, philosophers that emerged as intellectuals in Athens after the Peloponnesian Wars), they are particularly charged with the function of defining the 'absolute truth' and the 'state-of-affairs in general' – the *Zeitgeist* of a particular epoch. In post-Enlightenment Europe, this was a function

that was taken over by philosophers. Gramsci discusses Immanuel Kant, as well as his nemesis Benedetto Croce, in this light (eg. ibid: 56n; 374).

3 Developmental democracy is based on the idea that the tension between the need for political order and freedom can be resolved by shaping society so as to condition and encourage the moral and social development of individuals as active political citizens. This legacy of radical liberalism, which democratic socialists accept, should be seen in contrast to the 'protective democracy' advocated by, for example, Jeremy Bentham, where formal representative-democratic procedure is merely an instrument to ensure the defence of what he considers to be the essence of freedom and rationality in society – private property and market participation (Macpherson 1977: 1–2, 23–64; Held 1987: 36–37, 66–106).

4 Assar Lindbeck (who left the Swedish Social Democratic Party on the issue of wage-earner funds in the 1970s) chaired a major public commission in Sweden in 1992, which was formed by the Bildt administration. In their Final Report, Lindbeck and his colleagues provided comprehensive prescriptions for a neo-liberal transformation of Swedish society, including the curtailment of union power, labour market deregulation, and a move towards a residual welfare state (Sweden. SOU 1993; translated into English as Lindbeck *et al.* 1994). This report served as a legitimising reference-point for the reforms of the Bildt administration during their tenure of government, 1991–94. It might be worth pointing out, in this context, that as far back as in the 1970s Lindbeck was a member of the McCracken Group. Advancing their 'narrow path to growth-thesis' this group was important for laying the intellectual ground for neo-liberal restructuring of international economic governance (Cox 1987: 282–83).

5 Ironically, in the context of the British Labour Party, one of the arch villains of New Labour, Tony Benn, was an early champion of this type of analysis (Benn 1970).

6 Giddens cites as a model a Hewlett-Packard plant in Grenoble, which is kept open 24 hours a day, seven days a week, but where the average working week has been reduced to 37.5 hours. Work reductions have been made without loss of weekly income, since productivity increases have underwritten the reduction of working time.

7 It feels slightly odd to lay this charge against the author of the famous two-volume work titled *A Contemporary Critique of Historical Materialism* (Giddens 1981; 1987). The fact of the matter is, though, that Giddens does not cite this work in *The Third Way*. One could search for the implicit links and no doubt this would be an interesting exercise. I have chosen not to engage in such an exercise, however, since that might be to put words in Giddens' mouth, and it would be his responsibility to make the links explicit if he wanted to ground his argument in his previous research. Nevertheless such an exercise might begin with Giddens' invocation of his theory of structuration in the introduction of volume one of this work: '*Power and freedom are not opposites*; on the contrary power is rooted in the very nature of human agency, and thus in "the freedom to act otherwise"' (Giddens 1981: 4; my emphasis). This is probably true, and it provides the basis of a reasonable critique of a reductionist interpretation of the base-superstructure scheme as a method of analysing social *being* (in which Giddens is joined by Lukács, Gramsci and the critical theory of the Frankfurt School). However, if it is the basis of the passages in the *Third Way* I have just criticised, then we might conclude that it is a dubious alternative to Marxism, as a point of reference of social criticism (see Appendix: 201–02) of critical theory, concerned with the social ontology of 'becoming' and what ought to be.

8 In her comparative study of welfare state design in Britain, the United States, the Netherlands and Sweden, Sainsbury shows that the 'male breadwinner model'

has been less pervasive in the latter case than in the other exactly because of social citizenship and universalism. Hence, it is hard to sustain Giddens' inherent link between traditional social democracy and the male breadwinner model. First, social citizenship principles gave married women individual entitlements independent of their husbands. Second, married women's entitlements were enhanced by the demise of residual means-tested programmes in favour of universal programmes. Third, legislation has made the care of children rather than wives the referent object of welfare policy. The principle of care has strengthened women's entitlement based on their roles as mothers and care-givers, rather than wives (Sainsbury 1996: 63). This emphasis on care-giving has in the Swedish context been articulated with unionised wage earning, since reproductive work (health, education, welfare) has been displaced from the family to the public welfare sector to a much larger extent in the social democratic regime type (see chapter 2). This means that women hold a dual subject position as carers and unionised wage earners in the Swedish welfare state, which has increased the prospects of interpellating them into the extended working class. It should be pointed out in this context that whereas the other welfare states tend to configure wage work and entitlement due to care functions in opposition to one another (through means-tested benefits that are lost when employment is accepted), Swedish child-care related entitlements are to a larger extent conceived as supplementary to wage work (eg. universal child allowances, parental insurance based on the incomes maintenance principle, and advanced maintenance allowances) (ibid: 84–86; 122–25).

9 I have elaborated on this in Ryner (2000) on the basis of the comparative empirical research of Keith Banting (2000) in the same book. Whilst there can be no doubt that Sweden suffers from xenophobia and marginalisation of immigrants, it is nevertheless true that immigrants conceive the welfare state as a beneficial institution and a mechanism towards social inclusion in Sweden, and this can be attributed to its universal social citizenship nature. It is also true that Swedish welfare constituencies and organisations tend to respond to the threats that immigrants may pose to welfare state entitlements (for example, through wage competition) by including and tying immigrants to welfare state entitlements rather than excluding them. This is in contrast to the status segmenting conservative welfare states of continental Europe, where the movement is towards all-out exclusion, and in residual liberal welfare states where the norms of integration are based on 'making it' without the welfare state. This does not mean that there is no discrimination against immigrants in Sweden (where the label 'immigrant' tends to stick even after long periods of residence in Sweden). On the latter, see especially Knocke (1994; 2000). But contests and struggles over these issues tend to be posed in terms of the content of the universal welfare state.

10 In this context it might make sense to invoke Stefan Svallfors' (1989; 1994) extensive survey-based research on attitudes towards the welfare state in Sweden. His study confirms the importance of the ideological appeal of universalism as institutional form for the sustained legitimacy of the Swedish welfare state. While attitudes to the welfare state vary according to class belonging (rather than according to gender or sectoral employment), the degree of variation of attitudes is relatively small. And while there is evidence of critique of the administrative aspects of the welfare state and a sense that there are clients that abuse the system (expressed in relatively low support for means-tested systems), support for the central universal programmes remains strong and actually grew in the 1980s. This indicates that these programmes are experienced as 'fair' and not particularly 'bureaucratic' and intrusive, and there is a willingness to pay relatively high taxes to sustain them. In the latter book, however, he documents an increased

anti-welfarism in the Swedish political and cultural elite in the 1980s and early 1990s, which is out of step with the continued mass-support.

11 Knocke (2000), for example, show a clear relationship between full employment and integration of immigrants as segregation increases with a slackening of labour demand and increased unemployment.

12 We will return to the notion of popular movements in chapter 3 (which included, for example consumers' associations, co-operatives, pensioners' associations) and their significance for the construction of social democratic hegemony in Sweden. They are not to be understood as volunteer associations in the Anglo-Saxon sense, but as constituent entities in a network that constituted the labour movement as a movement for social change. The aforementioned pluralist and integrative strategy would depend on the continued vitality and prospects of transformation of the popular movements to reflect new antagonisms in society (i.e. including immigrants' rights movements). On research that points to the continued vitality of such movements and the link of this vitality to the universal welfare state, see Rothstein's study based on comprehensive time-series data and comparative analysis (1998b: 11–53).

2 The social democratic welfare state and the political economy of capitalist restructuring

1 Esping-Andersen reports that the participation rate decreased, for example, in Germany between 1960 and 1985 from 70 per cent to 66 per cent of the population between 15 and 64 years old (Esping-Andersen 1990: 197). The participation rate has subsequently recovered and was back at 70.7 per cent in 1995 (cf. OECD 1997: Table 2.6). Employment rates however, have not recovered. They were 69.6 per cent in 1960, 62.2 per cent in 1985 and 64.9 per cent in 1995 (ibid: Table 2.14). Moreover, in Germany employment has increasingly become part-time employment (for example, between 1973 and 1981 the ratio of part-time employment growth over total employment growth was 165 per cent) (Esping-Andersen 1990: 198, cf. OECD 1983a).

2 According to Esping-Andersen's own calculations of Luxembourg Income Study data (1996b: 75), 10–12 per cent of German families are now single-parent families, and 27 per cent of them are living in poverty.

3 According to Esping-Andersen, the Christian democratic policy regime makes demographic assumptions that no longer obtain. It assumes a male working-life from the age of 15 or 16 to the age of 65, and a short period of retirement before death. It also assumes that women will be available to rear children and take care of the elderly for free under the auspices of the family. Present realities are such that the working age has been reduced to include the age from about 18–20 to 55–59, with increased risks of unemployment within this period. Also, the nuclear family is under strain and women no longer are prepared to assume the role of family carer. Their unpreparedness to do so manifests itself in the form of low fertility rates that will exacerbate the age-dependency ratios further (ibid: 76, cf Kohli 1993 and Gustavsson and Stafford 1994).

4 Whereas manufacturing employment decreased in the USA as well as in Germany in 1960–84, the average annual rate of post-industrial service employment was much higher in the USA than in Germany (6.7 per cent compared to 3.5 per cent between 1960 and 1984), generating a 2.4 per cent average annual increase in employment in the former country and a 0.1 annual decrease in employment in the latter (Esping-Andersen 1990: 199 cf. Elfring 1988). During the period 1980– 94, employment increased by 25.5 per cent in the USA and by 10.5 per cent in Germany (Esping-Andersen 1999a: 100). Post-industrial employment increased

by an average annual rate of 2.7 per cent in the USA and by 1.8 per cent in Germany in 1980–90 (Esping-Andersen 1999a: 108, cf. ILO various years).

5 See Rein (1985). Female labour-market participation rates remained stagnant in Germany between 1960 and 1981 (49.2 per cent and 50.1 per cent), whereas they increased from 42.6 per cent to 60.7 per cent in the USA and from 46.1 to 57.5 per cent in the UK (ibid: 38, cf. OECD 1983: 2.6, 2.7, 2.8). More up-to-date figures are 69.6 per cent for the USA, 67.8 per cent for the UK and 60.8 per cent for Germany (OECD 1997: Table 2.8). In other words, German participation rates have increased subsequently but they still lag behind, and have not been matched by a corresponding increase in job opportunities (Esping-Andersen 1996b: 78).

6 See Esping-Andersen (1990: 197–99). The Swedish annual average employment growth rate was 0.8 per cent in 1960–85 (the US figure was 2.4 per cent), and the part-time ratio was 105 (as opposed to 165 in Germany). The participation rate increased in the same period from 74 to 81 per cent, in contrast to the more modest increase in the USA from 66 to 75 per cent. The increase in the female participation rate in Sweden was equally impressive (cf Rein 1985: 38, cf. OECD 1983a), from 50.1 per cent to 75.3 per cent between 1960 and 1983, whilst we recall that the increase in the USA was from 42.6 to 60.7 per cent. The trends in manufacturing and consumer service employment in Sweden are almost identical to those in Germany in that period (−0.7 per cent and 1.6 per cent). But with an increase of 8.6 per cent in health, education and welfare service employment in Sweden (as opposed to 4.8 per cent in Germany and 6.2 per cent in the USA), Swedish post-industrial employment growth matched that of the USA (6.7 per cent) (cf. Elfring 1988). See also Rein (1985: 41–43).

7 The Dutch 90/10 ratio increased by 17.2 per cent between 1985 and 1994. The American figures between 1979 and 1995 were 13.7 per cent, and the British figures were 18.6 per cent. These three countries stand out as the OECD countries where wage dispersion grows the fastest. By comparison, the percentage increase in Canada was 4.7 (between 1981 and 1994), in Australia it was +6.1 (1980–94). The Swedish rate increased slightly from a very low base rate between 1980 and 1993 (+4.4). In Norway and Finland, wage differentials actually narrowed slightly. In Germany, wage rates narrowed markedly between 1983 and 1993 (13.8 per cent). (Clayton and Pontusson, 1998, cf. OECD, 1993; 1996).

8 Lipietz' (1987: 25–26) formulation of the meaning of the term 'regime of accumulation' is as follows: '"Values in process capitals" march alongside each other, exchanging goods with each other, or exchanging goods for those very special values-in-process which are wage revenues. How is it possible that this interlacing of autonomous processes weaves a coherent social product, where all the private employments of labour (by means of the expenditure of capital) are affirmed as valid? As in every social relation, the acquired experience of the possibility of a solution is in itself one of the bases of the solution. The capitalists, by virtue of acquisitions (previous revenues) and knowledge of the market (tested in previous periods), bet that it is all right to renew the wage relation, to buy more constant capital, and by this fact already contribute to the validation of the products of colleagues and of the labour power offered by the wage-earning class. The conditions inherited from the past and the expectation of a continuing future are the conditions of the present social bond. The continuity of accumulation, the habits acquired regarding an allocation which is equilibrated between the different branches of the division of labour and the expectations with regards to the social orientations of the transformations of the norms of production and consumption all combine to dominate the private bets of entrepreneurs (and their bankers), like an immanent force, laying the foundations of a 'social mould', which is called in this context a regime of accumulation.'

9 The term 'Taylorism' refers to the paradigm of workplace organisation (or 'scientific management') associated with Frederick W. Taylor (b. 1911). Taylorism postulates that complex labour processes should be organisationally fragmented into the individual movements required to produce a product and the individual worker should specialise in one of these movements/tasks, where they were previously engaged in many or all of these movements (as in craft production). For example, where two workers had shovelled and pushed a cart, one would shovel and the other would push. Apart from the economies accruing from the division of labour as such, Taylor discovered that this fragmentation increased the possibilities for management to apply scientific methods to analyse and reorganise production so as to increase the *intensity* of work. This was because the set-up of the production process could be optimised through 'time-motion studies'. Most importantly, since the motion of workers was now available for observation, measurement and control, the Taylorist set-up facilitated a closer discipline of workers. This organisation of work was well suited to the mechanisation of the labour process (for example, through the conveyor belt), and this mechanisation of Taylorism is attributed to Henry Ford. The working class was ambigious towards Taylorism. On the one hand, it implied de-skilling and increased social control by the management (see Braverman 1974). On the other hand, productivity increases and the dependence of management on a stable and predictable supply of labour power, generated the material basis for mass consumption and relative job security.

10 *Ex ante* integrated wage norms imply that wages for a given turnover period of capital are set before the production process of that period begins. This ensures beforehand a given consumption market and wage cost. Thus, risk is minimised, and demand is stabilised and expanded according to anticipated productivity increases resulting from Taylorist incremental time–motion rationalisations in the labour process (see Braverman1974: 85–137). This type of wage determination is said to have been pioneered by Henry Ford, but it gained socio-economic significance through the collective bargaining regimes that were instituted in Western countries in the 1930s and 1940s. This type of wage relation was functional in the rather rigid industrial system of mass production, that resulted from the application of Taylorist principles of organisation of production, and product-specific machinery, yielding profits primarily through returns to scale. Hence mass consumption was expanded and deepened in order to absorb mass production, and the two were articulated into a stable reproductive circuit through the wage relation. Keynesian macroeconomic policy and Beveridgian social policy generally also helped facilitate such stable expansion of mass consumption, through demand management and public investment in welfare goods and services (such as health and housing). See, for example, Mishra (1984: 1–18).

11 The 'virtuous cycle' of Fordism is reflected in a number of indicators. Most OECD countries experienced an unprecedented phase of productivity growth after World War II (the exceptions were the USA, with high growth for a century, and the sluggish development in the UK). Output increased on average by 3.8 per cent per head in the advanced capitalist economies between 1950 and 1973. (For 1913–50 the figure was 1.2; 1870–1913: 1.4; and 1820–70: 1.0) (Armstrong *et al.* 1991: Table 8.1, p. 117, cf. Maddison, 1982: 91.) Between 1955 and 1970, productivity increased by 60 per cent in the advanced capitalist economies, and product wage increases had an almost identical development (ibid: Figure 8.3, p. 121). Profit rates remained at between 25 and 30 per cent of invested capital between 1955 and 1968 (except for 1958, when the rate diped to 21 per cent) (ibid: Figure 8.2, p. 120). Apart from the almost identical development of

productivity and wage increases, it is notable that wage elasticity to prices was exactly 1 in all G-5 countries as well as Italy, Austria, and Sweden during the post-war period up until the early 1970s: that is, a perfect indexation with respect to consumer prices. In the nineteenth century the corresponding figure was 0.1–0.2 and, as we shall see, it has changed markedly since the 1980s. This means, according to Boyer (1997), that the wage no longer is a pure market variable. It '[took] into account a minimum standard of living' and the idea of a 'sharing of the dividend of progress', as opposed to merely being a function of the developments of labour supply and labour demand. This, he argues, expresses the *ex ante* integration of mass production and mass consumption, based in the capital/labour accords.

12 However important the economies of scope have become in post-Fordism, as Robert Boyer (1991; 1997: esp. p. 23) has argued, they have not made economies of scale redundant and they are not in and of themselves sufficient to ensure a sustainable regime of accumulation. Adequate investment levels are still important. Also, economies of scope presuppose a stable environment in which the diffusion of 'best practices' (primarily through 'learning by doing') can take place, and this requires a stable expansion of aggregate demand. This, in turn, requires a wage relation that integrates *inter alia* productivity gains on the supply side with increases in effective demand, and generates growth via compatible social wage-, 'normal' profit-rate-, savings-, finance-, and investment-relations. This thesis is given empirical substantiation by Boyer and Petit (1991: esp. pp. 50–55, 61–62) who show that there continues to be a strong cumulatively causal relationship between prodctivity growth and growth in effective demand in the OECD area (the so-called Kaldor–Verdoorn relationship). 'Solow's productivity paradox' in the 1980s – the coexistence of rapid technological innovation and stagnant rates of productivity growth – is strongly related to the sluggish and uneven growth in aggregate demand. Boyer and Petit argue that this has inhibited the diffusion of new technology, which is verified by sectoral data (OECD 1988).

13 That is, because of the absence of a 'virtuous' 'Kaldor–Verdoorn' dynamic as discussed by Boyer and Petit as discussed in note 12.

14 See especially pp. 182–83, where he discusses this in terms of 'temporal displacement of overaccumulation'.

15 Strange points especially to the importance of fluctuations in the foreign exchange markets, and the demand of corporations to hedge exchange rate fluctuations risks on the futures market in this process. This is, however, a process that has a cumulative effect, because as traders on this type of market try to manage the risk, it adds further momentum to speculation and short-termism.

16 This subject is analysed by the classical Marxist theories of imperialism (the dynamic whereby profit rates are sustained by expanding into territory where higher rates of exploitation of labour are possible, and/or where surplus capacity and products can find a market outlet). This is not without relevance to the dynamic of the 'emerging markets'. Harvey (1990: pp. 183–84) discusses this in terms of 'spatial displacement'.

17 See Streeck (1995: pp. 22–25). This is not to say that the erosion of 'Rhineland capitalism' is a foregone conclusion, that there are not opposite and contradictory tendencies, nor even that there are not counter-tendencies (including 'tradition' and path dependency) (Rhodes and van Apeldoorn 1998). On the continued relevance of quasi-public lending instituions in regional industrial policy and for the finance of small high-tech enterprises in Germany (generally disregarded by larger banks), see Deeg (1997). But this hardly falsifies the contention that the 'globalised', short-term financial market is a powerful tendential development

that is increasingly challenging the institutions of state–business relations of the post-war 'Rhineland model'.

18 Michalet (1991: pp. 79–87) relates Solow's productivity paradox (see note 14) to exactly this.

19 A conceptual note: The term 'articulation' of social relations of production implies that any concrete economy is comprised of many different patterns of production organisation, that are nevertheless connected through external relations. (For example, the typical post-war economy was characterised by bipartite or tripartite Fordist organisation in key sectors, but these nevertheless co-existed with 'free-enterprise' labour markets, as well as with patriarchical relations in the household.) 'Hegemonic' in this context does not mean that all sectors, or even national economies, are characterised by this mode. Rather, it means that a certain mode is predominant in the economic dynamic, and that other modes are inserted in the economy so as to serve its imperatives (Cox 1987: Part I).

20 The data are taken from Christian Berggren's contribution in Sandberg (1995: 105–26). The interpretation that Uddevalla and Kalmar contained a production paradigm capable of competing with Toyotism has triggered controversy. Adler and Cole (1995: 171–78), whilst accepting that Uddevalla compared favourably with European and North American competitors, were not convinced that the plant could close the gap with the Toyota plant. They point to the fact that Berggren's argument hinges on the fact that the plant was in an early phase of its lifetime and that dramatic improvements in productivity would close the gap. They are less convinced that this is necessarily the case, since many plants experience a temporary steep learning-curve and 'crisis learning' in the early stages. Much of the debate hinges around scope for transcending standardisation (Adler and Cole 1995) and the more positive assessments of the scope for 'holistic learning' (and whether Uddevalla displayed this rather than 'crisis learning') (Nilsson 1995: 75–86). Be this as it may, it should be pointed out that Uddevalla matching Toyota is not the burden of proof here. First, even assuming Toyotism does represent best practice, whilst depending on a radical dualisation of 'established' and 'precarious' labour, it hardly represents the type of Americanised individual wage-setting that Calmfors associates with post-Fordism. Also, here there is a collectivist moral economy determining the wage norm (although a hierarchical one). Secondly, the productivity improvements at Kalmar and Uddevalla shows that it more than held its own with other competitors.

21 Though, of course, there were (and are) many other similar instances of production process innovation in Sweden. For overviews, see Mahon (1994a: 83–136) as well as Brulin and Nilsson (1994). Sandberg (1992) led a project looking at co-determination and technological change in six companies in six different sectors. Glimstedt (1993) analysed the (from the point of view of organised labour) more ambiguous – but by no means hopeless – situation in 'co-operation agreements' by Asea Brown Boveri in the heavy engineering sector. In their critical discourse analysis of struggles to determine the meaning of 'industrial democracy', and 'co-operation' in what they see as an open-ended shift towards post-Fordism, Elam and Börjesson (1991) focus on the steel and printing sectors. For a recent survey-based analysis that points to a positive relation between Swedish co-determination and economic efficiency, see Levinson (2000).

22 Freyssenet argues that this form of production presupposes a particular social and organisational context of negotiation and co-operation. Here he turns the debate around, and argues that, because the system is based on autonomy and active involvement of the workers, it also presupposes guarantees that labour-saving techniques do not translate into redundancies etc. Hence, the question is not so much whether the system can be rendered compatible with de-commodification

associated with social citizenship norms. The question is whether the potential of new technology can be fully realised in an organisational and social setting, when labour power is treated as a commodity to be shed when productivity increases. Here Freyssenet invokes research in Japan indicating that, in the process of extending lean production, Toyota has had to take on principles from the Uddevalla model (cf. Shimzu 1995). This corroborates well with arguments that Japanese lean production, which combines a loss of autonomy with a demand for involvement is likely to run into social limits in the form of shopfloor resistance (Skorstad 1994).

3 The formation and consolidation of social democratic hegemony in Sweden

1 'Socialisation' as used here has a very particular meaning: i.e. what the Germans call *Vergesellschaftung* (which, strictly speaking, ought to be translated as 'societalisation'). Socialisation in this sense is adopted from Marx's *Grundrisse* and should be understood as the dialectical counterpart of 'commodification'. The premise (related to that of regulation theory presented in chapter 2) is that the tendency to organise social entities and their interrelations through a market-determined money nexus (and hence define them as commodities) encounters inherent limits, because it is in the nature of certain aspects of social reality to resist commodification despite having a 'use value'. For Polanyi, this is inherently so for the 'fictitious commodities' of land, labour and money itself ('the postulate that anything that is bought and sold must also have been produced for sale is emphatically untrue in regard to them' [Polanyi 1957: 72, cited in van der Pijl 1998: 15]). But in addition, in different epochs, with different production and social technologies, other aspects of social reality may also not be amenable to commodification. Synthesising Marx with Weber, Habermas suggested that normative reproduction also cannot be subordinated to a pure commodity economic logic. The notion of socialisation, in this context, should be understood as the responses engendered in society as a result of the distintegrative effects of commodification and the 'planned or otherwise normatively unified interdependencies of functionally divided social activity' that are produced in the search for social order. Van der Pijl (1998: 14–30) gives an overview of the dialectic of commodification and socialisation and discusses its general effect on dynamics in the levels of production, state, culture and international relations.

2 The socio-political basis of this coexistence of landed autarky and commercial liberalism was based on power blocs constituted by the landed aristocracy and the commercial cum financial capitalist elite, with different balances of powers and different ethico-political normative frameworks prevailing in different states (Moore 1967). The commercial bourgeoisie was hegemonic in the Anglo-Saxon 'Lockeian' heartland but not in the 'Hobbesian contender-states' (van der Pijl 1998: 64–83).

3 The Cow Deal has the same connotation in Swedish as the term 'horse trade' in English. This was because it was perceived as an unprincipled deal between two parties with nothing in common. (The Agrarians had been reluctant to concede universal suffrage and the SAP had supported free trade in agriculture in order to lower the price of food). However, it proved to be the beginning of an enduring alliance between two parties representing social groups that had been hit hard in the depression and hence were united in their vulnerability to market forces.

4 The reforms in housing policy included housing subsidies for families with many children, maternity benefits to 90 per cent of all mothers, free maternity and child-birth services, state loans to newly married couples and two weeks statutory

holidays (Olsson 1987: 5). The main intellectual proponents of these reforms were Alva and Gunnar Myrdal, whose book *Kris i befolkningsfragan* set the tone of the debate. They successfully articulated the view that the family policy reforms were in the 'national interest' as they counteracted population decline (and hence the reproductive role of the welfare state was emphasised). The unemployment insurance scheme was formulated and implemented under the intellectual leadership of Gustav Möller, along the lines of the Ghent model, to which principles the SAP had subscribed since 1910. The state does not set up its own unemployment insurance programme in the Ghent model. Rather, it provides subsidies and grants to already existing trade union unemployment benefit societies, in exchange for the latter accepting norms set by the government on issues such as insurance premiums, benefit levels, and methods of control. Hence, unemployment insurance is administered by the trade unions. From the point of view of social democratic hegemony, this reproduces the idea that the 'normal' worker is a trade union member, and it does so apparently successfully, since there is a strong positive correlation between the Ghent model and trade union density. Furthermore, self-organisation of UI administration by organised labour provides a way to keep the micro-processes of state bureaucratic discipline at arms-length (Rothstein 1990: 317–45).

5 The factors behind the acute balance of payments crisis of 1931 and their links to the international crisis and the devaluation of the pound are analysed in Kock (1961: 90–98). In part, the balance of payments crisis was due to a decrease in exports caused by the depression abroad. But what is particularly notable is the rapid withdrawal of liquid foreign assets from Sweden in 1931, without a corresponding inflow of Swedish assets abroad because of the 'non-liquid' nature of the latter assets tied to the Young Plan credit package to Germany. The explanation seems to lie in the financial speculation by Krüger and Toll, the world monopolists of matches of this period. The 'match king' Krüger had amassed a fortune in the 1920s based on a highly speculative extension of credit in Europe, and on borrowing in North America, using his match monopoly as collateral (and links to the Skandinaviska Bank). By 1931, events caught up with him. He had locked much of his assets into long-term loans to Germany, as organised by the Young Plan. But these assets were financed by short-term loans that by 1931 he could no longer pay. Hence, Sweden went off the gold standard, and Krüger committed suicide.

6 The Saltsjöbaden Accord was a bipartite agreement that constituted negotiation procedures and rules of conduct in industrial conflict (including the protection of 'third party'). The agreement stipulated that wage agreements would be struck by peak associations at the branch level. However, the procedural rules also allowed for coordinated inter-branch level negotiations if the bargaining units considered this to be desirable. The agreement did not involve the government, but it was based on a government strategy that followed the recommendations of the so-called Nothin Commission. This public commission had been formed against the backdrop of highly polarised industrial relations where the clash of an increasingly strong trade union movement and an economic-liberal business-class had yielded one of the highest strike and lock-out rates in Europe. The Commission argued that it would be desirable if unions and the employers' federation could reach an agreement on rules of conduct in industrial relations. Only if such talks did not materialise, the commission argued, should the government prepare legislation (Sweden. SOU 1935b). It was against this backdrop, and the election result of 1936, which dashed their hopes of more restrictive labour laws and the repeal of social democratic welfare and economic policy, that SAF took the initiative to the Saltsjöbaden Accord (Johansson 1989: 135–49). The Salsjöbaden

Accord ushered in an era of 'labour market peace' and 'consensus' on the rules of conduct in industrial relations. Whereas an average of 80,000 workers were on strike or were locked out per year in the 1920s and the early 1930s in Sweden, the corresponding number for the period 1956–65 – the 'golden age' of the Swedish model – was 1500 workers. This reduction understates the trend since both labour force and unionisation rates increased from the first to the second period (Lewin 1992b: 38–39).

7 The term 'passive revolution' refers to when a power bloc modifies itself to pre-empt a hegemonic crisis and incorporates new forces (and displaces old ones) as a response to social transformations. It does so in order to maintain political order and its form of rule. However, in doing so it may unleash further transformations that require a further passive revolution: 'One may apply to the concept of passive revolution the interpretative criterion of molecular changes which in fact progressively modify the pre-existing composition of forces, and hence become a matrix of new changes' (Gramsci 1971: 109).

8 Popular movements were based on ideas of 'collective solidarity and self-organization and popular education for the cause of individual human development and social progress' (Therborn 1988: 352). On the development of popular movements, see also Samuelsson (1968: 168–72); Lundqvist (1975: 180–93); Scott (1988: 353–61; 409–37); Pontusson (1988: 40–45). As the rural poor were transformed into the urban proletariat, the popular movements also provided a contact area and a sense of belonging in the city; see, for example, the case study of Malmö by Billing *et al.* (1988: 118–22).

9 From 1906 onwards SAF compelled the unions to concede that all collective agreements must include a clause that invoked §23 of SAF's statutes which stated that management enjoyed the absolute right to manage the organisation of the labour process. They enforced this demand through threats of industry wide lockouts that would have drained union strike funds (Casparsson 1951: 215–60).

10 For a more detailed discussion of the notion of *folkhemmet* in the forging of hegemony at the national popular level, see Stråth (1996: 246–53). He emphasises the importance of the notion of '*folk*' (people) for a formal discursive field that social democrats and conservatives shared, but over whose content they engaged in struggle. The notion of *folk* was initially a conservative one that emerged in crisis of the Oscarian era at the turn of the century and was deployed in a project of 'national renewal'. Three factors triggered this project: the end of political union with Norway in 1905, mass emigration to the USA and the challenge of the labour movement. It also coincided with the development of a national industrial economy to be discussed below, and was directed towards a reform strategy that would rationalise state–society relations of the Oscarian bloc so as to incorporate labour and address the problem of emigration. This project did result in a formal rationalisation of the civil service, but did little in terms of content. By the late 1920s, a very different articulation of the notion of '*folk*' (associated with *folkrörelser*) carried the day in a project that had incorporated elements of the conservative discourse (such as how to deal with the decline of population growth through the social democratic welfare state) and that accepted the state framework of the rationalised civil service as the instrument of reform.

11 On the interaction of domestic 'development blocs' and the export system in the Swedish mode of growth, see Edquist and Lundvall (1993: 277–83).

12 On SNS, see also the memoirs of the former CEO and Chairman of Handelsbanken Tore Browaldh (1976: 68–95).

13 According to Åke Ortmark (1981: 105), one of Sweden's most prominent economic journalists, industrial consolidation and restructuring 'quickly became a forté of the Wallenbergs'. Marcus Wallenberg Sr took primary responsibility for

the relationship between the bank and its corporations. The following quote from Ortmark illustrates the intimate relationship between bank and industry and the control exercised: '[When Markus Wallenberg Sr] had hand-picked a CEO for the consolidation process of a company, he then kept regular contact with him subsequently. The need for contact was (and is) mutual. It is not only a question of the great capitalist [Wallenberg] wanting to control that all is going according to plan. It has just as often been the wish of the appointed CEO to take advantage of the experience and the sense of judgement of the family. A citation from Sigfrid Edström's [CEO of ASEA in the 1930s] calendar is illuminating with respect to this: "During the first years of ASEA's consolidation, I visited Marcus Wallenberg once a week at his office . . . he gave me much valuable advice" . . . The importance of the contacts between the capitalist [Wallenberg] and the company executive cannot be overestimated. Through them, the Wallenbergs have had formidable steering-instruments. With [their] perspective of the 'big picture', their memory, and command of the telephone conversation, Marcus Wallenberg [Sr as well as Jr] could participate in, or initiate decisions in about 10 [of Sweden's most prominent] corporations' (ibid: 119) (my translations).

14 See also Marcus Wallenberg's letters to Keynes that reveal his contemptuous and hostile attitude towards the new government and its policies (Gårdlund 1977).

15 The Salsjöbaden Accord coincided with a transition of generations in the Wallenberg sphere. The brothers Knut Agathon Wallenberg and Marcus Wallenberg Sr died in 1938 and 1943 respectively, and Marcus Sr's sons, Jacob and Marcus Jr (henceforth referred to as Marcus Wallenberg) took over the leadership. Knut Agathon, who also had served as Foreign Minister, had played an active role in inter-war financial diplomacy. Marcus Sr was less flamboyant and had focused his time much more strictly to the business of the bank. In the last year of his life, however, he assumed a more active political role, feeling that he was almost desperately fighting for his survival, as the new economic thinking of the 1930s took root. His sons disliked the new economic policy just as much, but they assumed a new tactical line in political society: 'the line of silence'. This was in part because they concluded that it was hopeless to oppose the political climate and in part because they considered that such verbal engagements, leading to defeat, devalued the reputation of the family. In a sense, the line of silence worked. Their economic power, combined with their Garboesque engagement with the public, definitely gave Jacob and Marcus Wallenberg an awesome aura in Sweden (see Ortmark 1981: 114–15).

16 SI became a coordinating centre for promoting research and education for example, through the development of a business school based on the German Handelshochschule model (i.e. Stockholm School of Economics was formed in 1909). But SI also promoted 'rationalisation ideas' in society at large. For example, they published Taylor's *The Principles of Scientific Management* in 1913.

17 The most unequivocal policy-relevant statement of this argument is Frans Severin's reservation about the neo-classical interpretation of unemployment in the Report of the Unemployment Commission of 1936 (Sweden. SOU 1935b: 293–337).

18 The relationship between Swedish social democrats and Keynes might require some elaboration. The change of economic policy in the 1930s has often been seen as a major rupture in the ideology of Swedish social democracy away from Marxism to Keynesianism. But Nils Unga (1976) – who seems to have the final word on the emergence of the new unemployment policy in the 1930s – has pointed out the continuity of social democratic ideology. Firstly, he showed that the policy of 1932 was not informed by Keynesianism in a strict sense, but by the quite immediate interests of the trade unions. Secondly, he persuasively argued

that when Keynesianism became a prominent element of social democratic policy during World War II, it became an instrument understood in the broader terms of the discourse of 'organised capitalism'. Keynesianism, then, as appropriated by the social democrats in the 1930s should not be understood in opposition to (Austro-)Marxism. And Keynes was only one of many influences.

19 On the utopian and rationalist conceptions of social policy that informed Swedish 'social engineers', defined their role, authority and self-definition, see Hirdman (1989: 11–13, 92–158, 176–215).

20 The forced sterilisation programme seems to have singled out so-called *tattare* (a dark skinned group traditionally subjected to prejudice in Sweden). The sterilisation policy was explicitly justified in terms of releasing the state from potential future burdens, as welfare entitlements expanded (Matl 1997).

21 On the intellectual background to this type of welfare reform, see Rothstein (1985a: esp. 156–59, 163–64). My distinction between the Myrdals and Möller probably oversimplifies and exaggerates their differences. Also, the Myrdals saw virtues in popular mobilisation, and construed bureaucracy as unfortunate but necessary for as long as the social conditions required to produce the democratic socialist citizen had not yet been achieved (Myrdal 1967). This being said, however, Möller's principled and stubborn opposition to administrative controls suggests, as Rothstein argues, that he was conscious of the danger that state bureaucracy posed for reformism in a way that the Myrdals and other social democratic were not. On the other hand, Möller was more prone to accept traditional gender relations as natural, whereas the Myrdal's demanded a transformation of the conditions of women (although from a technocratic-utopian, not 'organic', vantage point).

4 Social democratic regulation: the Swedish model

1 Unless otherwise stated, this account of the immediate post-war period is based on Lewin (1967).

2 The debates on social policy focused on the revenue side, that is taxation policy. Ohlin, the liberal Keynesian, advocated lower rates of taxation and deficit financing of the social policy reform programme.

3 Apart from the text of the 1951 LO Congress Report, my interpretation of the Rehn–Meidner model and its politico-economic implication relies heavily upon Martin (1984: 202–23), Hedborg and Meidner (1984), and Erixon (1994).

4 'Planned wage policy', for the purpose of generating productivity growth, rationalisation of industry, and the potential for real wage increases, was approved by the LO congress of 1941. The idea of solidaristic wage policy was formulated by Albin Lind in 1938 (Simonson 1988: 20–21, 23–35). Active labour market policy emerged in the late 1940s, in part as an outgrowth of the employment exchanges set up by social democratic municipalities during the inter-war period (Rothstein 1985b: 156–58).

5 Wage drift is defined as the difference between the statistically measured rate of total wage increases and the rate of total wage increases estimated on the basis of the collective agreement. Main causes of wage drift are held to be (uneven) productivity growth and overtime (which increases the total earnings of workers whose wage is significantly variable on quantity produced and hours worked eg. piece rates and overtime bonuses). Another alleged cause is voluntary payments that exceed the rate of the collective agreement, paid by some employers in order to recruit or retain 'core-workers' in a context of excess demand for labour. See, for example, Bergom-Larsson (1985: 374–75).

6 See Erlander (1974: 234–40; 1976: 37–47) and Rehn (1988: 217–47) for political deliberations between representatives for LO and the government. See also the theoretical and ideological debate in the official journal of the SAP, *Tiden*, during the decade after 1948. Apart from Rehn and Meidner's articles cited above, participants in the debate included Per Åsbrink, who would become the Governor of the Bank of Sweden during this time, Bent Hansen, Director of the Research Institute associated with the Ministry of Finance (*konjunkturinstitutet (KI)*), Per-Edvin Sköld, the Minister of Finance himself, and Karl Fredriksson, a prominent editor of the daily *Socialdemokraten*.

7 The concept of 'transformation pressure' is not contained in the original Rehn–Meidner model. Rather, it is integrated into it by Lennart Erixon in his interpretation and further theoretical elaboration of the model. Invoking industrial economists such as Åkerman, Dahmén and Svennilson, and indirectly Schumpeter, he tries to render the Rehn–Meidner model relevant to the economy of the 1990s, by embedding it in an explicit industrial-dynamic theorisation (Erixon 1994: 25–27; 1991: 239–399).

8 The first bargaining round that followed this principle was that of 1952, although LO had not managed to devise a coherent strategy at that time, and the result rather serendipitously arose by SAF forcing the issue of coordinated bargaining. As of the bargaining round of 1956, the LO progressively developed its strategy however, and through its low-wage deal (*låglönesatsning*) of 1966, solidaristic wage policy probably reached its zenith. In the late 1950s, low-wage groups were offered a fixed increase in öre, above the macro-level percentage increase ('the broken öre-percentage norm'). In 1963 the LO–SAF agreement included special low-wage pools for all agreement-areas where a fixed öre (as opposed to percentage) increase was allotted to low-wage workers. In addition there was a low wage supplement for special low-wage agreement areas. This 1966 agreement further developed the low-wage pool and included a 'wage development guarantee' to address the issue of uneven developments in variable wages, the area where wage drift was most prevalent (Meidner 1973: 35–38).

9 The real interest rate was only marginally over zero during the time period, and the net rate after tax rarely above zero (Lindbeck 1975: 127; Mjöset *et al.* 1986: 131).

10 On this point, see Martin (1984: 212) and (Sweden. SOU 1955: 338–45). This ambiguity is evident in the latter document – a major public commission report written by Bent Hansen, the Director of the National Institute of Economic Research (KI), which is a research branch of the Ministry of Finance. This report engaged in an explicit discussion with the trade union economists, Rehn and Meidner. Being very careful not to suggest that they had not defined the central relationships of economic policy, Hansen nevertheless suggested that the government may choose to order the aims of medium-term policy in other ways than Rehn and Meidner had suggested (i.e. favour balance of payments and savings over wage drift containment). He himself did not venture into defining the hierarchy of objectives. Thus the economic model he formulated left much room for contest and negotiation.

11 The average combined central and municipal rate of corporate taxation 1955–72 was about 52 per cent (Pontusson 1992: 70, cf. Bergström 1982 and Taylor 1982).

12 Tax depreciation rates exceeded real economic depreciation for capital equipment, and thus provided a form of interest free credit or subsidy for such investment. Depreciation allowances were more favourable for investments in capital equipment than in buildings. The IF system, however, made no distinction between the two forms of investment. The result of this was that there was a higher propensity to set aside funds for buildings investment in the IF system.

This served the governments contra-cyclical and employments policies well, since such investments have a more immediate employment effect (ibid: 71–72).

13 Regulations constraining the potential financial power of the AP funds were strict, which suggests that they were to minimise risk and to serve as guarantees that the terms of the historic compromise between capital and labour would not be changed. The 1959 funds were prohibited from acquiring equity capital and from lending directly to private corporations. However, corporations could reborrow 50 per cent of the fees they had paid into the system the preceding year (retroverse loans), provided a bank assumed the risk for such loans. The funds could be lent directly to the public sector, and be used to purchase bonds (private as well as public bonds) (Pontusson 1992: 82–83). The memoirs of Browaldh (1980), the CEO of the SHB bank, who it should be recalled, in contrast to the Wallenbergs, actively supported the spirit of compromise between capital and labour, illustrate that ATP threatened to challenge boundaries that he did not want to be challenged. He was appointed as the representative of business to the Public Commission in charge devising the ATP proposal, and he made it a priority to ensure that the AP funds should not be allowed to purchase shares 'because there was no need for another credit institute . . . and because, in an economic crisis, this might mean that a number of corporations must be taken over by the AP fund (my translation)'. In this respect, he was highly satisfied with the manner in which the chair of the committee, Åsbrink, the Central Bank Governor, narrowed the discussions by insisting on three specific aims: to develop effective bond market, to minimise the bureaucratic overheads of the AP funds, and to minimise the risks of ATP savings (Browaldh 1980: 178–79). At the time this was not a problem and Browaldh characterised the atmosphere in the committee (which included Meidner) friendly, resembling an economics seminar. As we shall see in chapter 6, this issue would become more contentious in the 1970s.

14 The emissions control implied that all bond issues had to be approved by the Central Bank. The Central Bank used this leverage to control the quantity of the emission and the rate of interest of the bond. Foreign exchange control was based on World War II legislation that was not repealed after 1945. It prohibited residents from acquiring foreign assets and nonresidents from dealing in Swedish assets without government permission. Trade credits (up to three months) were allowed as have generally been foreign direct investments (which, however, had to be financed through foreign currency loans).

15 Interviewee 8. While Marquis Childs put undue emphasis on the role of the co-operatives in the Swedish model in his book, *Sweden: The Middle Way*, other accounts have probably gone too far in ignoring them. Cooperatives played a significant role in the mode of consumption of the Swedish model. Two million Swedes (out of a population of 8.5 million) are members of the Consumer Cooperative Association (*Kooperativa förbundet* (KF)), and this conglomerate ranks as one of Sweden's ten largest corporations. KF is a key actor in food markets, vertically integrating production and retail petroleum retail, and insurance. Moreover, the housing cooperative, HSB, is a significant actor on the housing market, and BPA, a trade union cooperative, is a significant actor in the construction industry. Finally, LRF, the farmers' cooperative, dominates the wholesale of agricultural products (Pestoff 1991: ch. 1).

16 'Tripartism' as adopted from Jessop does not have the same meaning as it does in industrial relations. In industrial relations it denotes a direct participation of the state in deliberations together with employers and employees. Understood in the latter sense, Swedish industrial relations were emphatically not tripartite, but bipartite (as codified by the Saltsjöbaden Accord). However, when the point of reference is the overall regulation/mediation of civil society by the state – the

concern of neo-Marxist state theory – then Sweden clearly fits the definition tripartism. Jessop uses the term to describe what others refer to as 'democratic corporatist' to distinguish it from authoritarian corporatism. The defining feature is the coexistence of functional representation and liberal democratic representation, where the former is embedded in the latter.

17 This might be an appropriate place to clarify the different ways in which the word 'structural' is used in this book. At times I refer to the 'structural power of capital' or the capitalist class. Here I refer to the power that emanates from an overall essential structural characteristic of capitalism as a totality: that is the formal separation of capitalism into a 'political' and 'economic' as well as 'civil' sphere. At other places I talk about structural economic policies. This refers to policies that are directed towards the economic sphere with the intention of facilitating the development of the forces of production. They do not challenge the social relations of production – that is the overall structural configuration. Finally, I refer at times to the structural power of the American state. This refers to structural power in the stricter sense than the structural power of capital. It refers to structural power in the political sphere, as exercised in the international state system, which is part and parcel of transnational capitalism.

18 Two of the most prominent economists of this institutionalist brand of Keynesianism, Gunnar Myrdal and Bertil Ohlin, held prominent positions in the SAP and the Liberal Party, respectively. But this policy discourse was not monistic. It was a 'contradictory unity' with possible competing interpretations, informed by other theoretical and philosophical currents (Pekkarinen 1989: 312–14, 318–21). Marxism remained a latent legacy in the 'functional socialism' of the SAP. This party was also more directly influenced by the functionalist movement, and was optimistic about the possibility of using the state to rectify injustices and irrationalities in everyday life, through 'social engineering' (Olsson 1994: 48–50). The Liberals were less optimistic regarding the possibilities of the state and more optimistic about the role of the market. This is evident in a critique of Rehn and Meidner by the liberal economist, Erik Lundberg (Lewin 1967: 366–74). The Liberals tended to favour a more expansionary Keynesianism, with lower levels of taxation public consumption. Interestingly, Ohlin was one of the pioneers in advocating selective labour market policy in the 1930s. But, as Söderpalm (1976: 157) observes, he assumed a more *laissez faire* posture after he became the leader of the Liberals. The latter suggests that this change in orientation is a consequence of the strong connection between the Liberal Party and the export industry that existed through the 1930s to the 1950s.

19 On the relationship with the Central Bank, see Uusitalo (1984: 36–48) and also Notermans (1993: 140–41, 157), who emphasises the decisive importance of direct administrative credit rationing and strict exchange controls for restrictive fine tuning as a compensation for fiscal lags. For the importance of the relationship between the Finance Minister and the Prime Minister, see for example the memoirs of Kjell Olof Feldt (1991). This special relationship is empirically validated by Petersson (1989: 58–66). I am not aware of a systematic study of this relationship made in the early post-war period, but the importance of the relationship between the Prime Minister (Erlander) and the Minister of Finance (Sköld) in the process surrounding the acceptance of the Rehn–Meidner model seems to indicate its existence at this period as well (Rehn 1988). In his memoirs, Wigforss (1954: 329) explains that he could not support Gustav Möller as the successor of Per Albin Hansson as Prime Minister, because he felt that Möller had become too personally involved with the social policy reforms to provide adequate support for the Minister of Finance on internal governmental deliberations.

20 For an elaboration of the budget bargaining process in this period, see Amnå (1981).

21 The potential contradiction between the Ministry of Social Affairs, in charge of social welfare maintenance and expansion, and the Ministry of Finance, in charge of internal and external economic balance, is obvious (see Amnå 1981). For the relationship between the LO's negotiators and the Ministry of Finance, see Martin (1984: 207) and Åmark (1988: esp. pp. 69–70, 75–82). The tensions between macroeconomic managers and trade unionists stem from their different perspectives on the relationship between wages and their respective policy ends. For macroeconomic managers, macro-wage increases that were too high might endanger the balance of payments. For union negotiators, wage increases that were too low might jeopardise 'external wage levelling', and make it possible for individual entrepreneurs to offer market-determined extra wage increases (wage drift) that could undermine the internal fabric of the 'moral economy' (the socially constructed norms of relative wage relations), and threaten organisational unity and legitimacy within the union movement (Swenson 1989: chs 1 and 4).

22 The 'New Deal synthesis' defined the content of the power bloc that initially was organised through Roosevelt and the Democratic Party. It was based on the leadership of emerging (Fordist) capital intensive corporations that, whilst depending on internal mass consumption, also had vital interests in international expansion. Since their terms of economic openness were not based on wage competition, it was possible for these corporations to strike capital–labour accords with the trade union movement. It was also possible for them to unite with investment bankers in New York behind an accumulation strategy, given the relative weakness of the latter after the Wall Street Crash. The Republican Party had initially represented a 'protectionist' counter-bloc, but after World War II, Republicanism merely represented a slightly more aloof variant of the New Deal synthesis (van der Pijl 1984).

23 Embedded liberalism was a compromise between the economic nationalism that had emerged in the west in response to the economic crisis in the 1930s, and the free trade liberalism of the Pax Britannica era. While international multilateralism was affirmed, it would not be predicated on *laissez faire* economic philosophy. Rather, it would be predicated on domestic interventionism. For that purpose, the international monetary order of Bretton Woods was based on the principle of the double screen. Liberalisation and expansion of international trade would be facilitated by the gradual abolition of exchange controls, and a multilateral fixed exchange rate regime. However, in order to ensure that these imperatives for international trade did not undermine the possibility of states pursuing Keynesian economic policy and a full employment commitment, the IMF system would finance short-term payments of deficit countries from funds provided by membership contributions. (Due to the reluctance of the US administration to provide the IMF with adequate funds, this function would in reality be performed unilaterally by the USA.) In addition, the norms of the IMF stated that if 'fundamental disequilibrium' developed, exchange rates could be altered with IMF concurrence. Finally, in this system, governments maintained the controls on capital markets that had been implemented in the 1930s and 1940s. See Ruggie (1983: 209–11).

24 See for example, Armstrong *et al.* (1991: 68–135). In particular, Sweden obviously benefited from the reconstruction and gradual expansion of trade in Western Europe (which, excluding Scandinavia, comprised about 65 per cent of Swedish trade in the post-war period), particularly the reconstruction of Germany. In the 1960s, though, Sweden's neutrality policy created complications

since it prevented an entry into the EEC. This was offset primarily by the growth and relative diversification in the other Nordic (EFTA) markets (Olsson 1993: 24–31).

25 That is, after the anti-socialist American union leader, Gomper, who was a champion of a narrow economistic industrial unionism.

5 Neo-liberal globalisation

1 Time–space compression means that social communicative interaction is possible over an ever increasing spatial range within an ever shortening time-horizon. With the internet it is possible to communicate worldwide almost instantaneoulsy at a low cost.

2 As Jessop points out, in this respect, neo-Marxist state theory remains valid. The 'state' and 'market' are merely specific forms of the formal separation of 'the economic' and 'the political' in the capitalist mode of production, that then are interconnected in various ways in different historical contexts in order to make possible the maintenance of social order.

3 GDP growth slowed down in OECD-Europe from an annual average rate of 4.7 per cent in 1960–73, to 2.2 per cent in 1973–89, despite marked increases in inflation (Armstrong *et al.* 1991: Table 14.1 p. 234, cf. OECD *Historical Statistics and Economic Outlook*, various issues). Productivity growth declined from an annual average rate of 4.3 per cent in 1960–73 to 1.9 per cent in 1973–87 (ibid: Table 14.7, p. 245). Recurring budget deficits in the 1970s led to a doubling of government debt/GDP ratio in the OECD countries between 1973 and 1986, from 16 to 33 per cent (ibid: 256). Lipietz (1985; 1987) shows that decreases in productivity gains started before other crisis symptoms as early as the mid-1960s. They were originally 'counteracted' by an increase in the value of capital per head, which had an adverse effect on the profit rate. Oligopolies could initially 'pass-on' the welfare loss to its consumers through mark-up procedures, but the result of this was inflation. The cause for the slowdown in productivity, in turn, is to be found in the successful resistance of workers to, and the increasingly expensive organizational overheads of, further Taylorist refinement of the production process.

4 According to Ruigrok and van Tulder, the banks have tried to keep the equity share of the percentage of assets as low as possible. A more accurate statement would be that the spheres have pursued an aggressive strategy of issuing 'B shares' with weak voting rights, reserving for themselves preference shares with strong voting rights. Hence capital can be raised on the equity market without the loss of strategic control. In 1989, the Wallenberg sphere had only 3.8 per cent of the shares in Electrolux, for example, but since these were preference shares it controlled 45.9 per cent of the vote (Hermansson 1989: 195). The *Financial Times* journalist, Christopher Brown-Humes, suggests that the Marxist Hermansson underestimates the concentration of Wallenberg power in Electrolux. He argues that through cross-ownerships in 1994 the Wallenberg sphere could control 94.1 per cent of the votes (Brown-Humes 1994).

5 By 1994, foreign production as a proportion of total production had, in aggregate terms, approached 55 per cent for Swedish TNCs and 71 of total employment of the TNCs was abroad (Ekholm and Hesselman 2000).

6 Strange explains the logic behind this development in the following way. Under floating exchange rates companies engaging in foreign trade had an increased need to protect the value of their transactions, which would vary with the rates of exchange. Hence, their finance managers would buy their currency forward to ensure a particular rate of exchange. This purchase amounted to an investment

in the short-term money market, since the order from the trading corporation would create an imbalance in the balance sheet of its bank. The bank would then use the deposit to swap currencies in order to optimise its portfolio (according to expectations of exchange and interest rate movements) on the short-term 'overnight' financial markets). According to Strange, it is these swaps that are behind the growth of the inter-bank markets through which international liquidity is now provided. The price of the cover on the future markets tends to be determined by these inter-bank operations 'according to the differences between interest rates offered for Eurocurrency deposits in differenct currencies. This is the link that connects the foreign exchange market with the short-term credit market, and exchange rates with interest rates. And because of the greater volatility of exchange rates, the Eurocurrency markets became a channel by which any event which affected the exchange rate, whether that was a change in the trade account or some political event regarded in the market as a plus or a minus for a particular currency, was immediately transmitted to the credit markets' (Strange 1989: 11–12).

7 Turnover time is the time it takes for a unit of capital advanced (M) to realise its profit (M'). Post-Fordism essentially operates by rationalising the movement of the capital circuit, M–C–M', in various ways. Some sectors of financial capital involved in risk-management and speculation realise their profits (or losses) almost instantaneously (M–M').

8 Central in this respect was the decreased capacity of the American government to provide the reserve currency of the international money supply through the IMF finance system which was supposed to manage balance of payment surpluses and deficits according to Keynesian principles. This capacity decreased essentially because of the diminishing productivity gap between the USA and other OECD states, with its attendant effects on balance of payments. In more immediate terms, the problem manifested itself in the US deficit-financing of the Vietnam War and the Great Society programme which generated inflation which was 'imported' to other countries through the fixed exchange rates. Japan and European states, led by Germany and France, were increasingly reluctant to participate in such a system. The Special Drawing Rights were proposed as the basis of a global currency, but the USA was reluctant to cede its seignorage position. Amid increased tensions, the Nixon administration abandoned the Bretton Woods system in 1971.

9 Embedded liberalism was a compromise between the economic nationalism that had emerged in the west in response to the economic crisis in the 1930s and the free trade liberalism of the Pax Britannica era. While international multilateralism was affirmed, it would not be predicated on *laissez faire* economic philosophy. Rather, it would be predicated on domestic interventionism. For that purpose, the international monetary order of the Bretton Woods system was based in the principle of the 'double screen'. Liberalisation and expansion of international trade would be facilitated by the gradual abolition of exchange controls and a multilateral fixed exchange rate regime. However, in order to ensure that these imperatives for international trade did not debilitate the possibility of states to pursue Keynesian policies and a full employment commitment, the IMF system would finance short-term payments of deficit countries from funds provided by membership contributions. (Due to the reluctance of the US administration to provide the IMF with adequate funds, this function would in reality be performed unilaterally by the USA.) In addition, the norms of the IMF stated that if 'fundamental disequilibrium' developed, exchange rates could be altered with IMF concurrence. Finally, in this system, governments maintained the controls on

capital markets that had been implemented in the 1930s and 1940s. (Ruggie 1983: 209–11).

10 Indeed, while he insists that Fordist modes of regulation were autocentric, Lipietz (1987: 31) calls this an 'implicit (international) mode of regulation' based on a 'vast catching up movement by Europe and Japan in relation to the United States'.

11 That is, the dilemma of either restoring the domestic balance of payments equilibrium at the risk of triggering a world recession, or supplying dollars for the world market and exacerbating domestic inflation and balance of payments problems.

12 New constitutionalism initially (1979–84) took the form of *laissez faire* in the exchange rate determination between the US dollar and the European currencies (pooled in the ecu), and a regional fixed exchange rate regime between the European currencies through the European Monetary System (EMS). In the USA, the inflationary tendencies of expansionary fiscal policies, geared towards rearmament, were contained by monetarist policies. This led to higher interest rates that also attracted capital from abroad and increased the value of the dollar. This drainage of international finance away from other countries had an effect on interest rates worldwide, and these were in fact used in Europe to assert monetarist discipline. Due to balance of payments surpluses and reserves, and the inflation-fighting record and credibility in the eyes of the financial markets, the German mark became the anchor currency of the EMS. Other currencies 'imported' monetarist discipline through their fixed exchange rate to the German mark. Ultimately this discipline was enforced through German veto on the usage of EMS reserves to defend a currency that was subject to speculation. Eventually the imbalance between the dollar and the ecu as well as the Third World debt crisis became such that even the Reagan Administration agreed to a measure of policy coordination through the G7, IMF, OECD and the BIS, and henceforth such intergovernmental coordination has been the form of new constitutionalist policy content. Examples of new constitutionalist policy coordination include the IMF Structural Adjustment Policy regime towards the Third World debt states, as configured through the Baker and Brady Plans. This regime was subsequently extended with reference to post-Socialist transition states. Other fora of coordination include the G10 Central Bank coordination through the Basle Agreements (BIS), which coordinates central bank intervention in currency markets and is responsible for the management of risk in global financial markets. On a regional level in Europe, the EMS framework has, of course, been formalised and transformed through the formation of the EMU and the 'Stability Pact' managed by the European Council of Finance Ministers (Ecofin).

13 It might be worthwhile to explain why I rely on *both* Moses and Notermans in my account when the two have formulated their positions in mutual contrast to one another. In short, I think that they have overstated their difference, in part because their, in my opinion quixotic, search for 'the independent variable' leads them to overly reductionist explanations. (There is also an element of that American habit of caricaturing the opponent's position and overstating one's own, that often is more misleading than revealing.) Notermans is absolutely right that Moses cannot generate an argument that is sufficient to maintain his position, and that in the end he contradicts himself by invoking political decisions, such as EU membership applications and even conversion of elites to neo-liberalism! At the same time, Notermans himself goes too far in dismissing the importance of financial globalisation for capital deregulation. He makes a persuasive case that a 'grey' financial market grew up in Sweden (and Norway) as a result of domestic inflationary pressures, and that this eventually contributed to

the central bank giving up on capital controls. On the other hand, this does not preclude the fact that transnational currency swaps contributed just as much to this decision. (Indeed, references to the Central Bank, suggest that this is how they experienced it (eg. Sweden. Bank of Sweden 1987: 14–16).) Moreover, this diachronic question about primary 'causes' notwithstanding, it does not change the fact that global financial markets would have made it next to impossible to maintain political control over both exchange rates and interest rates even if an inflation-induced domestic market had not materialised (that is, if no other more radical credit rationing measures, such as the implementation of wage-earner funds, had been taken – see chapter 6). I also believe that Notermans' explanation is insufficient because if the issue could be reduced to one of containing inflation, why did policy-makers deregulate pro-cyclically so as to fuel inflation, especially as it violated the terms of negotiated wage-determination (to which Moses refers but that Notermans (in the Nordic context) wrongly dismisses as 'beggar-thy-neighbor policies')? Furthermore, he fails to account for why other methods of curbing inflation were precluded. This suggests that a particular *conception* of how to curb inflation had become predominant.

14 It could be argued that such self-interest policy is an expression of a lack of hegemony. But from a Gramscian perspective one must note that the USA managed to pursue such policy with the consent of other states, and even diffuse its norms of post-Fordist restructuring to other states.

15 Gill's and van der Pijl's research shows that, particularly in moments of crisis, informal and, strictly speaking, private fora, such as the Bilderberg Group, the Pinay Circle and the Trilateral Commission, have helped to construct and prepare the ground of the underlying norms of more formal multilateral cooperation. These 'private planning groups' are notable for the leading role that 'civil societal' actors, such as CEOs of TNCs and investment bankers, and to some extent selected intellectuals, play. Here business-actors play a direct and deliberate role in the shaping of the governance of the global political economy. These, then, are particularly important organisations where transnational political and civil society are fused and given a particular hegemonic-ideological direction. The private planning groups are also fora through which fractional class actors form a broader and more general class identity and interest. The European Roundtable of Industrialists (ERT) serves a similar function on the European level (eg. van Apeldoorn 1998). This is a point that Castells (1996) misses entirely in his rather economistic argument that capitalist agency is now so fragmented that it makes no sense to talk about a capitalist class.

16 This is as long as a stable macroeconomic environment, supervision of international financial activity, and international lender of last resort functions, are present to avert endogenously produced financial crises. According to Helleiner the 'weak regime' of BIS is sufficient in this regard. The management of the Peso Crisis, the Russian default on its loans and the Asian financial crisis 1997–98, certainly does not contradict this.

17 The end of Russia's euphoria with market-based solutions is definitely connected with the austerity and attendant social dislocation associated with 'shock therapy'. Arguably, the breakup and civil war in former Yugoslavia also needs to be considered with reference to centrifugal tendencies engendered by debt-induced austerity policies (Blokker and Waringo 1999).

18 Lafontaine's position was part and parcel of a political strategy geared towards maintaining the electoral alliance upon which the SPD victory was based. That is, a maintenance of the core working-class base, combined with an appeal to the mass unemployed in the former GDR, the Catholic workers in the south and the middle class concerned about the erosion of social insurance. Given the burden of

German reunification and the reduced multiplier effects of the German export sector, this required a pan-European demand-oriented economic strategy, according to Lafontaine (see Ryner 2002 forthcoming).

19 For an analysis of the relationship between unions, the technocratic elite of social democratic parties and new social movements, see Jenson and Ross (1993). For an account of issue-based politics radical groups, see McCann (1986).

20 In other words we can agree with Schwartz (1994), for example, that globalisation in the nineteenth century was rather narrow in sociological terms and even in economic terms, centred as it was around commerical capital circuits between a few trading cities and especially settler colonies.

21 Many works tend, rather confusingly, to treat 'globalisation' and post-modernisaiton' as synonymous. This, in my view, is more confusing than illuminating since it would imply that time–space compression is an inherent part of the changing aesthetic and socio-psychological determininants of social identity discussed under the heading of post-modernity and vice versa. No doubt they may be related and feed on one another, but to treat them as *a priori* internally related by definition would seem to preclude a detailed analysis of these inter-relations.

6 The organic crisis of the Swedish model

1 I interpret history as presented by Schiller and Simonson through the conceptual distinction between the 'logic of the literal' and the 'logic of symbolic' of a social antagonism which Laclau develops by invoking 'the dilemma of Rosa Luxembourg' in her comparison of the revolutionary situations in Germany and Russia in 1917. According to Laclau, 'the logic of the symbolic', i.e. broader ideological signification, is required for an antagonism to become politics of (counter-)hegemonic proportions. See Laclau (1988) and Laclau and Mouffe (1985: 8–14).

2 Swenson points out that the distributive demands made in the wildcat strikes were not typically to advance the share of the privileged workers in the corporation, but to take advantage of the local power that excess profits and labour shortage created to advance the lot of less privileged workers within the industry, such as those of unskilled workers and women, and to privilege the salary component over piece rates (ibid: p. 93, cf. Ohlström 1975). LO also concluded that the LKAB strikers' demands were consistent with their articulated demands and policy statements on industrial democracy (Simonson 1988: 66, cf. LO 1970).

3 The white-collar share of union members increased from just under one-fifth to just under one-third of union members between 1950 and 1970. Their unions, affiliated with TCO and SACO–SR, had seen it as their mandate to defend the relative pay position and status of their members compared to LO members, a mandate which employers viewed in a sympathetic light. Their bargaining rounds were consistently set after the LO rounds. This practice became highly contentious, especally in the light of the 1965 SACO–SR strike in the public sector, the outcome of which was very high compensatory wage increases (35 per cent over three years). It was in this context that Geijer attacked this practice on the grounds that it put the entire burden of ensuring economic stability on LO members and contravened LO efforts to improve the lot of those with the lowest wages. In the light of this, he argued, LO would have to pursue more aggressive wage-increase strategies in order to defend its members (Martin 1984: 238–41).

4 There is one notable exception. The municipal workers' union, *Kommunalarbetarförbundet*, is affiliated with LO. Indeed, it has become LO's largest affiliate-union in recent years.

5 Tommy Nilsson's dissertation is very important for the thesis about an 'extended working class'. It traces the genesis and changes of white-collar worker organisation from 1900 to 1980. The organisations initially pursued a strategy of status maintenance. However, as their sense of intimate affiliation with owners and management eroded, in the inter-war period the organisations were progressively transformed to trade unions and took the form of TCO and SACO. After the war, the strategy of TCO was to maintain the position of the 'middle class' and that of SACO was to maintain the position of the 'professional'. By 1970, however, routinisation and Taylorist rationalisation of work as well as a general social levelling of status in society brought the ideology of TCO-affiliated unions close to the ideology of LO. By 1970 solidaristic wage policy (including equal pay for equal work and a commitment to special representation of low wage groups) became official policy and the basis of negotiation strategy for KTK, SIF and TCO-S. The main difference between TCO and LO was that TCO insisted on the importance of wage differentials according to work tasks. This is not a difference of principle, however, since LO's 'equal pay for equal work' also implies 'different pay for different work'. SACO has not converted to solidarisitc wage policy, but it is notable that SACO has also been compelled to water down its ethos as 'professional association' and to take the form of a trade union.

6 The LO–SAF rounds had been the only significant ones in the 1940s to 1960s. Now three rounds, LO–SAF, TCO (PTK)–SAF and TCO (TCO-S)–the government (SAV), became macroeconomically determining.

7 Key economic indicators reflect the worsening performance of the Swedish economy. Average annual productivity growth declined to a mere 0.6 per cent between 1973 and 1979 (Boltho 1982: 22) and the annual average rate of real growth in the economy decreased to 2 per cent in the 1970s (from 4 per cent in the 1960s). Industrial production declined on average by 6.2 per cent annually between 1974 and 1982. Terms of trade deteriorated sharply, resulting in a serious deterioration in the balance of payments. By 1982, Sweden had accumulated a foreign debt of 21 per cent of GDP, in contrast with the net credit position equivalent to 5.3 per cent in 1974 (OECD *Economic Surveys: Sweden* 1985: 8–9). As a result of the fragmentation of the wage determination system average annual nominal wage increases increased from 8.4 per cent in 1965–70, to 12 per cent in 1970–79, while real wage increases declined from 6.2 per cent in 1965–70, to 2.2 per cent in 1970–75 and 0.5 per cent in 1975–79. Thus, wage-led consumer price inflation rose dramatically (OECD *Economic Surveys: Sweden* 1966, 1980). Profit rates decreased to less than 20 per cent of value added 1975–80 (it was about 30 per cent in the golden age of the Rehn–Meidner model) (Erixon 1989). Savings and investment levels fell. On average, business fixed investments declined 2.5 per cent annually between 1975 and 80 (OECD 1966, 1985).

8 The conventional interpretation is that this was caused by the rigidities associated with solidaristic wage policy. Erixon refutes this explanation with a comparative reference to the other Nordic models with a similar system of wage determination and finds that the deterioration of Swedish export perfomance (which was held to cause the crisis) was much worse. This means that the decisive variable must lie elsewhere.

9 Government net lending declined from +4 per cent/GDP in 1973 to −6 per cent/GDP in 1982. Government debt increased from 20.6 to 48.1 per cent/GDP.

10 Once connected to the Skandinaviska sphere that was taken over by the Wallenbergs, Volvo was without an obvious house-bank. Gyllenhammar sought to solve the problem of finance through independent means, by conglomerisation, and by tying financial operations to the company. Hence, Volvo was relatively open to joint ventures with the state, including an aborted joint venture with the

Norwegian state connected with oil exploration. On the failure of this venture, and the role that Marcus Wallenberg as a minority shareholder played in turning Volvo shareholders against the venture, see Browaldh (1984: 103–19) (who as Chair of Handelsbanken cooperated with Volvo on the venture).

11   These five spheres dominated ownership of Sweden's multinational corporations. Skanska and Volvo were about the same size. Boliden was about half their size. The degree of control of SHB was about 1.5 times the size of Skanska and Volvo. The Wallenberg/SE sphere was 3.5 times the size of Volvo or Skanska (Hermansson 1989: 164–70).

12   The devaluation of 1982 did restore the competitiveness of the Swedish export sector and, together with the 'Reagan boom' of the world economy, set the stage for export-led growth. From 1982 onwards, the Swedish trade balance was positive, and the current account was balanced in 1984. Investments consequently increased (by an average annual rate of 11 per cent from 1985 to 1990). This set the stage for export-led growth in the mid-1980s and increased tax revenues and the scrapping of industrial subsidies resulted in a budget balance in 1986. In 1987, Sweden had a budget surplus of 4 per cent. Unemployment remained at a remarkably low level: with a peak of 3.2 per cent in 1983, it was reduced to about 2 per cent by the mid-1980s. In 1989 the unemployment rate was 1.5 per cent (OECD *Economic Surveys: Sweden* 1989).

13   Elvander's study of Swedish wage determination in the 1980s is especially admirable in its detail. But his explanation of the erosion of coordinated bargaining is in my view too reductionist, blaming the ossified organisation structures of the trade unions for not facilitating logical bargaining over the white- and blue-collar divide. Whilst not incorrect, this seriously understates the unstable stance of macroeconomic policy in the period and its connection to the modalities of capitalist restructuring. Elvander also tends to take VF's conception of the nature of technological change at face value.

14   The SE bank was on the brink of bankruptcy when the recession bottomed out, but as interest rates were lowered in 1993 and as the business cycle turned it could secure adequate capital solidity through increased net-interest earnings and the largest emission of bank shares in Swedish history (SEK 5.3 billion). Swedish export earnings allowed the bank to recover further in 1994, although there is a 'speculative flavour' to the rapid turnaround after the share emission (Brown-Humes and Fossli 1993; Carnegy 1994).

15   The Peso Crisis indicates the peril of exposing debt to short-term financial markets. Sweden had nothing to do with the crisis in question, but it nevertheless generated a massive sell-off of Swedish bonds on the market. This was because high risk takers had borrowed short on American markets to invest in Swedish bonds in order to profit from interest differentials. However, when the American government presented the rescue package to Mexico, it cut into the margin of these investors and they divested from Swedish bonds. This in turn generated an accelerator-effect, as the value of the crown deteriorated sharply, despite the fact that Sweden had made significant headway in terms of financial consolidation. (I am grateful to Dan Olsson, financial reporter for *Tidningarnas Telegrambyrå*, for helping me clarifying the relationship between the Peso Crisis and the 1995 run on the crown.)

16   The actual developments of unemployment insurance retrenchment are actually more complex than this summary suggests. Benefit levels were actually reduced to 75 per cent on 1 January 1996, but amid union protests and debates at the Party Congress of the Social Democratic Party, benefit levels were restored at the 1993 levels of 80 per cent. Furthermore, the employee contributions to the finance of UI have been transferred to help fund the health insurance system. The non-

socialist government of 1993 also introduced a time limit after which it would no longer be possible to claim UI after participation in an active labour market policy programme and they removed the administration of UI from the unions. These latter measures were repealed by the Social Democrats after 1994, but instead they have tightened the eligibility criteria for UI.

18 Economic development in Sweden during this time was reviewed in chapter 2. Given the shortfall in revenue due to successive years of negative growth, the outlays due to unemployment insurance, steep interest payments and bank bailouts, the 5 per cent/GDP surplus in 1989s became a 15 per cent GDP per cent deficit by 1995 (OECD *Economic Surveys: Sweden* 1994: 14).

7 Why social democrats become neo-liberals: lessons from the Swedish case

1 This brief summary of events is based upon Åsard (1979; 1985).

2 Between 1973 and 1976 SAP did not have effective control over Parliament, since the bourgeois and Socialist blocs had exactly 175 representatives each.

3 Interviewee 6 speaks of a 'euphoric feeling' among the trade union leadership on finally being able to escape the blackmail situation they had always experienced in collective bargaining.

4 There was miscommunication between the LO working group and the party secretariat of SAP, which led to the unfortunate situation that SAP was taken quite by surprise when the Meidner Plan was endorsed by the LO congress in 1976. The party secretary who was in charge of the communications on the party side had a set of serious family tragedies, of which Meidner was not aware. Meidner interpreted that as a lack of interest on behalf of the party (Interviewee 14). The second major case of fumbling was the failure to have the 1978 proposal passed by the Party Congress.

5 Although I had no opportunity to interview Feldt himself, the other members of the LO/SAP working group that I interviewed attested to the constructive working environment in the group, and even suggested that Feldt (as well as Carl Lidbom) was at times quite enthusiastic. In his memoirs Feldt distances himself from the Meidner Plan, and regrets that the group did not have the courage to depart further from that proposal. But he does not distance himself from the 1981 construction and certainly not the 1983 Bill (Feldt 1991: 14, 28–30). Gunnar Sträng, Minister of Finance from 1956 to 1976, gave a very positive assessment of the 1978 funds, which he saw as an 'indispensable instrument' for economic policy in the 1980s (Sträng 1977: 148–49).

6 Senior representatives in the Ministry of Finance as well as corporate leaders took part in the Bilderberg meetings. Some Swedish corporate executives, such as Marcus Wallenberg, Sr, were members with high profiles in the International Chamber of Commerce and associated with Dawes and the Young Plan. Marcus Wallenberg II was involved with the Bilderberg Group. The current CEO of Investor, Percy Barnevik, is a member of the Trilateral Commission and as CEO of ABB he was also a member of the European Roundtable of Industrialists, in which former the CEO of Volvo, Gyllenhammar, was a leading figure. The social democratic 'grey eminence', C.J. Åberg, head of the AP funds, was a member of the Trilateral Commission. Handelsbanken's Tore Browaldh's had substantial experience with international work in public multilateral fora (such as the Council of Europe and various UN committees). But he, like many leading politicians, was also active in the Aspen Institute.

236   *Notes*

7 Indeed in 1983 the government explicitly evoked the Rehn–Meidner model in their budget statement (Sweden. Ministry of Finance 1984: 26–27).
8 See, for example, Kjell Olof Feldt's (1994: 12–24) characterisation of the crisis of economic policy in the 1970s and the 1980s (he calls it 'economic theory in practice').
9 The ground had been prepared for some time, however. First, it became increasingly rare to justify the new economic policy with reference to Marx, and during World War II the editor of *Tiden* for the first time explicitly defined Social Democratic policy in opposition to Marx (Gårdlund, 1941: 193–98.)
10 Wigforss (1954) gives the following portrait of Gunnar Myrdal in his memoirs: 'Myrdal had not, like some other intellectuals [in the movement] of an older vintage, received his socialism coloured in Marxism, and he had not himself had the experiences that taught of an unavoidable class struggle.'

Appendix: Theoretical premises and methodology

1 That is 'metaphysical' as defined by logical positivists: i.e. philosophical speculation of any kind. Positivists reject speculation and assert that knowledge should depart from the constant of something 'given' upon which everything is based. This 'given', it is asserted, can be determined through scientific observation of the empirical, which speaks for itself (Johansson and Liedman 1993: 14–22).
2 This is a different conception of historicism, then, than the one critiqued by positivists (Popper) and structuralist Marxists (Althusser), which is said to hold that history unfolds according to a predetermined logic.
3 Indeed, invoking Marx's third thesis on Feuerbach, one can argue that it is exactly this overdetermined conception of the objective and subjective that distinguishes historical materialism from vulgar materialism, which privileges the objective moment: 'The material doctrine that [human beings] are products of circumstances and upbringing, and that, therefore changed [human beings] are products of other circumstances and changed upbringing, forgets that it is [human beings] that change circumstances and that the educator him[/her]self needs educating' (Marx 1845 (1976): 28).
4 For discussions more broadly on the linguistic and metaphorical mediation of social patterns of determination, see especially Taylor (1985: 15–32), but also, for example, Outhwaite (1987: 62–64) as well as Hall (1988).
5 Michel Foucault's critique of hermeneutics, for example, seems to hinge on this fallacious attempt to ground meaning in a transcendental subject. It should be pointed out, however, that Foucault also failed to break out of the hermeneutic circle. His attempt to develop a self-referential theory of discursive formations faltered in part because it 'foreclosed the possibility of bringing critical analysis to bear on his social concerns'. His subsequent work on 'bio-power' and normalisation as discipline may be exactly about the way power manipulates meaning and culture to further itself (and therefore his critique of an idealised transcendental subject stands), but his argument that the organisation of society as 'bio-technico-power' is the central issue of our time is not empirically demonstrable, but rather emerges out of interpretation for pragmatic purposes. (See Dreyfus and Rabinow 1982: esp. xx–xxvi, 44–61, 79–100.) Interpretation for whom; pragmatic for whom?
6 The social structural accumulation school has the advantage over other forms of regulation theory in that it formulates its indicators in terms that are accessible in national accounts statistics. It has been criticised for not adequately reflecting on the value-theoretical foundations of capital accumulation (eg. Jessop 1990a).

This may be the case, but it should be pointed out that early regulation theory (eg. Aglietta 1979) can be criticised for making too direct quantitative deductions between abstract variables pertaining to regimes of accumulation and concrete modes of economic growth. (On the contingencies of the relationship between the abstract logic of capital accumulation and capitalist history, see Albritton (1991).) This makes the SSA indicators not only more readily available, but arguably also more useful, if not entirely unproblematic.

References

Interviews

Interviewee 1: Former Chief Negotiator of SAF, Former Acting Director-General of SAF, State mediator; interviewed in Stockholm, 23 September 1993.

Interviewee 2: Head of Staff and Administration of SAF; interviewed in Stockholm, 22 September 1993.

Interviewee 3: Deputy Minister of Finance of Sweden 1982–90, Minister without Portfolio (Ministry of Finance) 1990–91; interviewed in Stockholm, 15 April 1993.

Interviewee 4: Director of Research of FIEF (Trade Union Institute of Economic Research); Member of the SAP Working Group on Industrial Policy in the 1970s; interviewed in Stockholm, 20 September 1993.

Interviewee 5: Secretary of the Productivity Commission (SOU 1991: 82); interviewed in Stockholm, 19 April 1993.

Interviewee 6: Director of Economic Research of LO, Member of the LO Reference Group on Wage Earner Funds, Member of the LO–SAP Committees on Wage Earner Funds, Secretary of the SAP Crisis Committee, Responsible for the implementation of wage earner funds in the Ministry of Finance 1982–83; interviewed in Stockholm, 16 April and 13 September 1993.

Interviewee 7: Director of Timbro, Former Director of Social Information Branch of SAF; interviewed in Stockholm, 21 September 1993.

Interviewee 8: Former Chief Negotiator of LO, Member of the LO Reference Group on Wage Earner Funds, State Mediator; interviewed in Stockholm, 27 September 1993.

Interviewee 9: Member of the LO (Meidner) Working Group on Wage Earner Funds; interviewed in Stockholm, 7 September 1993.

Interviewee 10: Deputy Governor of the Central Bank of Sweden; interviewed in Stockholm, 31 August 1993.

Interviewee 11: Member of the LO (Meidner) Working Group on Wage Earner Funds; Member of the LO-SAP Working Groups on Wage Earner Funds; interviewed in Falun, 15 September 1993.

Interviewee 12: Deputy Minister of Finance of Sweden 1982–1985, Minister without Portfolio (Ministry of Finance) 1985–1988; interviewed in Stockholm, 1 September 1993.

Interviewee 13: Head of the International Brach, Swedish Ministry of Finance 1982–90; Deputy Minister of Finance, 1990–91; interviewed 9 September 1993.

Interviewee 14: Former Director of Economic Research of LO, Director for the LO Working Group on Wage Earner Funds, Professor at the Swedish Centre of Working Life; interviewed in Stockholm, 23 March and 14 April 1993.

Interviewee 15: Former Director of Economic Research of LO, Member of the 1967 LO–SAP Working Group on Industrial Policy, co-author of the EFO and FOS reports; interviewed in Stockholm, 3 September 1993.

Interviewee 16: Professor of Economic History, Stockholm School of Economics; interviewed in Stockholm, 15 September 1993.

Interviewee 17: Professor of History, University of Gothenburg; interviewed in Gothenburg, 26 April 1993.

Interviewee 18: Head of Budget Branch, Ministry of Finance 1982–88; interviewed in Stockholm, 7 April 1993.

Documents and Secondary Literature

Åberg, R. (1984) 'Market Independent Income Distribution: Efficency and Legitimacy', in J. J. Goldthorpe (ed.) *Order and Conflict in Contemporary Capitalism*, (Oxford: Clarendon Press).

—— (1988) 'Economic Work Incentives and Labour Market Efficiency in Sweden', in G. Olsen (ed.) *Industrial Change and Labour Market Adjustment in Sweden and Canada* (Toronto: Garamond Press).

Adler, P. S. and Cole, R. E. (1995) 'Design for Learning: The Tale of Two Auto Plants', in Å. Sandberg *Enriching Production* (Aldershot: Avebury).

Aglietta, M. (1979) *A Theory of Capitalist Regulation*. (London: New Left Books).

—— (1985) 'The Creation of International Liquidity', in L. Tsoukalis (ed.) *The Political Economy of International Money* (London: Sage).

—— (1998) 'Capitalism at the Turn of the Century: Regulation Theory and the Challenge of Social Change', *New Left Review* (232): 41–90.

Ahlén, K. (1989) 'Swedish Collective Bargaining under Pressure: Inter-Union Rivalry and Incomes Policy', *British Journal of Industrial Relations* 27 (3).

Ahrne G. and Clement W. (1994) 'A New Regime? Class Representation within the Swedish State', in W. Clement and R. Mahon (eds) *Swedish Social Democracy: A Model in Transition* (Toronto: Canadian Scholars' Press).

Albo, G. (1994) '"Competitive Austerity" and the Impasse of Capitalist Employment Policy', in R. Miliband and L. Panitch (eds) *The Socialist Register 1994* (London: Merlin Press).

Albritton, R. (1991) *A Japanese Approach to Stages in Capitalist Development* (London: Macmillan).

—— (1992) 'Levels of Analysis in Marxian Political Economy: An Unoist Approach', *Radical Philosophy* 60.

Åmark, K. (1988) 'Sammanhållning och intressepolitik: Socialdemokratin och Fackföreningsrörelsen i samarbete på skilda vägar', in K. Misgeld, *et al.* (eds) *Socialdemokratins samhälle* (Stockholm: Tiden).

Amin, A. (1994) 'Post-Fordism: Models, Fantasies and Phantoms of Transition', in A. Amin (ed.) *Post-Fordism: A Reader* (Oxford: Blackwell).

Amin, A. and Malmberg, A. (1994) 'Competing Structural and Institutional Influences on the Geography of Production in Europe', in A. Amin (ed.) *Post-Fordism: A Reader* (Oxford: Blackwell).

Amin, S. (1976) *Unequal Development* (New York: Monthly Review Press).

Amnå, E. (1981) *Planhushållning i den offentliga sektorn?* (Stockholm: Norstedts).

Anderson, K. (1998) 'Organized Labor, Policy Feedback, and Retrenchment in Swedish Pension and Unemployment Insurance', Paper Presented at the Council of European Studies, Baltimore, USA.

Andersson, J. O. (1990) 'Den europeiska inre marknaden i ett nordiskt och reguleringsteoretiskt perspektiv', *Nordisk tidsskrift för politisk ekonomi* 25/26.

Andersson, S. O. (1969) *Vilda strejker: En undersökning inom Svenska Metallindustriarbetar-förbundet* (Stockholm: Rabén & Sjögren).

Andrae, C. G. (1975) 'The Swedish Labour Movement and the 1917–1918 Revolution', in S. Koblik (ed.) *Sweden's Development from Poverty to Affluence* (Minneapolis: University of Minnesota Press).

Armstrong, P., Glyn, A. and Harrison, J. (1991) *Capitalism since 1945.* (Oxford: Basil Blackwell).

Åsard, E. (1978) *LO och löntagarfondsfrågan* (Stockholm: Rabén & Sjögren).

—— (1985) *Kampen om lbntagarfonderna* (Stockholm: Norstedts).

Ashley, R. (1986) 'The Poverty of Neorealism', in R. O. Keohane (ed.) *Neorealism and its Critics* (New York: Columbia University Press).

Banting, K. (2000) 'Looking in Three Directions: Migration and the European Welfare State in Comparative Perspective', in M. Bommes and A. Geddes (eds) *Immigration and Welfare: Challenging the Borders of the Welfare State* (London: Routledge).

Baude, A. (1979) 'Public Policy and Changing Family Patterns in Sweden 1930–1977', in J. Lipman-Blumen and J. Bernard (eds) *Sex Roles and Social Policy: A Complex Social Science Equation.* (London: Sage).

Baumol, W. (1967) 'The Macroeconomics of Unbalanced Growth', *American Economic Review* 57.

Beck, U. (1994) 'The Reinvention of Politics', in U. Beck, A. Giddens and S. Lash (eds) *Reflexive Modernisation* (London: Polity Press).

Bell, D. (1976) *The Cultural Contradictions of Capitalism* (London: Heinemann).

Benn, A.W. (1970) 'The New Politics: A Socialist Reconnaissance', *Fabian Tract 402*.

Berggren, C. (1992) *The Volvo Experience: Alternatives to Lean Production in the Swedish Auto Industry* (Ithaca, NY: Cornell University Press).

Berggren, C. (1995) 'The Fate of the Branch Plants: Performance versus Power', in Å. Sandberg (ed.) *Enriching Production* (Aldershot: Avebury).

Bergom-Larsson, M. (1985) 'Den svenska modellen ur branschperspektiv', SAF *Fred eller fejd: personliga minnen och anteckningar* (Stockholm: SAF).

Bergström, H. (1987) *Rivstart? Från opposition till regering* (Stockholm: Tiden).

Bergström, V. (1982) *Studies in Swedish Post-war Industrial Investments* (Stockholm: Alnqvist & Wichsell/IUI).

—— (ed.) (1993) *Varför överge den svenska modellen?* (Stockholm: Tiden).

Bieling, H. J. (2001) 'Employment Policy Between Neo-Liberalism and Communitarianism', in H. Overbeek (ed.) *The Political Economy of European (Un) Employment* (London: Routledge).

Billing, P., Olsson, L. and Stigendal, M. (1988) 'Malmö – vår stad', in K. Misgeld *et al.* (eds) *Socialdemokratins samhälle* (Stockholm: Tiden).

Blair, T. (1998) Interview with John Humphries in the *Today* Programme, BBC Radio 4, 30 September.

Blair, T. and Schröder, G. (1999 (2000)) 'Europe: The Third Way/Die Neue Mitte', in B. Hombach, *The Politics of the New Centre* (Cambridge: Polity Press).

Block, F. (1977) *The Origins of International Economic Disorder* (Berkeley: University of California Press).

Blokker, P and Warirngo, K. (1999) 'Reshaping Southeast Europe – EU strategies after the Kosovo crisis', mimeo, Research Centre of International Political Economy, University of Amsterdam.

Blyth, M. (1997) 'The Neoliberal Moment in Sweden: Economic Ideas and the Transformation of the State', mimeo, Department of Political Science, Johns Hopkins University, Baltimore, USA.

Bobbio N. (1996) *Left and Right: The Significance of a Political Distinction*, trans. Allan Cameron (Cambridge: Polity Press).

Boltho, A. (1982) *The European Economy: Growth and Crisis* (Oxford: Oxford University Press).

Boréus, K. (1994) *Högervåg: Nyliberalism och kampen om språket i svensk offentlig debatt 1969–1989* (Stockholm: Tiden).

Bosworth, B. and Rivilin, A. (eds) (1987) *The Swedish Economy* (Washington, DC: The Brookings Institute).

Bowles, S., Gordon, D. and Weisskopf, T. (1983) *Beyond the Waste Land* (New York: Anchor Press).

Boyer, R. (1987) 'Flexibility: Many Forms, Uncertain Effects', *Labour and Society* 12 (1).

—— (1991) 'The Eighties: The Search for Alternatives to Fordism', in B. Jessop *et al.* (eds) *The Politics of Flexibility* (Aldershot: Edward Elgar).

—— (1997) 'Capital–Labour Relations in OECD Countries: From the Fordist Golden Age to Contested National Trajectories', in J. Schor and J. Il You (eds) *Capital, the State and Labour: A Global Perspective* (Aldershot: Edward Elgar).

Boyer, R. and Petit, P. (1991) 'Technical Change, Cumulative Causation and Growth', OECD. Technology and Productivity Programme, *Technology and Productivity: The Challenge of Economic Policy* (Paris: OECD).

Braudel, F. (1958 [1980]) 'History and the Social Sciences: The *longue durée*', *On History* (Chicago: University of Chicago Press).

Braudel, F. (1977) *Afterthoughts on Material Civilization and Capitalism* (Baltimore: Johns Hopkins University Press).

Braverman, H. (1974) *Labour and Monopoly Capital* (New York: Monthly Review Press).

Browaldh, T. (1976) *Gesällvandring* (Stockholm: Norstedts).

—— (1980) *Vägen vidare* (Stockholm: Norstedts).

Brown-Humes, C. (1993) 'The slide from difficulty to disaster', *Financial Times*, 19 February.

—— (1994) 'Keeping Sweden in the Family: Analysis of the Power of the Wallenberg Empire', *Financial Times*, 3 May.

Brown-Humes, C. and Fossli, K. (1993) 'A burst of light for banks in Nordic gloom', *Financial Times*, 20 August.

Brulin, G. and Nilsson, T. (1994) 'The Modern Production System and its Consequences for the Swedish model', Paper Presented at the 2nd Meeting of the Scandinavian–Canadian Academic Foundation (SCAF), Stockholm, May 1994.

Burley, A. M. (1993) 'Regulating the World: Multilaterialism, International Law and the Projection of the New Deal State', in J. G. Ruggie (ed.) *Multilateralism Matters* (New York: Columbia University Press).

242   *References*

Cafruny, A. (1989) 'Economic Conflicts and the Transformation of the Atlantic Order', in S. Gill (ed.) *Atlantic Relations: Beyond the Reagan Era.* (New York: St Martin's Press).

Calmfors, L. (1993) 'De institutionella systemen på arbetsmarknaden och arbetslösheten', Sweden. SOU 1993: 16 Bil. 1 *Nya Villkor för ekonomi och politik* (Stockholm: Allmäna förlaget).

Calmfors, L. and Driffil, J. (1988) 'Bargaining Structure, Corporatism and Macroeconomic Performance', *Economic Policy* 6.

Carnegy, H. (1994) 'Swedish banking recovery gathers pace', *Financial Times,* 24 August.

Carr, E. H. (1945) *Nationalism and After* (London: Macmillan).

Casparsson, R. (1951) *LO under fem Årtionden,* 2 vols (Stockholm: Tiden).

Castells, M. (1996) *The Information Age Volume I: The Rise of the Network Society* (Oxford: Blackwell).

—— (1997) *The Information Age Volume II: The Power of Identity* (Oxford: Blackwell).

Cerny, P.G. (1995) 'Globalization and the Changing Logic of Collective Action', *International Organization* 49.

Clayton, R. and Pontusson, J. (1998) 'Welfare State Entrenchment Revisited', *World Politics* 51.

Clement, W. (1992) 'Continentalization and Regime Change: Labour, Capital and the State in Sweden and Canada', Paper Presented at the 1st Meeting of the Scandianavian Canadian Academic Foundation, Toronto, December, 1992.

Connerton, P. (ed.) (1976) *Critical Sociology* (Harmondsworth: Penguin).

Cox, R. W. (1976) 'On Thinking about Future World Order', *World Politics* 28 (2).

—— (1981 [1986]) 'Social Forces, States and World Order: Beyond International Relations Theory', in R. O. Keohane (ed.) *Neorealism and its Critics* (New York: Columbia University Press).

—— (1987) *Production, Power and World Order: Social Forces in the Making of History* (New York: Columbia University Press).

—— (1992) 'Global Perestroika' in R. Miliband and L. Panitch (eds) *New World Order? The Socialist Register 1992* (London: Merlin Press).

Crouch, C. (1997) 'The Terms of the Neo-Liberal Consensus', *The Political Quarterly* 68 (4).

Dahlström, E., Eriksson, K., Gardell, B., Hammarström, O. and Hammarström, R. (1971) *LKAB och demokratin* (Stockholm: Wahlström and Widstrand).

Davis, M. (1984) 'The Political Economy of Late Imperial America', *New Left Review* 143.

Dean, M. (1995) 'Governing the Unemployed Self in an Active Society', *Economy and Society* 24 (4).

De Cecco, M. (1979) 'The Origins of the Postwar Payments System', *Cambridge Journal of Economics* 3.

Deeg, R. (1997) 'Banks and Industrial Finance in the 1990s', *Industry and Innovation* 4 (1).

De Geer, H. (1978) *Rationaliseringsrörelsen i Sverige* (Stockholm: SNS).

—— (1989) *I vänstervind och högervåg.* (Stockholm: Allmäna förlaget).

Dexter, L. A. (1970) *Elite and Specialized Interviewing.* (Evanston: Northwestern University Press).

Dicken, P. (1998) *Global Shift: Transforming the World Economy* (London: Paul Chapman Publishing).

Dølvik, J. E. and Martin, A. (2000) 'A Spanner in the Works and Oil on Troubled Waters: The Divergent Fates of Social Pacts in Sweden and Norway', in G. Fajertag and P. Pochet, *Social Pacts in Europe – New Dynamics* (Brussels: European Trade Institute).

Dreyfus, H. and Rabinow, P. (1982) *Michel Foucault: Beyond Structuralism and Hermeneutics*, 2nd edn (Chicago: University of Chicago Press).

Eckstein, H. (1976) 'Case Study and Theory in Political Science', in F. Greenstein and N. W. Polsby (eds) *Handbook of Political Science*, vol. 7 (Reading, Mass: Addison Wesley).

Edquist, C. and Lundvall, B. Å. (1993) 'Comparing the Danish and Swedish Systems of Innovation', in R. R. Nelson (ed.) *National Innovation Systems: A Comparative Analysis* (Oxford: Oxford University Press).

Edgren, G., Faxén, K. O. and Odhner, C. E. (1970) *Lönebildning och samhällsekonomi* (Stockholm: Rabén and Sjögren).

Ehrencrona, O. (1991) *Nicolin: en svensk historia* (Stockholm: Timbro).

Ekholm, K. and Hesselman, M. (2000) 'The Foreign Operations of Swedish Manufacturing Firms: Evidence from a Survey of Swedish Multinationals 1998', *Industrins utredningsinstitut. Working Paper* No. 540.

Eklund, I. (1999) 'Kraven i arbetslivet', *Statistics Sweden. Välfärdsbulletinen* 4.

Elam, M. and Börjesson, M. (1991) 'Workplace Reform and the Stabilization of Flexible Production in Sweden', in B. Jessop, H. Kastendiek, K. Nielsen and O. Pedersen (eds) *The Politics of Flexibility* (Aldershot: Edward Elgar).

Elfring, T. (1988) 'Service Employment in Advanced Economies', Ph.D. Dissertation, Rijksuniversiteit Groningen.

Elvander, N. (1988) *Den svenska modellen* (Stockholm: Allmäna förlaget).

Eriksson, A. H., Nilsson, A. and Olsson, B. H. (1991) *Förnyelsefonder* (Stockholm: Arbetslivscentrum).

Erixon, L. (1984) 'Den svenska modellen i motgång', *Nordisk tidsskrift för politisk ekonomi* 15/16.

—— (1988) 'Structural Change and Economic Policy in Sweden during the Post-War Period', mimeo. (Stockholm: Arbetslivscentrum).

—— (1989) 'Den tredje vägen: inlåsning eller förnyelse?', *Ekonomisk debatt*. 3.

—— (1991) 'Omvandlingstryck och produktivitet', in Sweden SOU *Konkurrens, regleringar och produktivitet* (SOU 1991: 82 Expertrapport 7).

—— (1994) 'Rehn–Meidnermodellen: en tredje väg i den ekonomiska politiken', *Arbetslivscentrum. Research Report* 4.

Erlander, T. (1972) *1901–1939* (Stockholm: Tiden).

—— (1974) *1949–1954* (Stockholm: Tiden).

—— (1976) *1955–1960* (Stockholm: Tiden).

—— (1979) *Sjuttiotal* (Stockholm: Tiden).

Esping-Andersen, G. (1985a) 'Power and Distributional Regimes', *Politics and Society* 14 (2).

—— (1985b) *Politics Against Markets: The Social Democratic Road to Power* (Princeton: Princeton University Press).

—— (1990) *The Three Worlds of Welfare Capitalism* (Cambridge: Polity Press).

—— (ed.) (1996a) *'After the Golden Age': Welfare States in Transition: National Adaptations in Global Economies* (London: Sage in association with UNRISD).

—— (1996b) 'Welfare States without Work: The Impasse of Labour Shedding and Familialism in Continental European Social Policy', in G. Esping-Andersen (ed.)

Welfare States in Transition: National Adaptations in Global Economies (London: Sage, in association with UNRISD).

—— (1999a) *Social Foundations of Postindustrial Economies* (Oxford: Oxford University Press).

Esping-Andersen, G., Friedland, R. and Olin-Wright, E. (1976) 'Modes of Class Struggle and the Capitalist State', *Kapitalistate* 4/5.

European Community (1993) *Social Protection in Europe* (Brussels EC).

Faxén, K. O., Odhner, C. E. and Spånt, R. (1987) *Lönebildningen i 90-talets samhälls-ekonomi* (Stockholm: Rabén and Sjögren).

Feldt, K. O. (1961) 'Planhushållning i vår tid', *Tiden* 5.

—— (1989) 'Internationalization and National Economic Policy', in Hans Söder-ström (ed.) *One Global Market: Paper Proceedings from an International Conference* (Stockholm: SNS).

—— (1991) *Alla dessa dagar*. (Stockholm: Norstedts).

—— (1994) *Rädda välfärdsstaten!* (Stockholm: Norstedts).

Flora, P. and Heidenheimer, A. J. (eds) (1981) *The Development of Welfare States in Europe and America* (London: Transaction Books).

Forsgren, M. (1989) *Managing the Internationalization Process: The Swedish Case* (London: Routledge).

Foucault, M. (1970) *The Order of Things: An Archaeology of the Human Sciences* (New York: Random House).

Fredriksson, K. (1933) 'Kapitalbildningens roll i konjunkturförloppet', *Tiden*.

—— (1938) 'Till reformismens psykologi', *Tiden*.

Freyssenet, M. (1998) '"Reflective Production": An Alternative to Mass Production and Lean Production?' *Economic and Industrial Democracy* 19.

Fröbel, F. *et al.* (1980) *The New International Division of Labour* (Cambridge: Cambridge University Press).

Frykman, J. and Löfgren, O. (1987) *Culture Builders: A Historical Anthropology of Middle Class Life* (New Brunswick: Rutgers University Press).

Fulcher, J. (1991) *Labour Movements, Employers, and the State* (Oxford: Clarendon).

Furåker, B. (ed.) (1989) *Välfärdsstat och iönearbete* (Lund: Studentlitteratur).

Gårdlund, T. (1941) 'Efter marxismen', *Tiden*.

—— (1977) '1933 års krispolitik – Markus Wallenbergs brevväxling med Strakosch och Keynes', in J. Herin and L. Werin (eds) *Ekonomisk debatt och ekonomisk politik* (Stockholm: Norstedts).

Gezelius, M. (1992) *Bildt på väg* (Stockholm: Bonniers).

Giddens, A. (1981) *A Contemporary Critique of Historical Materialism* (London: Macmillan).

—— (1987) *The Nation State and Violence* (Berkeley and Los Angeles: University of California Press).

—— (1991) *Modernity and Self Identity: Self and Society in the Late Modern Age* (Cambridge: Polity Press).

—— (1998) *The Third Way: The Renewal of Social Democracy* (Cambridge: Polity Press).

Gill, S. (1990) *American Hegemony and the Trilateral Commission* (Cambridge: Cambridge University Press).

—— (1991a) 'Reflections on Global Order and Sociohistorical Time', *Alternatives* 16.

—— (1991b) 'Historical Materialism, Gramsci and International Political Econ-omy', in C. N. Murphy and R. Tooze (eds) *The New International Political Economy* (Boulder: Lynne Rienner).

—— (1992) 'The Emerging World Order and European Change' in R. Miliband and L. Panitch (eds) *New World Order: The Socialist Register 1992*. (London: Merlin Press).

—— (1993) 'Global Finance, Monetary Policy and Cooperation among the Group of Seven, 1944–1992', in P. Cerny (ed) *Finance and Global Politics* (Aldershot: Edward Elgar).

—— (1994) 'Structural Changes in Multilateralism: The G7-Nexus and the Global Crisis', Paper Presented UNU/MUNS-Symposium, 'Sources of Innovation in Multilateralism', Lausanne.

Gill, S. and Law, D. (1988) *The Global Political Economy* (Baltimore: Johns Hopkins University Press).

—— (1989) 'Global Hegemony and the Structural Power of Capital', *International Studies Quarterly* 33.

Glimstedt, H. (1993) 'Restructuring the Transformer Industry', *The Nordic Council of Ministers. Nordisk seminar og Arbejdsrapport* 645.

Golding, S. (1992) *Gramsci's Democratic Theory: Contributions to a Post Liberal Democracy.* (Toronto: University of Toronto Press).

Gordon, D. (1980) 'Stages of Accumulation and Long Economic Cycles', in T. Hopkins and I. Wallerstein (eds) *Processes in the World System* (London: Sage).

Gourevitch, P. (1986) *Politics in Hard Times: Comparative Responses to International Economic Crises* (Ithaca, NY: Cornell University Press).

Grahl, J. and Teague, P. (1989) 'The Cost of Neo-Liberal Europe', *New Left Review* 174.

Gramsci, A. (1971) *Selections from the Prison Notebooks* (New York: International Publishers).

Grassman, S. (1986) *Det plundrade folkhemmet* (Stockholm: Årstidernas förlag).

Gustavsson, S. and Stafford, F. (1994) 'Three Regimes of Childcare: The United States, the Netherlands and Sweden', in R. Blank (ed.) *Social Protection versus Economic Flexibility* (Chicago: University of Chicago Press).

Habermas, J. (1976) *Legitimation Crisis* (Boston: Beacon Press).

Hall, S. (1988) '"The Toad in the Garden": Thatcherism among the Theorists', in C. Nelson and L. Grossberg (eds) *Marxism and the Interpretation of Culture* (Urbana: University of Illinois Press).

—— (1998) 'The Great Moving Nowhere Show', *Marxism Today*, Special Issue, November/December.

Hall, S., Lumley, B. and McLennan, G. (1977) 'Politics and Ideology: Gramsci', in B. Schwartz *et al.* (eds.) *On Ideology* (Birmingham: Hutchinson).

Halliday, F. (1986) *The Making of the Second Cold War* (London: Verso).

Halvarsson, A. (1982) *Sveriges statsskick* (Stockholm: Esselte).

Hancké, B and Rubinstein, S. (1995) 'Limits to Innovation in Work Organisaiton', in Å. Sandberg (ed.) *Enriching Production* (Aldershot: Avebury).

Hansen, B. (1956) 'Penningpolitiken och penningvärdet', *Tiden* 2.

Hansson, S. O. (1984) *SAF i politiken* (Stockholm: Tiden).

Harmes, A. (1998) 'Institutional Investors and the Reproduction of Neoliberalism', *Review of International Political Economy* 5(1).

Harrod, J. (1998) 'Globalisation or Corporatisation: Labour and Social Forces in the Global Political Economy', Paper Presented at the Annual Meeting of the International Studies Association, Minneapolis, USA, 17–21 March 1998.

Harvey, D. (1990) *The Condition of Postmodernity* (Cambridge: Blackwell).

—— (1997) 'Betreff globalisierung', in W. Schumann *et al.* (eds) *Jeneseits der Nationalkökonomie* (Frankfurt a. M., Das Argument).

Häusler, J. and Hirsch, J. (1989) 'Political Regulation: The Crisis of Fordism and the Transformation of the Party System in West Germany', in Gottdiener, M. and Komninos, N. (eds) *Capitalist Development and Crisis Theory* (New York: St Martin's Press).

Hedborg, A. and Meidner, R. (1984) *Folkhemsmodellen* (Stockholm: Rabén and Sjögren).

Held, D. (1987) *Models of Democracy* (Stanford: Stanford University Press).

—— (1998) 'Globalisation: The Timid Tendency,' *Marxism Today* Special Issue, November/December.

Helldén, A. (1990) *Ernst Wigforss: en idébiografi* (Stockholm: Tiden).

Helleiner, E. (1990) 'States and the Future of Global Finance', *Review of International Studies* 18 (1).

—— (1994) *States and the Re-emergence of Global Finance* (Ithaca: Cornell University Press).

Hermansson, C. H. (1989) *Ägande och makt* (Stockholm: Arbetarkultur).

Himmelstrand, U., Ahrne, G. and Lundberg, L. (1981) *Beyond Welfare Capitalism: Issues, Actors and Forces in Societal Change* (London: Heinemann).

Hirdman, Y. (1989) *Att lägga livet till rätta* (Stockholm: Carlssons).

—— (1994). 'Sweden and the Woman Question: Social Engineering in the Thirties', in W. Clement and R. Mahon (eds) *Swedish Social Democracy: A Model in Transition* (Toronto: Canadian Scholars' Press).

Hirst, P. and Thompson, G. (1999) *Globalization in Question* (Cambridge: Polity Press).

Holman, O. (1992) 'Transnational Class Strategy and the New Europe', *International Journal of Political Economy* 22 (1).

Holman, O. and van Apeldoorn, B. (1995) 'Transnational Class Strategy and the Relaunching of European Integration: The Role of the European Round Table of Industrialists', Paper Presented at the Annual Meeting of the International Studies Association, Washington, DC, 1994.

Holmberg, S. (1982) *Valundersökning 1982* (Gothenburg: Statvetenskapliga institutionen, Göteborgs universitet).

Holmlund, B. (1993) 'Arbetslösheten – konjunkturfenomen eller systemfel?', Sweden. SOU 1993:16 *Nya villkor för ekonomi och politik* (Stockholm: Allmäna förlaget).

Hombach, B. (2000) *The Politics of the New Centre* (Cambridge: Polity Press).

Hörngren, L. (1993) '"Normer eller diskretion": Om möjliga och omöjliga val i stabiliseringspolitiken', in V. Bergström (ed.) *Varför överge den svenska modellen?* (Stockholm: Tiden).

Huntington, S., Crozier, M. and Watanaki, J. (1975) *The Crisis of Democracy: Report on the Governability of Democracies to the Trilateral Commission* (New York: New York University Press).

ILO (various years) *Yearbook of Labour Statistics* (Geneva: ILO).

IMF (various years) *Balance of Payments Statistics Yearbook* (Washington DC: IMF).

Ingham, G. (1974) *Strikes and Industrial Conflict: Britain and Scandinavia* (London: Macmillan).

IUI, DØR, ETLA, IFF and IØI (1984) *Economic Growth in a Nordic Perspective* (Bergen: Copenhagen, Helsinki and Stockholm: IUI, DØR, ETLA, IFF, IØI).

Jansson, K. (2000) 'Reformerad husållsstatistik förstärker bilden: Sverige har jämnast inkomstfördelning', *Statistics Sweden. Välfärdsbulletinen* 1.

Jenson, J. (1989) 'Paradigms and Political Discourse: Protective Legislation in France and the United States', *Canadian Journal of Political Science* XXII (2).

Jenson, J. and Mahon, R. (1993) 'Representing Solidarity: Class, Gender and the Crisis in Social Democratic Sweden', *New Left Review* 201.

Jenson, J. and Ross, G. (1986) 'Post-War Class Struggle and the Crisis of Left Politics', in R. Miliband and J. Saville (eds) *The Socialist Register 1985/86* (London: Merlin Press).

Jessop, B. (1979) 'Corporatism, Parliamentarism, and Social Democracy', in G. Lehmbruch and P. Schmitter (eds) *Trends towards Corporatist Intermediation* (London: Sage).

—— (1985) *Nicos Poulantzas: Marxist Theory and Political Strategy* (New York: St Martin's Press).

—— (1990a) 'Regulation Theories in Retrospect and Prospect', *Economy and Society* 19 (2).

—— (1990b) *State Theory: Putting Capitalist States in their Place* (Cambridge: Polity Press).

—— (1997) 'Die Zukunft des Nationalstaates: Erosion order Reorganisation?', in W. Schumann *et al.* (eds) *Jeneseits der Nationalokökonomie* (Frankfurt: Das Argument).

Johansson, Alf (1989) 'Arbetarklassen och Saltsjöbaden 1938: perspektiv ovan och underifrån', *Saltsjöbadsavtalet 50 år* (Stockholm: Arbetslivscentrum).

Johansson, A. L. (1989) *Tillväxt och klass-samarbete*. (Stockholm: Tiden).

Johansson, I. and Liedman, S. E. (1993) *Positivism and Marxism*, 4th edn (Gothenburg: Daidalos).

Jörberg, L. (1975) 'Structural Change and Economic Growth in Nineteenth Century Sweden', in S. Kobhk (ed.) *Sweden's Development from Poverty to Affluence* (Minneapolis: University of Minnesota Press).

Kalecki, M. (1943) 'Political Aspects of Full Employment', *The Political Quarterly* 14 (4).

Kaplinsky, R. (1984) *Automation: New Technology and Society* (Geneva: ILO).

Karleby, N. (1928) *Socialismen inför verkligheten* (Stockholm: Tiden).

Katzenstein, P. (1985) *Small States in World Markets* (Ithaca, NY: Cornell University Press).

Knocke, W. (1994) 'Gender, Ethnicity and Technological Change', in W. Clement and R. Mahon (eds) *Swedish Social Democracy: A Model in Transition* (Toronto: Canadian Scholars' Press).

—— (2000) 'Immigration or Segregation? Immigrant Populations Facing the Labour Market in Sweden', *Economic and Industrial Democracy* 21.

Kock, K. (1961, 1962) *Kreditmarknad och räntepolitik 1924–1958*, 2 vols (Uppsala: Almqvist and Wicksell).

Kohli, M., Rein, M. and Guillemard, A. (1993) *Time for Retirement* (Cambridge: Cambridge University Press).

Korpi, W. (1978) *The Working Class in Welfare Capitalism* (London: Routledge and Kegan Paul).

—— (1983) *The Democratic Class Struggle* (London: Routledge and Kegan Paul).

—— (1996) 'Eurosclerosis and the Sclerosis of Objectivity: On the Role of Values among Economic Policy Experts', *The Economic Journal* 106 (November).

Korpi, W., Olsson, S. E. and Stenberg, S. Å. (1982) 'Svensk socialpolitik', in B. Södersten (ed.) *Svensk ekonomi*, 3rd edn (Stockholm: Rabén and Sjögren).

Korpi, W. and Palme, J. (1993) 'Socialpolitik, kris och reformer: Sverige i internationell belysning', in Sweden. SOU 1993:16 Bil 2.

Kugelberg, B. (1985) 'De centrala avtalen', SAF *Fred eller fejd: Personliga minnen och anteckningar* (Stockholm: SAF).

Laclau, E. (1977) *Politics and Ideology in Marxist Theory* (London: Verso).

—— (1988) 'Metaphor and Social Antagonism', in C. Nelson and L. Grossberg (eds) *Marxism and the Interpretation of Culture* (Urbana: University of Illinois Press).

Laclau, E. and Mouffe, C. (1985) *Hegemony and Socialist Strategy* (London: Verso).

Lafontaine, O. (1999) *Das Herz schlägt links* (Munich: Econ).

Larsson, K. A. (1980) 'The International Dependence of the Swedish Economy', in J. Fry (ed.) *Limits of the Welfare State* (Aldershot: Gower).

Lash, S. and Urry, J. (1987) *The End of Organized Capitalism* (Madison: University of Wisconsin Press).

Leborgne, D. and Lipietz, A. (1988) 'New Technologies, New Modes of Regulation: Some Spatial Implications', *Environment and Planning D: Society and Space* 6.

Levinson, K. (2000) 'Codetermination in Sweden: Myth and Reality', *Economic and Industrial Democracy* 21.

Lewin, L. (1967) *Planhushållningsdebatten* (Stockholm: Almqvist and Wicksell).

—— (1979) 'Union Democracy', in J. Fry (ed.) *Industrial Democracy and Labour Market Policy in Sweden* (Oxford: Pergamon).

—— (1992a) *Ideologi och strategi*, 4th edn (Stockholm: Norstedts).

—— (1992b) *Samhället och de organiserade intressena.* (Stockholm: Norstedts).

Lindbeck, A. (1961) 'Inkomstfördelning, resursallokering och stabiliseringspolitik', *Tiden* 7.

—— (1975) *Svensk ekonomisk pohtik* (Stockholm: Aldus).

—— (1984) 'Tre grundproblem i svensk ekonomi', *Ekonomisk debatt* 3.

—— (1995) 'The End of the Middle Way?' *American Economic Review*, 11.

Lindbeck, A. *et al.* (1994) *Turning Sweden Around* (Cambridge, MA: The MIT Press).

Lipietz, A. (1985) *Mirages and Miracles* (London: Verso).

—— (1987) 'The Globalization of the General Crisis of Fordism', in J. Holmes and C. Leys (eds) *Frontyard/Backyard* (Toronto: Between the Lines).

—— (1988) 'Reflections on a Tale: The Marxist Foundations of the Concepts of Regulation and Accumulation', *Studies in Political Economy* 26.

—— (1989) 'The Debt Problem, European Integration, and the New Phase of World Crisis', *New Left Review* 178.

Ljunggren, S. (1993) 'Myt och verklighet i den ekonomiska krisen', *Zenit* 120/121.

LO(1951) *Fackföreningsrörelsen och den fulla sysselsättningen* (Stockholm: LO).

—— (1970) 'Gruvstrejken 1969–1970: Material rörande konflikten vid LKAB', unpublished memo. 13 January 1970.

—— (1972) 'Dagordningens Punkt 28: Motionerna 305–309, 311–344, 357 och 370: Näringspolitik, inflytande i näringslivet, AP-fonderna', *Protokoll: 18e kongressen 1971* (Stockholm: LO).

—— (1986) *Ekonomiska utsikter*, April.

—— (1997) *Bilaga och mötesmateriel om lönebildning: Supplement LO-tidningen*, 7 February.

—— (2000) 'LO's kommentar till lagrådremissen "Lönebildning för full sysselsättning"', Press release, Stockholm, March 31, 2000.

LO and SAP (1981) *Arbetarrörelsen och löntagarfonderna* (Stockholm: Tiden).

Lundqvist, S. (1975) 'Popular Movements and Reforms 1900–1920', in S. Koblik (ed.) *Sweden's Development from Poverty to Affluence* (Minneapolis: University of Minnesota Press).

Macpherson, C. B. (1977) *The Life and Times of Liberal Democracy* (Oxford: Oxford University Press).

Mahon, R. (1977) 'Canadian Public Policy: The Unequal Stucture of Representation', in L. Panitch (ed.) *The Canadian State* (Toronto: University of Toronto Press).

—— (1994a) 'From Fordism to ?: New Technology, Labour Markets and Unions', in W. Clement and R. Mahon (eds) *Swedish Social Democracy: A Model in Transition* (Toronto: Canadian Scholars' Press).

—— (1994b) 'From Solidaristic Wages to Solidaristic Work: a Post Fordist Historic Compromise for Sweden?', in W. Clement and R. Mahon (eds) *Swedish Social Democracy: A Model in Transition* (Toronto: Canadian Scholars' Press).

—— (1994c) 'Wage Earners and/or Co-Workers? Contested Identities', in W. Clement and R. Mahon (eds) *Swedish Social Democracy: A Model in Transition* (Toronto: Canadian Scholars' Press).

Maier, C. (1977 [1991]) 'The Politics of Productivity: Foundations of American International Economic Policy after World War II', in C. Maier (ed.) *The Cold War in Europe* (New York: Markus Wiener Publishing).

Marklund, S. (1988) 'Welfare State Policies in the Tripolar Class Model of Scandinavia', *Politics and Society* 16(4).

Martin, A. (1984) 'Trade Unions in Sweden: Strategic Responses to Change and Crisis', P. Gourevitch *et al.* (eds) *Unions and Economic Crisis* (London: Allen and Unwin).

Marx, K. (1844 [1975]) 'Economic and Philosophic Manuscripts', in Marx, K. and Engels, F. *Collected Works*, Volume 3 (New York: International Publishers).

—— (1845 [1986]) 'Theses on Feuerbach', in K. Marx and F. Engels *Selected Works* (New York: International Press).

—— (1857 [1973]) 'Introduction', *Grundrisse* (Harmondsworth: Penguin).

—— (1867 [1977]) *Capital: A Critique of Political Economy*, Volume 1 (London: Vintage Books).

—— (1885 [1986]) 'The Eighteenth Brumaire of Louis Bonaparte', in K. Marx and F. Engels *Selected Works* (New York: International Publishers).

Matl, W. (1997) 'Ein Alptraum vom reinen Schweden,' *Die Zeit* 37, 5 September.

McCann, M. (1986) *Taking Reform Seriously: Perspectives on Public Interest Liberalism* (Ithaca: Cornell University Press).

Meidner, R. (1948) 'Lönepolitikens dilemma vid full sysselsättning', *Tiden* 9.

—— (1973) 'Samordning och solidarisk lönepolitik under tre decennier', LO *Tvärsnitt*. (Stockholm: Prisma/LO).

—— (1980) 'Our Concept of the Third Way: Some Remarks on the Socio-Political Tenets of the Swedish Labour Movement', *Economic and Industrial Democracy* 1.

Meidner, R., Hedborg, A. and Fond, G. (1978) *Employee Investment Funds* (London: Allen and Unwin).

Merkel, W. (2000) 'Die Dritten Wege der Sozialdemokratie', *Berliner Journal für Soziologie* 1.

Michalet, C. A. (1991) 'Global Competition and its Implication for Firms', OECD. Technology and Productivity Programme *Technology and Productivity: The Challenge for Economic Policy* (Paris: OECD).

Mishra, R. (1984) *The Welfare State in Crisis* (Brighton: Harvester).

Mjøset, L. (1987) 'Nordic Economic Policies in the 1970s and the 1980s', *International Organization* 41 (3).

Mjøset, L. *et.al* (1986) *Norden dagen derpå* (Oslo: Universitetsforlaget).

Moore, B. (1967) *Social Origins of Dictatorship and Democracy* (London: Allen Lane).

Moses, J. (1994) 'Abdication from National Policy Autonomy: What's Left to Leave?', *Politics and Society* 22 (2).

Mossler, K., Torége, J. and Öström, A. (1999) '120 000 barn berörs av långvarigt socialbidrag', *Statistics Sweden. Välfärdsbulletinen* 2.

Mouffe, C. (1979) 'Hegemony and Ideology in Gramsci', in C. Mouffe (ed.) *Gramsci and Marxist Theory* (London: Routledge and Kegan Paul).

—— (1998) 'The Radical Centre: Politics without Adversary', *Soundings* 9.

Murray, R. (1971) 'Internationalization of Capital and the Nation State', *New Left Review* 67.

Myrdal, G. (1928 [1963]) *The Political Element in the Development of Economic Theory* (London: Routledge and Kegan Paul).

—— (1945) 'Tiden och partiet', *Tiden* 1.

—— (1960 [1967]) *Beyond the Welfare State* (New York: Bantham Books).

Nilsson, L. (1995) 'The Uddevalla Plant: Why Did it Succeed with a Holistic Approach and Why Did it Come to an End?', in Å. Sandberg (ed.) *Enriching Production* (Aldershot: Avebury).

Nilsson, T. (1985) *Från kamratförening till facklig rörelse: De svenska tjänstemännens organisationsutveckling 1900–1980* (Lund: Arkiv).

Notermans, T. (1993) 'The Abdication of Policy Autonomy: Why the Macro-economic Policy Regime Has Become so Unfavourable to Labor', *Politics and Society* 21 (2).

—— (1994) 'Social Democracy in Open Economies: A Reply to Jonathon Moses', *Politics and Society* 22 (2): 149–64.

Nussbaum, M. (1990) 'Aristotelean Social Democracy', in B. R. Douglas, G. Mara and H. S. Richardson (eds) *Liberalism and the Good* (London: Routledge).

OECD (1983a) *Employment Outlook* (Paris: OECD).

—— (1983b) *Historical Statistics* (Paris: OECD).

—— (1988) *Ageing Populations* (Paris: OECD).

—— (1988b) *New Technology in the 1990s: A Socio-Economic Strategy* (Paris: OECD).

—— (1992) *Employment Outlook* (Paris: OECD).

—— (1993) 'Earnings Inequality', *Employment Outlook* (July).

—— (1996) 'Earnings Inequality, Low Paid Employment and Earnings Mobility', *Employment Outlook* (July).

—— (1997) *Historical Statistics* (Paris: OECD).

—— (various issues) *Employment Outlook* (Paris: OECD).

—— (various years) *Economic Outlook* (Paris: OECD).

—— (various years) *OECD Economic Surveys: Sweden* (Paris: OECD).

—— (1999) *Economic Outlook* 66 (Paris: OECD).

Ohlström, B. (1975) *Vilda strjeker inom LO området 1974–75* (Stockholm: LO).

Offe, C. (1985) *Contradictions of the Welfare State* (Cambridge, MA: MIT Press).

—— (1996) *Modernity and the State* (Cambridge: Polity Press).

Offe, C. and Wiesenthal, H. (1985) 'Two Logics of Collective Action', in C. Offe (ed.) *Disorganized Capitalism* (Cambridge, MA: MIT Press).

Ohmae, K. (1995) *The Borderless World: Power and Strategy in the Interlinked Economy* (London: Fontana).

Olsen, G. (1994) 'Labour Mobilization and the Strength of Capital: The Rise and Stall of Economic Democray in Sweden', in W. Clement and R. Mahon (eds) *Swedish Social Democracy: A Model in Transition* (Toronto: Canadian Scholars' Press).

Olsson, H.(1991) 'Konkurrensförhållandenas betydelse för produktiviteten', Sweden. SOU 1991: 82 *Expertrapport 7.*

Olsson, S. E. (1987) 'Sweden', in P. Flora (ed.) *Growth to Limits* (Berlin: de Greuyter).

—— (1993) *Social Policy and Welfare State in Sweden* (Lund: Arkiv).

Olsson, U. (1993) 'Sweden and Europe in the 20th Century: Politics and Economics', *Scandinavian Journal of History* 18 (1).

—— (1994) 'Planning in the Swedish Welfare State', in W. Clement and R. Mahon (eds) *Swedish Social Democracy: A Model in Transition* (Toronto: Canadian Scholars' Press).

—— (1995) 'Swedish Commercial Banking During 150 Years', mimeo. Department of Economic History, Stockholm School of Economics.

Ortmark, Å. (1981) *Skuld och makt – En kapitalistisk historia: Famijerna Medici, Rothschild, Rockefeller, Wallenberg* (Stockholm: Wahlström and Widstrand).

Outhwaite, W. (1987) *New Philosophies of Social Science: Realism, Hermeneutics and Critical Theory* (New York: St Martin's Press).

Palme, O. (1987) 'Sveriges ekonomi: resultat och nya uppgifter', *Olof Palme: en levande vilja* (Stockholm: Tiden).

Panitch, L. (1981) 'Trade Unions and the Capitalist State', *New Left Review* 125.

—— (1994) 'Globalisation and the State', in R. Miliband and L. Panitch (eds) *New World Order? The Socialist Register 1994* (London: Merlin Press).

Patomäki, H. (2000) 'Beyond Nordic Nostalgia: Envisaging a Social/Democratic System of Global Governance', *Cooperation and Conflict* 35 (2).

Pekkarinen, J. (1989) 'Keynesianism and the Scandinavian Models of Economic Policy', in P. Hall (ed.) *The Political Power of Economic Ideas* (Princeton: Princeton University Press).

Perner, W. (1999) 'Von Wim Kok Lernen,' *Die Zeit* 42, 14 October.

Pestoff, V. (1991) *Between Markets and Politics: Co-operatives in Sweden* (Frankfurt am Main and Boulder, CO: Campus Verlag/ Westview Press).

Peterson, O. (1989) *Maktens nätverk* (Stockholm: Carlssons).

Petrella, R. (1999) 'Man nannte es den Dritten Weg', *Le Monde Diplomatique (German language version)* 6 October.

Pierson, C. (1998) *Beyond the Welfare State* (Cambridge: Polity Press).

Piore, M. and Sabel, C. (1984) *The Second Industrial Divide* (New York: Basic Books).

Poggi, G. (1978) *The Development of the Modern State* (Stanford: Stanford University Press).

Polanyi, K. (1957a) *The Great Transformation.* (Boston: Beacon Press).

—— (1957b) 'The Economy as Instituted Process', K. Polanyi *et al.* (eds) *Trade and Markets in Early Empires* (New York: The Free Press).

Pontusson, J. (1984) 'Behind and Beyond Social Democracy in Sweden', *New Left Review* 143.

—— (1987) 'Radicalization and Retreat of Swedish Social Democracy', *New Left Review* 165.

—— (1988) *Swedish Social Democracy and British Labour: Essays on the Nature and Conditions of Social Democratic Hegemony* (Ithaca, NY: Cornell Studies in International Affairs).

252   *References*

—— (1992a) *The Limits of Social Democracy* (Ithaca, NY: Cornell University Press).

—— (1992b) 'Unions, New Technology, and Job Redesign at Volvo and British Leyland', in M. Golden and J. Pontusson (eds) *Bargaining for Change* (Ithaca, NY: Cornell University Press).

Pontusson, J. and Swenson, P. (1993) 'Varför har arbetsgivarna övergivit den svenska modellen?', *Arkiv för studier i arbetarrörelsens historia* 50.

Poulantzas, N. (1978) *State, Power, Socialism* (London: New Left Books).

Przeworski, A. (1985) *Capitalism and Social Democracy* (Cambridge: Cambridge University Press).

Putnam, R. D. (1993) 'Social Capital and Institutional Success', in Putnam, R. D., R. Leonardi and R. Nanetti, *Making Democracy Work: Civic Traditions in Modern Italy* (Princeton, NJ: Princeton University Press).

Rehn, G. (1948) 'Ekonomisk politik vid full sysselsättning', *Tiden* 3.

—— (1952) 'The Problem of Stability: An Analysis and Some Policy Proposals', in R. Turvey (ed.) *Wages Policy under Full Employment* (London: William Hidge).

—— (1988) 'Finansministrarna, LO ekonomerna, och arbetsmarknadspolitiken', *Full sysselsättning utan inflaton* (Stockholm: Tiden).

Rein, M. (1985) 'Women, Employment and Social Welfare', in R. Klein and M. O'Higgins (eds) *The Future of Welfare* (Oxford: Basil Blackwell).

Rhodes, M. (1991) 'The Social Dimension of the Single European Market: National vs. Transnational Regulation', *European Journal of Political Research* 12.

Rhodes, M. and van Apeldoorn, B. (1998) 'Capitalism Unbound? The Transformation of European Corporate Governance', *Journal of European Public Policy* 5 (3).

Riester, W. and Streeck, W. (1997) 'Solidarität, Arbeit, Beschäftigung', Beitrag zur Schwerpunktkommission Gesellschaftspolitik beim Parteivorstand der SPD (Contribution to the Commission on Social Policy of the Party Executive of the SPD).

Rose, N. (1999) 'Inventiveness in Politics', *Economy and Society* 28 (3).

Ross, G. (1992) 'Confronting the New Europe', *New Left Review* 191.

Rothstein, B. (1985a) 'Managing the Welfare State: Lessons from Gustav Möller', *Scandinavian Political Studies* 8 (3).

—— (1985b) 'The Success of the Swedish Labour Market Policy: The Organizational Connection to Policy', *European Journal of Political Research* 13.

—— (1986) *Den socialdemokratiska staten* (Lund: Arkiv).

—— (1990) 'Marxism, Institutional Analysis and Working Class Power: The Swedish Case', *Politics and Society* 18 (3).

—— (1992) *Den korporativa staten* (Stockholm: Norstedts).

—— (1998a) *Just Institutions Matter* (Cambridge: Cambridge University Press).

—— (1998b) 'Social Capital in the Social Democratic State: The Swedish model and Civil Society', Paper presented at the 11th International Conference of Europeanists, Baltimore, USA, 26 February–1 March.

Ruggie, J. G. (1983) 'International Regimes, Transaction and Change: Embedded Liberalism in the Postwar Economic Order', in S. Krasner (ed.) *International Regimes* (Ithaca, NY: Cornell University Press).

Ruigrok W. and van Tulder, R. (1995) *The Logic of International Restructuring* (London: Routledge).

Ryner, M. (1992) 'Research Proposal: The World Economic Order and the Demise of the Swedish model', mimeo, Department of Political Science, York University, Toronto.

—— (1994) 'Economic Policy in the 1980's: The Third Way, the Swedish model, and the Transition from Fordism to Post-Fordism', in W. Clement and R. Mahon (eds) *Swedish Social Democracy: A Model in Transition* (Toronto: Canadian Scholars' Press).

—— (1997) 'Nordic Welfare Capitalism in the Emerging Global Political Economy', in S. Gill (ed.) *Globalization, Democratization and Multilateralism* (Tokyo and London: United Nations University Press/Macmillan Press).

—— (2000) 'European Welfare State Transformation and Migration', in M. Bommes and A. Geddes (eds) *Immigration and Welfare: Challenging the Borders of the Welfare State* (London: Routledge).

—— (2002) 'The Political Economy of Germany in Transition: Does the Equation of Disciplinary Neoliberalism and the Social Market Still Hold?', in A. Cafruny and M. Ryner (eds) *The Political Economy of the European Union* (Lanham: Rowman and Littlefield).

Sabel, C. (1994) 'Flexible Specialisation and the Re-emergence of Regional Economies', in A. Amin (ed.) *Post Fordism: A Reader* (Oxford: Blackwell).

SAF (1990) *Marknad och mångfald (Free Markets and Free Choice)* (Stockholm: SAF).

SAF (1991) *Farväl till korporativismen.* (Stockholm: SAF).

Sainsbury, D. (1980) *Swedish Social Democratic Ideology and Electoral Politics 1944–1948* (Stockholm: Almqvist and Wicksell International).

—— (1996) *Gender, Equality and the Welfare State* (Cambridge: Cambridge University Press).

Samuelsson, K. (1968) *Från stormakt till välfärdsstat.* (Stockholm: Rabén and Sjögren).

Sandberg, Å. (1994) 'Volvoism at the End of the Road?', *Studies in Political Economy* 45.

—— (ed.) (1995) *Enriching Production* (Aldershot: Avebury).

—— (ed.) (1998) *Good Work and Productivity: Special Issue of Economic and Industrial Democracy* 19 (1).

Sandberg, Å, Broms, A. G., Grip, A., Sundström, L. and Steen, J. (1992) *Technological Change and Co-determination in Sweden* (Philadelphia, PA: Temple University Press).

Sandner, G. (2000) 'Halbierter Sozialismus oder: Die Politische Theorie des Dritten Weges', *Österreichische Zeitschrift für Politikwissenschaft* 29 (1).

SAP (1981) *Framtid för Sverige* (Stockholm: SAP).

Sassen, S. (1991) *The Global City* (Princeton, NJ: Princeton University Press).

Sayer, A. (1992) *Method in Social Science* (London: Routledge).

Scharpf, F. (1996) 'Negative and Positive Integration in the Political Economy of European Welfare States', in G. Marks, F. Scharpf, P. Schmitter and W. Streeck (eds) *Governance in the European Union* (London: Sage).

Schiller, B. (1975) 'Years of Crisis 1906–1914', in S. Koblik (ed.) *Sweden's Development from Poverty to Affluence* (Minneapolis: University of Minnesota Press).

—— (1987) *Det förödande 70-talet* (Stockholm: Allmäna förlaget).

—— (1988) *Samarbete eller konflikt.* (Stockholm: Allmäna förlaget).

Scholte, J. A. (2000) *Globalization: A Critical Introduction* (London: Macmillan).

Schwartz, H. (1994) *States versus Markets* (New York: St Martin's Press).

Scott, F. (1988) *Sweden: The Nation's History* (Edwardsville: Southern Illinois University Press).

Shimzu, K (1995) 'Humanization of the Production System and Work at Toyota Motor Co. and Toyota Motor Kyushu', in Å. Sandberg (ed.) *Enriching Production* (Aldershot: Avebury).

254   References

SI and SAF (1976) *Företagsvinster, Kaipitalförsörjning, Löntagarfonder* (Stockholm: SI and SAF).

Simon, R. (1982) *Gramsci's Political Thought* (London: Lawrence and Wishart).

Simonson, B. (1988) *Arbetarmakt och näringspolitik*. (Stockholm: Allmäna förlaget).

Sköldebrand, B. (1989) *Anställd och ägande – konvertibler* (Stockholm: Arbetslivscentrum).

Skorstad, E. (1994) 'Lean Production, Conditions of Work and Worker Commitment', *Economic and Industrial Democracy* 15 (3).

Söderpalm, S. A. (1976) *Direktörsklubben: storindustrin i svensk politik under 30- och 40-talen* (Stockholm: Zenit/Rabén and Sjögren).

Söderström, H. T. (ed.) (1989) *One Global Market: Paper Proceedings from an International Conference* (Stockholm: SNS).

Standing, G. (1988) *Unemployment and Labour.Market Flexibility: Sweden* (Geneva: ILO).

Statistics Sweden (2000) 'Arbetsinkomst för helårs- och heltidsanställda individer', www.scb.se/befolvalfard/inkomster/hink/hinktab2.asp

Steffen, G. (1920) *Socialiseringsnämnden* (Stockholm: Riksarkivet).

Stephens, J. (1979) *The Transition from Capitalism to Socialism* (London: Macmillan).

Stopford, J. M. and Strange, S. (1994) *Rival States, Rival Firms: Competition for World Market Shares* (Cambridge: Cambridge University Press).

Sträng, G. (1977) 'Kommentar', in K. O. Feldt *et al.* (eds) *Ekonomisk politik inför 1980-talet* (Stockholm: Tiden).

Strange, S. (1987) 'The Persistent Myth of Lost Hegemony', *International Organization* 41 (4).

——(1989) *Casino Capitalism*, 2nd edn (Oxford: Basil Blackwell).

—— (1998) *Mad Money* (Manchester: Manchester University Press).

Straw, J. (1998) 'Building Social Cohesion, Order and Inclusion in a Market Economy', Speech to the Nexus Conference on Mapping Out the Third Way, 3 July. www.netnexus.org/events/july98/talks/szreter.htm

Stråth, B. (1996) 'Sweden: The Emergence and Erosion of a "Model"', in P. Pasture *et al.* (eds) *The Lost Perspective? Volume 1* (Aldershot: Avebury).

Streeck, W. (1992) *Social Institutions and Economic Performance* (London: Sage).

—— (1994) 'Pay Restraint without Incomes Policy: Institutionalized Monetarism and Industrial Unionism in Germany', in R. Boyer and R. Doré (eds) *The Return to Incomes Policy* (London: Pinter).

—— (1995) 'German Capitalism: Does it Exist? Can it Survive?', Max Planck Institut für Gesellschaftsforschung, Cologne, Discussion Paper 2.

Sunesson, S. (1974) 'Den socialdemokratiska statsideologin och fackföreningsrörelsen', in P. Dencik and B. Å. Lundvall (eds) *Arbete, Kapital and Stat* (Stockholm: Zenit/Rabén and Sjögren).

Svallfors, S. (1989) *Vem älskar välfärdsstaten?* (Lund: Arkiv).

—— (1994) *Välfärdsstatens moraliska ekonomi* (Umeå: Boréa).

Sweden. Bank of Sweden (1985) 'Deregulation Continues,' *Sveriges Riksbank Quarterly Review* 1.

—— (1987) 'Riksbankens räntepolitik – nya tekniker och ny miljö: Anförande av riksbankschefen Bengt Dennis', Lecture Presented at Stockholm School of Economics, Stockholm, 5 March.

—— (1988) *Statistisk årsbok*.

—— (1992) *Statistisk årsbok*.

Sweden. Ministry of Economic Affairs (1978) *Proposition om inriktningen av den ekonomiska politiken* Prop. 1977/78: 45.

Sweden. Ministry of Finance (1984) *Finansplanen* Prop. 1983/84: 100 Bil. 1.

—— (1985a) *Om den ekonomiska politiken på medellång sikt* Prop. 1984/85: 40.

—— (1985b) *Finansplanen* Prop.1984/85: 100 Bil. 1.

—— (1985c) *Valutautflödena 1985 och den ekonomiska politiken* Ds.Fi. 1985: 16.

—— (1986) *Prehminär nationalbudget för 1986* Prop. 1985/86: 100 Bil. 1.1.

—— (1988) *Om den ekonomiska pohtiken på medellång sikt* Prop. 1987/88: 36.

—— (1989) *The Revised Budget Statement 1989*.

—— (1990) *Sweden's Economy: April 1990*.

—— (1991) *Remissyttranden över långtidsutredningen 1990* Prop. 1990/91: 39.

—— (1992) *The Budget Statement 1991/92*.

Sweden. Ministry of Industry (1999) *Lönebildning för full sysselsättning* Prop. 1999/2000: 32.

Sweden. Riksdagen (1981) *Om den ekonomiska politiken och budgetregleringen* (Olof Palme *et al.*) Mot.1980/81: 1136.

Sweden. SOU (1935a) 'Särskilt yttrande av herr Severin', *Åtgärder mot arbetslöshet* SOU 1935: 6.

—— (1935b) *Betänkande om folkförsörjning och arbetsfred*, Volume I, SOU 1935: 65.

—— (1955) *Penningvärdesundersökningen 2: Finanspolitikens ekonomiska teori*, SOU 1955: 25.

—— (1990) *Demokrati och makt i Sverige* SOU 1990: 44.

—— (1991) *Konkurrens, regleringar och produktivitet*. Expert Report, Volume 7, SOU 1991: 82.

—— (1993) *Nya villkor för ekonomi och politik*. Main Report and Supplements, 2 vols, SOU 1993: 16.

—— (1997) *Medlingsinstitut och lönestatistik*, SOU 1997: 164.

Swenson, P. (1989) *Fair Shares: Unions, Pay and Politics in Sweden and West Germany* (Ithaca, NY: Cornell University Press)

—— (1991) 'Managing the Managers: The Swedish Employers' Confederation and the Suppression of Labour Market Segmentation', *Scandinavian Journal of History* 16 (2).

Taylor, C. (1985) 'Interpretation and the Sciences of Man', *Philosophy and the Human Sciences: Philosophical Papers 2* (Cambridge: Cambridge University Press).

Taylor, J. (1982) 'The Swedish Investment Funds System as a Stabilization Policy Rule', *Brookings Papers on Economic Activity* 1.

TCO and SACO (1999) 'Öbergsutredningen: TCO och SACO avvisar förslaget', Press release, 5 March 1999.

Therborn, G. (1980a) *What does the Ruling Class do when it Rules?* (London: Verso).

—— (1980b) *The Ideology of Power and the Power of Ideology* (London: New Left Books).

—— (1988) 'Nation och klass, tur och skicklighet. Vägar till ständig (?) makt', in K. Misgeld *et al.* (eds) *Socialdemokratins samhälle* (Stockholm: Tiden).

—— (1989) *Borgarklass och byrålkrati i Sverige* (Lund: Arkiv).

Thomsen, S and Woolcock, S (1993) *Direct Investment and European Integration* (London: Pinter).

Thrift, N. (1987) 'The Fixers: The Urban Geography of International Commercial Capital', in J. Henderson and M. Castells (eds) *Global Restructuring and Territorial Development* (London: Sage).

Thunberg, A. (ed.) (1970) *Strejken.* (Stockholm: Rabén and Sjögren).

Tilton, T. (1988) 'Ideologins roll i socialdemokratisk politik', K. Misgeld *et al.* (eds) *Socialdemokratins samhälle* (Stockholm: Tiden).

—— (1991) *The Political Theory of Swedish Social Democracy* (Oxford: Clarendon).

Titmuss, R. (1974) *Social Policy* (London: Allen and Unwin).

Unga, N. (1976) *Socialdemokratin och arbetslöshetsfrågan 1912–34* (Kristianstad: Arkiv).

Uusitalo, P. (1984) 'Monetarism, Keynsianism and the Institutional Status of Central Banks', *Acta Sociologica*, 27 (1).

Van Apeldoorn, B. (1998) 'Transnationalization and the Restructuring of Europe's Socioeconomic Order', *International Journal of Political Economy* 28 (1).

van der Pijl, K. (1984) *The Making of an Atlantic Ruling Class* (London: Verso).

—— (1989) 'Ruling Classes, Hegemony and the State System', *International Journal of Political Economy* 19 (3).

—— (1994) 'The Cadre class and Public Multilateralism', Y. Sakamoto (ed.) *Global Tansformation* (Tokyo: United Nations University Press).

—— (1998) *Transnational Classes and International Relations* (London: Routledge).

Visser, J. and Hemerijck, A. (1997) *'A Dutch Miracle': Job Growth, Welfare Reform and Corporatism in the Netherlands* (Amsterdam: Amsterdam University Press).

Wacquant, L. (1997) 'Vom wohltätigen Staat zum strafenden Staat: Über den politischen Umgang mit dem Elend in Amerika', *Leviathan* 1.

Webb, S. (1989) 'Sweden Braced for Bond Bonanza', *Financial Times*, 18 January.

Weir, M. and Skocpol, T. (1985) 'State Structures and the Possibilities for 'Keynesian' Responses to the Great Depression in Sweden, Britain and the United States', in P. Evans *et al.* (eds) *Bringing the State Back In* (Cambridge: Cambridge University Press).

Wibe, S. 'Regleringar och produktivitet', Sweden. SOU 1991:82 *Konkurrens, regleringar och produktivitet.* Expertrapport, Volume 7.

—— (1993) 'Vad skapade krisen?', *Zenit.* 120/121 (1993).

Wickman K. and Pålsson, R. (1948) 'Ideologisk upplösning och förnyelse', *Tiden* 3.

Wigforss, E. (1949) 'Socialismen i socialdemokratin, *Tiden* 4.

—— (1954) *Minnen*, volume 3 (Stockholm: Tiden).

—— (1971) *Vision och verklighet* (Stockholm: Prisma).

Wilensky, H. (1975) *The Welfare State and Equality* (Berkeley: University of California Press).

Williamson, O. (1975) *Markets and Hierarchies* (New York: The Free Press).

Zysman, J. (1983) *Governments, Markets and Growth* (Ithaca, NY: Cornell University Press).

Index

Ruigrok, W. 103, 105, 106, 228
Russian revolution (1917) 65
Ryner, M. 49, 132, 136, 146, 148, 151,
    152, 157, 158, 162, 203, 213, 231

SAAB 69, 134
Sabel, C. 52, 102, 103
SAF *see* Employers' Federation of
    Sweden
Sainsbury, D. 98, 212, 213
Saltsjöbaden Accord (1938) 62, 72, 74,
    76, 87, 93, 127, 133, 145, 220, 225
Samuelsson, K. 64, 67, 221
Sandberg, A. 52, 218
Sandner, G. 8
Sandvik 69
SAP *see* Social Democratic Workers'
    Party of Sweden
Sassen, S. 39, 47
Sayer, A. 39, 159
Scandinavia 21, 46, 59–60
Scharpf, F. 99
Schiller, Bernt 64, 127, 128, 144, 145,
    168, 170, 207
Scholte, J. A. 100, 119
Schröder, Gerhard 8, 12, 118
Schumpeter, J. 41, 46, 47
Schwartz, Herman 57, 232
scientific management 72, 74, 216
scientific rationality 77
second industrial revolution 58, 67
Second Socialist International 55, 60,
    123, 183
Second World War 61, 80, 81
Simon, R. 6, 200, 201
Simonson, B. 128, 129, 223
Skandinaviska 71, 147, 233
Skanska 147, 234
SKF 69
Skocpol, T. 62
Sköldebrand, B. 146
social citizenship
    de-commodification 48–50, 99
    discourse ethics 24
    new social movements 22
    norms 2
    post-Fordism 159
    social programmes 141
    traditional commitments 1
    universal-abstract conception 24
    universalism 9, 30, 55
social cohesion 16, 32, 58
social democracy
    Austria 75
    cadres 73, 77, 80, 173

compensatory neo-liberal
    restructuring 3
    de-commodification 22, 55
    Denmark 64, 78
    Germany 35, 64
    humanised capitalism 12, 13
    individualism 23
    meta-principles 25
    misrationalisation 9, 24, 25, 75, 133
    reconsideration 21–6
    social welfare 25
    Sweden *see* Swedish model
    universalism 22
    welfare state 27–54, 59–60, 214–19
social democratic labour movement
    agrarian forces 62
    emergence 64
    experts 77
    hegemony 58
    integrative democracy 58, 77
    modernity 58
    popular movements 65
    social engineering 77, 78, 80
Social Democratic Party (SPD)
    Germany 8, 116, 118
Social Democratic Workers' Party of
    Sweden (SAP)
    Agrarian coalition 61, 66
    Cow Deal 61, 66, 72, 219
    economic policy 79, 151
    electoral defeats 125, 152, 154, 167
    hegemony 74
    industrial democracy 134
    industrial policy 138, 142
    Liberal coalition 66
    Meidner plan 140, 166, 172, 173, 235
    National Government 79
    natural party of government 59, 60,
        93
    People's Home 66
    popularity 154–5
    public consumption 80
    reform agenda 124
social engineering 77, 78, 80
social exclusion 17, 21
social integration 58, 72–3
social linguistics psycho-analysis 60
social marginalisation 20
social movements
    new 22
    popular 23, 58, 64, 65
    social citizenship 22
    social democratic labour movement
        58
social policy 43, 81, 85

For Product Safety Concerns and Information please contact our
EU representative GPSR@taylorandfrancis.com Taylor & Francis
Verlag GmbH, Kaufingerstraße 24, 80331 München, Germany